Attorney Liability in Bankruptcy

Corinne Cooper, Editor
Catherine E. Vance, Contributing Editor

AMERICAN BAR ASSOCIATION
Defending Liberty
Pursuing Justice

GP|Solo

ABA General Practice, Solo & Small Firm Division

10 09   5 4 3 2

Library of Congress Cataloging-in-Publication Data

Cooper, Corinne, 1952-
    Attorney liability in bankruptcy / Corinne Cooper, Catherine E. Vance, American Bar Association.
    p. cm.
    ISBN 1-59031-582-0
    1. Bankruptcy lawyers—Malpractice—United States. 2. United States. Bankruptcy Abuse Prevention and Consumer Protection Act of 2005. 3. Consumer credit—Law and legislation—United States. 4. Consumer protection—Law and legislation—United States. 5. Bankruptcy—United States. 6. Attorney and client—United States. I. Vance, Catherine E. II. American Bar Association. III. Title.
    KF313.C66 2006
    347.73'5041—dc22   2006005213

Contents

Chapter 4
You Know You're a Debt Relief Agency When 75
by Corinne Cooper

Chapter 5
The DRA Quiz 95
by Catherine E. Vance

Chapter 6
Unbundling Legal Services 103
by Thomas J. Yerbich

Chapter 7
Bankruptcy Ethics Issues for Solos and Small Firms 121
by Nancy B. Rapoport

Chapter 8
Constitutionality of the Attorney Liability Provisions of the
Bankruptcy Reform Act **141**
by Erwin Chemerinsky and Barbara Glesner Fines

Chapter 9
Drop the Yellow Pages and Put Your Hands in the Air! The
Perils of Advertising Under the BRA **153**
by Corinne Cooper

Chapter 10
Representation, Consultation, and Termination Agreements **167**
by Marc S. Stern and Joel Pelofsky

Chapter 11
Complying with Debt Relief Agency Provisions: Notices,
Prohibitions, and Enforcement **179**
by Catherine E. Vance

Chapter 12
Attorney Liability and § 521: Dismissal for Failure to File
   Required Documents **217**
by Catherine E. Vance

Chapter 13
Section 707(b)(4): New Certifications, New Sanctions **227**
by Catherine E. Vance

Chapter 14
Reaffirming Debt after Bankruptcy 261
by Catherine E. Vance

Chapter 15
Creditors' Lawyers and Other White Meat 285
by Catherine E. Vance and Corinne Cooper

Chapter 16
Criminal Liability for the Bankruptcy Practitioner 303
by Ronald R. Peterson

Chapter 17
No Good Deed Goes Unpunished: *Pro Bono* Practice under
by Corinne Cooper and Thomas J. Yerbich

Chapter 18
by Catherine E. Vance

Index of Forms and Tables

Dedication

This book is dedicated to David D. Cooper, who never stopped fighting to improve American public policy and who died during the writing of this book.

Acknowledgments

The editors wish to thank the authors for their valuable insights, their professionalism, and their willingness to work on a tight deadline. They also thank Richard Paszkiet, John Rhead, Andrew Alcala, Jill Nuppenau, Katrina Krause, Lisa Burns, and the staff of ABA Publishing, who worked so hard to get this book done quickly.

Corinne Cooper wishes to thank Catherine E. Vance, Thomas Yerbich, Marc Stern, the Hon. Marilyn Shea-Stonum, Christopher R. Kaup, Robert Nadler, Prof. Jonathan Lipson, Richard B. Levin, Prof. Bruce A. Markell, Prof. Barbara Glesner Fines, Dean Nancy Rapoport, and Prof. Juliet Moringiello for contributing to this book. Thanks also to Law Professors for Bankruptcy Reform, the group that brought this legislation to her attention in 1998, and to the many lawyers and consumer advocates around the nation who fought this bill so relentlessly and gave so generously of their time to teach her bankruptcy law, particularly an anonymous congressional staff member, without whom this book could never have been written.

Catherine E. Vance wishes to thank the Hon. Steven Rhodes, Marc Stern, Prof. Charlie Wilson, Max Moses, Jan Ostrovsky, Sarah Jolie, and Shelby Nincehelser-Vance.

Preface

We spent much of our time during the period from 2000 to March 2005 fighting the passage of the Bankruptcy Reform Act. We wish it had not passed. It is terrible legislation for a whole variety of reasons.

This book highlights one very bad result of its passage. This book is not intended as legal advice for debtors, but as a guide to help attorneys—debtor and creditor, bankruptcy and non-bankruptcy—confront and understand the very profound and negative impact that this law will have on the practice of law.

Speaking around the country, we encountered many experts who are struggling, as we are, to make sense of the law. What we present here is the cumulative insight of dozens of people, and hundreds of hours spent parsing legislative language and history.

Please don't rely solely upon our interpretations of the statute. As you will see from a careful reading, the authors respectfully disagree on several points. Between the publication of *Nine Traps and One Slap: Attorney Liability under the New Bankruptcy Law,* 79 AM. BANKR. L. J. 283 (2005)—the article upon which much of this book is based—and the completion of this manuscript, the editors changed our minds many times about the meaning and impact of the law. Please forgive us! Because the statute is so poorly written, it is almost impossible to interpret.

In the course of speaking and writing about this law, we've been told that we were overreacting. We've been called "an egg-head Chicken Little," "an hysterical female," and "the girl who cried wolf"! We've been accused of using "overblown rhetoric."

After time to deliberate, we don't think so.

The attorney liability provisions incorporated in the new bankruptcy law represent as heinous an attack on the profession as anything written since Shakespeare. This book is an attempt to explain those provisions.

We don't expect you to read this book straight through. Here's a little tour:

- Please start with Chapter 1.
- If you are challenging the provisions, don't miss Chapters 3 and 8.
- If you advertise, go right to Chapters 4 and 9.
- If you don't want to get sued, sanctioned, or disbarred, see Chapters 7, 12, and 13.

- If you wonder what forms you need, go to Chapters 10 and 11.
- If you represent consumer debtors, memorize Chapters 11-14.
- If you want to know what a "debt relief agency" is, study Chapters 4 and 5.
- If you don't want to go to jail, don't miss Chapter 16.
- If you think you aren't covered by the law, better read Chapters 4, 5, and 15.
- If you share our political outrage, welcome to Chapters 2 and 18!

There was a recent Arizona opinion interpreting the BRA. Here is our favorite passage:

> It has been reported that a "technical amendments" bill is in the works to fix various glitches in BAPCPA, notwithstanding Congressional testimony that it was so perfect that not a word need be changed. Perhaps this is one of those glitches. If so, Congress can easily fix it. . . . Until Congress does fix it, however, the Court must apply the unambiguous statute as written.

In re McNabb, 326 B.R. 785, 791 (Bankr. D. Ariz. 2005).

Corinne Cooper
Tucson, Arizona

Catherine E. Vance
Columbus, Ohio

January 2006

About the Editors

Corinne Cooper is the principal of Professional Presence®—www.professionalpresence.com—a communication consulting firm that specializes in professional communication training and development for legal organizations. She is a professor *emerita* of law, having taught contracts and commercial law for almost two decades.

Her prior books include HOW TO BUILD A LAW FIRM BRAND (ABA 2005), THE NEW ARTICLE 9 (ABA 2nd ed. 2000), and THE PORTABLE UCC (ABA 4th ed. 2005).

Professor Cooper devoted several years to the development of non-verbal tools to teach law. She designed the graphics in this book. (Dean Rapoport is a master of graphics and created most of those found in her chapter.) Professor Cooper has written two books on the subject: GETTING GRAPHIC® (AALS 1993), on the use of non-verbal tools to teach commercial law, and GETTING GRAPHIC2® (Institute for Law School Teaching 1994), on the use of graphics to teach law.

Professor Cooper has been involved in book and magazine publishing for more than 20 years. She was a member of the Board of Editors of *The ABA Journal* from 1999 to 2005; prior to that, she served as Editor of *Business Law Today*.

Last century, Professor Cooper received a BA *magna cum laude*, and JD *summa cum laude* from the University of Arizona. She is a member of Phi Beta Kappa, Phi Kappa Phi, and the Order of the Coif. She also studied finance in the MBA program at the Wharton School of the University of Pennsylvania. She is a member of the bars of Arizona and Missouri. She was elected a member of the American Law Institute in 1994.

Catherine E. Vance is vice president of research and policy and associate general counsel at Development Specialists, Inc., resident in the firm's Columbus, Ohio, office. Ms. Vance has written extensively on matters related to bankruptcy, bankruptcy reform, privacy, and other matters affecting the debtor/creditor relationship and insolvency proceedings. Her recent articles include *Nine Traps and One Slap: Attorney Liability under the New Bankruptcy Law*, 79 AM. BANKR. L.J. 283 (2005), co-authored with Corinne Cooper; *The Facts & Fiction of Bankruptcy Reform*, 1 DEPAUL COM. & BUS. L.J. 361 (2003), co-authored with Paige Barr; and *Attorneys and the Bankruptcy Reform Act of 2001: Understanding the Imposition of Sanctions against Debtors' Counsel*, 106 COM. L.J. 241 (2001).

Prior to joining DSI, Inc., Ms. Vance served as the Commercial Law League of America's legal writer and analyst. In this capacity, she acquired a thorough understanding of bankruptcy reform legislation pending in the United States Congress since the late 1990s. Ms. Vance is a regular contributor to the *Bankruptcy Yearbook and Almanac*, co-authoring the publication's annual legislative update. She also served as associate editor for the 94th edition of the National Association of Credit Management's *Manual of Credit and Commercial Laws*.

A United States Army veteran, Ms. Vance received her bachelor's degree, *magna cum laude*, from Ohio State University and is a graduate of the university's College of Law, where she was awarded the American Bankruptcy Institute's Medal for Excellence in Bankruptcy Studies.

About the Contributors

Erwin Chemerinsky is an Alston & Bird Professor of Law and Political Science at Duke University. Prior to joining the Duke faculty in 2004, he was on the faculty of the University of Southern California Law School for 21 years. Professor Chemerinsky graduated from Northwestern University and Harvard Law School. He is the author of four books and more than 100 law review articles on constitutional law and he frequently argues appellate and U.S. Supreme Court cases.

Barbara Glesner Fines is the Ruby M. Hulen Professor of Law at the University of Missouri–Kansas City. Professor Glesner Fines has a J.D. from the University of Wisconsin and an LL.M. from Yale University. She researches and teaches professional responsibility.

Joel Pelofsky is of counsel to Spencer Fane Britt & Browne LLP, Kansas City, Missouri. He served as a U.S. Bankruptcy Judge from 1980 to 1985 and as a U.S. Trustee from 1995 to 2003.

Ronald R. Peterson is a partner in Jenner & Block's Chicago office and a member of the firm's Bankruptcy, Workout and Corporate Reorganization Practice. Mr. Peterson is AV Peer Review Rated, Martindale-Hubbell's highest peer recognition for ethical standards and legal ability. Mr. Peterson has concentrated his practice in the areas of commercial, insolvency, and bankruptcy law, focusing primarily on representing debtors, trustees, creditors' committees, landlords, and secured lenders in Chapter 11 cases.

Nancy B. Rapoport is dean and professor of law at the University of Houston Law Center. Her specialties are bankruptcy ethics and the interaction between popular culture and the law. In 2001 she was elected to membership in the American Law Institute, and in 2002 she received a Distinguished Alumna Award from Rice University. She is a Fellow of the American Bar Foundation and a Fellow of the American College of Bankruptcy.

Marc S. Stern is a solo practitioner in Seattle, Washington, where his practice emphasizes insolvency and bankruptcy. Since 1993, he has been board-certified as a Business Bankruptcy Specialist by the American Board of Certification. He represents creditors and debtors. He is admitted to practice in the U.S. Supreme Court, the Ninth Circuit, the Court of Appeals for the Armed Forces, the District and Bankruptcy Courts for the Eastern and Western Districts of Washington, and the Washington State Supreme Court. He earned his J.D. from the University of Idaho College of Law and his A.B. *cum laude* from Washington University, St. Louis, Missouri.

Thomas J. Yerbich received his J.D. (with distinction) and LL.M (business and tax) from the University of the Pacific, McGeorge School of Law. Prior to joining the U.S. District Court, Alaska, as Court Rules Attorney in 2001, he was in private practice for 30 years with an emphasis on bankruptcy and tax law. Previously board-certified in both business and consumer bankruptcy law, Mr. Yerbich has written numerous articles on bankruptcy law, and is the author of *Consumer Bankruptcy: Fundamentals of Chapter 7 and Chapter 13 of the U.S. Bankruptcy Code* (ABI 2003).

CHAPTER 1

Overview of the BRA:
New Rules for Bankruptcy Lawyers

by Catherine E. Vance

Ready or not, it's time to comply with the BRA[1] and its many provisions targeted at attorneys representing consumer debtors. This chapter offers an overview of these provisions, which fall into three general categories:

- New certification and sanctions provisions in Chapter 7 cases
- Regulation of attorneys as "debt relief agencies"
- Heightened certification requirements for reaffirmation agreements.

As a fourth category, we offer some discussion of BRA provisions that will affect other attorneys. Just because you are representing someone other than a consumer debtor doesn't mean you get a free pass under the BRA.[2]

In addition to the increased burdens on debtors' counsel, the BRA diminishes the distinction between the services that trained, licensed attorneys provide to their clients and the largely unregulated fields of credit counseling and bankruptcy petition preparation. Chapter 18 has more on this.

---

1.   The Bankruptcy Abuse Prevention and Consumer Protection Act of 2005, Pub. L. No. 109-8, 119 Stat. 23 ["BRA"]. The Act is rather euphemistically titled; some opponents refer to it as the Bankruptcy Act Reform Fiasco, or BARF; one named it "The Bankruptcy Prevention and Consumer Abuse Act." The editors of this book have decided to use "Bankruptcy Reform Act," "BRA," or "the Act" as a neutral middle ground. References to a section of the law passed will say "the Act." All references to "the Code" mean the Bankruptcy Code, codified at Title 11 of the United States Code.

2.   Although not nearly so onerous as those directed at consumer debtors' lawyers, there are provisions in the BRA that will affect attorneys representing creditors and other parties. Chapter 15 takes a closer look at some of the provisions affecting attorneys and others who act on behalf of parties other than consumer debtors.

Handy Dandy BRA Reference Table

The BRA is not a new Bankruptcy Code but an elaborate series of amendments. To avoid confusion, we use different language to refer to the Act and the Code.

Citations to the Act read, "BRA Section ###."

Citations to the Code read, "Code § ###."

This chart will help you keep track of the relevant Code sections amended by the Act

Act	Code	Provision
Section 102	§ 707(b)	Dismissal of Conversion of Chapter 7 Case
Section 203	§ 524	Reaffirmation Agreements
Section 226	§ 101	Definitions
Section 227	§ 526	Restrictions on Debt Relief Agencies
Section 228	§ 527	Disclosures
Section 229	§ 528	Requirements for Debt Relief Agencies

I. Certification and Sanctions in "Abusive" Consumer Chapter 7 Cases

Amended § 707(b) contains the new law's most prominent feature; the BRA substantially rewrote the section to include the much-discussed "means test" for consumers seeking Chapter 7 relief, as well as a less-noticed good faith filing requirement. Among these changes is new § 707(b)(4), directed at the attorney for the debtor, which:

- alters, for consumer debtors' attorneys, the certifications made by virtue of their signatures on bankruptcy documents, and
- permits the imposition of unprecedented sanctions against these attorneys.

Under Rule 9011 of the Federal Rules of Bankruptcy Procedure (largely the same as Rule 11 of the Federal Rules of Civil Procedure), all attorneys make certain assurances by signing any document submitted to the court. These rules are designed to prevent frivolous or bad faith filings; they require attorneys to conduct reasonable inquiries into the facts and law in their filings, and to file them only for a proper purpose.

Under the BRA, the signature of the debtor's attorney takes on greater significance through two distinct provisions. The first of these appears in § 707(b)(4)(C) and provides:

> The signature of an attorney on a petition, pleading, or written motion shall constitute a certification that the attorney has—
> (i) performed a reasonable investigation into the circumstances that gave rise to the petition, pleading, or written motion; and
> (ii) determined that the petition, pleading, or written motion—
>   (I) is well grounded in fact; and
>   (II) is warranted by existing law or a good faith argument for the extension, modification, or reversal of existing law and does not constitute an abuse under paragraph (1).[3]

The reference to "paragraph (1)" means that the filing is not an abuse as defined by the means test and good faith filing requirement in new § 707(b)(2) and (3). This provision creates an entirely new potential for attorney liability: representing a losing debtor.

The second certification, codified at § 707(b)(4)(D), says:

> The signature of an attorney on the petition shall constitute a certification that the attorney has no knowledge after an inquiry that the information in the schedules filed with such petition is incorrect.[4]

The schedules contain information about the debtor's assets and liabilities, some of which, like checking account balances, is in flux. Verifying that information is sure to be costly and, in some cases, impossible. Among other things, this rule apparently requires debtor's counsel to investigate and verify the accuracy of claims against the debtor. Since this information is largely in the control of creditors, it is not clear how an attorney is supposed to comply with this duty.

The courts will set the standards of conduct that apply to these two provisions, including defining what it means to conduct a "reasonable investigation" or when an attorney has "knowledge" of "incorrect" information in the schedules after "inquiry."[5] Still, it's clear that the BRA creates a significant risk of liability for consumer bankruptcy attorneys faced by no other attorneys.

New § 707(b)(4)(A) allows for sanctions to be imposed when the trustee wins a motion to dismiss the debtor's case based on "abuse." Specifically, if the court finds that the bankruptcy filing constituted:

---

3. Code § 707(b)(4)(C).
4. Code § 707(b)(4)(D).
5. An American Bar Association task force released a report recommending that "reasonable investigation" and "inquiry" be defined in a manner consistent with the standards developed under Rule 9011 and its "reasonable inquiry" standard. *See* Chapter 13 for more information about the task force report.

- abuse on the part of the debtor, and
- a violation of Rule 9011 on the part of the attorney,

the court may order the attorney to reimburse the trustee all reasonable costs and fees associated with the motion to dismiss. At its heart, this provision is little more than a fee-shifting statute, but with a remarkable distinction: the fees are shifted not to the debtor, but to the attorney alone. It's worth mentioning that this provision once *mandated* sanctions against the attorney; if there's any good news, it's the change to a discretionary standard.[6]

New § 707(b)(4) also has a generalized provision that appears to allow the court to assess a civil penalty if it finds the attorney for the debtor violated Rule 9011. The goal and operative effect of this provision are far from clear. Its language makes it subject to interpretive dispute and its point is in question, given that a violation of Rule 9011 already provides a basis for imposing sanctions. This provision was also mandatory in earlier versions of the BRA.

Chapter 13 discusses in detail new § 707(b)(4)'s certification requirements and its potential for sanctions against debtors' attorneys.

II. Regulating Consumer Debtors' Attorneys as "Debt Relief Agencies"

The BRA defines—and deprofessionalizes—debtors' attorneys as "debt relief agencies" and dramatically regulates an attorney's practice, from advertising to representation, mandating what the attorney must do and what the attorney is forbidden from doing, with no regard for the best interests of the client. To accomplish its mission, the BRA creates three important definitions:

- "Assisted Person" [AP] is any person whose debts consist primarily of consumer debts, and whose non-exempt assets are worth less than $150,000.
- "Bankruptcy Assistance" includes goods or services sold or otherwise provided to an assisted person, such as legal advice or representation, document preparation or filing, or attendance at a creditors' meeting or the like, in connection with a case or proceeding under the Bankruptcy Code.
- "Debt Relief Agency" [DRA] is any person who provides bankruptcy assistance to an AP in return for the payment of money or other valuable consideration, or who is a bankruptcy petition preparer under § 110 of the Code.

---

6. *See* Chapter 3 for more on this change.

WARNING!!

Just because your client isn't the debtor doesn't mean you get a free pass. Family lawyers, small business lawyers, tort lawyers, and many more may get caught up in the new "debt relief agency" provisions.

Chapter 4 discusses these definitions in intricate detail. Some folks are expressly (and inexplicably, in some cases) excluded from the BRA's definition of "debt relief agency." Chapter 5 discusses the counterintuitive and even dangerous results these definitions and their exceptions produce when determining who is and is not a "debt relief agency."

For debtors' attorneys, these definitions bring into play an alarming array of new restrictions and duties that apply in three main areas. The first is advertising. The second and third are flip sides of the communication coin: attorneys are prohibited from making some statements and forced to make others.

A. Attorney Advertising

Any attorney who fits the definition of a "debt relief agency" under the BRA must comply with its regulation of advertisements. If the attorney's advertisement is directed at the general public and:

- includes a description of bankruptcy assistance, or
- uses language that could lead a reasonable consumer to believe that debt counseling is being offered when in fact the services are directed to providing bankruptcy assistance, or
- offers assistance with credit defaults, mortgage foreclosures or eviction, excessive debt, debt-collection pressure, or an inability to pay any consumer debt,

then the attorney is required to disclose that the services relate to bankruptcy and to include this statement clearly and conspicuously in the advertisement:

"We are a debt relief agency. We help people file for bankruptcy relief under the Bankruptcy Code."

This provision is not only offensive, it's confusing. It may seem simple on its face, but there is plenty more to say about it. It's discussed at length in Chapter 9.

B. Required Disclosures

No fewer than five written disclosures are required to be given by the DRA attorney to the client—"assisted person" in the new bankruptcy parlance—under the BRA. Each of these has different rules about when the attorney is supposed to provide a given notice, whether its contents must be clear and conspicuous, whether proof of delivery is required, and how long the attorney is supposed to retain a copy in the client's file.

1. The § 342(b) Notice[7] must provide descriptions of the relief available under the different chapters of the Bankruptcy Code, and must also include language designed to scare the debtor about criminal liability and Attorney General investigations (although Congress sees this notice as informing debtors of "matters pertaining to the integrity of the bankruptcy system"[8]).

2. Mini-Miranda II sets out specific "advice" the attorney must give, some of which is actually inconsistent with the law. As in the first notice, the debtor's potential criminal liability must be mentioned.

3. The BRA mandates the Prescribed Language Notice, which is very much like those required under federal consumer protection statutes. The content of this notice is set out in the statute; attorneys must use the statutory language or language that is "substantially similar."

4. In the "How To" Notice, the attorney must provide "reasonably sufficient information" that, like the second notice, is inconsistent with what the law actually requires. Here, the attorney is also required to advise the client how to perform tasks—such as the valuation of assets—that have perplexed attorneys and courts for some time.

5. The attorney must provide the client with a written contract, which every lawyer should do anyway. This contract, however, has to make clear and conspicuous both the services that will be provided and the cost and payment structure for those services.

All of these notices are discussed more fully in Chapter 11.

C. Prohibited Statements

The flip side of the required statements is the BRA's prohibition on what an attorney can say or do. These prohibitions are discussed along with the mandated notices in Chapter 11.

In some respects, these prohibitions are unnecessary reiterations of ethics and disciplinary rules. For example, the BRA says an attorney can't advise a

---

7.   The names of the required disclosures used in this Chapter were taken from Chapter 11, which talks about all of them in detail.

8.   H.R. REP. No. 109-31, at 18 (2005).

debtor to make false statements in bankruptcy papers, which an attorney isn't allowed to do under any circumstances.

But some prohibitions are also foolhardy—and dangerous. They reach "prospective assisted persons" in addition to actual clients, preclude what could be the best legal advice for a particular client, and create thresholds for liability that are frightfully low. The attorney can't even tell the client, whose financial distress has become so dire that he sought out the attorney's help, that it's okay to borrow the money needed to pay the legal expenses of the bankruptcy.

D. Constitutional Implications

In many respects, as highlighted above and discussed in greater detail throughout this book, the BRA cuts right into the heart of an attorney's First Amendment rights. Most perniciously in the debt relief agency provisions, the BRA forces speech in some contexts and prohibits it in others. Chapter 8 looks at these very important issues.

III. Attorney Certification of Debtor Reaffirmation Agreements

Among the substantial changes the BRA makes to reaffirmation agreements is a new requirement for debtors' attorneys.

Attorney certifications in this context are not new. For some time, the law has required that a reaffirmation agreement must be accompanied by counsel's declaration stating that:

- the agreement represents a fully informed and voluntary agreement by the debtor;
- the agreement does not impose an undue hardship on the debtor or his or her dependents; and
- the attorney fully advised the debtor of the legal effect and consequences of the agreement itself and any default by the debtor.

The BRA adds an additional certification if the agreement triggers the statutory presumption of undue hardship; in those cases, the attorney must go further and give assurance that the client can perform the promise to pay the debt. The BRA provides:

> If a presumption of undue hardship has been established with respect to [a reaffirmation] agreement, such certification shall state that in the opinion of the attorney, the debtor is able to make the payment.[9]

---

9.   Code § 524(k)(5)(B).

Obviously, this creates a serious problem for the attorney. If the client wants to reaffirm a debt, that is the client's decision, even if doing so flies in the face of the attorney's sound legal advice. After all, attorneys can't *force* their clients to do anything. But the BRA goes a step further by requiring the attorney to certify that the debtor—who has a demonstrated *inability* to pay a reaffirmed debt—is nevertheless able to pay it. Chapter 14 provides more detail on reaffirmation agreements, including the potential liability for attorneys under the new certification: liability to the creditor for what the debtor owes.

IV. Ethics and Professionalism

Ethics and professionalism issues permeate the attorney liability provisions of the BRA, irrespective of whether the attorney represents consumer debtors or has some other role in the case. Many of this book's contributing authors raise ethical issues that arise in the context of the each chapter, but we also offer three distinct discussions in this area:

- Chapter 7 is an excellent primer on attorneys' ethical duties, especially in the world of bankruptcy, where the issues can get very thorny.
- Chapter 16 is an important companion to the ethics chapter, providing a thorough and detailed analysis of attorneys' criminal liability.
- This book concludes with a view of professionalism in an era of legislative regulation of attorneys, and the dangerous trend that is under way—for *all* attorneys, not just bankruptcy practitioners.

CHAPTER 2

The Politics of the BRA

by *Corinne Cooper*

It's a profession-wide crisis. "Why am I doing this?" they ask. "What's the point?" Consumer bankruptcy attorneys are depressed these days. Those who aren't depressed are angry. And they have every reason to be.

When you read the Bankruptcy Reform Act,[1] and study all the provisions aimed at consumer debtors' attorneys, the conclusion is inescapable. Congress has attacked an entire field of practitioners who represent ordinary people with lives that have become desperate because they are deeply in debt. Congress does not like the lawyers who midwife the financial rebirth of these clients.

Supporters of the law gave at least three justifications for their attack on attorneys:

1. **Congress wanted to curb the dramatic rise in consumer bankruptcies.**[2]

   Members noted the fact but did not wish to acknowledge the cause. Attorneys don't cause bankruptcy any more than obstetricians cause pregnancy. In each case, there is a supervening act that warrants mention.

---

1.   The Bankruptcy Abuse Prevention and Consumer Protection Act of 2005, Pub. L. No. 109-8, 119 Stat. 23 ["BRA"]. The Act is rather euphemistically titled; some opponents refer to it as the Bankruptcy Act Reform Fiasco, or BARF; one named it "The Bankruptcy Prevention and Consumer Abuse Act." The editors of this book have decided to use "Bankruptcy Reform Act," "BRA," or "the Act" as a neutral middle ground. References to a section of the law passed will say "the Act." All references to "the Code" mean the Bankruptcy Code, codified at Title 11 of the United States Code.

2.   H. REP. 109-31, Part I, 109th Cong., 1st Sess. 2 (2005), Bankruptcy Abuse Prevention and Consumer Protection Act of 2005 ["House Report"]. The House Report identifies these factors supporting the need for reform:

2. **Congress wanted to decrease bankruptcy fraud and abuse.**[3]
   Proponents of the law noted a few cases of debtor fraud, some aided and abetted by counsel. The apocryphal became factual.[4]

3. **Congress wanted to protect consumer debtors.**
   Here, instead of being in collusion with their clients, the same attorneys are unethical scoundrels who take the initial fee and run off, leaving their poor clients without adequate representation. Or they provide the promised representation and then have the audacity to expect payment prior to the existing creditors of the debtor.[5]

---

1. The escalation in consumer bankruptcy filings, because bankruptcy is too readily available;
2. The losses to the economy, resulting in a "bankruptcy tax" on all consumers;
3. The existence of loopholes and incentives that allow or encourage opportunistic personal filings and abuse, including misconduct by attorneys and other professionals; and
4. The ability of some debtors to repay some or all of their discharged debts.

Id.

3.   *Id.* In fact, the Report of the National Bankruptcy Review Commission found little evidence of widespread abuse of the bankruptcy system by conniving debtors, or of wrongdoing by attorneys. *See, e.g.,* the Report of the National Bankruptcy Review Commission 83-86, 108 (Oct. 27, 1997) ["Commission Report"]. It specifically discounted the proposition, advanced by a study for VISA, that increased lawyer advertising led to an increase in bankruptcy filings. *Id.* at 86-87. It did note that attorneys could do more to ensure the accuracy of the schedules. *Id.* at 110, 112. An article on bankruptcy shortly after the Commission Report issued posited a causation between attorney advertising and bankruptcy filing, based upon the VISA study, a report by the Federal Reserve, and the Supreme Court decision permitting lawyer advertising, but provided no data. Vern McKinley, *Ballooning Bankruptcies: Issuing Blame for the Explosive Growth*, Reg. Vol. 20, No. 4 (Cato Institute 1997) at 7. For some interesting data on the correlation between attorney advertising and bankruptcy filings, *see* Henry Jacobs, *The Subtle Serpent: Correlation of Bankruptcy Attorney Advertising to Consumer Bankruptcy Filing Rates* (2003), unpublished manuscript in the files of the author. The regulation of attorney advertising in the BRA is discussed in Chapter 9.

4.   For the best possible example of the "apocryphal becoming factual" in the political process that led to the BRA, *see* Elizabeth Warren, *The Phantom $400*, 13 J. Bankr. L. & Prac. 77 (2004).

5.   The House Report noted:

   Consumer Debtor Bankruptcy Protections. The bill's consumer protections include provisions strengthening professionalism standards for attorneys and others who assist consumer debtors with their bankruptcy cases. S. 256 mandates that certain services and specified notices be given to consumers by professionals and others who provide bankruptcy assistance. To ensure compliance with these provisions, the bill institutes various enforcement mechanisms.

Not all bankruptcy lawyers are angels. We all know of exceptions. There are bankruptcy lawyers who are incompetent, and those who aid their clients in committing fraud. But there is no evidence that they are even a significant minority, much less the majority. Consumer bankruptcy isn't the most fertile field for anyone—lawyer or debtor—seeking to profit by wrongdoing or fraud.

Nor are bankruptcy lawyers unique in their willingness to participate in bad behavior: on rare occasions, corporate lawyers, accountants, CEOs, judges, and even members of Congress have ignored their professional obligations.

In response to the caricature the bill's proponents painted, Congress enacted complex and often incomprehensible rules to control almost every aspect of practice by consumer debtors' attorneys. This chapter is an attempt to explain *why* these provisions were included in the new law.[6]

I. First, Let's Kill All the Lawyers

Why did Congress conclude that an attack on lawyers[7] was an effective way to reduce consumer bankruptcy "fraud and abuse"? The legislative history never explains.

Although there are no acknowledged authors of the attorney liability provisions in the BRA, there are fingerprints.[8] The banking and credit card lobbyists who drafted this bill in some plush, walnut-paneled conference room clearly understood that debtors would be severely disadvantaged by appear-

---

6. Chapter 3 will describe *how* they came to be included.

7. As a matter of pure politics, politicians lose very few points for attacking lawyers. The same Congress that passed the BRA also passed significant legislation curbing the conduct of plaintiffs' attorneys, The Class Action Fairness Act of 2005, Pub. L. No. 109-2, 119 Stat. 4. The Lawsuit Abuse Reduction Act of 2005, H.R. 420, introduced in January, amends Rule 11 "to improve attorney accountability." Like the original version of the BRA, this would make sanctions against attorneys mandatory. (For more on this issue, see Chapter 3.) It also mandates suspension of attorneys from practice for three or more violations of Rule 11. Still another pending bill describes tax and estate lawyers as performing "make work" that puts a strain on the national economy. The Family Heritage Preservation Act, H.R. 64, introduced January 4, 2005, at § 2: Findings.

8. *See, e.g.,* Testimony of George Wallace before the House Judiciary Committee, Hearing on H.R. 333 (Feb. 7, 2001), representing the Coalition for Responsible Bankruptcy Laws, which he describes as "a broad coalition of consumer creditors, including banks, credit unions, savings institutions, retailers, mortgage companies, sales finance companies and diversified financial services companies." *Id.* The *American Banker* identified Wallace as the author of the bill in 2001. *Top Creditor Lobbyist Tassey Goes for Broke,* AM. BANKER (May 17, 2001) at 1, *cited in* Elizabeth Warren, *The Phantom $400,* 13 J. BANKR. L. & PRAC. 77, at n. 60 (2004).

ing without the benefit of counsel.[9] Since supporters could not legislate away the right to representation, they advanced this result by incorporating disincentives that are certain to reduce the number of attorneys practicing,[10] increase the cost of filing,[11] and dramatically swell the ranks of *pro se* filers.[12]

The first moves in the game to "pin the blame on the lawyers" were made by the dissenters to the National Bankruptcy Review Commission.[13] The Minority Report made several recommendations that were ultimately incorporated into the BRA.

In its dissent, the Minority complained, among other things, that:

> [D]ebtor's counsel should be required to do their jobs in an ethical and proper fashion. Finally, it should be pointed out that the Commission has heard little on the subject of false creditors' claims; in contrast, it has repeatedly heard that debtors' schedules are generally incomplete and unreliable. In fact, one bankruptcy judge told the Commission that debtors' schedules were often "fiction."[14]

The Minority Report went on to recommend:

> Debtors' counsel should take an active role in certifying the accuracy of the information contained in the debtors' schedules, statements of affairs, and amendments thereto. Attorneys presently are not required to sign these official court documents . . . . Requiring attorneys to sign schedules, as they are required similarly to certify all other pleadings filed with the court,

---

9.   *See, e.g.,* Greg Stiles, *Bankruptcy Changes Discourage Attorneys,* MAIL TRIBUNE, August 23, 2005 at http://www.mailtribune.com/archive/2005/0823/biz/stories/01biz.htm; Romona Paden, *Lawyers reform their ways to meet bankruptcy changes,* KANSAS CITY BUS. J., Oct. 31, 2005, *at* http://www.bizjournals.com/kansascity/stories/2005/10/31/ focus2.html; John Caher, *New Law Raises Stakes for Debtors'Attorneys,* N.Y. L.J., Oct. 17, 2005, *at* http://www.law.com/jsp/article.jsp?id=1129280709784.

10.   *Id. See also* http://www.abiworld.org/consumerlive/overviews.html.

11.   *See, e.g.,* Jean Sahadi, *Rush to file for bankruptcy,* CNN MONEY, Oct. 14, 2005, *at* http://money.cnn.com/2005/10/10/pf/debt/bankruptcy_runup/index.htm (reporting fee increases of between 75% and 100%); Romona Paden, *Lawyers reform their ways to meet bankruptcy changes,* KANSAS CITY BUS. J., Oct. 31, 2005, *at* http://www.bizjournals.com/ kansascity/stories/2005/10/31/focus2.html (reporting fee increases of 33%); John Caher, *New Law Raises Stakes for Debtors' Attorneys,* N.Y. L.J., Oct. 17, 2005, at http:// www.law.com/jsp/article.jsp?id=1129280709784.

12.   *Id. See also* http://www.abiworld.org/consumerlive/overviews.html.

13.   National Bankruptcy Review Commission, Additional Dissent to Recommendations for Reform of Consumer Bankruptcy Law ["Minority Report"]. *See also* Chapter 3.

14.   Minority Report at 18.

would clarify their responsibility to inquire into the accuracy of the information, and will improve the quality of data in the bankruptcy files.[15]

And to argue:

Debtors' attorneys are also able, under current law, to take advantage of priority status for the payment of their fees in Chapter 13, such that in many cases attorney fees are paid from the first funds a debtor pays to the Chapter 13 trustee for distribution to creditors. Because a debtor's attorney is also a debtor's creditor, the attorney has a conflict of interest when counseling a debtor as to choice of chapter under which to file. In addition, because Chapter 13 cases often require more legal work and continuing involvement of the debtor's attorney than Chapter 7 cases, debtors may be left without effective representation after plan confirmation.[16]

And to accuse:

In addition, criticism has been directed against debtors' attorneys in Chapter 7 cases. The most strident complaints are those of debtors who complain that their attorneys abandon them after they file the petition and schedules and attend the meeting of creditors. Debtors' attorneys respond that they make minimal services available to debtors at a low cost, and that they satisfy their ethical duty to inform their clients early in the process. Consequently, their low fees do not include the cost of representation in, for example, adversary proceedings or motions for relief from stay. Such additional services are frequently priced separately from the agreed fee for the bankruptcy filing.

One proposal for reforming the attorneys' fee payment structure would require that fees be paid incrementally through the entire duration of the Chapter 13 plan. Debtors' attorneys would then have a stake in ensuring that plans are feasible and that debtors complete plans. A second proposal would require that at least a portion of the fees be held back until after payments to creditors have commenced. Debtors' attorneys criticize both these proposals as requiring attorneys to provide services to debtors without clear expectation of receiving payment.

Reformers should note that courts superintend the allowance of fees, and judges have the duty to police ethical violations and conflicts of interest between attorney and client. The proposed amendment to Federal Rule

---

15. *Id.* at 18-19 (citations omitted). The footnote goes on to say, "The onus must be placed squarely on the debtor and his counsel to file truthful, complete documents." *Id.* at n. 14.

16. *Id.* at 23 (citations omitted).

of Bankruptcy Procedure 9011 would give judges another source of information to allow more active supervision of debtors' attorneys by the courts.
Ethical lapses by attorneys can and should be more vigilantly pursued by
the courts and bar association grievance committees.[17]

And finally:

It is not the current law [governing reaffirmations] that is at fault; it is the
inability or unwillingness of the courts and/or the debtors' attorneys to do
their jobs and enforce it.[18]

These stinging critiques of lawyers in the Minority Report presage the
attorney liability provisions that appear in the BRA. But the allegations are
pure propaganda. No data are offered to support the contention that lawyers
are behind the rising number of bankruptcies filed, or participating in the
filing of fraudulent bankruptcies. The Minority Report conceded that a only
small percentage of debtors abuse the system, but argued that these cases
had become notorious and tainted the public's (and creditors') perceptions
of the system.[19] Exactly one example of attorney malfeasance is cited.[20]

Even if attorneys were largely responsible for abuse of the bankruptcy
system, Congress could have addressed the abuses more directly.[21] For example, the drafters could have:

- excluded certain debts from discharge (as they have in the past);[22]
- expanded standing to file a § 707(b) motion to include trustees and
  creditors;
- invited bankruptcy courts to encourage state bars to regulate the content of bankruptcy attorney advertising that they found to be deceptive; or

---

17.   *Id.* at 24 (citations omitted).

18.   *Id.* at 31 (citations omitted).

19.   *Id.* at 20.

20.   *In re* Davila, 210 B.R. 727 (Bankr. S.D. Tex. 1996), which involved 155 Chapter
13 cases. At the same time, the Minority Report found insufficient support to justify a
change in the law of reaffirmation. It noted a "single" case of creditor malfeasance, *In re*
Lantanowich, 207 B.R. 326 (Bankr. D. Mass. 1997), the *Sears* case, which involved 2,734
reaffirmation agreements. Minority Report at 29, 31. Rather than blaming creditors, the
Minority held debtors' lawyers and the courts largely responsible for problems with
reaffirmations. *Id.*

21.   The broad regulations that they chose may become important in analyzing the
constitutionality of the provisions, discussed in Chapter 8.

22.   The amendment prohibiting discharge of student loans closed one such avenue
of abuse. *See, e.g.,* Code § 523(a)(8). An amendment that permitted the discharge of old
credit card debt, while denying the discharge to recent debt, would have prevented much
of the abuse claimed by proponents of the bill. *See, e.g.,* Testimony of George Wallace
before the House Judiciary Committee Hearing on H.R. 333 (Feb. 7, 2001).

- specified the sanctions to be imposed by the court on an attorney who was found knowingly to have filed a bankruptcy in bad faith.[23]

Instead, Congress acted broadly, enacting provisions that apply to every consumer debtor's attorney.[24]

II. *Voodoo Economics, Part 1*

Perversely (and this is what sticks in the craw), the credit card industry lobbyists did not draft a bill that will reap their clients any great benefits. Here's how creditors are likely to suffer:

- Bankruptcies are going to be more expensive for creditors as well as debtors.[25]

---

23.   The authors believe that Bankruptcy Rule 9011, amended in 1997, and Rule 11 provide ample authority to act against this conduct, but sanctions could have been identified to punish specified acts.

24.   And many other attorneys as well. See Chapter 15.

25.   At a recent program in Boston, a lawyer who works with major consumer creditors stated that the *increased* costs to creditors caused by the Bankruptcy Reform Act could be substantial. Comments of Ricardo Kilpatrick, ALI-ABA Course of Study on New Bankruptcy Legislation, Bankruptcy Abuse Prevention and Consumer Protection Act of 2005, Thursday, July 21, 2005. *See also* Eileen Alt Powell, *Bankruptcy law gives creditors a small payoff,* at http://www.modbee.com/business/story/11298118p-12047613c.html:

> [B]anking consultant Bert Ely of Alexandria, Va., is skeptical that creditors will gain much under the new law. "A lot of folks just don't have the income to handle repayment plans, or they'll start out under a plan and a few years down the road, they'll get into some trouble and not be able to complete it as envisioned," he added.

In addition, he added, it could be a "win-lose" situation for creditors because higher administrative costs in dealing with long-term collection programs will eat into the money they recover.

News reports after the effective date also noted the dramatic increase in filings prior to the BRA's effective date. *See, e.g.,* Gregory Cresci, *Morgan Stanley Costs to Rise in 4th Quarter; Bankruptcy Law Blamed,* Nov. 1, 2005, *at* http://www.bloomberg.com/apps/news?pid=10000103&sid=axxb4HnOyYiI&refer=us (citing increased costs reported by Morgan Stanley, which owns Discover, Citigroup, JP Morgan Chase, and Capital One). MBNA reported similar losses in its SEC filing, although it said:

> This accelerated rate of filings will significantly increase the Corporation's net credit losses for the month of December because bankrupt accounts are charged off by the end of the second calendar month following receipt of notification of the filing from the applicable court. See "Net Credit Losses" for a discussion of the charge-off of bankrupt accounts. However, the number of bankruptcy filings and resulting credit losses could be significantly offset in the periods following the effective date of the Act as a result of the earlier acceleration in filings and restrictions in the Act.

Form 10-Q for MBNA dated November 9, 2005 *at* http://biz.yahoo.com/e/051109/krb10-q.html. We'll see if this rosy prediction comes true. *See also We're crying crocodile tears*

- The new law is not likely to result in increased recoveries by credit card companies.[26]
- Fear of the new law pushed almost half a million people into bankruptcy *in the week* before it became effective.[27] Undoubtedly, some who filed might not have sought bankruptcy protection but for fear of the changes.
- The BRA is expected to shift distribution in Chapter 13 cases from unsecured to secured debts—principally automobile lenders.[28]

It is the disparity between the small incidence of wrongdoing and the large cost of preventing it that is so frustrating. It's bad economics.

Suppose, as a society, we decided to curb drunk driving and therefore presumed every driver was drunk. Suppose the law obligated all drivers to prove their sobriety by installing a breathalyzer in every car. Imposing heavy

---

here at Magpie, at http://www.magpieblog.blogspot.com/2005_10_23_magpieblog_archive.html.

26.   Although the overall scheme of the BRA is to force more debtors into Chapter 13, there is no statistical evidence in the record to support the theory that this will result in higher recoveries. Nor is there evidence that the new law will lower the cost of credit. In fact, the famous "$400 per household bankruptcy tax" bandied about so frequently by BRA supporters is supported in the Minority Report by this authority: "cite." Minority Report at 71 n.121 (*Really*, that's what it says.). *See also* Elizabeth Warren, *The Phantom $400*, note 4, above.

27.   "In the weeks before the October 17th effective date of the 2005 bankruptcy reform act [sic], filing soared to a record 479,430 filings in one week (the average weekly filings total 30,000)." E-mail from David Goch, Commercial Law League of America, dated Nov. 22, 2005, on file with author. News reports confirmed record filings all across the country in the period immediately preceding the effective date. Ironically, bankruptcy filings had not been increasing dramatically up to that point. *See, e.g.,* Press Release dated Aug. 24, 2005 (filings up less than 1% in 12 months ending in June 2005) *at* http://www.uscourts.gov/Press_Releases/bankruptcyfilings82405.html.

28.   *See, e.g.,* Hank Hildebrand, *Survey Shows Big Impact of Anti-Lienstripping Provisions in S. 625* (document on file with the author). Among the conclusions, it notes:

- 44.78% of existing Chapter 13 cases would be confirmed under S. 625, with a substantial reduction in distributions to general unsecured creditors.
- Assuming the filings in January 1999 are representative, 72,758 Chapter 13 cases per year could not pay anything to unsecured creditors and an additional 156,435 Chapter 13 cases per year would distribute less to general unsecured creditors under S. 625.
- The average reduction to unsecured creditors in each case in which debtors would still be eligible for Chapter 13 relief under S. 625 is $3,210.22
- The reduction in proposed distributions to general unsecured creditors under S. 625, even among Chapter 13 cases still feasible, would be approximately $100,447,600 per year.

Id. at 2. *See also* Eileen Alt Powell, *Bankruptcy law gives creditors a small payoff, at* http://www.modbee.com/business/story/11298118p-12047613c.html.

costs on drivers who are not engaged in the prohibited behavior is not an efficient way to lower the risk.[29]

This law is even worse. It does nothing to curb the drunken consumption of credit and protects the credit industry entirely, providing absolutely no limits on the extension of credit, nor any incentive to reduce the practices that statistics suggest led to an increase in consumer bankruptcy.[30] Which leads me to:

III. Voodoo Economics, Part 2: Credit Card Debt

In politics, as in life, the real issue driving debate isn't always explicitly identified. Supporters of the BRA made many assertions about abuse and misconduct—abuse of the system by debtors and misconduct by their attorneys.[31] It was natural for creditors to oppose the attorneys who assist debtors in discharging debts, and to seek to limit their impact. But in the final analysis, this is not the key to the attorney liability provisions of the BRA.

The driving issue is credit card debt.

A. The Bankruptcy Review Commission's Findings

Historically, and particularly during the era of usury limits, unsecured creditors were the main losers in bankruptcy. They had, in good faith, lent good money to debtors who, for many reasons, could not pay it back.[32] As the

---

29. Professor Elizabeth Warren of Harvard Law School has said that this bill is like to trying to reduce car accidents by closing emergency rooms.

30. Robert M. Lawless, *The Relationship Between Nonbusiness Bankruptcy Filings and Various Basic Measures of Consumer Debt* (2004), *available at* http://www.law.unlv. edu/faculty/rlawless/busbkr/body_filings.htm.

31. *See, e.g.,* Statement of Rep. Goodlatte, March 19, 2003, at CONG. REC. H1995 ("In addition, H.R. 975 protects consumers from bankruptcy mills that encourage folks to file for bankruptcy without fully informing them of their rights and the potential harms that bankruptcy can cause."). *See also* Chapter 3.

32. So that I will not immediately be dismissed as a bleeding-heart liberal former law professor, let me explain that I spent most of 1979 and 1980 as a young lawyer collecting credit card debt for First Interstate Bank of Arizona. Much of that unpaid debt was the result of one of the first mass mailings of pre-approved credit card applications to middle- and low-income consumers. It proved to be surprisingly unprofitable, because it was ahead of its time. At that time, *credit card interest rates were still regulated.* Banks discovered that if they lent money to deadbeats (an industry term of art for high-risk borrowers) at the same rate that they lent money to good credit risks, they would not make money on the former. They sent very young lawyers to clean up this mess, get back the credit cards, and collect some, if any, of the debt. I was one. I did not have much sympathy for the deadbeats at that point in my career. Having studied economics in undergraduate school, I did not understand how people could borrow money that they had no ability (and to my mind, intention) to repay. The bank I represented did not hound people to pay judgments that they clearly could not repay, and seized assets only when they could recover more than the attorneys' fees expended to enforce the judgment.

Everybody Loses

The members of Congress who supported this legislation[33] and the credit industry lobbyists who paid for it did not bother to calculate the full cost of the BRA. There are no clear winners under the BRA (except credit counselors). Increased costs include, for example:

1. **Costs to the bankruptcy courts because:**
   - more consumer debtors will file *pro se* using more bankruptcy court time and resources, but with no increase in funding for staff
   - more will fail to comply with the stringent new requirements of the law and have their cases dismissed, and possibly refile
   - those that are not dismissed will last longer, and take more court resources, under both Chapter 7 and Chapter 13
   - additional hearings will be required to comply with the law

2. **Costs to creditors who now have to:**
   - attend more hearings
   - challenge missing or insufficient documents
   - monitor the repayment schedules for more debtors, and for longer, and often for sums so small it would cost less to write off the debt
   - collect their debts outside of bankruptcy when cases are dismissed
   - take back automobiles that debtors will not keep because of the anti-cramdown provisions

---

Three events changed my mind about the relative responsibility of credit card issuers and deadbeats. First, in 1988 (the year that Michael Milken was under indictment), I went to Wharton and studied finance in the MBA program. I learned about the new financial models that predicted huge rewards when unrestrained lending met *unregulated interest rates*. Second, I wrote *The Madonnas Play Tug-of-War With the Whores: An Essay on Lobbyists and the Uniform Law Process*, 26 Loy. L.A. L. Rev. 563 (1993), which summarized my experience with the power of special interests in the law reform process. Nothing I outlined in that article can compare with the financial muscle flexed by the credit card companies in their quest to obtain passage of the BRA. Third, I represented an elderly couple in a bankruptcy after they had accumulated almost $50,000 in credit card debt on 17 credit cards. Although they had initially used the credit cards to help bridge the gap between Social Security (their only source of income) and their modest expenditures (particularly the cost of prescription drugs), the vast majority of the debt resulted from fees and interest generated by cash advances taken out to pay existing credit card bills (a common practice among debtors). When they came to me, they were not in default. No amount of pleading or negotiating would persuade the credit card companies that there was no secret inheritance or tort judgment pending. We were forced to file a Chapter 7. After that, I didn't feel sorry for credit card companies whose debts were discharged.

33.   It will be interesting to see how the bankruptcy—and appellate—courts deal with these unintended consequences. "The fact that Congress may not have foreseen all of the consequences of a statutory enactment is not sufficient reason for refusing to give effect to its plain meaning." Union Bank v. Wolas, 502 U.S. 151, 158 (1991).

3. **Costs to debtors (many of which are imposed before filing on all consumer debtors, none of whom has been proven guilty of any wrongdoing) including:**
   - the additional fees they will pay to their attorneys
   - the cost of the faux credit counseling they will be forced to undergo
   - the costs of assembling the documentation required by the law
   - the lost time associated with these increased burdens
   - the lost pensions and Social Security benefits when a certain number of debtors lose hope in the legal system and go underground rather than face a lifetime of debt repayment

4. **Costs to other lawyers and clients, including:**
   - the cost to non-bankruptcy attorneys of learning about the law and deciding whether they wish to comply with the provisions so that they may continue to give bankruptcy advice to their clients
   - the cost to non-bankruptcy attorneys who do not learn about the law and run afoul of its provisions, although they represent no clients in bankruptcy
   - the lost fees for non-bankruptcy lawyers who refuse to give any advice related to bankruptcy to their non-debtor clients[34]
   - the cost to clients who do not receive needed advice related to bankruptcy law
   - the costs to non-bankruptcy lawyers who, having failed to give needed advice related to bankruptcy, are sued by their clients.

5. **Costs to federal, state, and local government that will result when:**
   - they lose tax payments from debtors who go underground
   - they lose sales tax payments debtors would have made if they had been given a fresh start
   - money that would have been injected into local economies is instead shipped to credit card companies in Delaware and New York
   - entrepreneurship declines because the risk of financial failure is dramatically increased, reducing employment and income tax revenues
   - Congress has to go back and fix the myriad flaws, errors, and bad judgments incorporated in the Act

---

34.   At a recent meeting of the American Association of Agricultural Lawyers in October 2005, there was a program to introduce members to the provisions of the BRA. Many of these attorneys represent clients who qualify as "assisted persons" under the terms of the law (see Chapter 4) but are not debtors. One lawyer responded to the program by saying that his representation agreement from then on would include a statement that he did not provide any information related to bankruptcy and that if the client had questions, to please direct them to a bankruptcy attorney. E-mail from Professor Barbara Glesner Fines dated Oct. 9, 2005, on file with the author. There is no answer whether this kind of defensive law will protect a lawyer from claims by the client if the lawyer fails to give needed advice relative to bankruptcy law.

number of consumer bankruptcies began to rise dramatically in the 1980s, it was natural to ask why.

Since a central force driving the Commission's creation was the increase in consumer bankruptcies, the Commission was concerned about the causes. Although it discussed various factors, the Commission Report highlighted a series of studies of the rise in consumer credit card debt, and specifically the correlation between the rise in consumer debt and the rise in consumer bankruptcies. The report noted:

> Between 1977 and 1997, consumer debt has grown nearly 799%. For generations, Americans have experienced divorces, illnesses and uninsured medical costs, and job layoffs. However, never before have so many families faced these setbacks with so much consumer debt.[35]

The report went on to analyze both anecdotal evidence and empirical research that support a correlation between the rise in consumer bankruptcies and the rise in consumer debt levels.[36] It noted that the Congressional Budget Office dismissed as "unscientific" a report by the credit card industry attributing the increase in consumer bankruptcies to social factors, such as reduced social stigma, and advertisements for bankruptcy assistance.[37]

The Commission Report pointed a finger at credit card lending. In the era of unregulated interest rates, the Commission Report suggested that irresponsible lending by unsecured (and some secured) creditors, and not moral laxity by debtors, was responsible for the rapid rise in consumer bankruptcies.

> [T]he empirical studies seem to indicate that the sharp rise in consumer bankruptcy—27% [in 1996] alone—may be more a function of a changing debt picture than of a sudden willingness to take advantage of the bankruptcy system.[38]

Commission review of that data culminated in this recommendation:

1.4.1 Credit Card Debt
Except for credit card debts that are excepted from discharge under section 523(a)(2)(B) (for materially false written statements respecting the debtor's financial condition) and section 523(a)(14) (debts incurred to pay nondischargeable taxes to the United States), debts incurred on a credit card issued to the debtor that did not exceed the debtor's credit limit should

---

35.   Commission Report at 84-85 (citation omitted).
36.   *Id.* at 84-86.
37.   *Id.* at 86.
38.   Commission Report at 87.

be dischargeable unless they were incurred within 30 days before the order for relief under Title 11.[39]

The Commission Report went on to point to testimony that tighter lending practices—not surprisingly—result in lower default rates and fewer bankruptcies.[40] It cited a study suggesting that 54% of consumer bankruptcies would be eliminated by withholding credit cards from the bottom 10% of the market.[41]

The Commission Report ended this discussion with a litany of predictions based upon this pattern of lending to those who are unlikely to repay, noting:

- Credit card issuers earn about 75% of their revenues from the interest paid by borrowers who do not pay in full each month, and some companies charge or cancel customers who pay in full each month;
- Cash advances on credit cards and home equity loans and locating ATMs in casinos enable gambling using consumer credit. Initial studies suggest legal gambling is positively correlated with bankruptcy.[42]
- Marketing by credit card companies resulted in 2.5 billion credit card applications a year during the three years prior to the report. Consumer credit is profitable even with high default rates, on average twice as profitable as other banking activities.[43]
- The fastest-growing segment of the consumer credit market is subprime lending, a practice that the FDIC issued a warning about in May 1997.
- Credit card companies are targeting young people, although they often have no income, no credit history, and no parental approval.
- Home equity lending places more homes at risk, and pre-approved credit lines are becoming common.

---

39.   *Id.* at 5.

40.   *Id.* at 87-89.

41.   *Id.* at 88.

42.   Not surprisingly, further studies after the Commission Report have observed this correlation. *See, e.g.,* Laura Parker, *Gambler Says Casino Played Him,* USA TODAY, Feb. 21, 2003, at 3A ("John Kindt, a professor of business and legal policy at the University of Illinois, says the economic cost of gambling addiction includes lost wages, bankruptcy filings, lost purchases of other consumer goods, and increased crime. 'People should ask why gambling was illegal in this country for 100 years,' Kindt says. 'Addicted gamblers cost society tens of thousands of dollars a year.' In 1999, the National Gambling Impact Study Commission estimated the number of addicted gamblers in the USA at 1.8 million to 2.5 million.").

43.   "According to Synovate, which tracks the industry through consumer surveys, an estimated 1.4 billion applications were sent in the first quarter [of 2005]. That's 5.8 applications per household every month." Bob Sullivan, *Deluged with credit card mail? Help is coming* (MSNBC, Aug. 8, 2005), *available at* http://www.msnbc.msn.com/id/8827007/.

- Credit is being extended to debtors immediately after they emerge from bankruptcy, since they cannot discharge their debts again for six years.[44]

B. The Industry Response

As Cyndi Lauper sang so eloquently, "Money changes everything."[45] That sentiment efficiently sums up what happened to the recommendations of the Bankruptcy Review Commission.[46] The Minority Report ignored the Commission's concerns about credit card debt completely and focused instead on the irresponsibility of debtors and their attorneys.[47] The credit card industry was undaunted by the Commission's opinion of its practices; its response can be characterized by the maxim, "The best defense is a good offense." In hindsight, it is not hard to see that the Commission Report triggered the BRA.[48] Given this frontal assault on its practices, it is not surprising that the credit card industry reacted preemptively, relentlessly wielding money and political pressure, to impose a bankruptcy revision more to its liking.

One notable response to criticisms of the credit industry's practices has been rhetorical: whenever the BRA was nearing a vote, or the editorial attacks on its practices heated up, the industry—in particular, Citibank—would run

---

44.   Commission Report at 91-94. In early 1997, The Consumer Federation of America issued a report blaming credit card debt on the increase in consumer bankruptcies. It recommended limiting credit card debt to 20% of household income. Stephen Brobeck, *The Consumer Impacts of Expanding Credit Card Debt*, February 1997 (Consumer Federation of America). One writer attacked the Consumer Federation Report, arguing that expansion of lending to low-income households was positive, and that the decision to extend credit should be made not by the government but by consumers, "limited only by a financial institution's willingness to supply such credit." Vern McKinley, *Ballooning Bankruptcies: Issuing Blame for the Explosive Growth*, Reg. Vol. 20, No. 4 (Cato Institute 1997) at 5.

45.   The song was written by Tom Gray in 1978 and recorded by Lauper on her 1983 album, *She's So Unusual*:

> Money changes everything
> money changes everything
> we think we know what we're doing
> we don't pull the strings
> It's all in the past now
> money changes everything.

46.   See Chapter 3.

47.   In fact, the Minority Report takes no position on Commission Recommendation 1.4.1. Minority Report at 41.

48.   *See* Susan Jensen, A *Legislative History of the Bankruptcy Abuse Prevention and Consumer Protection Act of 2005*, 79 Am. Bankr. L.J. 485, 489-90.

extremely clever "Use Credit Responsibly" ads, similar to the liquor industry's responsible drinking campaigns.

There is one hilariously obvious difference between these two industries: once liquor is shipped, the manufacturer has no control over who consumes it or how much they consume. In marked contrast, the credit card industry controls every penny of credit that is consumed, and could stop excess borrowing instantaneously even after it ships out the billions of applications. They choose not to, because it remains profitable for them to lend to overextended debtors. If they really wanted people to use credit responsibly, they would watch the ads themselves, and apply the cost saved by not airing them to the losses caused by bankruptcies.

Unwilling to curb its addiction to this highly profitable segment of the market,[49] the credit card industry has only increased its questionable lending practices in the period since the Commission Report issued.[50] Even the economic

---

49.   As reported in *Business Week*:

> Last year, credit-card issuers reported record profits of $30 billion—much of it earned on liberal lending policies and punishing fees that often exacerbate the financial woes of cardholders who have gotten in over their heads. Borrowers who make a late payment—whether it's for the phone bill, a credit card, or a house payment—often are charged punitive rates averaging 29% on all their cards. These on-the-edge borrowers are the most profitable part of any bank's card operations, as long as they don't default.

Mara Der Veanesian, *Tough Love for Debtors*, BUS. WEEK, Apr. 25, 2005, at 98. Shortly after the passage of the BRA, the Senate scheduled hearings on the practices of the credit card industry, which Republicans promised to do during the BRA debate. *See* U.S. Senate Committee on Banking, *Examining the Current Legal and Regulatory Requirements and Industry Practices for Credit Card Issuers With Respect to Consumer Disclosures and Marketing Efforts*, May 17, 2005, *available at* http://banking.senate.gov/index.cfm?Fuseaction =Hearings.Detail&HearingID=154. *See also* Chapter 3.

50.   There were news stories in 2003 describing a downturn in credit card portfolio profits. *See, e.g., Morgan Stanley's Second-Quarter Profit May Fall on Credit Cards,* BLOOMBERG NEWS SERVICE, June 17, 2003, *at* www.bloomberg.com. This report noted a probable profit drop at Morgan Stanley to 68 from 72 cents a year earlier, due primarily to a drop of 8% in its Discover card unit. MBNA reported an increase in uncollectible loans to 5.35% from 5.14% a year before. Capital One reported an increase in losses in May to 6.4% from 6.36% in May 2003. Note that none of these accounts reports a loss on the credit card portfolios; these are reports of *falling profits*, which have been at record levels in recent years. *But see* "The Profitability of Credit Card Operations of Depository Institutions," Report by the Board of Governors of the Federal Reserve (June 2004), which noted that for 2003:

> [R]eturns for large credit card banks increased 38 basis points or 11.6 percent from 2002. Returns on credit card operations have been increasing over the past four years and compare favorably with returns experienced during the mid-1990s. Despite improved earnings in recent years, returns on credit card operations in 2003 remain below their high point attained in 1993. . . . [C]redit card

downturn early in the decade did not curb enthusiasm for lending to consumers for whom repayment of the principal is a mathematical impossibility.[51]

IV. A Note About Interest Rates

As noted above, the credit card companies make enormous profits lending to people who do not or cannot pay off their credit card debts. Since interest rates rise with risk, the profitability of debt actually *increases* over time as the creditworthiness of the borrower decreases.

The higher interest rate includes a risk premium, which is intended to compensate lenders for this increased risk. It's a form of insurance, and the longer the risk is deferred, the greater the pool of funds that theoretically[52] should be set aside to pay when risk becomes reality. But the risk premium assumes that a certain percentage of all loans will not be repaid, and this is also true for credit card lending to low-income borrowers. Even when the predicted percentage of debt is discharged in bankruptcy, these loan portfolios have made money.[53]

Still, the risk of major, and rising, default rates has made the credit card companies nervous. They sought and received congressional assistance in collecting these debts even while they reaped the rewards of the risk premiums they charged. It is as if the life insurance industry came to Congress and asked it to outlaw death, because they had paid out all the premiums to their shareholders, and now could not pay death benefits when they came due.

---

earnings have been consistently higher than returns on all commercial bank activities. For example, for all commercial banks, the average return on all assets, before taxes and extraordinary items, was 2.05 percent in 2003, well below the returns on credit card activities in that year.

Id. at 2-3.

51.   *See, e.g.,* Commission Report at 83.

52.   I say "theoretically" because credit card companies are not required to account for their anticipated losses in quite the way that insurance companies are. In fact, credit card companies do have reserve accounts, but most of these profits have been paid out to investors, not set aside to offset defaults.

53.   As I wrote in an editorial on this topic:

[T]he bill benefits the credit card industry, whose insatiable hunger for customers has pushed more cards and higher limits into the hands of consumers, including many who should never have received credit. Some cards bear interest rates of 29 percent. Such high rates should compensate the credit card companies for the risk of nonpayment.

But the credit card lobby didn't feel secure even as it reaped record profits. It went to Congress and bought—at an estimated cost of $30 million during the last election, and even more this year—a bankruptcy bill that will make it much harder for people to discharge credit card debt.

Corinne Cooper, *An Odious Bankruptcy Measure,* Kansas City Star, Aug. 11, 2002, at B8.

Critical to their plan is to burden entry into the bankruptcy system, and raise the cost of filing so that people will be precluded from filing because they cannot navigate the system, or because they are too broke to go bankrupt. A key component is to drive up the cost of legal assistance, accomplished in the BRA by increasing every debtor's burden and every attorney's financial risk. Attorneys who remain in practice will raise prices because of increased time spent complying with the new provisions, and increased risk if they fail to police their debtors' filings sufficiently.[54]

V. My Bad?

The real insult—the slap in the face to all consumer debtors' attorneys—is not that the BRA's treatment of lawyers appears to be unjustified by the facts.[55] It's that the law forces consumer debtors' attorneys to behave in ways that are detrimental to their clients:

- by requiring lawyers to describe themselves as "debt relief agencies," lumped in with petition preparers, a group with a less than illustrious history,
- by forcing them to give bad legal advice, and preventing them from offering some good advice, and
- by placing unnecessary burdens, risk, and expense on the practice of consumer bankruptcy law.

WARNING!!

There's no question that the cumulative effect of all these provisions will be to drive some lawyers who currently file consumer bankruptcies out of the practice, to increase the number of *pro se* filers, and to increase the number and business of bankruptcy petition preparers.

Let's not forget that the BRA will raise the cost of filing by forcing debtors to undergo "re-education" with consumer credit counselors,[56] just another

---

54. *See* notes 9-11, above.

55. This is particularly true in comparison to its treatment of two groups with a demonstrated record of preying on the financially vulnerable: credit counseling agencies and bankruptcy petition preparers. See Chapter 18.

56. I call this "the Barn Door" provision because it comes a tad late! If we genuinely want to educate consumers about the danger of excessive debt, a laudable objective, we'd probably pick a time earlier than the eve of bankruptcy for these lessons. This provision is not intended to provide consumers with much-needed insight into the nature of debt, its

punitive measure to make it more difficult for people to get to the courthouse and discharge their debts.

Here's what Senator Hatch, a prime mover of the bill, had to say on the Senate floor the day of the bill's passage by that body:

> It is getting to the point where some might even forget why we initiated this legislation. We have been at it for 8 years now. Some of those who oppose the bill and are offering final postcloture amendments are flying in the face of years and years of hard work and bipartisan compromise. By the way, the ones who bring up the amendments will never vote for this bill no matter what you do, unless it is a complete cave-in, so we cannot solve the problems that are eating our country alive in bankruptcy. And they do it under the guise that they are trying to protect the weak and the infirm and those who really cannot help themselves.
>
> Give me a break. We over here get so tired of those populist arguments. . . . Yet it happens every time—they get up and act like the world is coming to an end because their populist rhetoric is not being listened to. Unfortunately, there are people out there who really believe this stuff when somebody starts yelling, screaming, and shouting on the Senate floor. [57]

We began this chapter admitting that there are examples of abusive bankruptcy filings and complicit attorneys. But none of the conduct alleged by the BRA's supporters is borne out by the facts: there is no empirical evidence proving a significant growth in these problems, nor any other practices that justify this punitive reaction. Congress has reached out and slapped the face of our profession, with no more justification than that it suited their contributors to do so.

---

individual and social costs, or to discourage in any way the excessive consumer borrowing that has been driven in large part by the barrage of credit cards that are offered to American consumers.

In fact, the credit industry fought every attempt to give real information to consumers that might curb their hunger for debt. *See, e.g.,* the vote on proposed Senate Amendment 15 to Senate Bill 256, the bill that became the BRA. This amendment, which was offered by Senator Akaka, was entitled: "To require enhanced disclosure to consumers regarding the consequences of making only minimum required payments in the repayment of credit card debt, and for other purposes." The proposed amendment was defeated in the Senate on March 2, 2005, by a vote of 59-40.

57.   151 Cong. Rec. S2339 (daily ed. Mar. 9, 2005) (statement of Sen. Hatch).

CHAPTER 3

A History of Attorney Liability
in the Bankruptcy Reform Act

by *Corinne Cooper*[1]

The Bankruptcy Reform Act[2] has a long and complicated history.[3] It contains many provisions distasteful for reasons ranging from policy and politics

---

1.   Most of those who assisted in the preparation of this Chapter wish to remain anonymous, but the author thanks Marc S. Stern for his assistance in drafting the section on lobbying by the ABA. The author is also very grateful to Catherine E. Vance, Thomas J. Yerbich, and Christopher Kaup for helping with this chapter and teaching her so much about bankruptcy law.

   Interesting insights undoubtedly came from other people, but they are absolved of responsibility for all errors, which are my own. This isn't just politesse; I am a novice in this process, having begun to follow the issue in earnest only in 2000. Many people have been actively involved with this issue since the creation of the National Bankruptcy Review Commission.

2.   The Bankruptcy Abuse Prevention and Consumer Protection Act of 2005, Pub. L. No. 109-8, 119 Stat. 23 ["BRA"]. The Act is rather euphemistically titled; some opponents refer to it as the Bankruptcy Act Reform Fiasco, or BARF; one named it "The Bankruptcy Prevention and Consumer Abuse Act." The editors of this book have decided to use "Bankruptcy Reform Act," "BRA," or "the Act" as a neutral middle ground. References to a section of the law passed will say "BRA." All references to "the Code" mean the Bankruptcy Code, codified at Title 11 of the United States Code. This Chapter is based in large part upon work that previously appeared in Corinne Cooper, Barbara Glesner Fines & Catherine E. Vance, "The Attorney Liability Provisions of the BRA: A Short History of the War on Bankruptcy Lawyers," Program Materials for "Business Bankruptcy for the Rest of Us," ABA Annual Meeting, San Francisco, California, August 2003.

3.   For an extraordinarily comprehensive history of the BRA, *see* Susan Jensen, *A Legislative History of the Bankruptcy Abuse Prevention and Consumer Protection Act of 2005,* 79 AM. BANKR. L.J. 485 (2005) [cited here as "Jensen"]. As both general counsel to the National Bankruptcy Review Commission and majority counsel to the Subcommittee on Commercial and Administrative Law of the House Judiciary Committee, she was in a unique position to observe the law's development. If this account differs from hers in any detail of chronology, trust her version.

to good writing and statutory construction. But among its many troubling provisions is an assault on the independence of bankruptcy attorneys, particularly those representing consumer debtors. This is a history of the attorney liability provisions.[4]

Since its initial introduction in 1997, every version of the BRA contained some variation of provisions regulating the conduct of attorneys who practice consumer bankruptcy law. The version enacted into law contains several of these provisions.[5]

I. The History Begins: The National Bankruptcy Review Commission

Any history of the attorney liability provisions must begin with the final Report of the National Bankruptcy Review Commission.[6] The Commission was created by Congress to recommend revisions to the bankruptcy system without disturbing "the fundamental tenets of current law."[7] As described in its final report,

> The Commission was created as an independent commission to investigate and study issues relating to the Bankruptcy Code, to solicit divergent views on the operation of the bankruptcy system, to evaluate the advisability of proposals, and to prepare a report to be submitted to the President, Congress and the Chief Justice not later than two years after the date of its first meeting, which took place on October 20, 1995.[8]

The Commission sought with its recommendations to balance the competing interests inherent in bankruptcy, noting:

> Balance is essential. Without it, the American bankruptcy system can be neither equitable nor efficient. The laws enacted over the last 100 years have had balance as their goal and their common theme, spoken or unspoken, trying to provide both fair treatment for creditors and a fresh start for debtors.[9]

---

4.   During the writing of this Chapter, one reviewer asked, "Why are you writing this chapter? It's nothing but bad news!" Indeed, there is no way to slant the overall history as a positive story for debtors' lawyers. But at least they will not be blindsided by adversaries who are aware of the history, and they will not argue that "Congress could not have intended . . ." when this Chapter makes clear that, in many cases, it probably did.

5.   See Chapter 1.

6.   Report of the National Bankruptcy Review Commission, October 20, 1997, Vol. 1 (U.S. Government Printing Office 1997) ["the Commission Report"].

7.   *Id.* at iv.

8.   The Commission Report at 47 (citations omitted).

9.   *Id.* at vi.

In retrospect, this objective seems charmingly naive. The provisions of the BRA are neither balanced nor efficient. Yet the report itself points to some of the forces that would result in the wholesale rejection of the Commission's recommendations.

A. The Commission Recommendations

Two recommendations in the Commission report are directly relevant to the history of attorney liability:

Recommendation 1.1.2 *Heightened Requirements for Accurate Information*
The Bankruptcy Code should direct trustees to perform random audits of debtors' schedules to verify the accuracy of the information listed. Cases would be selected for audit according to guidelines developed by the Executive Office for the United States Trustees.[10]

Recommendation 1.1.4 *Rule 9011*
The Commission endorses the amended Rule 9011 of the Federal Rules of Bankruptcy Procedure, to become effective on December 1, 1997, which will make an attorney's presentation to the court of any petition, pleading, written motion, or other paper a certification that the attorney made a reasonable inquiry into the accuracy of that information, and thus will help ensure that attorneys take responsibility for the information that they and their clients provide.[11]

The Commission Report explained that accurate information was essential to the integrity of the bankruptcy system:

Serious questions were raised about the basic information the parties put into the system. These concerns prompted the Commission to recommend audits of debtors' schedules to ensure accurate disclosure of information. Attorneys representing all parties also have been criticized, prompting a continuing discussion of the responsibility of an attorney for the accuracy of the information filed. The Commission developed recommendations to deal with these specific problems that call into question the integrity of the system.[12]

The next sentence of the report stated that there "is evidence of questionable use of the bankruptcy process by both debtors and creditors."[13] To

---

10.   *Id.* at 1.
11.   *Id.* at 112.
12.   *Id.* at 80.
13.   *Id.*

address abuse by creditors' lawyers, the recommendations included this provision:

1.1.3 *False Claims*

Courts should be authorized to order creditors who file and fail to correct materially false claims in bankruptcy to pay costs and the debtors' attorneys' fees involved in correcting the claim. If a creditor knowingly files a false claim, the court could impose appropriate additional sanctions.[14]

The report stated:

Some creditors also have found ways to take advantage of the system. Abusive post-bankruptcy debt collection, documented in the courts and reported widely in the news media, led the Commission to recommend banning the reaffirmation of unsecured debts and providing more supervision for reaffirmation of secured debt. The 1970 Commission recommended similar restrictions that might have avoided many of the current problems. Some creditors reportedly threaten to bring unfounded non-dischargeability actions that debtors cannot afford to defend as another way to collect dischargeable debt through reaffirmations. They would lose this option with the Commission's recommendation to set clear dischargeability rules for credit card debt.[15]

B. The Minority Report

These Commission recommendations, while supported by a majority of the members of the Commission, were not unanimously endorsed. A "minority report"[16] submitted by two members contained these alternative recommendations:

---

14.   *Id.* at 81.

15.   *Id.* More about the credit card issue in Chapter 2.

16.   Although this is generally known as the Minority Report, technically there was no such document. The Commission Report refers to these submissions as "Individual Commission Views." One was signed by two members of the Commission: Hon. Edith R. Jones, a member of the 5th Circuit Court of Appeals and a resident of Texas (appointed to the Commission by Chief Justice Rehnquist) and James I. Shepard, a tax and insolvency consultant from California (appointed by former Senate Minority Leader Bob Dole). Two other members of the Commission generally concurred in the document—which they referred to as a "dissent"—but wrote a separate opinion. They were John A. Gose, a real estate lawyer from Seattle (appointed by former Speaker Thomas Foley), and Jeffery J. Hartley, an Alabama lawyer who had served as majority counsel to the Senate Subcommittee on Courts and Administrative Practice (appointed by Senator Robert Byrd, former President *pro tem* of the Senate, and George Mitchell, then Majority Leader of the Senate). Commission Report at 56-57.

1.1.2 *Random Audits*
The U.S. Trustee should supervise random audits to verify the accuracy of representations made in debtors' schedules. Cases would be selected for audit according to guidelines developed by the U.S. Trustee. A debtor's discharge could be revoked or other penalties imposed based on deficiencies uncovered in an audit.[17]

The random audit provision was a slightly stronger recommendation than that of the Commission. In its discussion of random audits, the Minority Report noted that the Commission received "testimony that the information reported in the debtors' schedules is often unreliable."[18] It recommended specific amendments to §§ 727 and 1328 to deny or revoke discharge if an audit uncovered material inaccuracies.[19] The Minority members went on to suggest that failure to cooperate with the audit should also result in a denial of discharge.[20] The report also noted that irregularities might subject the debtor to prosecution.[21]

1.1.4 *Federal Rule of Bankruptcy Procedure 9011*
Bankruptcy Rule 9011 should be revised to require an attorney's signature, subject to Rule 9011 sanctions, to the debtors' lists, schedules, statements of affairs and of intention, and amendments thereto.[22]

The Minority's Rule 9011 proposal was also stronger than the Commission's. It focused very clearly on the responsibility of debtor's counsel to police the schedules, noting:

Requiring attorneys to sign schedules, as they are required similarly to certify all other pleadings filed at court, would clarify their responsibility to inquire into the accuracy of the information, and will improve the quality of data in the bankruptcy files.[23]

---

17.   The Commission Report at Chapter 5: Recommendations for Reform of Consumer Bankruptcy Law by Four Dissenting Commissioners, submitted by The Honorable Edith H. Jones and Commissioner James I. Shepard, at Executive Summary 8 [cited here as "the Minority Report"].

18.   *Id.* at 14. It cannot go unmentioned that only two examples are offered as authority for this assertion, one of which clearly does not support the statement in the text.

19.   *Id.* at 15.

20.   *Id.*

21.   *Id.*

22.   *Id.* at 18.

23.   *Id.* at 19.

The report noted that the then-proposed (now promulgated) Rule 9011 amendment would still not clearly apply to schedules. It went on to note that the revision of 9011 would conform to Rule 11:

> ... by allowing a party threatened with sanctions to 'withdraw or correct' [amend] the challenged pleading voluntarily. The policy that supports voluntary amendments in ordinary federal court litigation does not apply in bankruptcy where ... deadlines for action spawn gamesmanship. The onus must be squarely on the debtor and his counsel to file truthful, complete documents.[24]

This discussion clearly delineates two key tenets of the Minority Report:

1. Debtors are expected to file absolutely complete, accurate schedules from the initiation of the case, or pay the consequences.
2. Debtors' attorneys are expected to police the process, or similarly pay the consequences.

Although these requirements seem perfectly reasonable in the abstract, they ignore the realities of consumer bankruptcy, where poor record-keeping and a lack of financial sophistication are common. As the Commission Report noted:

> Realistically, malfeasance is unlikely to be the cause of much of the alleged inaccuracy. Rather, in a system designed to deal with financial failure, it would not be surprising if many debtors had difficulty complying fully with detailed financial disclosures. Debtor representatives and judges have reported that the financial affairs of individual debtors often are in complete disarray. Bills and pay stubs, if available at all, often are brought to a lawyer's offices in a shoe box or a paper bag. A debtor without legal representation may have no assistance in putting together the pieces of his financial life to make the requisite disclosures.[25]

This fundamental difference in perspective between the majority and minority Commissioners illuminates the disparate approaches taken by the two factions. The Minority Report went on to recommend additional reforms designed to enhance the integrity of the bankruptcy system, including:

---

24. *Id.* at 19, n.14. There is no explanation of the bracketed text, which appears in the original.

25. Commission Report at 108.

- limiting debtors' benefits from amendments to the schedules,
- requiring debtors to submit the prior three years' filed tax returns with their petitions,
- conditioning discharge on a trustee's certificate of cooperation and that all tax returns and other documents have been furnished,
- revoking a discharge if a random audit shows acts or omissions justifying revocation, and
- barring or revoking discharge if the debtor makes material false statements or omissions, and allowing a non-dischargeable fee and costs award to a party who uncovers the conduct.[26]

While acknowledging that the percentage of cases involving debtor abuse is small, the Minority Report stated that these cases "taint the public's and the creditors' perceptions of the system."[27] Obviously, these Commissioners did not calculate the cost to the bankruptcy system of their proposals, which are imposed before filing on every consumer debtor, none of whom has been found guilty of any wrongdoing.

At this point, the presumption of wrongdoing abruptly stopped. The Minority Report dismissed the Commission recommendation on false claims, stating bluntly, "There is no need for redundant rules to deter false claims";[28] it did not find that additional penalties for false statements by debtors were similarly redundant.

The report recommended an additional provision aimed at debtors' lawyers:

1.1B *Debtors' Attorneys' Fees*
Payment of consumer debtor attorneys' fees should be structured to remove attorneys' incentives to direct debtors' filing choices toward any particular chapter for fee-related reasons and to encourage more effective debtor counseling and representation.[29]

The Minority noted that the ratio of Chapter 13 to Chapter 7 filings is the result of many factors, varying throughout the United States, including legal culture, preference, and training. But it also raised a more sinister cause:

Critics suggest that the number of Chapter 13 filings relative to Chapter 7s is linked to the ability of debtors' attorneys to earn a higher fee in Chapter 13 cases than in Chapter 7 cases. Debtors' attorneys are also

---

26. Recommendation 1.1A of the Minority Report at Executive Summary 8-9.

27. *Id.* at 20. The report notes that bankruptcy has been described as "legalized theft" and "a haven for criminals." *Id.*

28. *Id.* at 8.

29. Minority Report at 9.

able, under current law, to take advantage of priority status for the payment of their fees in Chapter 13, such that in many cases attorney fees are paid from the first funds a debtor pays to the Chapter 13 trustee for the distribution to creditors. Because a debtor's attorney is also a debtor's creditor, the attorney has a conflict of interest when counseling a debtor as to choice of chapter under which to file.[30]

The Minority Report went on to point to ethical lapses by debtors' attorneys that result from unstructured payment of attorneys' fees in bankruptcy, including the failure to provide representation after plan confirmation in Chapter 13, and the failure to appear in adversary proceedings or motions for relief from the stay when a low fixed fee is paid for filing.[31] In response to the protestation of debtors' attorneys that this proposal required them to provide services for which they have no expectation of payment, the Minority Report responded:

[R]eformers should note that courts superintend the allowance of fees, and judges have the duty to police ethical violations and conflicts of interest between attorney and client. The proposed amendment to Federal Rule of Bankruptcy Procedure 9011 would give judges another source of information to allow more active supervision of debtors' attorneys by the courts. Ethical lapses by attorneys can and should be more vigilantly pursued by the courts and bar association grievance committees.[32]

Again, the Minority failed to consider the impact on the bankruptcy system as a whole if attorneys were required to represent debtors in matters for which they have not been paid, if attorneys were obliged to charge higher fees to account for this possibility, or if, as recommended by the Minority, fees were held back during the pendency of the case.

If you believed the assertions of the Minority, enhanced regulation and liability of attorneys in bankruptcy appeared warranted. The Minority Report painted debtors' attorneys as willing participants in their clients' "legalized theft"—scofflaws who could be forced to submit honest pleadings only on penalty of personal liability.

---

30.   *Id.* at 23. This is a puzzling point to find in the history of a piece of legislation that is intended to force thousands of people from Chapter 7 into Chapter 13. It also ignores good free-market theory: if lawyers indeed could make more money filing 13s, and that incentive was affecting the choice of filing, then why weren't Chapter 13 cases growing by leaps and bounds?

31.   See Chapter 6 for discussion of unbundling in bankruptcy cases.

32.   *Id.* at 24. Note again, however, that no increased scrutiny of creditors' attorneys' ethics is viewed as necessary, nor are they expected to perform services for their clients without payment of their fees.

Viewed in this light, who would doubt that debtors' attorneys deserved the increased scrutiny and regulation they were about to receive?

II. The Congressional Response: The History of the BRA Provisions

A. The 105th Congress

The BRA began its tortured life as H.R. 2500, in October 1997, just as the Report of the National Bankruptcy Review Commission was about to be released.[33] Viewed as a preemptive strike on the Commission Report recommendations, H.R. 2500 included a means test, limitations on filing, and a longer period between discharges. That bill, however, contained nothing on Bankruptcy Rule 9011, nor any other provision explicitly creating liability for debtors' attorneys. Although subcommittee hearings were held, the bill was not reported out of the subcommittee.[34]

Instead, in February of 1998, H.R. 3150 was introduced by then-Congressman Gekas.[35] By the time it passed the House, it contained the first iteration of almost every final attorney liability provision:

- Section 101 included a definition of "projected monthly net income" that permitted an adjustment of the statutory formula in extraordinary circumstances.[36] The adjustment process included a requirement that the debtor file a signed statement with his petition declaring that he was eligible for relief, and required the debtor's attorney to certify the correctness of the debtor's filing:[37]

---

33. H.R. 2500, The Responsible Borrower Protection Act, introduced in the 105th Cong. in the House on Sept. 18. 1997, sponsored by Rep. McCollum. Its introduction was noted in the Bankruptcy Reform Commission Report at 89, referring to the means test, which was the most significant feature of that bill.

34. H.R. 2500 Bill Summary and Status for the 105th Cong.

35. H.R. 3150, The Bankruptcy Reform Act of 1998, introduced in the 105th Cong. in the House on Feb. 3, 1998, sponsored by Cong. Gekas and 75 other members.

36. *Id.* at Section 101, adding Code § 109(h)(3).

37. *Id.* at Section 101, adding Code § 109(h)(4) (emphasis added). The entire provision read:

(4) In the event that the debtor establishes extraordinary circumstances that require allowance for additional expenses or adjustment of current monthly total income, projected monthly net income for purposes of this section shall be the amount calculated under paragraph (3) less such additional expenses or income adjustment as such extraordinary circumstances require.
(A) This paragraph shall not apply unless the debtor files with the petition—
(i) a written statement that this paragraph applies in determining the debtor's eligibility for relief under chapter 7 of this title;
(ii) if adjustment of current monthly total income is claimed, an explanation of any income that has been lost in the 6 months

(A) This paragraph shall not apply unless the debtor files with the petition—

. . .

(v) a sworn statement signed by the debtor and, if the debtor is represented by counsel, *by the debtor's attorney*, that the information required under this paragraph is true and correct.[38]

- Section 102 required that adequate income be committed to a Chapter 13 plan that paid unsecured creditors and provided a statutory formula for making that determination.[39] Section 102 added a section to the Code permitting adjustments to income or expenses under that formula, which required a written statement of extraordinary circumstances when seeking an adjustment. This section also required a sworn statement by the debtor and the debtor's attorney:

(E) a sworn statement signed by the debtor and, if the debtor is represented by counsel, by the debtor's attorney, of the amount of monthly net income that the debtor has pursuant to this subsection and that the information provided under this subsection is true and correct . . . .[40]

- Section 103 contained the rule requiring dismissal or conversion of an "inappropriately filed" Chapter 7.[41] Subparagraph (4)(B) was a state-

---

preceding the date of determination and any replacement income that has been offered or secured, or is expected, and an itemization of such lost and replacement income;

(iii) if allowance for additional expenses is claimed, a list itemizing each additional expense which exceeds the expenses allowances provided under paragraph (3)(A);

(iv) a detailed description of the extraordinary circumstances that explain why each loss of income described under clause (ii) will not be replaced or each additional expense itemized under clause (iii) requires allowance; and

(v) a sworn statement signed by the debtor and, if the debtor is represented by counsel, by the debtor's attorney, that the information required under this paragraph is true and correct.

Id.

38. *Id.* at Section 101, adding Code § 109(h)(4)(A)(iv) (emphasis added).

39. *Id.* at Section 102(1), amending Code § 101 by adding subsection (39A), Definition of "Monthly Net Income."

40. *Id.* at Section 102(3), adding Code § 111(a)(1)(E) (emphasis added). Section 111(a)(2) went on to provide that if a party challenged a debtor's statement of "extraordinary circumstances," the prevailing party would be entitled in some cases to attorney's fees and costs. *Id.* at Section 102(3), adding Code § 111(a)(2).

41. *Id.* at Section 103, amending Code § 707(b) by modifying the language of subsection (b) and adding subparagraphs 1-4. Subparagraphs (b)(1)-(3) provided:

ment that the signature of the debtor's attorney on any petition, pleading, motion, or other paper filed with the court constituted her certification that the attorney had:

> (i) performed a reasonable investigation into the circumstances that gave rise to the petition, schedules, and statement of financial affairs or the pleading, as applicable; and
> (ii) determined that the petition, schedules, and statement of financial affairs or the pleading, as applicable, including the choice of this chapter—
>> (I) is well grounded in fact; and
>> (II) is warranted by existing law or a good-faith argument for the extension, modification, or reversal of existing law and does not constitute an inappropriate use of the provisions of this chapter.[42]

SEC. 103. DEFINITION OF INAPPROPRIATE USE.
Section 707(b) of title 11, United States Code, is amended to read as follows:
(b)(1) After notice and a hearing, the court—

> (A) on its own motion or on the motion of the United States trustee or any party in interest, shall dismiss a case filed by an individual debtor under this chapter; or
> (B) with the debtor's consent, convert the case to a case under chapter 13 of this title;

if the court finds that the granting of relief would be an inappropriate use of the provisions of this chapter.
(2) The court shall determine that inappropriate use of the provisions of this chapter exists if—

> (A) the debtor is excluded from this chapter pursuant to section 109 of this title; or
> (B) the totality of the circumstances of the debtor's financial situation demonstrates such inappropriate use.

(3) In the case of a motion filed by a party in interest other than the trustee or United States trustee under paragraph (1) that is denied by the court, the court shall award against the moving party a reasonable attorney's fee and costs that the debtor incurred in opposing the motion if the court finds that the position of the moving party was not substantially justified, but the court shall not award such fee and costs if special circumstances would make the award unjust.

Id. Subparagraph (4)(A) provided an award of attorney's fees and costs to the trustee who wins a motion under the provision to dismiss or convert. *Id.* at subparagraph 707(b)(4)(A).

   42.   *Id.* at Section 103, amending Code § 707(b) by adding § 707(b)(4)(B).

- Section 103 also contained the first appearance[43] of the language explicitly making the debtor's attorney liable if a Chapter 7 was converted or dismissed:

  (C) If the court finds that the attorney for the debtor signed a paper in violation of subparagraph [(4)(B), quoted above], at a minimum, the court shall order—
    (i) the assessment of an appropriate civil penalty against the attorney for the debtor; and
    (ii) the payment of the civil penalty to the trustee or the United States Trustee.[44]

- Section 410 addressed Federal Rule of Bankruptcy Procedure 9011:

  It is the sense of the Congress that rule 9011 of the Federal Rules of Bankruptcy Procedure (11 U.S.C. App.) should be modified to include a requirement that all documents (including schedules), signed and unsigned, submitted to the court or to a trustee by debtors who represent themselves and debtors who are represented by an attorney be submitted only after the debtor or the debtor's attorney has made reasonable inquiry to verify that the information contained in such documents is well grounded in fact, and is warranted by existing law or a good-faith argument for the extension, modification, or reversal of existing law.[45]

- The Debt Relief Counseling Agency provisions included in this bill were virtually identical to the provisions of the BRA. They included:

---

43.   Susan Jensen, in her history of the bill, explains how this came to be included:

   The amendment in the nature of substitute added a requirement to § 103 of H.R. 3150 mandating the imposition of civil penalties against a debtor's attorney if the attorney signed any pleading in a bankruptcy case that was not well-grounded in fact and warranted by existing law.

Jensen at 507. She notes earlier in this discussion that because minutes of Judiciary Committee markups were not published prior to the 107th Cong., the references she provides are to "unpublished stenographic minutes." *Id.* at n.108. (And I thought I had it rough!)

44.   *Id.* at Section 103, amending Code § 707(b) by adding § 707(b)(4)(C).

45.   *Id.* at Section 410 (as passed in the House; Section 411 in the bill as originally filed in the House).

- The definitions of "assisted person,"[46] "bankruptcy assistance,"[47] and "debt relief counselling [sic] agency"[48]
- The elaborate disclosures demanded of a "debt relief counselling agency"[49]
- The conduct mandated of the "debt relief counselling agency," including:
  - the requirement of a written contract,[50]
  - the advertising provisions,[51] including the mandated description "We are a debt relief counselling agency. We help people

---

46. *Id.* at Section 113(a)(1), amending Code § 101 by adding § 3A.

47. *Id.* at Section 113(a)(2), amending Code § 101 by adding § 4A.

48. *Id.* at Section 113(a)(3), amending Code § 101 by adding § 12A. ["Counselling" is spelled as it is spelled in this bill.] One notable difference is that this version of the bill only contains three exclusions to the definition. The current first exclusion, applicable to officers and directors of debt relief agencies, and the current final exclusion, applicable to authors of copyrightable material, did not appear until later in the process.

49. *Id.* at Section 114(a), adding Code § 526.

50. *Id.* at Section 115, adding Code § 527(a)(1).

51. *Id.* at Section 115, adding §§ 527(a)(2) and 527(a)(3). The advertising provisions are much clearer in this version of the bill than in the BRA (see Chapter 9) providing:

> (a) A debt relief counselling [sic] agency shall—
>
> . . .
>
> > (2) disclose in any advertisement of bankruptcy assistance services or of the benefits of bankruptcy directed to the general public (whether in general media, seminars or specific mailings, telephonic or electronic messages or otherwise) that the services or benefits are with respect to proceedings under this title, clearly and conspicuously using the following statement: "We are a debt relief counselling agency. We help people file Bankruptcy petitions to obtain relief under the Bankruptcy Code." or a substantially similar statement. An advertisement shall be of bankruptcy assistance services if it describes or offers bankruptcy assistance with a chapter 13 plan, regardless of whether chapter 13 is specifically mentioned, including such statements as "federally supervised repayment plan" or "Federal debt restructuring help" or other similar statements which would lead a reasonable consumer to believe that help with debts was being offered when in fact in most cases the help available is bankruptcy assistance with a chapter 13 plan; and
> >
> > (3) if an advertisement directed to the general public indicates that the debt relief counselling agency provides assistance with respect to credit defaults, mortgage foreclosures, lease eviction proceedings, excessive debt, debt collection pressure, or inability to pay any consumer debt, disclose conspicuously in that advertisement that the assistance is with respect to or may involve proceedings under this title, using the following statement: "We are a debt relief counselling agency. We help people file Bankruptcy petitions to obtain relief under the Bankruptcy Code." or a substantially similar statement.

Id. The confusing hierarchy found in the current BRA does not exist in the original version of these provisions.

file Bankruptcy petitions to obtain relief under the Bankruptcy Code."[52]
- the prohibition on counseling the debtor to incur debt,[53] and
- myriad prohibitions on failure to act and misleading conduct,[54] and
- The enforcement provisions,[55] including:
  - the prohibition on enforcing contracts when the disclosure provisions have not been satisfied,[56] and
  - the disgorgement of fees paid and the obligation to continue the representation without fee.[57]

H.R. 3150 passed the House by a 3-1 margin in June of 1998[58] and was sent to the Senate the next day.[59]

The Senate version of the bankruptcy bill was S. 1301.[60] It did not contain all of the attorney liability provisions, but it did include several that largely paralleled the provisions in H.R. 3150:

- Section 102 of the bill amended § 707 to revise the rules on dismissal and conversion of a Chapter 7, including:
  - the requirement that the debtor's attorney pay the trustee fees and costs if the debtor loses a motion to convert or dismiss;[61]

---

52.   *Id.* at Code §§ 527(a)(2) and 527(a)(3).

53.   *Id.* at Code § 527(b)(4).

54.   *Id.* at Code §§ 527(b)(1) to 527(b)(3).

55.   *Id.* at Section 116(a), adding Code § 528.

56.   *Id.* at Code § 528(b)(1).

57.   *Id.* at Code § 528(b)(2).

58.   H.R. 3150 Bill Summary and Status for the 105th Cong. The recorded vote was 306-118, which occurred on June 10, 1998.

59.   *Id.*

60.   S. 1301, Consumer Bankruptcy Reform Act of 1998, 105th Cong.

61.   *Id.* at Section 102(a), amending Code § 707 by modifying subsection (b) and adding subsection 707(b)(3)(A):

> If a panel trustee appointed under section 586(a)(1) of title 28 brings a motion for dismissal or conversion under this subsection and the court grants that motion, the court shall order the counsel for the debtor, if the debtor is represented by counsel, to reimburse the trustee for all reasonable costs in prosecuting the motion, including reasonable attorneys' fees.

Id.

- the requirement that the debtor's attorney pay the trustee a civil fine if the attorney is found to have violated Rule 9011;[62] and
- the provision that the debtor's attorney's signature certifies that the attorney has performed a reasonable investigation and determined that the petition is well grounded in fact and warranted by existing law.[63]

- S. 1301 also contained a provision not included in H.R. 3150 that required the debtor's attorney to certify that she gave a statutory notice to the debtor that described bankruptcy as well as alternatives to bankruptcy.[64]

---

62. *Id.* at Code § 707(b)(3)(B):

(B) If the court finds that the attorney for the debtor violated Rule 9011, at a minimum, the court shall order—
(i) the assessment of an appropriate civil penalty against the counsel for the debtor; and
(ii) the payment of the civil penalty to the panel trustee or the United States trustee.

Id.

63. *Id.* at Code § 707(b)(3)(C):

In the case of a petition referred to in subparagraph (B), the signature of an attorney shall constitute a certificate that the attorney has—
(i) performed a reasonable investigation into the circumstances that gave rise to the petition; and
(ii) determined that the petition—
(I) is well grounded in fact; and
(II) is warranted by existing law or a good faith argument for the extension, modification, or reversal of existing law and does not constitute an abuse under paragraph (1) of this subsection.

Id.

In this case, it isn't clear what the reference to subparagraph (B) means, since Code § 707(b)(3)(B), quoted in note 62, does not refer to the filing of any motion. The "subparagraph (B)" reference makes more sense in H.R. 3150, since the immediately preceding provision in 707(b)(4)(B) contains the language in *this* provision, referring to the debtor's attorney's signature on a petition, pleading or motion. H.R. 3150, in the 105th Cong., Section 103, amending Code § 707(b) by adding subsection 707(b)(4)(B). In essence, paragraphs (B) and (C) are reversed in the Senate version (and in the Conference Report) so the reference to (B) makes no sense in either.

64. *Id.* at Section 301(a), amending Code § 342 by adding subsection (b) [requiring notice] and amending Code § 521 by adding subsection (a)(1)(B)(iii)(I) [requiring the attorney to certify by signing that the required notice was delivered].

When the Senate received H.R. 3150, it struck the provisions,[65] inserted some of the provisions from S. 1301, and passed its version of H.R. 3150 virtually unanimously in September of that year.[66]

The Conference Report on H.R. 3150 was issued on October 7, 1998. It combined provisions from the Senate bill with those from the House bill to put in place the basic elements of attorney liability that were enacted in the BRA.[67] In particular:

- Section 102 contains all the provisions on conversion and dismissal that amended § 707(b) of the Code, tracking the language of S. 1301.[68]
- Sections 105 to 108 contain all the Debt Relief Agency provisions, tracking the language of H.R. 3150.[69]
- Section 607 contains the "Sense of the Congress" provision on Rule 9011, from H.R. 3150.[70]

The only element of the current attorney liability scheme that had not appeared in the legislation by the end of the 105th Congress was the provision

---

65.   H.R. 3150 Bill Summary and Status for the 105th Cong., Sept. 23, 1998. The Senate acted on the bill on September 23, striking the provisions and substituting in H.R. 3150 the provisions from S. 1301.

66.   *Id.* at Sept. 23, 1998. The vote was 97-1 in favor of the bill. The late Sen. Wellstone was the sole negative vote.

67.   *Id.* at Oct, 19, 1990, H. REP. 105-794, Bankruptcy Reform Act of 1998. The House Report is available on the Web. You can locate it on Thomas by going to the 105th Cong., searching for H.R. 3150, selecting the bill presented to the Senate, going to the "Status and Summary" page for that bill, clicking on "Full Status and Summary," and scrolling down the status page until the House Report appears on October 19, 1998. You can then click H.Rpt. 105-794 to view the Conference Report.

68.   H. REP. 105-794 at Section 102(b), adding subsection 707(b)(2)(B) (see note 63 above for a discussion of the problem with the cross-references in the Senate version and the Conference Report) and subsections (b)(3)(A), (B), and (C). Note that another typographical error appeared in the Conference Report: Section 102(b)(2) of the Conference Report notes that the text is intended as an amendment to Code § 704. The first three changes that follow apparently belong in Code § 704. But the text denominated (3)(A), (B), and (C), cited here, is probably intended as an amendment to Code § 707(b), not 704. This can be determined from the fact that in both the House and Senate versions of the bill, the provision amended is § 707. In addition, House Report 105-540, containing the interlineated version of the Code as intended to be amended, shows the amendments to Code § 707 (although the language of the House bill differs slightly). *See* H. REP. 105-540 at 199.

69.   H. REP. 105-794 at Sections 106-108.

70.   *Id.* at Section 607.

requiring debtors' attorneys to certify their clients' ability to repay in certain reaffirmations.[71]

The Conference Report passed the House, again by a 3-1 margin.[72] Despite overwhelming support (and the fact that the Conference Report largely reflected the Senate version of the bill) the legislation did not get through Senate because time ran out in the session.[73]

B. The 106th Congress

In February 1999, the provisions of the Conference Report on H.R. 3150 reappeared as H.R. 833, sponsored again by then-Congressman Gekas.[74] There were numerous hearings and mark-up sessions, first in the House Judiciary Committee, then in the House Banking Committee.[75]

After lively discussion[76] and a number of amendments on the House floor, the bill passed the House on May 5, 1999.[77]

---

71.   The notes to the Conference Report describe the reaffirmation provision of that bill:

REAFFIRMATIONS
The House bill contained no comparable provision to the Senate bill, which imposed a requirement for a hearing before a judge for certain types of reaffirmations by debtors. The Conference Committee streamlined these judicial procedures by ensuring that every debtor who reaffirms unsecured debt has the opportunity to appear before a judge. Under the compromise, an enhanced standard is provided for the review of certain reaffirmation agreements. The judge is now required to determine that the reaffirmation was in the best interest of the debtor, would not impose an undue hardship, and was not the result of coercion.

Id. at Joint Explanatory Statement of the Committee of Conference. At this point, the debtor's attorney was not yet required to certify the reaffirmation when it imposed an "undue hardship" within the meaning of the bill.

72.   H.R. 3150, Bill Status and Summary for the 106th Congress, at Oct. 9, 1990. The vote was 300-125. *Id.*

73.   Testimony of George Wallace, House Judiciary Committee Hearing on H.R. 333, February 2, 2002, at 317. One of the reasons is that the Congress was busy with the impeachment of President Clinton. *See* Jensen at 518.

74.   Bill Summary and Status for the 106th Cong., H.R. 833, Full Summary and Status.

75.   *Id.* at Mar. 11. 1999 to April 29, 1999.

76.   Much of the debate was between two factions of House Republicans who differed on the stringency necessary for an effective means test. *See* Jensen at 523-28.

77.   *Id.* at May 5, 1999. The bill passed the House on a vote of 313 to 108, and was received in the Senate the next day.

The Senate version of the bill was S. 625.[78] It contained the now-familiar litany of attorney liability provisions, in somewhat streamlined form:

- Section 102 contained the amendments to § 707(b) and § 704:[79]
- The provision requiring the debtor and the debtor's attorney to certify under oath the accuracy of the information offered to rebut the presumptions in the means test;
- The provisions on dismissal or conversion that:
    - made the debtor's attorney strictly liable for the trustee's costs and fees if the debtor lost a motion to dismiss or convert;[80]
    - required the court to award the trustee a civil penalty paid by the debtor's attorney if the court found a violation of Rule 9011;[81]
    - provided that the signature of the debtor's attorney constituted a certification that an investigation had been performed and that the petition was well grounded in fact and warranted by law.[82]
- The bill also contained the "Sense of the Congress" provision relating to Rule 9011.[83]

Addressing the penalties exacted from debtors' attorneys when a case is converted or dismissed, the Senate Report on S. 625 clearly outlined the Senate's intent:

> If a motion is brought by a chapter 7 trustee, and the court determines that the debtor's case should be dismissed or converted, the court must order the debtor's counsel to reimburse the trustee for all reasonable costs associated with prosecuting the motion for dismissal or conversion if the motion was

---

78. S. 625, The Bankruptcy Reform Act of 1999, introduced in the 106th Congress in the Senate on Mar. 16, 1999 by Sen. Grassley.

79. *Id.* at Section 102(b), amending Code § 707(b) by modifying the language and by adding subsection (b)(2)(B)(ii).

80. *Id.* at Section 102(b) amending Code § 704 by adding subsection (3)(A). Note that in this bill, the problems described in note 63 above on the numbering of the provision and its inclusion in § 704 (as opposed to § 707, where this provision originally appeared) have been resolved by rewriting the bill's (but not the amendment's) language.

81. *Id.* 'at Section 102(b), amending Code § 704 by adding subsection (3)(B).

82. *Id.* at Section 102(b), amending Code § 704 by adding subsection (3)(C). Note that this provision carried forward the problem, referred to in note 63 above, with the cross-reference to subsection (B) that doesn't quite match the actual provisions of the preceding subsection.

83. *Id.* at Section 319.

granted and the action of the counsel was not substantially justified. The court must further order fines against the debtor's attorney if the court finds that the debtor's attorney violated rule 9011. *The Committee intends these fines to serve as financial incentive for chapter 7 trustees to discover and eliminate abusive chapter 7 cases.*[84]

Here is what two members said about this section of the bill:

S. 625 currently includes a provision which would make a debtor's attorney liable if he or she was not substantially justified in filing the petition in chapter 7. We believe that this would have a chilling effect on the system of justice in our nation. A debtor's attorney should not be faced with a financial disincentive to file in chapter 7 unless in so doing they violate rule 11 standards of attorney conduct. To require a penalty in any other case is not only unjust, but will force attorneys to run afoul of their ethical obligations to act in their client's best interest. In Committee, an amendment was offered by Senator Feingold to eliminate this provision from the bill. The Feingold amendment was narrowly defeated by a vote of 9–9. We will continue to support efforts to drop this provision from the S. 625.[85]

Four other dissenters shared this concern and expanded upon the impact of the attorney liability provisions. Under the subheading "Disincentives to Represent Consumer Debtors," they wrote:

From beginning to end, the bill is likely to increase costs that will fall the hardest on poorer families. Increased complexity as previously described, is not the only culprit. Rather, the bill will limit lower income debtor representation by imposing financial disincentives on professionals to represent debtors. For example, section 102 of the bill requires that a debtor's attorney reimburse the trustee if the debtor's case is converted or dismissed because the debtor is found to have the ability to pay a portion of her debts. This creates a conflict of interest between a debtor's attorney and his client.
This provision marginally improved last year under the leadership of Senators Feingold and Specter. Their amendment permitted imposition of this penalty only if the attorney was not substantially justified in helping a client file under chapter 7. The provision, however, still takes an unprecedented and unwarranted step, and because this bill creates entirely new requirements and standards, lawyers are not likely to know what will be considered not substantially justified. Every other fee-shifting provision in federal law that holds the attorney liable is premised on affirmative wrong-

---

84. S. Rep. 106-49 on S. 625, at 23 (emphasis added). See Section III below on the change from mandatory to discretionary sanctions.

85. *Id.* at 83, Additional Views of Senators Torricelli and Kohl.

doing by the attorney, and there is no legitimate basis for different and more punitive standards for consumer bankruptcy attorneys. Our justice system recognizes that everyone deserves representation, yet this provision undermines that basic principle.

This provision may achieve its goal of keeping some debtors from seeking access to the system altogether, but also will produce a greater number of pro se filings, some of whom will be given assistance by nonlawyer petition preparers. Pro se cases already are more likely to be dismissed for procedural mistakes, and the inherent disadvantages of filing pro se will be exacerbated by this bill due to the increase in the number of administrative rules and hair triggers for case dismissal. Many debtors who file for bankruptcy without lawyers will be denied debt relief due to administrative error and will have a difficult time re-entering the system due to the new repeat filing prohibitions.

Deterring lawyers from representing debtors may have an effect on the filing rate, but it will not keep out the abusive cases and it will occur at a potentially steep cost. Preventing financially burdened families from having decent legal representation is an untenable policy.[86]

Even the footnotes provide valuable insight into the concerns of these senators:

- The lawyer faces dubious incentives to counsel the client to file chapter 13, or not to file at all, in order to protect the attorney's financial interests. Rule 1.7(b) of the Rules of Professional Conduct specifically prohibits a lawyer from handling a case "if representation of that client may be materially limited by the lawyer's . . . own interests." Under this bill, debtors' attorneys would arguably be in violation of this Rule on a regular basis, setting the stage for extremely problematic attorney-client dynamics that will ultimately harm vulnerable consumers.[87]
- The amendments originally offered by Senators Specter and Feingold were designed to ensure that the chapter 7 trustee was compensated for his or her efforts in seeking the dismissal or conversion of potentially abusive cases. However, Senator Grassley made clear last year that this provision was inserted not to ensure reimbursement of trustees, but rather to discourage lawyers from directing their clients to chapter 7.[88]
- Although Senator Feinstein's amendment to revise section 110 of the Bankruptcy Code takes an important step toward preventing petition preparers from engaging in the unauthorized practice of law, it remains

---

86.   *Id.* at 119, Minority Views of Senators Leahy, Kennedy, Feingold, and Schumer (citations omitted).

87.   *Id.* at n. 49.

88.   *Id.* at n. 50.

unfortunate that this bill seeks to limit the options for legal representation.[89]

- The House Judiciary Committee amended H.R. 833 to provide that debtors' attorneys face sanctions for helping their clients file under chapter 7 only if the debtor's actions were sanctionable under Rule 9011 of the Federal Rules of Bankruptcy Procedure. This approach is much preferred. However, it remains troublesome that both bills continually single out attorneys who represent consumer debtors, when all attorneys should be subject to similar standards.[90]

These comments make clear that the consequences of these provisions were not the result of oversight or poor drafting, but a conscious decision by the members controlling the debate in Congress to create exactly these kinds of barriers to legal services for consumers.

The Senate also estimated the cost of complying with the provisions of the bill. Here is the estimate it offered with respect to the certification of the schedules:

Sections 102 and 319 would make bankruptcy attorneys liable for misleading statements and inaccuracies in schedules and documents submitted to courts or trustees. To avoid sanctions and potential civil penalties, attorneys would need to verify the information given to them by their clients regarding the list of creditors, assets and liabilities, and income and expenditures. Based on 1,286,000 projected filings under chapter 7 and chapter 13 and an estimated increase in attorneys' costs of $150 to $500 per case, CBO estimates that *the costs to attorneys of complying with this requirement would be between $190 million and $640 million in fiscal year 2000. With the rise in projected filings over the next 5 years, annual costs would be $280 million to $940 million for fiscal year 2004.* CBO expects bankruptcy attorneys to pass some of the cost on to debtors, reducing the pool of funds available to creditors.[91]

On May 11, 1999, S. 625 was reported out of committee. At that point, it still did not contain the requirement that the debtor's attorney certify the debtor's ability to pay in reaffirmation agreements.[92] Nor did it contain the Debt Relief

---

89. *Id.* at n. 51.

90. *Id.* at n. 52.

91. S. Rep. 106-49 on S. 625, at 73-74 (emphasis added).

92. *See* S. 625 in the 106th Cong., as reported in the Senate, Section 204. Senator Sessions had offered a reaffirmation amendment but withdrew it during Judiciary Committee consideration of the bill. S. Rep. 106-49 on S. 625, at 16 (amendment offered) and 17 (withdrawn). Subsequently, Senator Sessions co-sponsored the technical amendments to Sen. Reed's Amendment 2650; as explained in the text, that technical amendment added the attorney certification provision.

Agency provisions, which were stricken in committee.[93]

On November 5, 1999, Senator Reed submitted an amendment to address concerns about ill-advised reaffirmation agreements.[94] It contained provisions intended to ensure that reaffirmation agreements were based upon complete and accurate information, and required disclosure whether the amount of the monthly payment was greater than the debtor's net income.[95] If the debtor was represented by an attorney during the negotiation, the amendment required the attorney to file the declaration or affidavit mandated by existing Code § 524(c)(3).[96] If the debtor was not represented by an attorney, he or she was required to overcome the presumption of "undue hardship" at a hearing.[97]

On February 2, 2000, Senator Reed substituted a technical amendment to his prior amendment, which was accepted by unanimous consent.[98] That amendment required disclosures and certifications similar to those found in

---

93.   *See* S. 625 in the 106th Cong., Sections 221-224, and compare the bill as introduced and as reported in the Senate. *See also* S. REP. 106-49.

94.   *See* S. 625, Bill Status and Summary for the 106th Cong., Senate Amendment 2650 at Nov. 5, 1999; the text of the amendment is found in the CONG. REC. at S14156-14157. There were reaffirmation provisions in the bill when it was introduced, and the Senate Report addressed the issue by saying:

> Section 204 of the [bill] gives every debtor who intends to reaffirm a wholly unsecured debt a right to a fairness hearing. Debtors represented by counsel may waive this hearing if they so choose.

S. REP. 106-49 on S. 625 at 25.

95.   CONG. REC. at S14156, adding Section 204 to the bill, amending Code § 524.

96.   *Id.* at Section 204(a)(1)(C), adding Code § 524(g)(7)(B). Code § 524(c)(3) required and still requires the attorney to file with the reaffirmation agreement a "declaration or an affidavit of the attorney that represented the debtor during the course of negotiating an agreement" that the agreement does not impose an undue hardship on the debtor and the attorney fully advised the debtor of its legal effect and consequences. *Id.*

97.   *Id.* at Section 204(a)(1)(c), adding Code § 524(g)(7)(D), which provided:

> If the debtor was not represented by counsel during the course of negotiating the agreement and the debtor's net monthly income [as defined above] is less than the monthly payments required by the agreement, or if applicable, aggregation of agreements, there shall be a presumption that the agreement imposes an undue hardship. The court shall hold a hearing at which the debtor may rebut the presumption by demonstrating the existence of financial circumstances that would enable the debtor to undertake the agreement without undue hardship.

Id. in the CONG. REC. at S14156-14157.

98.   *See* S. 625, Bill Status and Summary for the 106th Cong. at Feb. 2, 2000; the text of the amendment is found in the CONG. REC. at S234-235. Sen. Sessions co-sponsored this amendment.

the current BRA. The two provisions requiring the debtor's attorney's certification were:

- the disclosure provision (which, since it mandated language to be disclosed to the debtor, spoke to the debtor in the second person):

  If you were represented by an attorney during the negotiation of the reaffirmation agreement, the attorney must have signed the certification in Part C.[99]

- the certification provision (which, since it mandated language for the debtor's attorney's certification, spoke as the attorney in the first person):

  (5)(i)[100] The declaration shall consist of the following:
  Part C: Certification by Debtor's Attorney (If Any).
  I hereby certify that (1) this agreement represents a fully informed and voluntary agreement by the debtor(s); (2) this agreement does not impose an undue hardship on the debtor or any dependent of the debtor; and (3) I have fully advised the debtor of the legal effect and consequences of this agreement and any default under this agreement.

  Signature of Debtor's Attorney: Date:

  (ii)[101] In the case of reaffirmations in which a presumption of undue hardship has been established, the certification shall state that in the opinion of the attorney, the debtor is able to make the payment.[102]

The Senate did not vote on S. 625. Instead, it took up H.R. 833 in February of 2000.[103] Again, the Senate struck all the provisions of the bill and inserted the provisions of S. 625.[104] The provisions requiring attorney certification of reaffirmation agreements that were presumed to impose an undue hardship were retained in the Senate version of H.R. 833.[105]

---

99. *Id.* at Section 204, amending Code § 524 by adding subsection (c)(2)(i)(3)(J)(3).

100. This became subsection 5(A) in the Senate version of H.R. 833.

101. This became subsection 5(B) in the Senate version of H.R. 833.

102. S. 625 Bill Status and Summary for the 106th Cong. at Feb. 2, 2000; the text of the amendment is found in the Cong. Rec. at S234-235, amending Code § 524 by adding subsections (c)(2)(i)(5)(A) and (B).

103. H.R. 833, Bill Status and Summary for the 106th Cong. at Feb. 2, 2000.

104. *Id.* at Feb. 2, 2000, inserting the language from S. 625 into H.R. 833 as introduced in the Senate, 106th Cong., Feb. 2, 2000.

105. H.R. 833 as amended in the Senate, at Section 203, amending Code § 524 to add subsections (c)(2)(i)(1-8) and subsections (c)(2)(j) and (k).

The Senate version of H.R. 833 passed the Senate in February 2000.[106] It contained the Section 102 amendments relating to the means test,[107] the reaffirmation certification provisions,[108] and the Rule 9011 "Sense of the Congress" provision.[109] It did not contain the Debt Relief Agency provisions.

Again the bill went to conference. This time, a Conference Report containing all of the attorney liability provisions was issued and passed both houses of Congress as H.R. 2415.[110] But the bill—which had sufficient support in the

---

106.   H.R. 833, Bill Summary at Status, at Feb. 2, 2000. The vote was 83-14.

107.   *Id.* at Section 102.

108.   *Id.* at Section 203.

109.   *Id.* at Section 319.

110.   At this point, it becomes almost impossible to follow both the bill numbers and provisions. Although H.R. 833 had passed both houses in some form and should have been the subject of the conference, the bill that actually passed after the conference was H.R. 2415, originally a State Department appropriations bill. The machinations were undertaken to avoid Sen. Wellstone's threatened filibuster (at this point, of a vote to go to conference). I spent many hours trying to figure out what happened (and in an earlier version of this Chapter, I came pretty close). Here is how Susan Jensen explains it:

> Finally, a legislative vehicle was found. H.R. 2415 was originally an authorization bill for the State Department . . . . On August 3, 1999, the Senate passed H.R. 2415, as amended and thereafter appointed conferees. On November 17, 1999, however, another version of this legislation was introduced, and an amended version of it was subsequently incorporated by reference in the conference report on an omnibus appropriations bill that was later enacted.
>
> As a result of these events, the need to proceed further on the conference for H.R. 2415 was rendered moot. H.R. 2415 was particularly attractive to the leadership because the Senate had already agreed to go to conference on that bill and, thus, was not subject to any filibuster by Senator Wellstone or any other Senator at least with respect to the motion to proceed to conference. At around 6:20 p.m. on October 11, 2000, the House agreed to the Senate's request for a conference on H.R. 2415 and appointed as its conferees House Majority Leader Dick Armey . . . and Representatives Hyde, Gekas, Conyers, and Nadler. It also agreed to a motion by Representative Nadler instructing the conferees to hold open and public meetings by a vote of 398 to 1. Approximately two hours later, however, a majority of the conferees filed the H.R. 2415 conference report. The text of the report was actually that of S. 3186, the Bankruptcy Reform Act of 2000, a bill that Senator Grassley introduced earlier that day. S. 3186 consisted of the compromise legislation that was the product of the informal conference negotiations. Later that evening, the House Rules Committee reported a rule allowing for consideration of the conference report the following day.

See Jensen at 535-36. She goes on to detail the differences between this bill and the Senate and House versions of H.R. 833. On Oct. 12, 2000, the Conference Report passed the House on a voice vote. On Nov. 1, 2000, the Conference Report was considered by the Senate. On Dec. 7, 2000, the Senate passed the Conference Report by a vote of 70-28. On Dec. 7, 2000, it was presented to President Clinton, and was pocket-vetoed by him on Dec. 19, 2000.

Senate to override a veto—was the subject of a pocket veto by President Clinton. So ended the bankruptcy legislation in the 106th Congress.

C. The 107th Congress

In the first days of the 107th Congress, then-Congressman Gekas introduced H.R. 333, which was identical to the text of H.R. 2415, the Conference Report from the 106th Congress.[111] After hearings in the House, the bill came to the floor on March 1, 2001.[112]

H.R. 333 passed the House that day on a vote of 306-108.[113] As passed, the bill contained all of the attorney liability provisions:

- Section 102 contained the amendments to § 707(b), making the debtor's counsel liable for fees if a case is dismissed or converted, and making the attorney's signature a certification that the attorney had made a reasonable investigation and determined that the filing was justified by the facts and the law;[114]

---

111.   H.R. 333 Bill Status and Summary, 107th Cong., introduced on Jan. 31, 2001.

112.   *Id.* at Mar. 1, 2001.

113.   *Id.*

114.   H.R. 333, 107th Cong., as passed by the House, Section 102, adding Code § 707(b)(4):

(4)(A) The court shall order the counsel for the debtor to reimburse the trustee for all reasonable costs in prosecuting a motion brought under section 707(b), including reasonable attorneys' fees, if—

   (i) a trustee appointed under section 586(a)(1) of title 28 or from a panel of private trustees maintained by the bankruptcy administrator brings a motion for dismissal or conversion under this subsection; and
   (ii) the court—
      (I) grants that motion; and
      (II) finds that the action of the counsel for the debtor in filing under this chapter violated rule 9011 of the Federal Rules of Bankruptcy Procedure.

(B) If the court finds that the attorney for the debtor violated rule 9011 of the Federal Rules of Bankruptcy Procedure, at a minimum, the court shall order—

   (i) the assessment of an appropriate civil penalty against the counsel for the debtor; and
   (ii) the payment of the civil penalty to the trustee, the United States trustee, or the bankruptcy administrator.

(C) In the case of a petition, pleading, or written motion, the signature of an attorney shall constitute a certification that the attorney has—

   (i) performed a reasonable investigation into the circumstances that gave rise to the petition, pleading, or written motion; and
   (ii) determined that the petition, pleading, or written motion—
      (I) is well grounded in fact; and

- Section 203 contained the reaffirmation amendments requiring the debtor's counsel to certify the ability to pay;[115]
- Sections 227-229 included the Debt Relief Agency provisions;[116] and
- Section 319 expressed the sense of the Congress with regard to Rule 9011.[117]

The version in the Senate went through several iterations and bill numbers.[118] Perhaps the falling economy, the shift in the control of the Senate, and an increase in effort by the opponents of the bill, or some combination of these factors caused a slight decrease in the enthusiasm for the bill. Whatever the cause, at this point there were significant amendments to the bill.[119]

To understand what happened next, we have to look at issues having nothing to do with attorney liability. There were two politically significant differences between the House and Senate bills:[120]

- the Senate limitation on state unlimited homestead exemptions,[121] and

---

(II) is warranted by existing law or a good faith argument for the extension, modification, or reversal of existing law and does not constitute an abuse under paragraph (1).

(D) The signature of an attorney on the petition shall constitute a certification that the attorney has no knowledge after an inquiry that the information in the schedules filed with such petition is incorrect.

Id. at Section 102(a)(2)(C), adding Code §§ 707(b)(4)(A-D). I am sure that it is of interest to no one but the author that the prior references to § 704 had been deleted, and all the provisions were again amendments to § 707(b).

115.   *Id.* at Section 203(a)(2), adding Code §§ 524(k)(3)(J)(i) and (k)(5)(A-C).

116.   *Id.* at Section 226, amending Code § 101(3) and adding Code §§ 101(4A) and (12A); Section 227, adding Code § 526; Section 228, adding Code § 527; and Section 229, adding Code § 528.

117.   *Id.* at Section 319.

118.   The bill was originally introduced as S. 220 by Senator Grassley on Jan. 30, 2001. No action was taken on that bill. Bill Summary and Status for the 107th Cong., S. 220. Another bill was introduced as S. 420, again by Senator Grassley, on Mar. 1, 2001, reported from the Judiciary Committee. There were hearings in the Senate on this issue in January, 2001, but none is reflected in the record of either S. 220 or S. 420.

119.   See Section III below on lobbying by the American Bar Association and other groups opposed to the attorney liability provisions.

120.   An excellent analysis of the differences between the House and Senate versions of the bill was done by the National Bankruptcy Conference and is on their Web site at http://www.nationalbankruptcyconference.org/pending.htm.

121.   S. 420 at Sections 307 and 308, amending Code § 522.

• the Schumer Amendment, making nondischargeable certain judgments for violation of the Freedom of Access to Clinic Entrances law (also called the FACE amendment).[122]

S. 420 passed the Senate on March 19, 2001, on a vote of 85 to 15.[123]

The bill again went to conference, with the first meeting scheduled for September 12, 2001. The events of 9/11 delayed consideration of the bill (but not as long as opponents had expected). Neither the events of 9/11 nor the ensuing downturn in the economy deterred proponents of the bill for long. The Committee began meeting in May 2002.[124]

---

122.   S. 420 at Section 328. This amendment became important, and ultimately prevented the bill from becoming law. It provided:

SEC. 328. NONDISCHARGEABILITY OF DEBTS INCURRED THROUGH VIOLATIONS OF LAWS RELATING TO THE PROVISION OF LAWFUL GOODS AND SERVICES.

. . . Nothing in paragraph (19) shall be construed to affect any expressive conduct (including peaceful picketing or other peaceful demonstration) protected from legal prohibition by the first amendment to the Constitution of the United States;

. . . .

(19) that results from any judgment, order, consent order, or decree entered in any Federal or State court, or contained in any settlement agreement entered into by the debtor, including any court-ordered damages, fine, penalty, citation, or attorney fee or cost owed by the debtor, arising from—
(A) an action alleging the violation of any Federal, State, or local statutory law, including but not limited to violations of sections 247 and 248 of title 18, that results from the debtor's—
(i) harassment of, intimidation of, interference with, obstruction of, injury to, threat to, or violence against, any person—
(I) because that person provides or has provided lawful goods or services;
(II) because that person is or has been obtaining lawful goods or services; or
(III) to deter that person, any other person, or a class of persons from obtaining or providing lawful goods or services; or
(ii) damage or destruction of property of a facility providing lawful goods or services; or
(B) a violation of a court order or injunction that protects access to a facility that provides lawful goods or services or the provision of lawful goods or services.

Id. at Section 328, amending Code § 523(a) by adding subsection 19.

123.   S. 420, Bill Summary and Status for the 107th Cong. at Mar. 19, 2001. This wide margin of support for the bill was a deep blow to opponents, who had lobbied hard in the Senate, who were fearful that the dramatic downturn in the economy would make the provisions of the bill disastrous for both consumers and small businesses. This sense of foreboding grew in the economic disarray that followed 9/11.

124.   *Id.* at May 22, 2002.

After two months of wrangling, and much pressure on Senator Schumer by bill supporters in his own party, the conference ultimately agreed to a Schumer/Hyde compromise on FACE, as well as compromises on unlimited homestead and resolution of several other important issues.[125] The Conference Report was issued on July 26, 2002.[126]

The report retained the Senate version of the debtors' attorney sanctions provision, but with one important difference: the § 707(b)(4)(A) and (B) sanctions became discretionary and not mandatory.[127] With the death of Senator Wellstone in the fall of 2002, the chance of a filibuster against the bill diminished, although Senator Feingold stated that he would filibuster in Senator Wellstone's memory.[128]

Debate in the House took place in mid-November of that year.[129] With the FACE language agreed to by Congressman Hyde, a staunch opponent of abortion, it seemed that passage was inevitable. The negotiating went on late into the night, and to the surprise of opponents—and the shock of the House leadership, which did some serious midnight arm-twisting—there was not a majority to support the report because of the FACE issue. The House managers could not bring the bill to a vote.[130]

The text of the bill was stripped of the Schumer/Hyde compromise language,[131] introduced[132] and passed by the House, and sent to the Senate, where no vote was taken.[133]

---

125.   H. REP. 107-617: Bankruptcy Abuse Prevention and Consumer Protection Act of 2002.

126.   H.R. 333, Bill Summary and Status for the 107th Cong., at July 26, 2002.

127.   *Id.* at Section 102, adding Code §§ 707(b)(4)(A) and (B). Before the conference, these provisions said that the court "shall" order imposition of the penalties. After the conference, the word in both subsections was "may." *See* Section III below on lobbying by the ABA and other organizations. Candor requires me to disclose that I was involved in the lobbying that led to this change. At the time, I was deeply disappointed that this minimal change was the only amendment to the attorney liability provisions.

128.   *Feingold, Others to Take Up Wellstone's Bankruptcy Fight*, CONGRESS DAILY, Nov. 1, 2002. In the end, no filibuster occurred.

129.   *Id.* at Nov. 13, 2002 to Nov. 15, 2002.

130.   *Id.*

131.   The provision requiring additional judges was also removed. *See* Jensen at 558.

132.   H.R. 5745, The Bankruptcy Abuse Prevention and Consumer Protection Act of 2002 (Nov. 15, 2002).

133.   H.R. 5745, Bill Summary and Status for the 107th Cong. The status notes: "On Nov. 15, 2002, the House agreed with an amendment to the Senate amendment to H.R. 333. This inserted the text of H.R. 5745 in H.R. 333." *Id.* After the early-morning passage of H.R. 5745, the House proceeded to honor Congressman Gekas, with Rep. Tom DeLay saying that Gekas "has worked on the bankruptcy reform bill for over 10 years . . . just stood up here and took all the abuse that could be hurled at him . . . and passed that bill and sent it over to the Senate . . . ." CONG. REC. H8877, daily ed. Nov. 14, 2002.

D. The 108th Congress

The version of the BRA introduced as H.R. 975 by Congressman Sensenbrenner[134] in February 2003 was the text of the Conference Report on H.R. 333, stripped of the Schumer/Hyde compromise.[135] The bill passed the House on March 19, 2003, with some housekeeping amendments but no substantive change.[136]

The bill was received in the Senate and read twice.[137] Senator Leahy requested that the Judiciary Committee observe regular order, but the bill was placed on the Senate calendar for floor action.[138] In spite of that maneuver, no action was taken in the Senate before the end of the 108th Congress.[139]

E. The 109th Congress

President Bush's reelection and Republican wins in the House and Senate in 2004 set the stage for the final act.

The final version of the BRA, in the form of S. 256, was introduced on February 1, 2005.[140] At that point, it contained all of the attorney liability provisions ultimately enacted; the sanctions provisions in Code §§ 707(b)(4)(A) and (B) remained discretionary.

The bill was referred to the Senate Judiciary Committee, and hearings were held on February 10. A number of amendments to the bill were accepted but none affected the liability provisions.[141] The bill was reported out of the Judiciary Committee on February 17, 2005.

---

134.   Congressman Gekas, one of the staunchest proponents of bankruptcy legislation, was no longer available to sponsor the bill, having been defeated by Democrat Tim Holden in the 2002 election.

135.   H.R. 975, 108th Cong., introduced on Feb, 27, 2003, by Rep. Sensenbrenner.

136.   H.R. 975, Bill Summary and Status for the 108th Cong., at Mar. 19, 2003. The vote was 313-113.

137.   *Id.* at Mar. 20, 2003 and Mar. 21, 2003.

138.   *Id.*

139.   When I asked parties involved about the reasons that the bill stalled, I was told only that there were other, more pressing priorities. Susan Jensen describes the steps that were taken in the House to overcome "certain procedural hurdles" in the Senate. This included stripping a Senate bill extending Chapter 12 of all its provisions, inserting the provisions of H.R. 975, slightly amended. This passed the House 265-99. The House then asked for a conference on that bill, but the Senate refused. *See* Jensen at 561-62.

140.   H.R. 685 was introduced in the House on Feb. 9, 2005.

141.   There is no official Judiciary Committee record of the amendments offered or votes taken in the Judiciary Committee, but there are press reports. *See* Michael Posner, *Senate Judiciary Passes Major Bankruptcy Reform Bill,* CONGRESS DAILY, Feb. 17, 2005, *at* http://nationaljournal.com/members/markups/2005/02/200504802.htm#.

Senator Schumer said that he would fight the bill on the floor unless it contained the compromise language on FACE.[142] But efforts to include the amendment failed. This time around, without the Schumer/Hyde language, pro-choice Democrats and Republicans in the Senate were directly facing a decision whether to support the bill on its own terms.[143]

The amendments to remove the attorney liability provisions, proposed by the American Bar Association,[144] found sponsors when the bill moved to the floor. Senator Feingold filed an amendment that would have deleted attorneys from the definition of debt relief agencies:

(12A) "debt relief agency" means any person, *other than an attorney or an employee of an attorney,* who provides any bankruptcy assistance to an assisted person in return for the payment of money. . . .[145]

The Feingold amendment also changed the notice required by Code § 527 to delete some of the references to attorneys:

IMPORTANT INFORMATION ABOUT BANKRUPTCY ASSISTANCE SERVICES FROM A BANKRUPTCY PETITION PREPARER.
If you decide to seek bankruptcy relief, you can represent yourself, you can hire an attorney to represent you, or you can get help in some localities from a bankruptcy petition preparer who is not an attorney. THE LAW REQUIRES A BANKRUPTCY PETITION PREPARER TO GIVE YOU A WRITTEN CONTRACT SPECIFYING WHAT THE BANKRUPTCY PETITION PREPARER WILL DO FOR YOU AND HOW MUCH IT WILL COST. Ask to see the contract before you hire anyone.[146]

---

142.   Michael Posner, *Senate Judiciary Passes Major Bankruptcy Reform Bill,* CONGRESS DAILY, Feb. 17, 2005, at http://nationaljournal.com/members/markups/2005/02/200504802.htm# (Schumer vowed to prevent action on the bill without the amendment).

143.   Despite the fact that he had supported the bill before, Senator Schumer ultimately voted against the BRA after failing to reinsert the Schumer/Hyde compromise language. Many other pro-choice Democrats and Republicans voted in favor of the bill, including Senators Biden, Collins, Snowe, and Stabenow.

144.   The ABA-proposed amendments can be found at http://www.abanet.org/poladv/brattyamendments7205.pdf. *See* the discussion below on lobbying by the ABA against the attorney liability provisions.

145.   Senate Amendment 93 to S. 256, filed March 7, 2005, CONG. REC. S2136-S2137, at S2136 (emphasis added).

146.   *Id.*

Senator Bingaman filed another of the ABA-proposed amendments, which would have deleted attorneys entirely from the § 707(b)(4) sanctions provision, and made the sanctions on debtors slightly tougher:[147]

> (A) The court, on its own initiative or on the motion of a party in interest, may order the debtor to reimburse the trustee for all reasonable costs in prosecuting a motion filed under section 707(b), including reasonable attorneys' fees, and reasonable trustee fees based upon the trustee's time in prosecuting the motion, if—
>> (i) a trustee files a motion for dismissal or conversion under this subsection; and
>> (ii) the court grants such motion.
> (B) Any costs and fees awarded under subparagraph (A) shall have the administrative priority described in section 507(a)(2) of this title in the current or any successor cases filed under this title.[148]

Senator Bingaman's amendment—similar to that proposed by the ABA—would have removed the attorney certification of hardship reaffirmation agreements in Code § 524.[149] Finally, the amendment would have changed BRA Section 319 to read:

> SENSE OF THE CONGRESS REGARDING ENFORCEMENT OF RULE 9011 OF THE FEDERAL RULES OF BANKRUPTCY PROCEDURE
> It is the sense of Congress that fraud and abuse exist in the bankruptcy system and that in order to curb this fraud and abuse, Federal bankruptcy courts should vigorously enforce rule 9011 of the Federal Rules of Bankruptcy Procedure (11 U.S.C. App.).[150]

---

147. The language in the amendment that gave costs and fees awarded by this amendment administrative priority was hotly contested by some members of the ABA who had fought to gain ABA support for amendments. *See* the section on ABA lobbying below.

148. Senate Amendment 51 to S. 256, filed March 4, 2005, CONG. REC. S2085-2086. The amendment also would have deleted attorneys from the sanctions in Code § 707(b)(5)(A)(ii)(II), so that it no longer contained the phrase, "the attorney (if any) who filed the motion did not comply with the requirements of clauses (i) and (ii) of paragraphs (4)(C) and". Finally, it would have amended Code § 523(a) to make the fees and costs nondischargeable.

149. Senate Amendment 51 to S. 256, filed March 4, 2005, CONG. REC. S2085-2086. The amendment accomplished this by changing the introductory language of subsection (5) to read:

> (5) The declaration shall consist of the following certification:
> 'Part C: Certification by Debtor's Attorney (if Any).'

and deleting subsections (B) and (C) entirely. *Id.*

150. Senate Amendment 51 to S. 256, filed March 4, 2005, CONG. REC. S2085-2086. The amendment proposed by the ABA used the phrase "significant fraud and abuse"; the word "significant" was not included in the Bingaman amendment.

On March 10, the bill came to the Senate floor. Again, several amendments were offered and several were passed. But attempts to alter the attorney liability provisions were unsuccessful. After several failed attempts to amend the bill, Senator Feingold withdrew Amendment 93 as a part of a compromise that led to the acceptance of a few unrelated amendments.

Senator Bingaman spoke in favor of his amendment. His remarks constitute the *entire discussion* on the floor of the Senate of the attorney liability provisions:

> Mr. President, this amendment would help to ensure that legal representation remains affordable and accessible to lower-income Americans who are forced into bankruptcy.
>
> As currently written, the bill contains provisions that would significantly increase attorney's fees and expenses related to the filing of a bankruptcy petition. Under existing law, attorneys can rely on information that a client provides regarding the extent and the value of their assets, such as the worth of a car, household furniture, and that sort of item.
>
> In an effort to combat the perceived abuse of the bankruptcy system, this proposed bill requires an attorney to certify that the attorney has made an inquiry into the client's assertions, and it subjects the lawyers to personal liability for inaccuracies in a debtor's list of assets. Although the proponents of this provision may argue that the change will prevent abuse, I believe it is an unnecessary change that will have significant unintended consequences.
>
> Under existing law, attorneys are already required to certify that pleadings, motions, and other materials have factual support pursuant to bankruptcy rule 9011. Attorneys are also prohibited from knowingly making any legal or factual misrepresentation to the court or assisting a client in any abuse. If we want to address misconduct by attorneys, what we need is better enforcement of those existing rules. If we want to address abuse by debtors in submitting their lists of assets, we should seek to hold those individuals responsible. My amendment would do that by making specific debts nondischargeable if the debtor lied about them in their bankruptcy schedule.
>
> With regard to the unintended consequences of these changes, in order to protect themselves from harsh sanctions, attorneys would be forced to conduct a costly investigation into the value and the actual existence of the client's claimed assets. This would not only directly increase the attorney's expenses, it would also likely raise very significantly other costs such as malpractice insurance. The Attorneys' Liability Protections [sic] Society, Inc., which is a malpractice carrier that insures 15,000 lawyers in 27 jurisdictions around the country, has estimated that the impact of this provision could result in the immediate increase of insurance premiums for bankruptcy lawyers from 10 to 20 percent.

The bankruptcy bill contains another provision with regard to reaffirmation agreements that will also likely result in higher attorneys' fees and costs.

Current law provides that debtors can reaffirm a debt and therefore keep a specific asset, as long as the attorney certifies the decision to do so is voluntary and will not create undue hardship for the debtor.

As drafted, S. 256 would require attorneys, where there is a presumption of hardship, to certify that debtors would be able to make future payments under the agreement. Attorneys are not accountants and would have to conduct extensive audits of their client's finances in order to determine if that client would be able to afford specific payments. Of course, that would drive up attorneys' fees as well.

These additional costs would negatively impact on the accessibility of legal representation and court administration in two primary ways. First, they would reduce the ability of lawyers to take on pro bono cases and would make these legal services unavailable to many indigent debtors. In my own state, the law clinic at the University of New Mexico Law School has said if the bill passes in its current form, it would likely have to stop doing bankruptcy work for indigent clients due to the additional cost and concerns related to the attorney sanction provision. Second, these costs would place additional administrative burdens on the nation's courts by increasing the number of individuals who would be representing themselves in the court proceeding due to their inability to afford an attorney. According to the Chief Bankruptcy Judge for the District of New Mexico, cases involving pro se debtors, debtors who are representing themselves, can take up to 10 times as much time to process as cases where debtors are represented by counsel. As such, even a small increase in the number of cases being processed without counsel could create substantial administrative burdens on our bankruptcy courts.

So the amendment I have called up would do three things. First, it would replace the attorney liability language in section 102 of the bill with new language that would impose nondischargeable sanctions on debtors who lie on their bankruptcy schedules. Second, it would urge bankruptcy courts to more vigorously enforce existing rules regarding the sanctioning of attorneys where misconduct has been demonstrated. These changes would properly address abuse in the bankruptcy system by holding debtors responsible for intentional misrepresentations in listing the worth of their assets and holding attorneys responsible if they assist in any such abuse. Last, the amendment would maintain existing law with regard to the certification of reaffirmation agreements by attorneys.

I understand the need to punish attorneys for abuse of the bankruptcy process, but there are ways to do this without unnecessarily driving up the cost of legal representation. This, in my view, is an amendment that is reasonable. The American Bar Association has endorsed it. I urge my colleagues to support it as well.[151]

---

151. *Id.* at S2319.

Recognizing the futility of proceeding, Senator Bingaman then withdrew his amendment prior to a vote.[152] S. 256 passed the Senate on March 10, 2005, supported by 74 senators.[153]

On March 14, 2005, the bill was received in the House. At the Judiciary Committee mark-up of the bill, Representative Watt offered the ABA amendments:

> Amendment 04, which is supported by the American Bar Association and a whole host of other people, accomplishes two things. It eliminates provisions in the bill that would require the debtor's attorney to certify the accuracy of the debtor's schedules under penalty of harsh court sanctions, and it modifies provisions that would require attorneys to certify a debtor's ability to make future payments under a reaffirmation agreement.
>
> Section 102 unnecessarily imposes a harsher standard on debtor attorneys to certify pleadings filed on behalf of the debtor. No similar heightened standard is imposed on [creditors'] attorneys, nor for attorneys outside the bankruptcy context. By holding the debtor's attorney personally liable for the accuracy of their clients' schedules, these provisions would force the attorney to hire private investigators and appraisers to verify information, adding thousands of dollars to the cost of representing a debtor in bankruptcy. Without this amendment, I believe that the bankruptcy representation—that bankruptcy representation would become unaffordable for most debtors.
>
> Also, the impact on the pro bono bar providing bankruptcy services would dwindle, with the likely result that thousands of pro se debtors would clog up the court system or debtors will not seek the relief they need at all.

152. *Id.*

153. Roll call vote number 44 on passage of S. 256 as amended, March 10, 2005. The vote was 74 yeas, 25 nays, 1 not voting, *at* http://www.senate.gov/legislative/LIS/roll_call_lists/roll_call_vote_cfm.cfm?congress=109&session=1&vote=00044. Interestingly, it was Sen. Clinton who did not vote. Her position on the bill changed dramatically when she moved from the White House to the Senate. As noted in Jensen, in 1998 she used her syndicated column to state that, while she supported "responsible bankruptcy reform," she opposed provisions of the bill that would force parents to compete with banks collecting credit card debt. *Id.* at 508, *citing* Hillary Rodham Clinton, *Talking It Over*, May 6, 1998, *at* http://clinton2.nara.gov/WH/EOP/First_Lady/html/columns/HRC0506.html. Mrs. Clinton reportedly advocated for the pocket veto of the bill by her husband in 2000. *See* Jensen at 515, *citing* HILLARY RODHAM CLINTON, LIVING HISTORY 650-51 (2003); and *id.* at 534, *citing* Hillary Rodham Clinton, *Talking It Over*, Sept 15, 1999, *at* http://clinton3.nara.gov/WH/EOP/First_Lady/html/columns/HRC091599.html. As senator, she voted in favor of the bill in 2002. *See* U.S. Senate Roll Call Votes, 107th Cong., 1st Session, Vote No. 36 on S. 420 *at* http://www.senate.gov/legislative/LIS/roll_call_lists/roll_call_vote_cfm.cfm?congress=107&session=1&vote=00036.

Amendment 05 corrects the provisions that would require bankruptcy attorneys to identify and advertise themselves as debt relief agencies and comply with intrusive new regulations that would interfere with the confidential attorney-client relationship. Sections 227 and 220 [sic] through 229 of the bill would seriously interfere with the attorney-client relationship by prohibiting debtor's bankruptcy attorneys and many non-bankruptcy attorneys from giving their clients certain proper bankruptcy planning advice. These provisions would also have a chilling effect on debtors' lawyers and their firms by requiring all of their newsletters, seminars, and advertising materials to include awkward and misleading statements identifying themselves as debt relief agencies.[154]

The amendments were defeated on a voice vote.[155] Although Rep. Cannon stated that he would be willing to consider the amendments in the future, he did not support amending the bill at that time.[156]

Many amendments were proffered by opponents of the bill, both in the Committee[157] and on the floor,[158] but none was adopted. The BRA passed the House on April 14, by a vote of 302-126,[159] and was signed into law by President Bush on April 20, 2005.[160]

III. *Lobbying Efforts of the American Bar Association*

For much of the pendency of the BRA, the legal community—even the bankruptcy bar—was largely oblivious to the impact that these provisions would have on the practice of bankruptcy law, and to the precedent that this level of intervention would set for the attorney-client relationship in all areas of practice.

There was some general grumbling about the impact of these provisions on various bankruptcy-related listservs, but no organized action.[161] Lawyers

---

154.   H. Rep. 109-031 Pt. 1, Bankruptcy Abuse Prevention and Consumer Protection Act of 2005, at 373. (Original contains the word "credential" where the brackets appear.)

155.   *Id.* at 374.

156.   *Id.*

157.   S. 256, Bill Summary and Status for the 109th Cong. *See also* H. Rep. 109-031 pt. 1, Bankruptcy Abuse Prevention and Consumer Protection Act of 2005. Chairman Sensenbrenner was not going to risk another conference on this bill, and announced at the outset that no amendments would be added. Many were offered and all were voted down.

158.   S. 256, Bill Summary and Status for the 109th Cong.

159.   *Id.*

160.   *Id.*

161.   Members of the ABA General Practice, Solo & Small Firm Section Committee on Bankruptcy Law had discussed the provisions as early as 1999, in a joint meeting with the members of the Consumer Bankruptcy Committee of the Section of Business Law, at the Annual Meeting in Atlanta. A statement objecting to the provisions was drafted, but no action was taken at that time. E-mail from Marc Stern, on file with the authors.

who represented debtors in bankruptcy viewed the entire bill with alarm, and did not single out the attorney liability provisions for special concern.[162] There was some evidence that the debtors' bar was suffering from "wolf crying" malaise: the alarm had been raised again and again over this provision or that of the BRA, and they might have reacted this time or that, but the bill hadn't passed. And hadn't passed. And hadn't passed.

In 2001, the author issued a call to action on one bankruptcy listserv, asking "Where is the ABA?" A response issued from Marc Stern, then vice-chair[163] of the Bankruptcy Committee of the ABA Section of General, Solo, and Small Firm Practice [GP]. He noted that his committee had passed a resolution that opposed these provisions in the bill.

After revisiting the issue in 2001, the GP Bankruptcy Committee leadership decided to ask the ABA for permission—called "blanket authority"[164]—to write a letter to Congress asking that the provisions be removed. At that point, the GP Section objected only to Section 102 of the bill, which amended Code § 707(b) of the Code and created liability for the debtor's attorney if the case was converted or dismissed.[165]

---

162.   The National Association of Consumer Bankruptcy Attorneys (NACBA) had vigorously opposed the BRA and led a coalition of organizations that opposed the bill. But it never singled out the attorney liability provisions for special attention and did not join in the ABA's effort to remove the provisions from the bill. Indeed, Henry Sommer, currently president of NACBA, has consistently taken the position that the attorney liability provisions are not that significant: "Much has been written about the new provisions requiring additional duties and certifications of attorneys, referred to by some as the 'attorney liability provisions.' (Citing the statute.) A careful examination of these provisions reveals that many of the statements predicting impending doom for consumer bankruptcy attorneys are overblown, to say the least. Indeed, those most likely to innocently violate the provisions will be attorneys who do not regularly represent consumer debtors." Henry Sommer, *Trying to Make Sense Out of Nonsense: Representing Consumers under the "Bankruptcy Abuse Prevention and Consumer Protection Act of 2005,"* 79 Am. Bankr. L.J. 191, 204 (2005). As the aforementioned but unidentified overblower, I certainly hope he is right. I haven't found many other consumer debtors' bankruptcy attorneys who share this perspective.

163.   Now co-chair.

164.   Bylaws of the American Bar Association, Section 25.1, as adopted by the House of Delegates in 1981 and interpreted in 1991. The Policy provides, in part, that any section of the Association may present a statement on matters within its primary or special expertise and jurisdiction to a federal, state or municipal legislative body or governmental agency (or to a court with respect to procedural rules only) subject to certain conditions, including that the position taken is not in conflict with any ABA policy, that no other Section of the ABA objects, that the blanket authority issues for a limited period (normally 90 days) and that the statement make clear that it represents only the views of the Section and not ABA policy. *Id.*

165.   *See* discussion above on the change in this provision before the 107th Congress.

The request for blanket authority was approved by the leadership of the GP Section and forwarded to the ABA. There were no objections, and the blanket authority issued in May 2001.

On May 18, 2001, the chair of the GP Bankruptcy Committee wrote to the Conference Committee on S. 420/H.R. 333.[166] The letter included the Resolution passed by the GP Section and the report supporting its conclusions. The letter stated:

> The Resolution . . . has broad implications for many general practice, solo, and small firm attorneys around the country. In short, the proposed section of the Bill substantially increases the duties and requirements of debtor's counsel in bankruptcy, creating a situation where the new duties of counsel may, in fact, create an unwaivable conflict of interest.[167]

The accompanying resolution stated:

> The General Practice, Solo & Small Firm Section of the ABA . . . opposes Section 102(4)(a) and 4(b)[168] of SR [sic] 420 and HR 333, which would impose strict liability on the attorney for the debtor in a Chapter 7 bankruptcy proceeding for all costs and fees incurred by the trustee . . . if the case is converted from Chapter 7 to Chapter 13 or is dismissed because of abuse.[169]

The accompanying report explained:

> It has been demonstrated that bankruptcy proceedings function more efficiently and with less loss of rights when all parties are represented by competent counsel who are aware of the rules of Bankruptcy Procedure and obligations imposed by the Code upon debtors. . . . Bankruptcy attorneys are already subject to BR 9011, which provides sanctions if an attorney signs pleadings without sufficient justification. They are also subject to 28 U.S.C

---

166. Letter from Larry B. Feinstein to the Joint Conference Committee on Proposed Bankruptcy Legislation S. 420/H.R. 333, dated May 18, 2001. A copy of that letter is on file with the ABA.

167. *Id.*

168. The actual provisions are in Section 102(a) of those bills (not 102(4)(a) and 4(b)), amending Code § 707, and the provisions are proposed Code §§ 707(b)(4)(A) and (B). *See* the text of these provisions above.

169. Resolution of the Missouri Bar and the General Practice, Solo & Small Firm Section of the ABA, dated May, 2001. A copy of the resolution is on file with the author. The author wishes to express her gratitude to the Missouri Bar Association, which acted with alacrity when requested to sponsor this resolution, which permitted it to be placed on House of Delegates' calendar prior to the 2001 Annual Meeting.

1927 for causing the vexatious or frivolous lengthening of lawsuits. Enactment of the subject clause could be read to create a different or higher standard, which would impose liability regardless of what the attorney knew. . . . [The provision] changes the attorney from an advocate for and representative of the client to his policeman. The legislation creates an unwaivable conflict of interest because the attorney must, in effect, inform against his client if he even suspects that the client may be hiding or misrepresenting something. Further the attorney will then be required to verify independently the representations of his client. The cost of verification will make competent bankruptcy attorneys shy away from representing debtors, and will require attorneys to essentially become furniture appraisers . . . .[170]

The report identified two major problems with the provision:

- It predicted that the provision would make settlement of questionable cases more difficult, because the trustee would have no incentive to settle, knowing that the debtor's attorney would be liable for fees and costs if the case was later converted or dismissed.
- It noted that unscrupulous trustees could offer the attorney an escape from potential liability in exchange for selling out the client.

It asked the conference to eliminate the provision from the bill.[171]

Following up on this letter, the GP Section, together with the Missouri Bar Association, offered a resolution to the ABA House of Delegates in August 2001 at the ABA annual meeting. The resolution, entitled "Recommendation: Resolved, that the American Bar Association opposes the enhanced attorney liability provisions in S. 420/H.R. 333," was ultimately co-sponsored by several additional entities.[172] The resolution passed the ABA House of Delegates

---

170.   *Id.* at report, page 2.
171.   *Id.* at report, page 3.
172.   In addition to the GP Section and the Missouri Bar, the resolution was co-sponsored by the ABA Section of Business Law, the ABA Section of Family Law, the ABA Standing Committee on Lawyer Professional Liability, and the ABA Tort and Insurance Practice Section [TIPS]. The author expresses gratitude to each of the co-sponsors of this resolution and their many members, who worked tirelessly to remove these provisions from the BRA prior to its passage. Special recognition for the passage of the resolution is due to Dwight Smith, who presented the resolution to the House of Delegates, Marc S. Stern, Larry Feinstein, Chris Kaup, Jeff Solomon of the GP Section, Professor Amelia Boss, William Schorling, Professors Juliet Moringiello and Jonathan Lipson of the Section of Business Law, Robert Minto of the Standing Committee on Lawyer Professional Liability, Marshall Wolf and Shayna Steinfeld of the Section of Family Law, Tim Lupinacci of the Young Lawyers Division, Francine L. Semaya of TIPS, Catherine Barrie, Theresa Levings, and Lee Viorel of the Missouri Bar Association, and to an unnamed but highly skilled bankruptcy judge who helped participants draft the report and the original proposed amendments.

on August 7, 2001, with 97 percent of the delegates voting in favor. At that point, for the first time, it became ABA official policy to oppose those provisions of the bill.

The report that accompanied the resolution[173] identified three aspects of attorney liability that were objectionable:

1. The certification of the bankruptcy schedules and the application of Rule 9011 to the schedules:

   Under current law, the debtor alone is responsible for the truthfulness and accuracy of the debtor's bankruptcy schedules. Bankruptcy Rule 9011 ..., which requires the attorney to certify that filings are warranted by the facts, does not apply to schedules, because attorneys naturally rely on financial information provided by their clients. ... [T]he proposed law would specifically apply Rule 9011 to schedules, and the Bankruptcy Code itself would require attorneys to make an affirmative investigation and inquiry into the accuracy of the schedules, and then to warrant that the inquiry revealed no inaccuracy. Current Rule 9011 grants the court discretion to impose penalties against attorneys, but the proposed legislation forces the court to im-

---

On the day after the resolution passed the House of Delegates, I sent an e-mail to 120 lawyers in my address book, asking them to forward the resolution to their state and local bar associations and encourage them to adopt the resolution, and to contact their congressional delegations and ask that the provisions be deleted from the bill. That was the beginning of my Attorney Liability Listserv (which survives to this day). Several other listservs were instrumental in raising opposition to these provisions, including the GP Section Bankruptcy Committee Listserv, the UNLV Bankruptcy Listserv, and Solosez.

173. Although it was submitted with the resolution and was available to the House of Delegates members at the time of the vote, the resolution made clear on its face that the report was not official ABA policy. Subsequent to the adoption of the resolution, one attorney who was involved in the process, and who recommended adoption of the resolution, disagreed with the text of the attached report. In order to resolve this conflict, a working group composed of several attorneys nominated by sponsoring entities changed the information that was submitted to Congress with the resolution. The information provided to Congress relative to this resolution went through several changes, none of which was approved by the House of Delegates, but which nonetheless were permitted by the ABA policy in support of the resolution. The amendments proposed by this working group differed dramatically from the proposal offered by the original proponents of the resolution. The amendments proposed by the ABA increased sanctions on debtors and changed the priority of attorneys' fees owed by debtors after the imposition of sanctions. These provisions—which shifted responsibility from attorneys at the expense of their clients— were not in the original resolution, nor in the accompanying report. At times, while lobbying for these amendments, opponents of the attorney liability provisions encountered distaste and even rejection by members of Congress and their staffers who were generally supportive of the effort. As noted above, Senator Bingaman refused one amendment proposed by the working group and wrote his own.

pose a fine on any debtor's attorney found to violate the rule, even inadvertently. In contrast, attorneys representing creditors are not subject to mandatory sanctions. If the debtor's schedules are found to violate Rule 9011, and the debtor is denied immediate discharge under the means test, the debtor's attorney will be liable for the fees of the trustee who contested the discharge.[174]

The report went on to note the conflict of interest, and the fundamental change in the attorney's role, that this provision would create.[175]

2.   The report next addressed—the first time for the ABA—the reaffirmation provision of the bill:

Under the proposed legislation, the debtor's attorney alone will be responsible for determining the appropriateness of reaffirmations. The debtor's attorney will be required to certify that "in the opinion of the attorney the debtor is able to make the payment," even in cases where there is a presumption of undue hardship under the debtor's budget. Bankruptcy attorneys currently do not make financial and household budgeting decisions for their clients. This requirement will create strong conflicts of interest between the attorney and a debtor, when the debtor wants to reaffirm a debt, and instructs the attorney to make the certification. If the attorney follows the client's directive, the attorney becomes subject to mandatory sanction under Rule 9011 if the reaffirmation is found to have been inappropriate.[176]

3.   The report also objected to many aspects of the debt relief agency provisions, including the mandated disclosure statement and record-keeping requirements, the loss of all fees for failure to observe any of these provisions in addition to being subject to additional penalties, and the advertising regulations. The report noted, "Many lawyers who represent both debtors and creditors will stop handling debtor cases rather than display this notice."[177]

The report closed with this statement:

The proposed changes, taken together, will have a massive negative impact on the availability of legal counsel in bankruptcy. More importantly, it is

---

174.   Report accompanying Recommendation on S. 420/H.R. 333, Approved by the House of Delegates on Aug. 7, 2001.

175.   *Id.* This statement is not the official policy of the ABA, but was merely included in the report accompanying the Resolution passed by the House of Delegates. (This footnote is included at the insistence of the American Bar Association Governmental Affairs Office.)

176.   *Id.*

177.   *Id.*

a dangerous precedent to permit Congress to mandate different degrees of professional responsibility, accountability, and liability simply because of an attorney's area of practice. If the proposed legislation is enacted with these provisions, it would not be difficult to imagine the Attorney General urging Congress to amend the United States Code to provide similar degrees of accountability on the criminal defense bar, or for the Internal Revenue Service to urge Congress to impose similar accountability upon the tax bar. The proposed legislation alters the most critical attributes of the attorney-client relationship, and should be opposed by the Association and by all participants in the legal system.[178]

After the Resolution passed the ABA, the ABA Government Affairs Office issued a Fact Sheet to members of Congress outlining the provisions that were targeted by the Resolution. It noted:

These three attorney liability provisions, taken together, will have a massive negative impact on the availability of quality legal counsel in bankruptcy. These provisions will discourage many attorneys from agreeing to represent debtors at all, while significantly increasing the fees and expenses of clients who are able to obtain legal representation. In addition, these provisions will discourage lawyers from volunteering their services for pro bono bankruptcy cases. Unless they are removed, these provisions pose a serious threat to the efficient operation of the bankruptcy system.[179]

After the adoption of the Resolution, many other state and local bar associations passed resolutions mirroring that of the ABA.[180]

After the passage of the Resolution, many lawyers in the ABA and state and local bar associations began to contact members of Congress concerning these provisions. In April, 2002, the Chair-elect of the Section of Business Law wrote to the conference members strongly opposing the attorney liability provisions, and asking the members to remove them from the bill.[181]

---

178. *Id.*

179. ABA Fact Sheet on Attorney Liability and Regulations on Debtors' Attorneys in Bankruptcy Cases, dated September 2001.

180. Among the many entities that have passed resolutions opposing these provisions are the state bars of Arizona, Arkansas, Illinois, Iowa, Maryland, Minnesota, Missouri, New Jersey, New Mexico, North Carolina, Ohio, Oregon, Pennsylvania, Tennessee, Utah, Virginia, Washington State, Wisconsin, and the bar associations of Boston, Chicago, the City of New York, Philadelphia, Richmond, and the Standing Committee on Insolvency of the California State Bar. Other organizations that have passed resolutions opposing these provisions include the Federal Bar Association and the United Auto Workers (*see, e.g.,* http://www.detnews.com/2005/autosinsider/0509/18/A01-318432.htm).

181. Letter from Harold S. Barron, Chair-elect of the ABA Section of Business Law, to Members of the H.R. 333 Conference, dated April 22, 2002.

As a result of this flurry of activity, one small but significant change did take place. As discussed above, the Conference Report on H.R. 333,[182] and all the subsequent versions of the bill, changed the standard of attorney liability found in the provision amending § 707(b). In each case, the word "shall" in the subsection imposing penalties against the attorney was changed to "may," making discretionary the imposition of penalties.[183]

- Where the text of proposed § 707(b) had previously read, "The court *shall* order the counsel for the debtor to reimburse the trustee . . ." before the conference, after conference the bill read, "The court *may* order the counsel for the debtor to reimburse the trustee . . . ."[184]
- Where the text had previously read, "If the court finds that the attorney for the debtor violated rule 9011 . . . the court *shall* order . . ." now read, "the court *may* order . . . ."[185]

This slight shift of language is a significant change in impact, giving the bankruptcy court discretion in every case whether or not to impose trustees' fees, costs, or penalties on the debtor's attorney. It is worth noting that this change was made during conference, despite the fact that the issue was technically "non-conferenceable,"[186] suggesting that the lobbying by members of the bar had an impact on this amendment.

None of the other provisions imposing liability and obligations on the debtor's attorney was altered as a result of lobbying by the ABA[187] or other bar associations. As noted above, although amendments were filed by Senators Feingold and Bingaman, they were withdrawn prior to a vote.

---

182.   Conference Report on H.R. 333, H. Rep. 107-617: Bankruptcy Abuse Prevention and Consumer Protection Act of 2002.

183.   Compare S. 420 as passed by the Senate and H.R. 333 as passed by the House with the Conference Report on H.R. 333.

184.   Compare S. 420 as passed by the Senate, Code § 707(b)(4)(A), with the same section in the Conference Report. (Emphasis added.)

185.   Compare S. 420 as passed by the Senate, Code § 707(b)(4)(B), with the same section in the Conference Report. (Emphasis added.)

186.   By "technically non-conferenceable," I mean that the amendments should not have been permitted in conference, because the provision was the same in both S. 420 and H.R. 333. The point of the conference is to resolve differences between the bills, and this was not a difference.

187.   In a last-ditch attempt to motivate the rank-and-file members of the ABA to contact their congressional delegations, the author created an advertisement in the ABA journal *e-Report*, an electronic journal that appears every Friday. With the financial support of the GP Section, the Section of Business Law, and the Standing Committee on Lawyer Professional Liability, the ad ran for three weeks, beginning on Friday, Feb. 18, 2005.

The impact of these provisions is amply illustrated by the other chapters in this book. The provisions have one goal, and that is to discourage attorneys from representing debtors in consumer bankruptcy cases. Consumer debtors will either be unable to obtain representation or will pay an increased fee.[188] This will be the result both of individual attorneys' decision to avoid the onerous and distasteful regulatory provisions—decreasing the available pool of debtors' attorneys—and of the increase in fees charged by those who remain in the practice, to account both for the added risk and the additional time associated with these provisions.[189]

WARNING!!

Deterring lawyers from representing consumer debtors will not stop bankruptcy filings, but it will increase the cost, as more debtors file *pro se*, dramatically increasing the administrative burden to the bankruptcy court system. More challenges and hearings will drive up the costs for creditors as well.

It is wrong to assume that this is an unintended consequence. There is every reason to believe that this is precisely the motivation that drove these provisions.[190]

---

188. *See, e.g.,* Jeanne Sahadi, *Rush to file for bankruptcy*, CNN Money, Oct. 14, 2005, *at* http://money.cnn.com/2005/10/10/pf/debt/bankruptcy_runup/ (attorneys' fees are expected to rise between 75% and 100% in response to the new law); Thomas Adcock, *Pro Bono Bankruptcy Push Trying to Beat the Clock,* N.Y. Lawyer, Oct. 7, 2005, *at* http://www.nylawyer.com/display.php/file=/probono/news/05/100705a (reporting on difficulties convincing attorneys to work on pro bono bankruptcy).

189. *Id. See also* Douglas Sherwin, *New Federal Law Puts Added Burden on Bankruptcy Attorneys*, San Diego Daily Transcript, Oct. 18, 2005, *at* http://www.sddt.com/News/article.cfm?SourceCode=20051018tba; *Mississippi Judge Calls New Federal Law "Meat-ax Approach,"* Picayune Item, Oct. 19, 2005, *at* http://www.picayuneitem.com/articles/2005/10/19/news/15reform.txt.

190. In discussions about the purpose of these provisions, one congressional staffer suggested that there was a widespread feeling that the schedules filed for debtors are not factual but fictional, and that debtors' attorneys view them as a starting point for negotiations rather than factual representations to the court of the debtor's financial health. This staffer felt that the inclusion of the attorney liability provisions was an attempt by the proponents to add a layer of responsibility in order to ensure that decisions were being made based upon factual information. *See* discussion above. The conclusion that factual information is essential to the effective operation of the bankruptcy system is supported by the Report of the National Commission as well. *See* Commission Report at Recommendation 1.1.2 and pages 107 to 110. However, as noted above, nothing in the Commission Report recommends holding debtors' counsel personally liable for inaccurate information.

IV. Now What?

As the BRA was about to become effective, the devastation wrought by Hurricane Katrina led some members of Congress to press for delay of the effective date,[191] while others offered legislation to make its provisions inapplicable to Katrina victims.[192] There was inescapable evidence that these victims would not be able to comply with the increased documentation required by the BRA.[193]

---

191.   *See, e.g.,* Congressional Research Service, RS22275: (Proposed Bankruptcy Legislation to Address Natural Disaster Victims), Sept. 22, 2005, *at* http://opencrs.cdt.org/document/RS22275.

192.   *See, e.g.,* Press Release by Congressman Jerrold Nadler, *Nadler, Conyers, Watt, Jackson Lee to Introduce Bill (to Relieve Debt Burden on Katrina Survivors*, Sept., 1, 2005, *at* http://www.house.gov/apps/list/press/ny08_nadler/DebtreliefKatrina090105.html. By my last count, at least nine bills were introduced to address the impact of the BRA on Katrina victims, including:

- S. 1765: A bill to provide disaster relief and incentives for economic recovery for Louisiana residents and businesses affected by Hurricane Katrina, sponsored by Sen. Landrieu (introduced 9/22/05)
- H.R. 3662: To delay for two years the general effective date of the Bankruptcy Abuse Prevention and Consumer Protection Act of 2005, sponsored by Rep. Slaughter (introduced 9/6/05)
- H.R. 3958: A bill to provide disaster relief and incentives for economic recovery for Louisiana residents and businesses affected by Hurricane Katrina, sponsored by Rep. Melancon (introduced 9/29/05)
- S. 1766: A bill to provide disaster relief and incentives for economic recovery for Louisiana residents and businesses affected by Hurricane Katrina, sponsored by Sen. Vitter (introduced 9/22/05)
- H.R. 3697: A bill to provide relief with respect to disaster-related debts incurred by victims of Hurricane Katrina and other natural disasters, sponsored by Rep. Conyers (introduced 9/8/05)
- S. 1647: To amend title 11, United States Code, to provide relief to victims of Hurricane Katrina and other natural disasters, sponsored by Sen. Feingold (introduced 9/8/05)
- H.R. 4197: A bill to provide for the recovery, reclamation, restoration, and reconstruction of lives and communities and for the reunion of families devastated by Hurricane Katrina and to address the issues of poverty exposed by Hurricane Katrina, sponsored by Rep. Watt (introduced Nov. 2, 2005)
- S.1637: A bill to provide emergency relief to meet the immediate needs of survivors of Hurricane Katrina for health care, housing, education, and financial relief, and for other purposes, sponsored by Sen. Reid (introduced Sept. 8, 2005)
- S. 1787: To provide bankruptcy relief for victims of natural disasters, and for other purposes, sponsored by Sen. Vitter (introduced Sept. 8, 2005).

193.   Not to belabor the obvious, *see, e.g.,* Alan Zarembo & Thomas H. Maugh II, *Lives and History Adrift in Soggy Paper Trail*, L.A. TIMES, Sept. 9, 2005, at A1.

But with Republicans in control of the both the Senate and the House,[194] and Republican leadership standing firmly against reopening the bill, none of this legislation is likely to pass.[195] Rep. Sensenbrenner made clear that he was unwilling to entertain any changes in the law:

> Representative F. James Sensenbrenner [sic] (R-WI), chairman of the House Judiciary Committee, has indicated he will not hold a hearing on waiving the law for purposes of disaster relief.

> "If someone in Katrina is down and out, and has no possibility of being able to repay 40 percent or more of their debts, then the new bankruptcy law doesn't apply," Sensenbrenner said.[196]

On the Senate side, there was a similar reaction by another of the law's strongest proponents, Senator Grassley:

> Beth Levine, press secretary for Senate Finance Committee Chairman Charles Grassley, R-Iowa, who sponsored the bankruptcy legislation, said Grassley included the special circumstances language to give judges "leeway" to help people who fall on hard times.
> . . . Still, she said, the senator expects debtors to pay back their creditors if they have the means to do so. He "just wants to be sure that those

---

194. It should be noted that, while the Republican Party is currently in control of Congress, the Democrats were in control of the Senate for most of the 107th Congress. Once Sen. Jeffords became an Independent, Democrats outnumbered Republicans by 50 to 49. The balance shifted back to the Republicans in the 2002 election, but the effect didn't come into play until January 2003. Many, many Democrats have supported this law repeatedly. Support for the bill was led in the Senate by a Democrat, Sen. Joseph Biden, the senior senator from Delaware, the home of MBNA, which holds one of the largest credit card portfolios in the world. *See, e.g.,* http://www.dkosopedia.com/index.php/Joseph_Biden.

195. *See* Martin H. Bosworth, *No Bankruptcy Relief for Katrina Victims,* CONSUMERAFFAIRS.COM, Sept. 15, 2005, *at* http://www.consumeraffairs.com/news04/2005/katrina_bankruptcy03.html; Carl Jones, *When Disaster Strikes: Bankruptcy Law's "Special Circumstances" Loophole,* DAILY BUS. REVIEW, Oct. 28, 2005, on Law.com *at* http://www.thedailylaw.com/when-disaster-strikes-bankruptcy-law-s-special-circumstances-loophole,6195.html.

196. Martin H. Bosorth, *No Bankruptcy Relief for Katrina Victims,* ConsumerAffairs.com, Sept. 15, 2005, *at* http://www.consumeraffairs.com/news04/2005/katrina_bankruptcy03.html. Rep. Sensenbrenner is actually quite wrong (although there are certainly cases for which his statement would hold true). For example, every person filing must comply with many of the provisions of the new law, including going through credit counseling and providing proof of income and expenses.

who abuse the system and have the means to pay part of what they owe pay [their debts]," Levine said.[197]

In order to ameliorate the impact of the law on Katrina victims—and, presumably, to reduce the political pressure on the Congress to make changes in it—the U.S. Trustee's Office announced that it would not enforce the new law against the victims of Katrina:

- On October 4, 2005, the U.S. Trustee announced that it was waiving the credit counseling requirement;[198]
- On October 7, 2005, the U.S. Trustee announced that it was waiving the debtor education requirement;[199] and
- On October 5, 2005, it announced temporary bankruptcy enforcement guidelines for hurricane victims, including:
  - Not enforcing document requirements
  - Considering income loss, expense increase, and other effects of a natural disaster in determining whether there are "special circumstances" sufficient to rebut the presumption of abuse under the means test
  - Exercising flexibility regarding the ability of the debtor to appear in person at the mandatory meeting of creditors
  - Not raising venue objections
  - Not taking enforcement actions against Chapter 11 small-business debtors.[200]

In addition to the legislation proposed in response to Katrina, there have been rumors of "technical amendments bills" that might include the ABA-proposed amendments. Indeed, a discussion draft of one such bill has sur-

---

197.   Carl Jones, *When Disaster Strikes: Bankruptcy Law's "Special Circumstances" Loophole*, DAILY BUS. REVIEW, Oct. 28, 2005, on Law.com *at* http://www.thedailylaw.com/when-disaster-strikes-bankruptcy-law-s-special-circumstances-loophole,6195.html (brackets in original).

198.   Department of Justice, Executive Office for United States Trustees, Press Release, Oct. 4, 2005, *available at* http://www.usdoj.gov/ust/press/pr20051004.pdf (announcing that the credit-counseling requirements of the BRA were temporarily being waived for residents of Louisiana and Mississippi affected by Katrina).

199.   U.S. Department of Justice, Executive Office for United States Trustees, Press Release, Oct. 7, 2005, *at* http://www.usdoj.gov/ust/press/pr20051007.pdf (announcing that the debtor education requirements of the BRA were temporarily being waived for residents of Louisiana and Mississippi affected by Katrina).

200.   U.S. Department of Justice, Executive Office for United States Trustees, Press Release, Oct. 5, 2005, http://www.usdoj.gov/ust/press/pr20051005.pdf (announcing temporary bankruptcy enforcement guidelines for hurricane victims in the Gulf Coast region).

faced, which purports to be sponsored by Senator Kyl.[201] It contains amendments that substantially track the ABA's attorney liability proposals.[202]

There is little likelihood that the credit card industry will stand by and let substantive changes be made to the law. They have long memories[203] and deep pockets.[204] Although support for the new law had weakened, it still passed with strong bipartisan support.[205] Absent a catastrophic economic event bringing consumers back into the forefront as voters, no dramatic change in this legislation is likely any time soon.

---

201.   Copy on file with the author. I say "purports" because that is what it says, but I did not receive it from Sen. Kyl's office, nor do I have any independent confirmation that he is its source.

202.   Although the bill is called a "technical amendments bill," it is hardly that. Only one provision arguably solves a technical problem in the law. It also contains far-reaching new matter beyond the attorney liability provisions, including a workout provision. *Id.*

203.   A participant in this process reminded me recently that the financial services industry has vast patience when it comes to protecting its interests, for example, working 20 years to repeal Glass-Steagel. Correspondence on file with the author.

204.   The financial services industry alone has contributed over $40 million to candidates for support of this law. *See* http://www.opensecrets.org/industries/indus.asp?Ind=F06, the Center for Responsive Politics Web site that tracks contributions by issue, industry, and party.

205.   Eighty-two members of the Senate voted in favor of the bill when it came to the floor in 2002. *See* Senate vote number 236, for passage of H.R. 333 in the 107th Congress. The vote was 82 yeas, 16 nays, 1 present, 1 not voting. *Available at* http://www.senate.gov/legislative/LIS/roll_call_lists/roll_call_vote_cfm.cfm?congress=107&session=1&vote=00236.

CHAPTER 4

You Know You're a Debt Relief Agency When . . .

by Corinne Cooper[1]

The most pernicious provisions of the BRA for lawyers are the debt relief agency sections. The BRA brands consumer debtors' attorneys "debt relief agencies" (DRAs) and uses that label to regulate an attorney's practice, controlling what an attorney must do and is forbidden from doing, regardless of the best interests of the client.

The regulations fall into three main areas. The first is advertising. The second is mandated "disclosures"—written notices with statements the attorney is required to make, even some that are not true. The third is prohibited statements and conduct.[2] Several chapters that follow discuss the rules that apply to attorneys once they fall within the definition of a debt relief agency.[3] This chapter explores the definition itself.

To accomplish its regulatory mission, the BRA incorporates three new definitions into § 101:

---

1. I can hardly remember everyone who contributed to this Chapter, but here are a few: Cathy Vance, Marc Stern, Chris Kaup, Thomas Yerbich, and an anonymous judge. Thanks also to the lawyers attending seminars who asked such hard questions.

2. Since following these instructions could be detrimental to the client's best interests, these provisions could place an attorney in violation of Rules of Professional Conduct. *See, e.g.*, MODEL RULES OF PROF'L CONDUCT § 2.1 (ABA 2002). See Chapter 7.

3. See Chapters 9, 10, and 11.

- "Assisted Person" (AP) is any person whose debts consist primarily of consumer debts, and whose non-exempt assets have a value less than $150,000.[4]
- "Bankruptcy assistance" means any goods or services sold or otherwise provided[5] to an AP with the express or implied purpose of providing—

  - information, advice, counsel, document preparation, or
  - filing, or
  - attendance at a creditors' meeting, or
  - appearing in a case or proceeding on behalf of another, or
  - providing legal representation with respect to a case or proceeding under the Bankruptcy Code.[6]

- "Debt Relief Agency" is any person who provides bankruptcy assistance to an AP in return for the payment of money or other valuable consideration, or who is a bankruptcy petition preparer under § 110 of the Code.[7]

Some folks are expressly (and in some cases, inexplicably) excluded from the BRA's definition of debt relief agency. We'll get to them in just a moment. Chapter 18 discusses the results the definitions and exceptions produce when applied to credit counselors—organizations that logically fit the DRA label.

What's missing from all these definitions? Any reference to a bankruptcy *debtor*! Common sense would suggest that these provisions apply only to

---

4.   BRA Section 226(a)(1), amending Code § 101 to add subsection (3). It is beyond the purview of this Chapter, but nonetheless interesting, to note in passing that the definition of "assisted person" appears to be a failed attempt to identify small consumer bankruptcies, thus limiting the reach of these provisions to lawyers who represent poorer debtors. In fact, substantial wealth can still be shielded through state exemptions (even with the BRA's homestead exemption cap) and asset protection trust statutes. Even with the changes to the unlimited homestead, some wealthy debtors (who have not moved or committed fraud, or whose assets are in an asset protection trust) will fall into the scope of the DRA provisions. Of course, some of those debtors will fall outside of the provision if the debts are not primarily consumer debts (for example, if they consist of guaranties of business obligations), but some will undoubtedly remain. One can only assume that the attorney who represented Bowie Kuhn does not advertise!

5.   That "otherwise provided" language is ripe to cause trouble. *See* the discussion below.

6.   BRA Section 226(a)(2), amending Code § 101 to add subsection (4A).

7.   BRA Section 226(a)(3), amending Code § 101 to add subsection (12A).

those attorneys assisting debt-laden consumers who are looking at bankruptcy as an option. Those who followed the adoption of this law know these provisions were meant to apply to debtors' counsel.[8]

But the language of the statute contains no such limitation. The plain language defies common sense—and common understanding—but unfortunately, in a battle like this, plain language usually prevails.

I. The Exceptions

Before we delve into who's included, let's mention the parties who are excluded. The DRA definition specifically excludes:

- officers, directors, employees, or agents of persons (including petition preparers) providing bankruptcy assistance
- 501(c)(3) organizations
- a creditor of an AP, but only if the creditor is assisting in the restructuring of that creditor's debt
- a depository institution or credit union
- an author, publisher, or seller of works subject to copyright protection (thank goodness!)[9]

A. Debtors' Attorneys v. Their Firms

A debtors' attorney in solo practice or with a firm that does only bankruptcy is a DRA, and the firm is a DRA. But suppose you practice in a law firm that has no other bankruptcy lawyers. You're a DRA. Is the firm? Let's look at the exceptions:

- The firm isn't an officer, director, employee or agent of a DRA.
- Unless you work in a clinic, the firm probably isn't a 501(c)(3).
- It isn't a creditor of an assisted person (see the discussion of creditors' lawyers below).[10]
- The firm isn't a bank, credit union, or other institutional lender.[11]

---

8. See Chapter 2. It's interesting to note the level of denial that still exists about this conclusion. While speaking around the country between the enactment and effective dates, the authors were astounded to discover how many bankruptcy attorneys were not familiar with the provisions. Reactions ranged from horror to denial. "You *can't* be reading that right," I was told after explaining the advertising provisions at a seminar.

9. BRA Section 226(a)(3), amending Code § 101 to add subsection (12A).

10. Or are you? Suppose you represented a client in a divorce who failed to pay you. The client comes to you to discuss filing bankruptcy. Are you a creditor of an assisted person, or a DRA representing one?

11. Is this list an example of *inclusio unius est exclusio alterius*? For example, does it also exclude credit card companies that are not banks? Since the statute does not include language like "including but not limited to," we have to read the exceptions narrowly.

• It isn't an author or publisher of a work (at least not in this capacity).

As counterintuitive as it may seem, the firm falls within the definition, and not within any of the exceptions, so it's a DRA. Labeling the *firm* a DRA and sanctioning it makes sense if the *firm* fails to comply with the law—for example, by failing to include the mandated language in its Yellow Pages ad. But is the firm a DRA because of its single bankruptcy lawyer? Since the firm fits the definition of DRA and doesn't fall into the exceptions, there's no escaping the impact of this designation.[12]

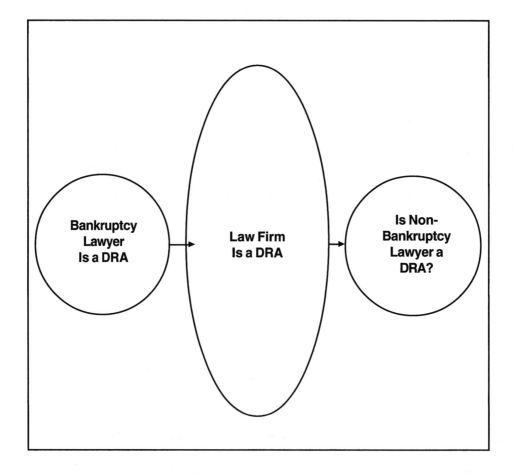

12.   It also makes sense because the client is the client of the firm, not just the individual lawyer.

What about the other lawyers in the firm? You could argue that non-partners are excluded under the employee exception. Partners could be excluded under the same provision because, under partnership law, they are agents of the firm. In that case, all lawyers in the firm fall within the exception.[13]

Whoa! Could the statute possibly mean that the firm is a DRA but all lawyers—even *the bankruptcy attorney*—fall within the exception? A strict reading of § 101(12A)(A) could lead to that conclusion.[14] A more logical interpretation is that the firm and all its bankruptcy lawyers are DRAs, but not the other firm lawyers,[15] employees, or agents.

---

13.   Here's the argument that the attorney is *not* a DRA, eloquently stated by Thomas Yerbich, author of Chapter 6:

> I am firmly convinced that my interpretation that the attorneys are excepted from the definition under §101(12A)(A) is consistent with the plain meaning of the statute, normal rules of statutory construction, the well-established laws of agency, partnership, LLCs, and corporations, and the "true" Congressional intent. . . .
>
> Let me pose one last question for thought. If the attorney member of the firm is a DRA, why . . . not the in-house counsel for a financial institution? In both instances, the attorney is acting as an employee/agent of another: the in-house counsel for the financial institution and the attorney for the firm. The fact that the financial institution is itself excepted (and I think we agree that the financial institution is excepted under §101(12A)(D)) is irrelevant unless the §101(12A)(D) exception flows down to embrace the attorney by its own force. I cannot read that into the statute. In that case, the attorney's exception is based on § 101(12A)(A) because the financial institution, not the attorney, is deemed under well-established laws of agency to be providing "such assistance." Try as I may, I cannot interpret § 101(12A) in a way that treats differently the attorneys who are members of the firm who are also acting as employees/agents.

Thomas J. Yerbich, e-mail on file with the author. I disagree; the debtor's attorney is an agent of the debtor client in exactly the same way that the creditor's attorney is the agent of the creditor, but that agency relationship is not the same as the debtor's attorney's relationship with his law firm.

14.   Bankruptcy Rules distinguish in other contexts between lawyers and their firms, but they don't treat them differently. Both terms are used in the rules on compensation. Bankruptcy Rules 2014(b) and 2016(a) and (b). There is also authorization in Rule 9011 to sanction "attorneys, law firms, or parties." The last sentence of Rule 9011(c)(1)(A) states: "Absent exceptional circumstances, a law firm shall be held jointly responsible for violations committed by its partners, associates, and employees."

15.   Until that lawyer falls within the DRA language by advising another client. (I understand; I feel like I need a drink, too.)

B. Creditors' Attorneys

One unanswered question is whether creditors' attorneys are DRAs. The answer isn't as easy as it appears at first glance. There's no indication of a "legislative intent" to exclude creditors' lawyers, and we never even get to legislative intent if the "plain meaning" of the statute is clear. To those who followed the development of the law, creditors' lawyers certainly weren't the intended victims, and it's natural to assume they fall under the exclusion for creditors. In some cases, they will. But consider these examples:

1. If attorneys are acting in their traditional, adversarial role on behalf of a bank, credit card issuer, or other institutional creditor, they fall outside the DRA definition because they are providing bankruptcy assistance to the creditor, and institutional creditors do not fit the definition of "assisted persons."

2. What if you represent any creditor—institutional or not—and work with the AP debtor to restructure your creditor client's debt? Don't you fall within the specific exception for creditors restructuring their own debt?[16] You aren't a creditor of an assisted person—your client is.

    The statute excepts the creditor, not the creditor's *attorney*.[17] But you aren't a DRA unless you are providing bankruptcy assistance to an AP. Here, you're providing services with respect to bankruptcy *not* to an AP, but to your client. Creditors' attorneys who are careful to give no bankruptcy assistance to debtors in the debt restructuring process are not DRAs.[18]

3. Suppose an elderly couple sells their house, taking back a mortgage on the property to provide a small income for their retirement. Let's assume the couple owes only consumer debts, and owns non-exempt property of less than $150,000. If you give them legal advice with respect to a bankruptcy filed by the *buyer*, you're a debt relief agency! The same is true if you give legal advice to an individual landlord about the bankruptcy of a tenant. If the creditor fits the definition of an AP, and the advice is bankruptcy assistance, you're a DRA.

---

16.   BRA Section 226(a), adding Code § 101(12A)(C).

17.   And there isn't any exception for agents and employees of creditors, as there is for DRAs.

18.   Indeed, ethical rules require the attorney for the bank to make clear to the debtor that he is representing the bank and not the debtor. See Chapter 7.

4. Let's change the facts and make you in-house counsel employed by a corporation that owns apartments. You scoff at a tenant's threat to file bankruptcy, and go on to explain the barriers to filing created by the new law. *You* aren't a DRA (you're excluded as an employee) but the corporation arguably is, if it's held to be offering (through you) bankruptcy assistance to an AP, and not with respect to restructuring its own debt.[19] Oops!

5. Finally, consider the avoidance problem. Right before Construction Company files, it pays off a past-due balance to Sally, who owns the coffee cart. If Sally is an AP who received a preferential transfer from a corporate debtor, her lawyer is a DRA under the plain meaning of the statute. The language in these definitions is not tied to consumer bankruptcies or representing a bankruptcy debtor. This type of transaction could reach out and snag more than a few members of the creditors' bankruptcy bar.

This little exercise is an important reminder that not all creditors, and not all attorneys for creditors, escape the reach of this law.

C. 501(c)(3) Organizations

Another specific exception is for 501(c)(3) organizations.[20] The irony is that those entities that we normally think of as debt relief agencies—that is, credit counselors and other organizations that purport to help people deal with their creditors and restructure their debts—are likely to be *excluded* by this exception.[21] AmeriDebt, for example, once one of the nation's largest credit counselors, would be exempt due to its nonprofit status.[22]

The non-profit exception raises an interesting question: can debtors' attorneys evade the DRA provisions by creating nonprofits that pay them nice salaries? They would fall within the exception for nonprofits. But courts are unlikely to condone a deliberate attempt to evade the impact of the law.

---

19. Again, assume that the debtor has primarily consumer debt and non-exempt assets of less than $150,000, which is certainly likely.

20. *See* BRA Section 226(a), adding Code § 101(12A)(B).

21. *See* BRA Section 226(a), adding Code § 101(12A)(B).

22. *See* the discussion of this result in Chapter 18.

> **WARNING!!** ━━━━━━━━━━━━━━━━━━━━━━━━━━━━
> Giving *any* advice concerning a bankruptcy proceeding to *any* person who falls with the definition of "assisted person" makes the person giving the advice a DRA if they receive consideration from anyone.

What about legitimate clinics set up to help debtors who cannot afford counsel? If they don't charge, there's no problem, since a DRA has to receive consideration. If they have a sliding scale for clients—as many clinics do—this will trigger DRA coverage.

Suppose the clinic operates within a private law school, but not as an independent legal entity? If it was operating as a non-profit before the BRA was enacted, it's hard to argue that it is trying to evade the statute. But bankruptcy clinics that charge anything for their assistance should clarify their status as 501(c)(3) entities or they may be subjected to the DRA provisions.

What about prepaid legal services plans, like those offered by many unions? The consideration isn't coming from the AP, but nothing in the statute says it has to. It says you're a DRA if you provide bankruptcy assistance in return for the payment of money or other valuable consideration. If the advice isn't provided by a nonprofit entity, that is enough to trigger the law.

D. Depository Institutions and Credit Unions

If the client is a type of creditor excluded by this language, the creditor will not be a DRA. The attorney will be fine, but not because of the agent/employee exception. That applies to agents and employees of DRAs. In this case, the attorney is an agent/employee of a non-DRA. Still, as long as the attorney sticks to restructuring the bank's debt, and does not give advice to the debtor relating to other creditors, she is not a DRA. As soon as she does, she runs the risk of giving bankruptcy assistance to an AP.

E. Authors and Publishers

The final exception is for authors, publishers, and sellers of works subject to copyright protection. Personally, I'm very grateful for this exception. But it doesn't go nearly far enough to protect all the people out there trying to provide information.

Note that law professors are not excluded when they are teaching class (and most of their students fit the requirements for an AP). Nor are CLE speakers exempt: they may not receive money, but if they get meals or travel, that is consideration. If even one member of the audience meets the AP requirement, they've provided bankruptcy assistance.

Professors can argue that this assistance is not being given with the express or implied purpose of being "in a case or proceeding on behalf of another" or "with respect to a case or proceeding under" title 11. There is no current case, nor is one specifically contemplated. What is being provided is general information in an educational setting to those who may be providing such assistance in the future. But that argument isn't as strong for a CLE speaker with an audience of bankruptcy attorneys with pending cases. And don't forget that students in the class may be clerking at a bankruptcy firm.[23]

What about the people providing general bankruptcy information to consumers? If the information could be subject to copyright, you're okay. So newspapers, television and radio, even blogs are protected. But there's no copyright protection for live, unrecorded speeches.

II. What Exactly Is a DRA?

Four elements make you a debt relief agency. You're a DRA if you:

- are a person
- who provides "bankruptcy assistance"
- to an "assisted person"
- for money or other consideration.[24]

---

23. See Chapter 7 for a discussion of the distinction between bankruptcy assistance and legal advice.

24. BRA Section 226(a), adding Code § 101(12A).

What Is a DRA?

"Debt Relief Agency" is defined in § 101(12A).

> The term "debt relief agency" means any person who provides any bankruptcy assistance to an assisted person in return for the payment of money or other valuable consideration, or who is a bankruptcy petition preparer under Section 110 . . . .

This definition has four elements. Let's explore them a step at a time.

- **What's a Person?**

To be a DRA, you first have to be a "person" under the Code. If you aren't a person, you aren't a DRA.

> § 101(41) The term "person" includes individual, partnership, and corporation, but does not include governmental unit, except that a governmental unit . . . .

This one is easy enough to apply to attorneys, if you aren't a governmental unit.[25] Whether you practice law as an individual, or in a law firm, you qualify as a person.

- **What is Bankruptcy Assistance?**

Second, you must provide bankruptcy assistance. As noted above, this doesn't mean just assistance in filing a bankruptcy.

Under § 101(4A) "Bankruptcy assistance" means any goods or services sold or otherwise provided to an assisted person with the express or implied purpose of providing:

- information, advice, counsel, document preparation, or
- filing, or
- attendance at a creditors' meeting, or
- appearing in a case or proceeding on behalf of another, or
- providing legal representation

with respect to a case or proceeding under the Bankruptcy Code.

---

25.   Attorneys general who appear in bankruptcy cases on behalf of consumers will no doubt be grateful for the exception. But there are *exceptions* to the exclusion for governmental units that are dealing with assets as a result of loan or pension guaranties. Code § 101(41). Chapter 5 notes, but offers no opinion, on whether legal services lawyers are part of a governmental unit or a "private nonprofit corporation."

- **What's an Assisted Person?**

Bankruptcy assistance must be provided to an assisted person. That definition in turn has three parts:

1. Person (see above)

2. Primarily consumer debts:

"Consumer debts" is a defined term in the Code:

> § 101(8) The term "consumer debt" means debt incurred by an individual primarily for a personal, family, or household purpose . . . .

This definition is used in many state and federal laws in addition to the Code, and its meaning is well established.

3. Non-exempt assets value is less than $150,000

This may be the trickiest part of the definition (see the discussion in the text). If the client has no non-exempt assets, she's an assisted person. If the debtor has non-exempt assets in excess of $150,000, then she is not an AP and, *as to that case,* you are not a DRA.

- **What Is Money or Other Consideration?**

On its face, there isn't much controversy here. Bankruptcy clinics that provide free advice to debtors are not DRAs.[26] Any consideration is sufficient, and nothing in the statute says it has to come from the AP.

---

26. Could a promise made by a debtor to the attorney as a condition of representation—as in, "I promise to deliver my pay stubs and tax returns to you by next Friday"—constitute consideration? It does under contract law, but surely this wasn't intended by the BRA.

If any of the four elements doesn't apply to you, you aren't a "debt relief agency" and you are relieved of the many obligations and restrictions placed on these entities. If you don't receive any form of consideration (including a promise of payment), you aren't a DRA.[27] It's safe to assume that consumer debtors' attorneys are included, and bankruptcy petition preparers are definitely included.[28]

It turns out that the most complex part of the definition is the one that looks the simplest on its face: the $150,000 non-exempt asset cap.

Let's work it through. The definition says you are a DRA if you provide bankruptcy assistance to an AP, which includes only those people with non-exempt assets of no more than $150,000. It's fascinating to contemplate what this implies: people with few non-exempt assets are entitled to the "protections" given to APs, such as mandatory disclosures and notices. People with lots of non-exempt assets are not protected. The distinction isn't whether the debtor is rich or poor, because debtors with millions in exempt assets are APs, and a retired person with a modest house is not. And because state exemptions vary dramatically, debtors with identical assets are treated differently in different states.

The confusion doesn't end there. The whole concept of "non-exempt asset" is a slippery one. Does it mean:

- an asset that is property of the estate but is not exempt?
- an asset that is not property of the estate?
- the total value of property that is not subject to any exemption, like a lottery ticket, but none of the value of an asset that is subject to any exemption, like a house?
- property that is subject to an exemption, to the extent the value exceeds the exemption?
- property that is not exempt, because the debtor has no equity to exempt?

A debtor who has a home worth $200,000 in Missouri (which has a $15,000 homestead exemption) has more than $150,000 of non-exempt property. As a result, that debtor is not an AP. Move one block west and the same debtor in the same house, who has lived for years in Kansas with its unlimited homestead exemption, has no non-exempt property, and is an AP.

---

27. But they *are* bound by other provisions of the Act, including the certification and reaffirmation provisions. See Chapters 13 and 14.

28. See BRA Section 226(a)(3), adding Code § 101(12A). Although the consideration requirement in § 101(12A) doesn't apply to bankruptcy petition preparers, § 110 defines "petition preparer" to include only people who prepare documents "for compensation." Code § 110(a)(1). I wonder if "compensation" means something different from "money or other consideration"!

We could also read this definition to mean that because a house is subject to a homestead exemption, *no* portion of the value of the home should count toward the $150,000 ceiling. The home is not "non-exempt property." Under this reading, only the value of assets not subject to *any* exemption would count toward the ceiling. This interpretation would exclude from the AP definition almost every debtor, except those having very valuable holdings in assets not subject to any exemption.

If this reading is correct, lawyers in states that have a longer list of exemptions will not be DRAs, but lawyers in states with fewer exemptions will be.

WARNING!!

Don't assume the safest choice is to treat all your debtor clients as if they have non-exempt assets worth less than $150,000 and comply with the DRA provisions in every case.

It might not be in your client's best interest to comply with the law when you aren't required to do so! For example, could a client who is not an AP—who would otherwise have been entitled to receive pre-filing advice about incurring debt—have a claim against an attorney who decided to treat her as an AP and obey the prohibition on this advice?

Remember that your obligation is to act in your client's best interest in each case, and ignore your own concerns.[29]

Let's talk about equity. The definition doesn't use the words "equity in" or "unencumbered" to describe non-exempt property. In other provisions, the Code uses the word "equity" to describe equity.[30]

You can argue that Congress *must* have intended to deduct the value of encumbrances from the value of the non-exempt asset, because existing case law applies *exemptions* only to the debtor's equity. But more than one commentator has taken the position that non-exempt property is not the same as non-exempt equity, and that Congress knew how to refer to equity if that's

---

29.   See Chapters 7 and 11.

30.   *See, e.g.,* § 362(g)(1) ("the party requesting such relief has the burden of proof on the issue of the debtor's equity in the property . . ."). On the use of "equity" in the BRA, *see* BRA Section 907, adding Code § 561(b)(2)(A), referring to the net equity in a commodity account.

what was meant.[31] So the equity v. total value argument will have to await court resolution.

If you consider the value of non-exempt assets before and after filing, the confusion only gets worse. A debtor with a new mansion that is entirely exempt under state law prior to filing is an AP until the bankruptcy is filed. If a homestead cap kicks in at the moment of filing, the debtor ceases to be an AP because her non-exempt assets now exceed $150,000.

Under any interpretation of the statute, a strange conflict of interest is developing between the interests of the debtor and her lawyer. If the lawyer wants to avoid the DRA requirements, it is in his interest to represent only clients with assets above the cap. Meanwhile, the debtor may be interested in keeping the asset value lower to obtain the benefit of exemptions.

Now consider assets that are not property of the estate. Is the value included in the calculation of non-exempt assets? There is no answer in the Code.

Think about the opposite problem: Under the BRA, no asset is exempt against a support creditor.[32] If the debtor owes a support obligation, does that mean that all of his assets are non-exempt? Again, no answer.

Here's a reality check: Unless you want to make law on the issue, this isn't worth litigating. The time you spend defending your decision in court will never be less than the time it will take you to comply with the law. For this and all purposes, make sure the client values property accurately.[33] Calculate the value of non-exempt assets in a rational (or at least consistent and defensible) manner, and ignore the implications that decision may have for you.

III. Applying the Law

Now that we have the elements of the DRA definition in place, let's apply them. Who else may be swept up in its terms?

1. Suppose a woman goes to an attorney and says, "My ex-husband has just filed for bankruptcy. How will this affect me?" Like most folks, this woman's own debts are primarily consumer obligations, and her non-exempt assets are worth less than $150,000. Now, suppose the attorney:

---

31. *See, e.g.,* posting dated Sept. 29, 2005, to bankr-unlv@law.unlv.edu, by Daniel M. Press (dpress@chung-press.com) entitled, "Subject: Re: [Bankr-UNLV] Creditor Only Lawyers as Debt Relief Agencies" which states: "Your guy is not an assisted person, as 'non-exempt property' is not the same as 'non-exempt equity.' If the real estate is worth $500K, even if it's fully encumbered, he has $500K of non-exempt property and is not an assisted person." E-mail on file with the author.

32. BRA Section 216, amending Code § 522(c)(1).

33. Or, if irrationality is required by the BRA, according to law! See Chapter 11.

- looks over the property and debt allocation in the divorce decree and tells the woman which items might be excepted from the ex-husband's discharge.
- attends the ex-husband's § 341 meeting of creditors.
- files a complaint to determine the dischargeability of any of the divorce debts.

Under the plain language of the statute, the woman is an assisted person and the attorney has rendered bankruptcy assistance. This attorney is a debt relief agency and must comply with all the mandates of Code §§ 526-528.

2. Suppose the attorney says to the woman, "Let me look over the papers and I'll get back to you." That might be enough to become a DRA; the definition of "bankruptcy assistance" includes "services sold or otherwise provided . . . with the express or implied purpose of providing information, advice, [or] counsel."[34]

3. Suppose, instead of the debtor's ex-wife, it's the debtor's mother who shows up at the attorney's office because the trustee served her with a complaint to recover her Mother's Day gift as a fraudulent transfer, or a loan repayment as a preference. The debt relief agency definition would apply, as long as Mom's debts and assets meet the "assisted person" standard. Informing, advising, or counseling Mom about the complaint is bankruptcy assistance, as is representing her against the trustee.

   If no consideration has changed hands yet, the DRA definition hasn't kicked in. If the attorney realizes the problem and declines to represent her, no consideration has been *paid.*

   But isn't the client a *prospective* assisted person? If "prospective assisted person" doesn't include potential clients who haven't yet entered into a relationship with the attorney, it's hard to know what the term means.

4. As noted above, some creditors' lawyers are DRAs as well. Lawyers who do no more than fill out a proof of claim form on behalf of their consumer clients could get swept into the chamber of DRA horrors. "Document preparation," without more, appears to be enough to constitute bankruptcy assistance.[35]

5. Plaintiffs' personal injury lawyers are in the same boat. Suppose you represent a person who has been seriously injured by a defendant who then files bankruptcy. When you and the client, who qualifies as an AP, begin discussing the impact that this will have on the case, you are giving bankruptcy assistance and are a DRA.

---

34. BRA Section 226(a), adding Code § 101(4A).

35. Document preparation, without more, might also make the attorney a bankruptcy petition preparer. See Chapter 6.

The same is true if the plaintiff has thousands in unpaid medical expenses, his mortgage is in default, and the credit card companies are hounding him. He comes to you to file suit against the person who injured him. But he's worried about his ability to stave off foreclosure during the pendency of the suit. Wouldn't bankruptcy be one of the options on the table for discussion? If so, he's an assisted person, you're giving bankruptcy assistance, and you're a DRA.

6. Just to drive home the point, imagine one last example. The pharmaceutical giant Merck goes into bankruptcy. What becomes of counsel in the individual and class-action suits over Vioxx? What about counsel for the creditors' committee, whose constituents include those individual and class-action plaintiffs? Again, the definition of "bankruptcy assistance" is broad enough to apply, and the matter comes down to the nature of the claimants' debts and the value of each claimant's non-exempt assets.

We are not trying to argue that scooping non-bankruptcy attorneys into the law is the right result.[36] This is all patently ridiculous. But that's the problem with the poorly-written language of the statute. It doesn't clearly identify its intended targets and, having failed to name them, it could trap lots of unintended victims. And the "plain language" regime that governs bankruptcy law seems destined to reach these cases. Let's hope that the courts can apply the magic descriptor "absurd" to results like these and free themselves from interpretations that elevate words over practicalities, common sense, and good law.

IV. Update

As this book was going to press (and the BRA going into effect), the first "opinion"[37] on lawyers as DRAs was written. On the day that the DRA provi-

---

36.   If an attorney who does not practice bankruptcy law inadvertently becomes a DRA under one of these examples, it raises another layer of questions. For how long does the DRA label attach? What are the penalties if the attorney does not comply with the advertising requirements? Who enforces the provisions of Code §§ 526-528? Does the bankruptcy court have jurisdiction if the attorney never appears or files a document? Is a violation of Code §§ 526-528 a violation of the Rules of Professional Conduct or state bar rules?

37.   I put opinion in quotes because, while there is an order, there is no case. *In re Attorneys at Law and Debt Relief Agencies*, order dated October 17, 2005 (the effective date of the BRA), Bankr. Ct. Misc. Proceeding No. 05-00400 (Bankr. S.D. Ga. 2005). I don't know anything about civil procedure, but this order raises many procedural issues: Who can appeal a decision with no parties? Will the U.S. Trustee have standing? The court based its authority on Code § 526(c)(5):

sions became effective, Judge Lamar W. Davis, Jr., Chief Bankruptcy Judge of the Southern District of Georgia, issued a very interesting order finding (holding?) that attorneys are not DRAs. His argument goes like this:

1. The definition of "debt relief agency" does not include the word "attorney" or "lawyer." "Attorney" is a defined term, so the two terms cannot be synonymous, "nor do they in common understanding include each other."

   Even though "providing legal representation" is included in the definition of "bankruptcy assistance," it must refer to non-lawyers providing legal assistance, which constitutes the unauthorized practice of law. Since states may not be very effective in enforcing their unauthorized practice statutes, this provision was "Congress's effort to empower the Bankruptcy Courts presiding over a case with authority to protect consumers who are before the Court, who may have been harmed by a debt relief agency that may have engaged in the unauthorized practice of law. . . ."[38]

2. Section 527(b) requires DRAs to inform APs that they have the right to an attorney or to represent themselves, and that only an attorney can provide legal advice.

   It is hard to imagine that the language which, again, conspicuously omits the word "attorney" really *requires* an attorney to tell an assisted person that he/she has the right to hire an attorney or how to prepare the documents *pro se* that the attorney is poised to prepare on that person's behalf.[39]

   He found that Congress enacted the DRA provisions intending to regulate entities—that are *not* attorneys—that assist persons, and to bolster the regulation of bankruptcy petition preparers.

3. Since the regulation of attorneys has historically been a matter of state law, "it would be a breathtakingly expansive interpretation of federal law to usurp state regulation of the practice of law via the ambiguous provisions of this Act, which in no clear fashion lay claim to the right

---

which authorizes the Court *on its own motion* to enjoin violations of the debt relief agency provisions or impose civil penalties on the violator. If the Court has that broad jurisdiction to both initiate a disciplinary action *and* punish a violation, it must of necessity have jurisdiction on its ownmotion to conclude that certain types of persons or certain types of activity are not covered at all, since the first step in enforcing the provision is to determine whom *[sic]* is encompassed within its grasp.

Id. at 4 n.1 (emphasis in original).

38. *Id.* at 5-6.
39. *Id.* at 6.

to do any such thing."[40] He states that he cannot conceive that Congress would regulate lawyers without expressly stating its intent to do so. In fact, the court theorized that such a regulation could "possibly" violate the 10th Amendment.

I commend Judge Davis for his bravery. I hope his position takes hold. His first argument—that since "attorney" is a defined term under the Code, if Congress meant attorneys it would have used the word—is quite clever, and a classic application of the rules of statutory construction.

The second and third arguments (excluding the 10th Amendment issue) are not supported by the legislative history or the law. Congress clearly intended to regulate attorneys when it enacted the DRA provisions,[41] and the federal government has regulated attorneys practicing bankruptcy before. Neither Rule 11 nor Rule 9011 usurps the states' role as the primary regulator of lawyers.[42] Nor do federal court rules on regular or *pro hac vice* admission to practice interfere with state regulation of the practice of law.

This order was appealed by the U.S. Trustee. In its brief, the U.S. Trustee argues that the case should be dismissed for lack of a case or controversy under Article III, or "action, case or proceeding" under title 28.[43] The brief goes on to argue—using the language of the BRA and the legislative history—that the order misconstrues the clear intent of Congress to regulate attorneys under the DRA provisions.[44] Finally, the brief argues that there is no

---

40.   *Id.* at 7-8.

41.   See Chapter 2 on the politics of the BRA, and Chapter 3 on the history of the BRA.

42.   There have also been specific attempts by the federal government to regulate attorney speech. See Chapter 8 on constitutional issues. *See also* Erwin Chemerinksy, *Constitutional Issues Posed in the Bankruptcy Abuse Prevention and Consumer Protection Act of 2005,* 79 Am. Bankr. L.J. 571 (2005). The problem (according to experts—and I am not one!) is that there has never been a definitive showdown between the states and the federal government on the regulation of the practice of law. The issue comes up from time to time, as it did during the Clinton administration, when the Justice Department issued a rule that its lawyers were not bound by state ethics requirements that prohibited contact with a defendant known to be represented by counsel. *See, e.g.,* Allen Samelson & Robert Maxwell, *State Ethics Rules Now Apply to Federal Prosecutors,* at http://www.rjop.com/publish22.htm. A current issue involves admission to the bar to practice purely federal law. *See, e.g.,* George Riemer, *Limited Practices: Is There a "Federal Law Only" Exception to the Oregon Bar Examination?* Ore. State Bar Bull., June 2001, *at* http://www.osbar.org/publications/bulletin/01june/barcounsel.htm.

43.   Brief of the U.S. Trustee, filed on Nov. 18, 2005, Dist. Ct. No. 4:05-CV-00206-WTM (S.D. Ga. 2006) at 2-3 and 6-10.

44.   *Id.* at 14-19 (citing, among other things, Sen. Feingold's comments, quoted in Chapter 4).

Tenth Amendment bar to Congress regulating the attorneys who practice before bankruptcy courts.[45]

No opinion has issued, but we can expect this issue to be litigated in a variety of forums over the next months and years.[46]

---

45. *Id.* at 18-19.
46. See Chapter 9 for a discussion of the advertising cases pending at the time of publication.

CHAPTER 5

The DRA Quiz

by Catherine E. Vance

Chapter 4 provides a lot of details about "assisted persons" and "debt relief agencies" (DRA). But there's still a lot of gray between who's clearly in and who's clearly out of the definition of a DRA. To show how complicated this new area of law could become, let's take a look at a hypothetical. The focus here is on other aspects of the definition of a DRA, so just assume that the debtors are "assisted persons."

Paul and Sheila Gray are in the red and worried about what to do. Paul, an internet junkie, does some searching on the Web and runs across a press release announcing the publication of *We The People's Guide to Bankruptcy*. The press release says the book "provides a step-by-step, easy-to-read guide for filing for bankruptcy, without an attorney, and gaining a fresh financial start in life," and that the book was written by We The People's co-founders, Ira and Linda Distenfield.[1]

Intrigued by the idea of a fresh financial start without having to pay for a lawyer, Paul does some more research. We The People (WTP), he discovers, calls itself "the national leader in legal document preparation services" and offers its business as a franchise opportunity. Paul can't find bankruptcy specifics at WTP's web site. (He does, however, learn that WTP is owned by Dollar Financial, a self-described "leading international financial services company offering a range of consumer financial products to our customers, many of whom receive income on an irregular basis or from multiple employers."[2] "Sounds like they're talking to me," Paul muses.) Paul gets a better description of bankruptcy services from a WTP franchise, WTP Mid-Atlantic:

---

1.   Press Release, We the People, New Do-It-Yourself Bankruptcy Book Helps Consumers File for Bankruptcy Before Recently Enacted Federal Law Closes the Door Forever (May 4, 2005).

2.   *See* http://www.dfg.com.

We The People provides a broad range of services that offer an economically attractive alternative to anyone who has a need to handle a legal action that does not require the advice of an attorney. We are best in support of customers who have a need for uncontested legal actions. These range from activities as simple as preparing a bill of sale for an automobile to a divorce to that of a complex bankruptcy.

Our process generally involves certain simple steps to accomplish the end result which is the preparation, and where appropriate, the filing of a legal action:

1. **Decide**—The Customer comes to a We The People office and tells us the action he/she has decided to take.
2. **Purchase**—Once the decision is made to proceed with our help, the customer purchases the service commitment for the action and we provide a workbook to be completed by the customer. This workbook simply documents all of the relevant facts and detailed decisions that the you [sic] must provide us so that we can prepare the appropriate forms and documents required to accomplish your desired goal.
3. **Questions**—In the event that you have questions about the legal issues with respect to the action your are [sic] taking, you will be given access to our supervising attorney. Our supervising attorney will answer simple and general questions you may have with respect to the actions. He will not give you advice about your specific action; simply answer questions about the law. This level of service is provided free to all customers as a part of the forms and document preparation fee paid. If you need more legal advice, you will need to hire an attorney.
4. **Advice from an Attorney if Required**—Should you need more complex legal advice and counsel and/or legal support during your action, our supervising attorney could conclude that you need the representation of an attorney. In that case you are free to either consult with another attorney or to engage our supervising attorney.
5. **Workbook Completion**—Once we have received the completed workbook, we check it for completeness and then the workbook is sent to our paralegal department and they begin the process of preparing the forms and documents.
6. **Completed Documents**—Within a few days, we will notify you of the completion of the documents and request that you make an appointment to return to the office to review the documentation for accuracy.
7. **Sign Documents & File**—When you are satisfied with the accuracy, you will sign the documents and, if a filing is required with the courts, we will handle that part of the process for you.
8. **At Your Service**—In some instances, there are follow-up actions required that may cause you to use our services again, or it might cause you to need further work from an attorney.

9. **Services Not Listed**—Please also recognize that, even if you do not find the specific action you need to take, we probably can still help you. We have offices throughout the country and many lawyers on our staff. They are all available to find a way to help us help you.[3]

"Sheila, I think I've found the answer to our problems," Paul tells his wife. "We can't get out of this financial mess we're in with our paychecks alone, but we can get a fresh start if we file for bankruptcy. And the best part is that we'll save a bundle because we won't have to hire a lawyer."

The next day, Paul and Sheila show up at their local WTP franchise. They receive a packet of information, including a workbook they're supposed to complete, for which they pay WTP $250.

While filling out the workbook at home, Paul and Sheila get confused and call WTP's supervising attorney on several occasions. The book says they are supposed to value their furniture at replacement value, but their furniture is old, and they think that's too high. They also want to keep their two cars, but can't figure out if they'll be able to afford the payments, or how much of the car loans (which far exceed the value of the cars) they're required to repay.

Paul and Sheila finally complete the workbook and take it back to WTP for processing. That night, Paul goes to the web site of a credit counselor because WTP told them that a briefing with a credit counselor is required before they can file for bankruptcy. At the conclusion of the online briefing—which cost the Grays $50—the web site generates a certificate with the following instruction: "Keep this Certificate in a safe place. You are required to file it with the bankruptcy court when you file your bankruptcy petition."

The next day, the Grays pick up their completed forms from WTP, head to bankruptcy court, and file for Chapter 7 relief.

"Whew," says Sheila. "I'm glad that's over."

Little do they know that their problems are just beginning. A few weeks after they file, Paul and Sheila find in their mailbox a motion for relief from stay filed by their mortgage company, and a motion by one of their car lenders to dismiss their Chapter 7 case as an "abuse." Paul immediately calls WTP, but the person on the phone tells him there's nothing WTP can do because it doesn't give legal advice. They transfer the call to the WTP supervising attorney, who tells Paul the same thing but offers to represent them independent of WTP for $250 an hour.

"To hell with you!" shouts a frustrated Paul as he slams down the phone.

Paul and Sheila turn to Legal Aid for help. Being broke, they find, finally has its bright side, because they qualify for help and only have to pay a nominal fee.[4] Their attorney, Elizabeth Anthony, works things out with the mort-

---

3. *See* http://www.wethepeoplema.com/services.asp.
4. See Chapter 17 for more about eligibility for Legal Aid.

gage company, amends a number of the documents that the Grays filed with their petition, and the creditor withdraws the § 707(b) motion.

Halfway through their ordeal, Ms. Anthony calls to tell the Grays that she is leaving Legal Aid to join a private firm, where she will leave consumer work behind and concentrate on business bankruptcy cases. The good news is that her new firm agreed to let her complete the rest of her consumer cases and to charge them the same rate they'd been paying Legal Aid.

Time for the Quiz

From this hypothetical, who do *you* think is a DRA?

1.   WTP
2.   WTP's supervising attorney
3.   Ira & Linda Distenfield, WTP's founders and co-authors of "We The People's Guide to Bankruptcy"
4.   Dollar Financial, WTP's owner
5.   The online credit counseling agency
6.   Legal Aid
7.   Elizabeth Anthony, the Grays' Legal Aid attorney
8.   Elizabeth Anthony, the Grays' private attorney
9.   Elizabeth Anthony's new law firm
10. Elizabeth Anthony and her new firm, after the Grays' bankruptcy is over

Take your time. Be careful!

Now let's compare answers.

1. We The People

WTP *is* a debt relief agency. This one is a no-brainer because WTP's services make it a bankruptcy petition preparer [BPP], which is expressly included in the DRA definition. A BPP is defined in the Code as "a person, other than an attorney for the debtor or an employee of such attorney under the direct supervision of such attorney, who prepares for compensation a document for filing."[5] Since WTP prepared documents for filing and received a fee, it is a BPP.

---

5.   Code § 110(a)(1).

2. WTP's Supervising Attorney

Up to the point that the Grays file their bankruptcy petition, the WTP supervising attorney *is not* a debt relief agency because he is an employee or agent of a DRA, one of the DRA's exclusions. But, as explained in detail in Chapter 15, he may still be a DRA because he fits within the definition of a BPP.

Now let's fast-forward to the call to the attorney after the case is filed and the problems start. At that point he may be a DRA as a result of having offered to represent the Grays in his individual capacity. Before they made a decision about hiring him, they were "prospective assisted persons," and therefore they were entitled to certain rights under the DRA provisions.

To add another twist, suppose the Grays had taken the WTP supervising attorney up on his offer to hire him independent of his relationship with WTP. In that case he *is* a DRA for the same reason any attorney would be. On the other hand, if he acted solely in his capacity as the WTP supervising attorney, he *is not* a DRA because he's within the employee/agent exception, although he's likely outside of permissible conduct under state ethical rules.[6]

3. Ira & Linda Distenfield, Co-authors of *We The People's Guide to Bankruptcy*

The Distenfields are off the hook so far as the book goes, even though it provides bankruptcy assistance to assisted persons. The book is a work subject to copyright, so the Distenfields *are not* a DRA because they are specifically excluded from the definition.

4. Dollar Financial, WTP's Owner

The answer here is tricky and may be affected by the company's corporate structure and how WTP is treated within it. The important thing to note is that there's no exception in the DRA definition for related corporate entities. So it's possible that Dollar Financial *is* a debt relief agency because it is, through WTP, providing bankruptcy assistance to assisted persons. The creditor exception doesn't apply because Dollar Financial isn't working out an arrangement with respect to its own debt, but to all the debtor's obligations.

5. The Online Credit Counselor

The credit counselor *might be* a debt relief agency. Here's why: The counseling agency charged the Grays $50 and at the end of the briefing produced a certificate confirming their participation. Under § 521(b), this certificate must be filed with the court.

---

6. *See* MODEL RULE OF PROF'L CONDUCT 5.4. WTP's probably in trouble here, too, because if the supervising attorney represents the Grays while an employee of WTP, then it is engaged in the unauthorized practice of law.

At the very least, the credit counseling agency looks an awful lot like a bankruptcy petition preparer. Remember that the definition of a BPP doesn't require the preparation of the *petition* but any "document for filing," which means "a petition or any other document prepared for filing by a debtor . . . in connection with a case under" title 11.[7] The certificate fits perfectly within this definition.

By definition, a BPP is a DRA. The one question that remains is how the courts resolve the statutory conflict that puts the counselor *in* as a BPP, but also pulls it *out* by virtue of its nonprofit status. Whether a DRA or not, the credit counselor gets the job of complying with the BPP provisions. Poetic justice.

6. Legal Aid

If Legal Aid offers bankruptcy assistance without charge, then it *is not* a debt relief agency because the consideration requirement is not met. In the hypothetical, however, Paul and Sheila were offered assistance at a reduced cost. That means Legal Aid *is* a debt relief agency unless one of the exceptions applies.

Odds are the Legal Aid clinic that helped the Grays operates as a 501(c)(3) nonprofit (as most, if not all, legal clinics do[8]), which would place it in one of the DRA exclusions. Clinics that are not 501(c)(3) nonprofits might still get out of the DRA definition if they can convince the court they aren't "persons." The argument is too complex to deal with here completely, but a clinic that is statutorily created and authorized may be a "governmental entity" instead of a "person," depending on its structure, funding, and the extent to which the legislature controls its activities.[9]

7. Elizabeth Anthony, the Grays' Legal Aid Attorney

The answer here depends on the status of Legal Aid. If Legal Aid is a debt relief agency, then Ms. Anthony *is not* a DRA because, like WTP's supervising attorney, she is the employee or agent of a DRA.

If Legal Aid is *not* a DRA, what becomes of Ms. Anthony? If it weren't for the language of the relevant exception, this would be a no-brainer; it's illogical and contrary to agency law that an employee would be a DRA when her employer clearly is not.

The DRA definition specifically excludes any person who is an "officer, director, employee, or agent" of a DRA, but here we have the reverse situation.

---

7.   Code § 110(a)(2).

8.   Section 1003(a) of the Legal Services Act, 42 U.S.C. § 2996b, requires that any recipient of grants from the Legal Services Corporation must be a 501(c)(3) organization.

9.   *See, e.g.*, Catherine E. Vance, The Federal Priority Statute (unpublished manuscript on file with author) (discussing when an entity is "the government").

Is an officer, director, employee, or agent of a non-DRA a DRA? Ms. Anthony otherwise fits the definition of a DRA. She is providing bankruptcy assistance to assisted persons and, by virtue of her salary, the consideration requirement might be met. So, she could be a DRA even if her employer is not.[10]

8. Elizabeth Anthony, the Grays' Private Attorney

If Ms. Anthony wasn't a DRA before she left Legal Aid, she *is* one now. There's no escaping the conclusion because, as the Grays' private, rather than Legal Aid, attorney, she's not doing anything different from all those hapless consumer debtors' lawyers that the DRA provisions were intended to snag. Ms. Anthony is providing bankruptcy assistance to assisted persons, and she's charging for it. Sadly, she gets no credit for working out the reduced fee with her new firm.

9. Elizabeth Anthony's New Law Firm

If you look carefully at the definition of DRA, you'll see that the new firm is also a DRA, since it is providing, via Elizabeth, bankruptcy assistance to an assisted person for consideration. See Chapter 4 for a more thorough discussion of the confusing relationship between attorneys and their firms.

10. Elizabeth Anthony and Her New Firm After the Grays' Bankruptcy Is Over

A question that has lingered in the minds of attorneys worrying about the DRA provisions is whether this statement is true: "Once a debt relief agency, always a debt relief agency."

Implicitly, the DRA provisions indicate that, yes, if you are a DRA with respect to just one case, then you are forever a DRA. But this seems to arise less from intent than from the mistaken assumption that the DRA provisions will apply only to consumer debtors' attorneys, and that all lawyers—and their firms—who do consumer bankruptcies practice in no other field of law. In other words, the bankruptcy "mill" seems to be the assumed model for the DRA provisions. Chapter 4 makes clear the error of this assumption.

The BRA could easily have provided clarification. For example, under the Fair Debt Collection Practices Act (FDCPA), the definition of "debt collector" includes:

> . . . any person who uses any instrumentality of interstate commerce or the mails in any business *the principal purpose of which* is the collection of any debts, or who *regularly* collects or attempts to collect, directly or indirectly, debts owed or due or asserted to be owed or due another.[11]

---

10. *But see* discussion of this issue in Chapter 4.
11. 15 U.S.C. § 1692a(6) (emphasis added).

With this definition, the FDCPA allows for the possibility that an attorney will sometimes undertake debt collection activity without being a "debt collector" and having to comply with the mandates of the FDCPA.

WARNING!!

Implicitly, the DRA provisions indicate that if you are a DRA with respect to just one case, then you are forever a DRA.

By contrast, the BRA makes no similar allowance based on how often a lawyer gives bankruptcy advice to an assisted person compared to the rest of the work the lawyer handles. The divorce attorney with one client whose ex-husband filed for bankruptcy is treated the same as the firm doing nothing but consumer debtor representation.

And think about the DRA advertising provisions. A single relationship with an assisted person is sufficient to transform the attorney into a DRA, and that transformation triggers an ongoing duty that the attorney refer to himself as a debt relief agency in any ad directed at the general public for bankruptcy assistance, and a host of other legal matters. (See Chapter 9 for more information on DRA advertising.)

Since the BRA assumes the bankruptcy mill model and, as a result, contemplates continued regulation and application of the DRA designation, Ms. Anthony, although she plans to handle only business matters for the rest of her career, may forever be a DRA, as might her firm, even if it never previously represented a single assisted person.

That's the end of the quiz. How did you do?

Keep in mind that the point of this Chapter has been to demonstrate that application of the DRA provisions is far from easy. Reasonable minds differ on some of the conclusions,[12] but few will doubt that the range of possibilities when applying the DRA label is beginning to seem limitless.

---

12. *See, e.g.*, *In re* Attorneys at Law, 2005 Bankr. LEXIS 1998 (Bankr. S.D. Ga. Oct. 17, 2005) (attorneys are not debt relief agencies).

CHAPTER 6

Unbundling Legal Services

by *Thomas J. Yerbich*

The enactment of the Bankruptcy Abuse Prevention and Consumer Protection Act of 2005[1] will no doubt result in significant growth in two areas of bankruptcy practice:

- fees charged by debtors' counsel, and
- *pro se* filings.

The Bankruptcy Reform Act (BRA) has added several procedures to the consumer bankruptcy process and imposed significant additional requirements to which counsel for consumer debtors must adhere. These, taken together, require counsel for consumer debtors to expend more effort than was necessary prior to the Act, which, quite naturally, will require counsel to expend more time on each consumer case. More time spent translates into higher fees charged for consumer cases.[2] The higher the fees attorneys charge, the fewer debtors that can afford them, and *presto!* More *pro se* filers.

In the old days, for debtors who had no complicating factors, proceeding *pro se* was not particularly difficult and presented no serious problems. The amendments wrought by the BRA, however, make the process for consumer

---

1. Pub. L. No. 109-8, 119 Stat. 23. Some opponents of the law refer to it as the Bankruptcy Act Reform Fiasco, or BARF. The editors of this publication have decided to use "Bankruptcy Reform Act" or "BRA" or "the Act" as a neutral middle ground. Each reference to a section of the law passed will say "the Act." All references to the Code mean the Bankruptcy Code, which is codified in Title 11 of the United States Code, and references to Rules are to the Federal Rules of Bankruptcy Procedure.

2. Various surveys have shown a general consensus that fees will rise; the amount of the expected increase varies from as little as 10% to more than 100%.

cases more complex and, in some areas, confusing and convoluted, creating a maze of pitfalls for the unwary. The penalty for falling into one of these pits can (and, too frequently, will) be devastating. It will be the rare case where a debtor—even those with no apparent complicating factor—can safely navigate the maze created by the Act without some legal assistance. Two principal avenues exist to address this situation: *pro bono* representation and limited representation (unbundling). This chapter addresses unbundling.[3]

Limited representation in litigation—often called "unbundling"—although still in its infancy, is emerging across the country, principally in family law. While there is some philosophical hostility to the concept that an attorney may limit representation of a client in a judicial proceeding, it is an issue that is not going to fade into the sunset. Acceptance of limited representation is gaining momentum across the country. This trend is driven primarily by two factors: economics, and the view that some representation is better than none.

A closely related issue is ghostwriting by attorneys—preparation of documents for filing by a client *pro se*. Both are antithetical to traditional "full service" representation where, absent a grant of permission to withdraw for cause, you are expected to represent the client throughout all stages of litigation from beginning to end.

In this chapter, I do not attempt to explore all the nuances of, justifications for, or arguments against limited representation. It seems to me that the same economic factors driving state courts to recognize the need for limited representation in family law exist with equal, if not greater, force in consumer bankruptcy proceedings. People filing bankruptcy are broke! Limited representation is not only inevitable in consumer bankruptcies but may very well be in the best interests of debtors, creditors, and the courts.

I have divided this discussion into four areas:

1. Basic rules governing limited representation
2. A summary of the current status of "unbundling" in states that permit it
3. Ghostwriting
4. Representation limited to discrete tasks.

I. The Basic Rule

As with any other aspect of the attorney-client relationship, discussion starts with the rules governing the conduct of an attorney. ABA Model Rule 1.2(c),[4] as amended in 2002, states:

---

3. For a discussion of *pro bono* representation, see Chapter 17.
4. Unless otherwise indicated, all references to the Model Rules are to the 2002 Model Rules of Professional Conduct promulgated by the American Bar Association.

A lawyer may limit the scope of the representation if the limitation is reasonable under the circumstances and the client gives informed consent.

Limited representation must pass both parts of this two-pronged test:

1. Reasonable under the circumstances, and
2. Informed consent by the client.

Broadly stated, what is reasonable is a question of whether the lawyer's limited scope of responsibility would amount to a violation of the lawyer's ethical or legal obligations, a determination that must necessarily take into consideration all the facts and circumstances. What is reasonable also requires recognition that the ethical responsibilities of an attorney do not necessarily end at the same time as representation. Some continue, like the obligation to respond to or forward to the debtor any subsequent inquiries or information. For example, if your limited representation does not include reaffirmation, you must nevertheless forward to the client any proposed reaffirmation agreements received and advise the creditor that the debtor is unrepresented.

WARNING!!

Limited representation should not be seen as a means to avoid the obligations imposed on attorneys by the rules of professional conduct and the requirements of the Bankruptcy Code. Courts are likely to look with disfavor on unbundling if used by an attorney to escape ethical and legal responsibilities. Limited representation is for the benefit of the client, not the attorney. As discussed below, the concept of reasonableness limits the extent to which services may be unbundled.

Informed consent, on the other hand, is a more generic or universal standard. You must clearly explain the limitations of your representation, including what services are not being provided and the probable effect of limited representation on the client's rights and interests.

So, you might ask, how do I do this? First, keep in mind two things:

1. your client's state of mind is important, and
2. you are a debt relief agency and must comply with the requirements imposed by §§ 526–528.[5]

---

5.   Debt relief agencies are discussed in Chapters 4 and 11.

For many consumer debtors, bankruptcy is their first encounter with the legal system. They are apprehensive because they have not the foggiest idea of what the process is or what to expect. The typical consumer debtor is also quite understandably depressed and scared, if not in a panic. In many cases, the debtor is facing an imminent foreclosure on a home, repossession of a car, wage garnishment, or seizure of a bank account. They, like the rest of the population, also have varied views of lawyers—some are hostile, while others may view you as a magician who, with the wave of a wand, will make their woes disappear. Obtaining "informed consent" under these circumstances is not going to be easy.

Once the preliminaries are completed—the debtor has communicated her sad tale of woe and flunked the "flinch test" (you informed her of your full-service fee and she flinched)—you must discuss the extent of your representation and your charges. I recommend you use a written checklist identifying *at a minimum* matters that are likely to arise based on the facts disclosed by the debtor.

That checklist should also provide a means for clearly identifying the services you will and will not be providing. You should have the client not only acknowledge that she understands that some services are not being provided but also clearly identify those services. It should clearly state the charges for the services you provide (and those not included) for a flat fee.[6] A checklist might look something like this, with the attorney and the client each initialing each service:[7]

---

6.   While you might think this a bit onerous, having this may provide your salvation in the event a controversy arises over what services you agreed to perform.

7.   As Chapters 7, 10, and 11 explain, you need a written contract with your client. A form is provided in Chapter 10. This is not a substitute for the contract, but an exhibit to it, so be sure that the contract either refers to this checklist or accurately reflects its terms.

Atty Will Provide		Not Provided		Service	Agreed Fee
Atty	Client	Atty	Client		
				Prepare Petition, including . . .	$75
				Prepare Schedules, including . . .	$250
				Attend § 341 Creditors' Meeting	$150/hour
				Reaffirmation Agreements (including court appearance)	$200/hour

Checklist

For each service, explain in plain language[8] not only what the client should expect but also should do. Some items should be covered in all cases. For example:

- proper preparation of the schedules and statements,
- attending the creditors' meeting and the documentation that must be produced,
- cooperation with and turnover of assets to the trustee,
- the automatic stay and the remedies available if a creditor violates it, and
- utility deposits under § 366.

Others depend on the client's particular situation.[9] For example, if the client has a car loan or is leasing a car, you should also explain:

- the procedures, limitations, effect, and the strict time periods associated with reaffirmation, redemption, or surrender of personal property securing consumer debts and consumer leases (including appearing at the hearing), and
- how and under what circumstances the automatic stay may be terminated, giving the creditor the right to repossess the car.

---

8. We recommend that all documents directed to the client be written at the 8th-grade level in a language in which the client is literate.

9. It's useful to have the client complete a questionnaire, prior to the initial interview, providing general background information such as marital status, children, whether a home or car is owned, and the nature and approximate amount of debts, with the common nondischargeable debts, *e.g.*, taxes, specifically identified. While I recommend you use an intake questionnaire, the structure and detail of the questionnaire is up to you.

If the debtor has debts that are not dischargeable—taxes, student loans, support, and other obligations arising out of a divorce—you should explain if the debt is automatically excepted from discharge and, for those that are not, the procedure involved. In a Chapter 13 case, the formulation and confirmation of a Chapter 13 plan should be thoroughly reviewed and explained.[10]

After going over the form with the client and explaining the process, ask the client if there are any questions. The form should also affirmatively reflect the client's questions and the fact that they were answered. At this point you might well be saying to yourself, "Why, with all this bother, might I want to even consider unbundling?" Well, for starters, as outlined in Chapter 4, if you charge even one penny for your services, whether you like it or not, you're a debt relief agency. As shown in Chapter 11, the disclosures you're required to make as a DRA require you to explain much, if not most, of the basic matters involved in a consumer bankruptcy.

The 2002 revision of Model Rule 1.1 states: "A lawyer shall provide competent representation to a client. Competent representation requires the legal knowledge, skill, thoroughness and preparation reasonably necessary for the representation."[11] The comment explains:

> Although [Model Rule 1.2] affords the lawyer and client substantial latitude to limit the representation, the limitation must be reasonable under the circumstances. If, for example, a client's objective is limited to securing general information about the law the client needs in order to handle a common and typically uncomplicated legal problem, the lawyer and client may agree that the lawyer's services will be limited to a brief telephone consultation. Such a limitation, however, would not be reasonable if the time allotted was not sufficient to yield advice upon which the client could rely. Although an agreement for a limited representation does not exempt a lawyer from the duty to provide competent representation, the limitation is a factor to be considered when determining the legal knowledge, skill, thoroughness and preparation reasonably necessary for the representation. See Rule 1.1.[12]

II. State Action

Several states have officially sanctioned limited representation in litigation. Here are some of the various approaches taken.

- **Alaska**: Permits limited representation in all civil cases in state courts.
- **California**: Permits limited representation. In family law cases, true ghostwriting is permitted (an attorney is not required to disclose his or her involvement in the process).

---

10. *See, e.g., In re* Castorena, 270 B.R. 504, 529–31 (Bankr. D. Idaho 2001).
11. MODEL RULE OF PROF'L CONDUCT R.1.1 (ABA 2002).
12. MODEL RULE OF PROF'L CONDUCT R.1.2, cmt. [7] (ABA 2002).

- **Colorado**: Permits an attorney to prepare documents for filing *pro se* but requires the attorney be identified by name, address, and bar registration number. Although assisting a *pro se* litigant in preparing a document does not constitute an appearance, it does subject the attorney to the same sanctions as if the attorney had appeared in the action. By district court general order, the change to the Colorado rules does not apply in the bankruptcy court in adversary actions or contested matters governed by Rule 9014; however, the general order prohibition does not extend to the main case.[13]
- **Florida**: Permits true ghostwriting and does not require that the attorney either sign or be identified in the document. However, a pleading or other paper prepared by an attorney or with the assistance of an attorney must indicate on the document "prepared with the assistance of counsel" to avoid misleading the court, which otherwise might be under the impression that the person, who appears to be proceeding *pro se*, has received no assistance from a lawyer.
- **Washington**: Adopted, with modification, Model Rule 1.2(c) and generally permits limited representation in both civil and criminal cases.
- **Wyoming**: Adopted a modified version of Model Rule 1.2(c), limiting it to nonprofit limited legal service programs under Model Rule 6.5.

Other states that have adopted the 2002 revision of Model Rule 1.2(c), or some variation, include Arizona, Delaware, District of Columbia, Idaho, Indiana, Iowa, Louisiana, Maryland, Minnesota, Montana, Nebraska, New Jersey, New Mexico, North Carolina, Oregon, Pennsylvania, South Carolina, South Dakota, and Tennessee. Several other state courts have initiated or commissioned studies of the issue of limited legal representation.

- Additional information on limited representation may be found on the Internet at www.unbundledlaw.org.
- In October 2003, the ABA released a 155-page Handbook on Limited Scope Legal Assistance, which may be accessed on the Internet at www.abanet.org/litigation/taskforces/modest/home.html.
- In addition, the ABA has a Pro Se/Unbundling Resource Center available on the internet at www.abanet.org/legalservices/delivery/delunbund.html.

All three contain guides, suggestions, and related information on practical and ethical concerns associated with limited representation.

---

13.   *See In re* Merriam, 250 B.R. 724, 735-36 (Bankr. D. Colo. 2000).

III. Ghostwriting

You are generally permitted to provide limited background advice and general counseling to *pro se* parties. It is impossible to avoid, let alone prohibit, because most initial interviews by an attorney include at least that much.

Ghostwriting—the drafting of documents for filing by a party *pro se* without disclosing that an attorney was involved—presents a different situation. If you prepare documents for a *pro se* debtor to file, you may not want to be identified. Very few jurisdictions permit true ghostwriting. Courts have generally considered ghostwriting misleading, because it appears that the ostensible *pro se* party is proceeding without the assistance of counsel. Ghostwriting tends to give litigants an unfair advantage because courts generally construe *pro se* pleadings liberally and grant *pro se* litigants far greater latitude in hearings and trials. Ghostwriting can also allow attorneys to evade obligations imposed on them by statute, code, and rule, and involve lawyers in litigants' misrepresentation of *pro se* status in violation of ethical rules.

Even if otherwise permitted by the Rules of Professional Conduct and court rules of practice, ghostwriting is practically impossible when you represent a debtor in bankruptcy, unless you prepare the documents on a *pro bono* basis or more than a year preceding the filing. Here's why:

- The debtor is required to disclose all compensation paid in the year preceding the filing for bankruptcy counseling.
- If you represent a debtor "in connection with such a case," you must file the disclosure statement required by § 329(a) ("in contemplation of or in connection with such a case") and Rule 2016(b).
- · Finally, by its literal language, § 329(a) requires disclosure even in the absence of an attorney's appearance in the case.[14]

These provisions eliminate your ability to remain anonymous. Of course, if you do not "represent" the debtor, which in most cases would be difficult to avoid, you don't need to comply with the requirements of § 329(a) and Rule 2016(b).[15] If you provide the services on a *pro bono* basis, the debtor has nothing to disclose. If both conditions coalesce, it is possible for your involvement to remain undisclosed.

---

14.   Some have suggested that if the attorney performs the services on a *pro bono* basis, he need not comply with Code § 329 and Rule 2016. I disagree. Section 329 requires disclosure of the compensation "agreed to be paid." If the agreement is that there is no compensation, it is nonetheless an agreement of the compensation to be paid, *i.e.*, that the debtor will pay nothing, and must be disclosed.

15.   However, as discussed later in this Chapter, that not only poses potential significant problems for an attorney providing legal assistance to a debtor for which the attorney receives compensation but also will not avoid disclosure of the fact that the debtor obtained legal assistance.

Even if you represent a creditor, you cannot go beyond a proof of claim without disclosing your participation. Unless the bankruptcy (or district) court has expressly adopted the state rules permitting ghostwriting, you should assume that the court will adhere to the "traditional" rule precluding that practice.

WARNING!!

If you are asked to ghostwrite for a *creditor* in a bankruptcy case, other than preparing a proof of claim, you should proceed with extreme caution, even in those jurisdictions in which the Rules of Professional Conduct permit an attorney to ghostwrite.

IV. Limitations

Assuming that unbundling is permissible under the applicable rules governing the attorney-client relationship, should there be any limitation on your ability to limit representation in bankruptcy proceedings? First, remember that unbundling is already recognized, at least implicitly, by the Federal Rules of Bankruptcy Procedure. A bankruptcy case is divided into three separate component parts:

- the main case,
- contested matters under Rule 9014, and
- adversary proceedings under Rule 7001, *et seq.*

By dividing the process into separate components, it may be logically assumed that unbundling is, at least to that extent, permissible.

While most, if not all, agree that adversary proceedings are separate actions, some debate whether contested matters are separate. The better view is that contested matters are severable from the main case, and representation of a debtor in a bankruptcy case does not automatically include representation in contested matters. Rule 9014 specifically provides that service of a contested matter is governed by Rule 7004. Service under Rule 7004 is made on the party, not the attorney for the party. It is only the service of subsequent documents to which Rule 7005 applies. The rules do not require service of a contested matter on the attorney for any party except the debtor.[16] Service on an attorney for a party to a contested matter (other than the debtor) is either a

---

16. Rule 7004(b)(9) requires service on the attorney for the debtor.

requirement of local rule, custom or practice, or a matter of professional courtesy. Logically, if the rules deemed the opposing party in a contested matter to be represented by counsel appearing in the main case, service of the motion would be under Rule 7005, not Rule 7004. In addition, Form B203, Disclosure of Compensation of Attorney for Debtor, and the accompanying instructions promulgated by the Judicial Conference of the United States clearly indicate that some unbundling is contemplated.

Can you limit the services rendered to a debtor to assistance in preparing the petition, schedules, and statements in a Chapter 7 case? If unbundling is to be permitted at all, the attorney for a Chapter 7 debtor should probably be permitted to limit services rendered to preparing the petition, accompanying schedules, and statements. The schedules and statements are the heart of every bankruptcy proceeding, from the simplest to the most complex. The schedules and statements give the trustee and other interested parties, *i.e.*, the creditors, information concerning the debtor's assets and liabilities, income and expenses, entitlement to exemptions, and eligibility for relief, as well as certain prepetition financial and property transactions. Schedules and statements that are properly, completely, and accurately prepared materially assist the trustee and creditors in identifying the areas that deserve further exploration at the creditors' meeting. A substantial percentage, if not the majority, of the problems that arise in consumer cases could be avoided by adequate schedules and statements.

On the other hand, a strong argument can be made for compelling an attorney who assists the debtor in preparing the schedules and statements to at least appear at the creditors' meeting. First, appearance at the creditors' meeting can be a deterrent to the debtor using the "but the attorney told me not to" response if confronted with a material error or omission. Second, presence at the creditors' meeting, which to the uninitiated can be somewhat daunting, can be a source of reassurance to the debtor. Third, an attorney who assisted in the preparation of the schedules and statements can provide background and help explain the schedules and statements, in particular how assets were valued and the sources of the valuation information.

Assuming you are permitted to limit representation to preparation of the petition, schedules, and statements, should you—in addition to being identified as having prepared or assisted in the preparation of the petition and schedules—also be required to sign the petition? In my opinion, the answer is an unequivocal yes. You should not be held to a lesser standard than that imposed by § 110 on bankruptcy petition preparers. You may fear becoming the attorney of record and, if listed as the attorney of record, being served instead of the debtor. You can avoid this problem by including a specific statement in the § 329(a)/Rule 2016 disclosures that you are not appearing on behalf of the debtor.[17] The debtor would be listed as appearing *pro se,* and interested parties would not mistakenly believe they must go through you, the attorney.

Requiring you to sign the petition removes any question of whether you are subject to Rule 9011 or § 707(b)(4)(C) and (D).[18] You might argue that that is unnecessary because the court can use § 329(b) and Rule 2017, which permit the court to order disgorgement even if you do not make an appearance. But that is not the only purpose served by signing the petition. If you assist a debtor in preparing the petition and accompanying schedules, you should be required to certify to the court and all interested parties, as well as the debtor, that you have made a reasonable investigation of the debtor's affairs and the petition is filed in good faith. Signing the petition, which is covered by Rule 9011 and § 707(b)(4)(C) and (D), satisfies this requirement.

Limiting representation of a debtor in a Chapter 13 case is probably economically unnecessary. The economic argument for unbundling is not the same in Chapter 13. While many Chapter 7 debtors are true "economic basket cases," if this is true in a Chapter 13, it is unrealistic to assume the debtor can propose a confirmable plan, let alone consummate it. If a debtor has the financial wherewithal to fund a Chapter 13 plan, the debtor can also afford representation, even under BRA. Indeed, the reverse is probably true: the debtor cannot afford to forgo representation. If you are retained post-petition in connection with the preparation of a Chapter 13 plan, the scope of your representation should include not only the plan preparation but confirmation as well. As a practical matter, in most cases it would take you less time to prepare a Chapter 13 plan and represent the debtor in obtaining confirmation than you would spend explaining to the typical consumer debtor the requirements for confirmation of a Chapter 13 plan under the BRA.

To what extent should unbundling—other than the preparation of the petition, schedules, and statements in Chapter 7 cases—be permitted? If you appear in a case on behalf of a debtor, other than a contested matter or adversary proceeding, you must provide certain minimum services in addition to preparing and filing the schedules. You should, at a minimum, be required to:

- attend the creditors' meeting;
- represent and assist the debtor in carrying out the debtor's duties under § 521 and Rule 4002;
- in Chapter 7 cases, assist and counsel the debtor with respect to reaffirmations and redemptions; and
- in Chapter 13 cases, formulate and confirm the Chapter 13 plan.

---

17. *See, e.g., In re* Merriam, 250 B.R. 724, 735-36 (Bankr. D. Colo. 2000).

18. "The signature of an attorney on the petition shall constitute a certification that the attorney has no knowledge after an inquiry that the information on the schedules filed with such petition is incorrect." Code § 704(b)(4)(D), added by BRA Section 102(a). See Chapter 13 for a complete discussion of the new certification requirements.

Anything less and a debtor may as well be appearing *pro se* throughout.

V. *Post-petition Representation*

Suppose the debtor initiates the case *pro se* and seeks your advice or assistance with respect to a matter arising post-petition.[19] A debtor may be (or believe himself to be) capable of handling a no-asset main case in which the presumption of abuse does not arise. But when a contested matter arises (relief from stay), or an adversary proceeding (a challenge to discharge or dischargeability), a *pro se* debtor can "get creamed."

A. Reaffirmation Agreements

Let's look at an example to illustrate the potential ethical problems that may confront you when you are asked to provide post-petition limited representation.[20] Suppose a debtor comes into your office with a proposed agreement reaffirming a loan secured by the debtor's automobile. Can you and the client agree that you will not make the "undue hardship" certification that the Code requires from the attorney?[21]

Analysis starts with the recognition that § 524(c)(3)(B)—which was not amended—has always required the attorney who represents a debtor in connection with a reaffirmation to certify that the reaffirmation agreement does not impose an undue hardship on the debtor. You should not make a certification under § 524(c)(3)(B) unless you, exercising your independent judgment after verifying the facts, determine that:

- it will not be an undue hardship,
- reaffirmation is in the debtor's best interests, and
- there is a reasonable probability that the debtor can make the payments.

Unfortunately, in far too many situations, attorneys have simply acceded to the debtor's wishes and made a § 524(b)(3)(B) certification without any investigation and without exercising independent judgment.

Now move to the BRA. Section 524(k)(5)(B)[22] requires that when the "undue hardship" presumption arises you, as the attorney, must certify that "in the opinion of the attorney, the debtor is able to make the payment." What purpose this additional certification serves is unclear. If the debtor is unable to make the

---

19.   If representing a debtor post-petition, attorneys must comply with the disclosure requirements of Code § 329(a) and Rule 2016(b) within 15 days of being retained.

20.   Reaffirmations are discussed in detail in Chapter 7.

21.   See Chapter 14.

22.   BRA Section 204(a), adding Code §§ 524(k)(3)(J) and 524(m).

payment under the reaffirmation agreement, irrespective of whether the presumption arises, reaffirmation necessarily imposes an undue hardship by making default inevitable. The very execution of the agreement perpetrates a constructive fraud—the making of a promise without the ability to perform.

So the answer to the question whether you may exclude the undue hardship certification requires a two-step analysis:

1. the authority of the court to regulate practice before it, and
2. the purpose served by the limitation.

The court certainly has no authority to compel you to make the "undue hardship" certification if you say "I cannot certify that, your Honor, because in my opinion it would be an undue hardship and the debtor will not be able to make the payments." The court unquestionably has the authority to make its own independent assessment and to approve the reaffirmation agreement notwithstanding your refusal or inability to certify that it does not impose an undue hardship and that the debtor can make the payment.

Conversely, the court is not bound by your certification and may disapprove the reaffirmation agreement if it finds insufficient evidence to establish the lack of undue hardship or that the debtor could make the payments.

On the other hand, if you can, consistent with your obligation to exercise independent judgment, make the certification, what purpose is served by an agreement not to do so? Under pre-BRA law, if the debtor was represented by counsel in negotiating the reaffirmation agreement and the attorney made the required § 524(c)(3)(B) certification, the agreement was not subject to judicial review before becoming effective. However, under the BRA, unless the creditor is a credit union, in *any* case, including where the debtor is represented by counsel, the court must review and approve a reaffirmation agreement in which the presumption of undue hardship arises before the agreement is effective.[23] If the presumption of undue hardship does not arise, a reaffirmation agreement containing the requisite attorney certification is effective when filed under the BRA just as it was under pre-BRA law.

An agreement that excludes the certification under § 524(c)(3)(B) in the normal case means that judicial review and approval of a reaffirmation agreement is required in all cases, not just those in which the presumption of abuse arises. This is not in the interests of the debtor or judicial efficiency, and the courts are not likely to sanction it.

If you cannot, under the facts and circumstances, make the required undue hardship certification, you must, consistent with your ethical and legal obligations to the client (not to mention those to a malpractice carrier), advise

---

23. *Id.*

the client not to enter into the reaffirmation agreement. If the debtor persists in going forward with reaffirmation, what is your responsibility? Must you always go along with the client and present the reaffirmation to the court, or may you decline to do so and require the debtor to present the reaffirmation agreement *pro se*? In my opinion you should, if requested by the client (preferably in writing), file the motion without the attorney's certification.

However, because this is an *ex parte* matter, you must also inform the debtor that you must include a full explanation of your position and the reasons for it.[24] In the event the client forbids that disclosure, you have no choice but to decline to file the motion, withdraw from representation,[25] and, to prevent misleading the court, advise the debtor to inform the court that he or she has consulted with an attorney and the attorney declined to make the undue hardship certification.[26]

Let's turn to the more practical aspects. If you exclude the "undue hardship" certification from your representation, what service are you providing the debtor in connection with a reaffirmation agreement? If the "undue hardship" certification is excluded, all you can do is review the agreement for form and content. Since § 524(k) spells out in minute detail the form and content of the agreement, there is little, if any, likelihood that any institutional creditor will provide a form that does not comply with § 524(k). In that case, you have provided nothing of substance. On the other hand, if you advise the client on obtaining judicial approval of the reaffirmation agreement (the critical reason for attorney involvement), you will by necessity have to follow the same procedures as you would in making the certification—for example, determine it would not be an undue hardship and that the debtor has the ability to make the payments. If the answer is yes, there is no reason not to make the required certification. On the other hand, if the answer is no, you should not make the required certification, *even if you have not excluded that from the scope of the representation*, and follow the procedure outlined above.

Bankruptcy courts are not likely to permit a limitation that excludes the "undue hardship" certification, which also necessarily excludes representing the debtor at the reaffirmation hearing. Expect to be required to appear at the reaffirmation hearing and explain why you will not, or cannot, make the certifi-

---

24.   *See* MODEL RULES OF PROF'L CONDUCT R. 3.3(d) and cmt. [14]; R. 1.2, cmt. [13] (ABA 2002).

25.   *See* MODEL RULES OF PROF'L CONDUCT R. 1.16(a)(1), (b)(4), and cmt. [2] (ABA 2002); MODEL RULES OF PROF'L CONDUCT (ABA 2002); *cf.* MODEL RULES OF PROF'L CONDUCT R. 3.3, cmt. [15] (ABA 2002).

26.   *Cf.* Rule 9011(b). Although the Rules of Professional Conduct do not directly apply to *pro se* parties, most, if not all, courts have by custom, usage, or rule held *pro se* parties to the same standard of full, complete, and accurate disclosure of the facts required of attorneys.

cation. The risk is that if you attempted to exclude the "undue hardship" certification, you may not be paid for the appearance, and if the court finds that your refusal to make the required certification was unjustified, you may be compelled to disgorge fees paid in connection with the reaffirmation agreement.

VI. *Contested Matters and Adversary Proceedings*

The situation is different for contested matters and adversary actions. First, as noted above, current rules at least tacitly permit an attorney for the debtor either to exclude contested matters and/or adversary proceedings or to limit representation to a particular contested matter or adversary proceeding. These limitations are particularly appropriate where your retainer is a flat-fee agreement. In that case, you are setting the fee based upon the expected time and effort to be expended in the case, which is, in turn, based on the extent to which you have agreed to provide representation.[27] To preclude limitation would either require you to provide services for which you are not being paid or force you to abandon flat-fee agreements.

In a "time and expense" retainer agreement, the parties may reasonably believe that the debtor cannot afford the legal fees that would be incurred if contested matters or adversary proceedings arise in the case. In that situation, unless the representation was excluded at the outset, you will be compelled to file, and the court to hear, a motion to withdraw.[28]

At the beginning of a consumer case, it is often impossible to identify all the potential proceedings that may be initiated either by or against a debtor. In those cases where an excluded contested matter or adversary proceeding is initiated against the debtor, or the circumstances require the debtor to file one, a new retainer agreement, with the required disclosures, is necessary. From the debtor's perspective, this provides an opportunity to weigh the costs of retaining counsel against the risks involved by proceeding *pro se*.

Whether an attorney should be permitted to limit representation *within* a contested matter or adversary proceeding is a different matter. Some jurisdictions permit an attorney to limit representation in litigation to a particular segment of the litigation, such as discovery, a single motion, or the trial itself. While that might be workable in the context of a complex adversary action, given the nature of most contested matters in consumer proceedings, which do not generally have components as do adversary proceedings, it is of questionable practicality.

---

27. That fee must be reasonable and is subject to disgorgement if it is not under Code § 329(b) and Rule 2017.

28. MODEL RULES OF PROF'L CONDUCT R. 1.16(b)(5), (6), and cmt. [8] (ABA 2002).

VII. Limited Representation of Creditors

Limited representation of creditors presents a different situation. Unlike representation of debtors and the trustee, there is no provision in the Code or rules requiring you to disclose the terms of employment, or providing for judicial oversight of your employment. Representing creditors in bankruptcy is extremely varied and depends on the nature of the creditor's claim.

Many creditors in bankruptcy cases file a proof of claim, but do not get directly involved in the process; for them, representation is unnecessary. Representing many creditors in bankruptcy cases involves nothing more than explaining the process and their rights under the Code, and preparing a proof of claim or helping the creditor do so.[29] These services have often been performed by attorneys who are true "ghosts," in that their involvement is undisclosed. On the other hand, secured creditors, lessors and lessees, recipients of preferential or fraudulent transfers, those whose claims are objected to, and those holding potentially nondischargeable debts are likely to appear and require representation in the proceeding at some point.

Appearance for a creditor may take different forms, depending on the level and degree of representation the creditor needs or desires. For example, you may be retained to monitor the case and alert the creditor to actions to be taken to protect or preserve the creditor's rights. In that case, you would make a "general" appearance in the main case, request to be included on the master mailing matrix, and receive notice on behalf of the represented creditor. You may be retained solely to appear in a contested matter—a motion for relief from stay, or an adversary proceeding like a preference recovery or dischargeability action—but not make a general appearance in the case. No generally applicable policy would be served by precluding the creditor and attorney from restricting the representation to a particular contested matter or adversary proceeding. Nor is there a general policy advanced by preventing the attorney from making an appearance in the main action but excluding representation of the creditor in contested matters or adversary proceedings. And, as noted previously, Rule 7004 does not require that a contested matter or adversary proceeding be served on counsel for a creditor. Because the nature and scope of contested matters and adversary proceedings vary widely, it is impossible to formulate a general rule for cases where limited representation may be permissible in a contested matter or adversary proceeding. These should be addressed by local rule on a district-by-district basis.

---

29.   The vast majority of creditors in bankruptcy proceedings never "appear" in the case beyond filing a proof of claim. In a Chapter 11, if the claim is correctly scheduled, it is not even necessary to file the proof of claim.

VIII. When Is an Attorney Not an Attorney?

Providing limited representation for a debtor is not without hazards, independent of the obvious ethical and potential malpractice concerns discussed above. One of the little-noticed changes wrought by the BRA is an amendment to the definition of a bankruptcy petition preparer (BPP). Under pre-BRA law, the definition of a BPP excluded all attorneys. As amended by the BRA, Code § 110(a)(1) now defines a BPP as "a person other than an attorney *for the debtor* or an employee of *such attorney under the direct supervision of such attorney*, who prepares for compensation a document for filing."[30] Take, for example, Robert, the tax attorney in Chapter 15 who prepared the return for the debtor; let's change the facts a bit. Assume a creditor has requested that postpetition tax returns be filed under § 521(f). Robert prepares a tax return for the debtor, which the debtor files. As noted in Chapter 15, Robert may not be acting as an attorney in that situation, let alone attorney for the debtor. As such, Robert may very well be a BPP.

In amending § 110(a), Congress has (inadvertently, perhaps) created a trap with potentially disastrous consequences if an attorney falls within the definition of a BPP.[31] For example, if you—other than as the debtor's attorney—prepare a document for filing by the debtor and then provide any legal advice in connection with the case, because § 110(e)(2) prohibits BPPs from giving legal advice, you have engaged in the unauthorized practice of law. On the other hand, if you actually represent the debtor, you need not fear this consequence. Instead, you must comply with the disclosure requirements of Code § 329 and Rule 2016. While failure to comply should not result in your becoming a BPP, it does subject you to possible sanctions for violation of those provisions.

IX. Conclusion

Although the Rules of Professional Conduct may permit limited representation, unbundling in bankruptcy is governed by court rules and should be addressed on a district-by-district basis, not by a set of national rules. First, state rules of professional conduct governing limited representation are not uniform. Second, different jurisdictions face different considerations; the solution in one district may not work in another. In some districts, a *laissez-faire*

---

30. BRA Section 221(1) amending Code § 110(a)(1) (added language emphasized). The definition of a document for filing in Code § 110(a)(2) remains unchanged: "a petition or any other document prepared for filing by a debtor in a United States bankruptcy court or a United States district court in connection with a case under [title 11]."

31. *See* Code § 110, as amended by BRA Section 221(1), for the full panoply of "bad things" that can apply to you if you are classified as a BPP. See also Chapter 15.

approach may be appropriate, in others a complete prohibition, and yet others something in between. Whatever the approach, in states where unbundling is permitted under the rules of professional conduct, the bankruptcy or district court should adopt local rules delineating the extent, if any, to which limited representation is permissible in bankruptcy cases. In fairness to the bar and debtors alike, the rules must be set in advance; the determination cannot be on an ad hoc basis.

Is limited representation inevitable in consumer bankruptcies? Probably. With more than 1.5 million consumer filings a year, if only 30 percent are *pro se*, there will be over 450,000 *pro se* filings a year. The majority of those are likely to be individuals who cannot afford "full service" representation. For them, limited representation is probably their only access to legal assistance.

But unbundling alone will not stem the tide. We need to look at an integrated solution combining *pro bono* representation, limited representation, and *pro se* assistance. This will take a joint effort by the bench and bar, and perhaps even Congress. Where the case involves issues beyond the capability of a *pro se* debtor, a sliding-scale fee arrangement may be appropriate where the attorney is providing the services partially compensated and partially on a *pro bono* basis. Using an attorney paid a salary by the court to assist *pro se* debtors, somewhat similar to the *pro se* law clerk system utilized in district courts, has also been suggested. The bench and bar should take a hard look at approving limited representation in consumer bankruptcy cases so that available *pro bono* hours can be more effectively allocated. Unless all participants work together, the bankruptcy system is destined to become clogged with *pro se* debtors. Far too many individuals will not receive the relief to which the law says they are entitled because they are unaware of the law or their rights under it.

CHAPTER 7

Bankruptcy Ethics Issues for Solos and Small Firms

by Nancy B. Rapoport [1]

Now that you've decided to work on a bankruptcy case, you need to make sure that you understand enough about the quirks of bankruptcy practice to keep yourself, your client, and your bar card safe for years to come. As with any other new representation, you should start by determining whether you can take on a new matter. A conflicts check is essential, but in bankruptcy cases, it can be extremely tricky to do correctly. Here's why.

I. "DTACs" and Conflicts Checks

I fell in love with bankruptcy law when I tried to do a conflicts check at my law firm, and I marked everyone in the case as "potentially adverse" to everyone else in the case. The conflicts check came back several inches high, the law firm wasn't amused, and I realized that there were some tricky conflict of interest issues in this field.

Normally, a conflicts check just isn't that hard: buyers are adverse to sellers; plaintiffs are adverse to defendants. State ethics rules (discussed below) can handle these easy situations. But what happens in those fields where parties can switch sides over and over, regrouping several times over the course of a given case? Such a possibility isn't as rare as you might think. For example, in family or probate law, Mom and Dad might be on opposite sides of a divorce but on the same side when contesting Grandma's will. Then Mom

---

1.   The views expressed in this Chapter are mine alone and not those of the faculty or administration of the University of Houston or the UH Law Center. Special thanks go to Cathy Vance and Corinne Cooper for their invitation to contribute to this book, to Jeff Van Niel and Morris Rapoport for their always-helpful edits, and to Kelli Cline for always helping me find the time for my projects.

and one of the 2.5 kids might agree on the best interest of Child .5, but Dad and the other kids might disagree. The combinations will depend on the choices that Mom, Dad, and their 2.5 kids make during the course of their lives.

Bankruptcy law has the same side-switching problem. During the course of a bankruptcy case, each party may potentially oppose every other party—or not—depending on the choices made during the case. If the conflicts check that you do at the beginning of the case doesn't take this potential side-switching into account, you might find yourself conflicted out of one or more representations in the middle of the case.

The problem with conflicts of interest in bankruptcy is that there are several types of conflicts, and state ethics rules can cope with only a few of those types. There are:

- obvious actual conflicts;
- obvious and likely potential conflicts (which you should treat as if they were actual conflicts);
- obvious and unlikely conflicts;
- conflicts that, if they crop up, will continue for the duration of the case; and
- conflicts that, if they crop up, will disappear after the issue that triggered them gets resolved.

Whew! That's a lot to remember.

If two parties are adverse at the beginning of the bankruptcy, you're not going to be able to represent both sides during the case. But what of those potential conflicts listed in the previous paragraph—they might or might not ever happen, so what should you do about them? Do you simply say, "This whole idea is too complex—I'm only going to represent one party in this case?" Well, you *could* say that (and I wouldn't blame you), but you might not want to say that. What if you've done a very tiny representation for one client (for example, you've filed a proof of claim on behalf of that client), and then a more interesting (read: lucrative) client comes along? That second client doesn't look adverse to the first client—at least not at first—but can you be sure?

Many conflicts in bankruptcy cases are single-issue conflicts that may or may not pop up, depending on the various parties' decisions in the case. I call these issue-specific conflicts "DTACs" (dormant, temporary, actual conflicts):[2]

---

2.   I first wrote about DTACs in 1994. *See* Nancy B. Rapoport, *Turning and Turning in the Widening Gyre: The Problem of Potential Conflicts of Interest in Bankruptcy,* 26 CONN. L. REV. 913 (1994). Since then, I've made the issue of conflicts of interest in bankruptcy cases the focal point of my career, at least so far. Some would say I'm obsessed by

- They're dormant because they might never arise.
- If they do arise, they're temporary because they're only single-issue conflicts.
- But while they're "on," they're actual conflicts, and they may present a real problem for you.

Take a look at Exhibits 7-1, 7-2, and 7-3, describing some simple DTACs. When you review these charts, remember that the dotted lines represent conflicts and the solid lines represent an alignment of parties in interest.

Exhibit 7-1

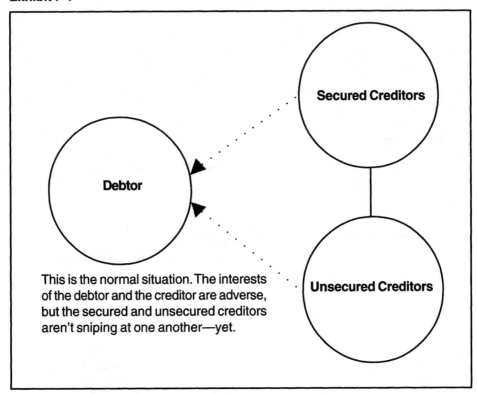

Secured Creditors

Debtor

Unsecured Creditors

This is the normal situation. The interests of the debtor and the creditor are adverse, but the secured and unsecured creditors aren't sniping at one another—yet.

---

the issue. For a partial listing of my work in this area, see Nancy B. Rapoport, *The Intractable Problem of Bankruptcy Ethics: Square Peg, Round Hole*, 30 HOFSTRA L. REV. 977 (2002); Nancy B. Rapoport, *Our House, Our Rules: The Need for a Uniform Code of Bankruptcy Ethics*, 6 AM. BANKR. INST. L. REV. 45 (1998); C.R. Bowles & Nancy B. Rapoport, *Has the DIP's Attorney Become the Ultimate Creditors' Lawyer in Bankruptcy Reorganization Proceedings?*, 5 AM. BANKR. INST. L. REV. 47 (1997); Nancy B. Rapoport, *Seeing the Forest* and *The Trees: The Proper Role of the Bankruptcy Attorney*, 70 IND. L.J. 783 (1995); *cf.*, Nancy B. Rapoport, *Avoiding Judicial Wrath: The Ten Commandments for Bankruptcy Practitioners*, 5 J. BANKR. L. & PRAC. 615 (September/October 1996) (obsessing about bankruptcy lawyers' behavior in bankruptcy cases more generally).

Exhibit 7-2

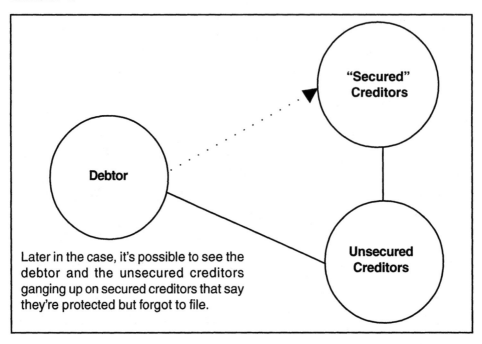

Later in the case, it's possible to see the debtor and the unsecured creditors ganging up on secured creditors that say they're protected but forgot to file.

Exhibit 7-3

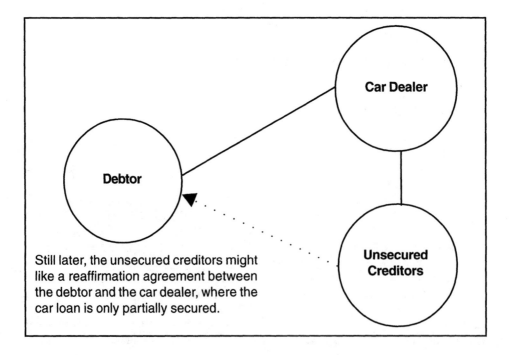

Still later, the unsecured creditors might like a reaffirmation agreement between the debtor and the car dealer, where the car loan is only partially secured.

What's the take-away lesson I want you to learn? Don't be lazy when you do your conflicts check—think hard about the parties' relationships and what they might become.[3]

Let's make things even more complicated: bankruptcy practice is a federal practice, but the ethics rules in the U.S. Bankruptcy Court in which your case has been filed could include:

1. the ethics rules of the state in which the court sits;
2. the rules that the court has, itself, decided to adopt; or
3. a combination of the two.[4]

So before you can take on a new matter for a potential client, you're going to have to clear two separate hurdles—the non-bankruptcy ethics rules and those additional rules imposed by the Bankruptcy Code.

II. State Ethics Rules and Conflicts of Interest

Most state ethics rules prohibit you from representing concurrent clients whose interests are directly adverse (see, e.g., Model Rule of Professional Conduct 1.7). Concurrent client ethics rules are designed to protect client confidences from being used against the client(s), and they're also designed to protect the clients from a "Mom always loved you more" situation (pulling your punches in favor of one client, also known as zealousness). When it comes to representing two current clients in the same matter, you have to make sure that confidentiality and zealous representation (on behalf of both clients) are foremost in your thoughts.

Those same state ethics rules also prohibit you from taking on a new client whose interests are materially adverse to those of a former client[5] (one whom

---

3. If I weren't compulsive in addition to being obsessive, I'd leave off nagging you about conflicts checks. But I do need to remind you that you need to be accurate in conducting your check. Don't forget that people change names (and some don't, even after they marry). Assumptions here can get you in a heap of trouble.

4. Feeling queasy yet about taking on this new representation? To make matters worse, if you are admitted in more than one jurisdiction (check your wallet—how many bar cards are you carrying?), then an ethics violation in one jurisdiction may create a snowball effect, leading to reciprocal discipline in all of your other jurisdictions. This problem gets more complicated if a particular behavior is well within the bounds of ethics in one state but is prohibited in another state.

5. Many lawyers are awfully sloppy when it comes to closing files, to the consternation of their malpractice carriers. When you are done with a matter, send a termination letter politely closing your file. See Chapter 10. The more definite you can make the separation between "current client" and "former client," the more likely it is that a court will apply the less-stringent "former client" rule (protecting confidentiality only) rather than the more-stringent "current client" rule (protecting confidentiality and zealousness).

you no longer represent) if the new matter and the former matter are substantially related to each other. With former clients, your duty is to protect all confidences you obtained in the course of the former client's representation. Because the former client is, well, former, you don't have the issue of pulling your punches on the former client's behalf.

Can you represent more than one client in a bankruptcy case? Don't forget about DTACs: you might think, at the beginning of the case, that the interests don't conflict, but developments in the case could change that calculus. If no DTACs appear likely, and no actual conflicts exist, then you may represent more than one client in the case—at least under the state ethics rules (see Exhibit 7-4).

Exhibit 7-4
Checklist: State Ethics Rules

1. Can you take on the new representation under the state ethics rules?[6] *It depends.*

   a. Do you have a current client whose interests appear to be directly adverse to the interests (or materially limited by your representation) of the new client?

      - If the answer is yes, unless you can get informed consent in writing from both clients, you can't take on the new representation.

      - Don't count on getting informed consent in this situation. The closer the interests of the two clients are to a concurrent conflict, the less likely it is that you'll be able to persuade a court that you acted reasonably in seeking the conflict waiver letters, even if you were able to get those letters signed.

      - Remember: when you have a current client and are thinking of taking on a new client, you have to protect the current client's confidences and assure yourself that you won't be tempted to pull your punches against either client in representing the other. (*Confidentiality* and *zealousness* ethics issues.)

   b. Do you have a former client whose interests may be materially adverse to the interests of the potential client?

      - If the answer is yes, then you need to determine whether the matter in which you represented the former client is substantially related to the matter in which you want to represent the potential client.

        1. If there's a substantial relationship, then it's likely that you'll have confidential information from the former client that you will not be allowed to use in representing the potential client. You won't be able to take on the potential client.

        2. If there's not a substantial relationship between the old and potential matters—and there's little risk that you'd be able to use confidential information that you obtained from the former client against the former client in your representation of the potential client—then you may take on the potential client's new matter.

   The trick is, of course, the specific facts that you're facing. Before you agree to take on a new representation, look at your state's ethics rules and make sure that you fit within the case law interpreting those rules.

---

6. We'll get to the special bankruptcy ethics rules next.

III. Bankruptcy Ethics Rules—Creditor (or Other Non-estate) Representation

Now that you think your state bar card will be safe, let's add those extra bankruptcy ethics rules. These rules govern two types of representation in bankruptcy:

- those for which the debtor's estate pays your bills, and
- those for which the estate doesn't pay your bills.

Let's do the easy one first—where the estate doesn't pay your bills (where you're representing, say, a creditor).

A. Representing Creditors

The good thing about representing a creditor or other, non-estate entity in a bankruptcy case is that you don't need to get the bankruptcy court's permission before you take on the representation. As long as your representation passes muster under your state's ethics rules, you may take on that representation. The only twist occurs when you represent more than one creditor (or equity security holder) in a Chapter 9 (unlikely) or in a Chapter 11 case. Even this twist doesn't require court approval, but it does require that you file something called a Rule 2019 statement.[7] That statement acts as a brief cross-check

---

7. Rule 2019 says:

Representation of Creditors and Equity Security Holders in Chapter 9 Municipality and Chapter 11 Reorganization Cases
  (a) Data required
       In a chapter 9 municipality or chapter 11 reorganization case, except with respect to a committee appointed pursuant to § 1102 or 1114 of the Code, every entity or committee representing more than one creditor or equity security holder and, unless otherwise directed by the court, every indenture trustee, shall file a verified statement setting forth (1) the name and address of the creditor or equity security holder; (2) the nature and amount of the claim or interest and the time of acquisition thereof unless it is alleged to have been acquired more than one year prior to the filing of the petition; (3) a recital of the pertinent facts and circumstances in connection with the employment of the entity or indenture trustee, and, in the case of a committee, the name or names of the entity or entities at whose instance, directly or indirectly, the employment was arranged or the committee was organized or agreed to act; and (4) with reference to the time of the employment of the entity, the organization or formation of the committee, or the appearance in the case of any indenture trustee, the amounts of claims or interests owned by the entity, the members of the committee or the indenture trustee, the times when acquired, the amounts paid therefor, and any sales or other disposition thereof. The statement

for the court (and anyone else) to determine how many entities you're representing in the case.

B. Representing the Estate

When the bankruptcy estate pays your bills, you do need prior court permission to represent the particular estate entity. Different chapters have different estate entities (see Exhibit 7.5).

Exhibit 7.5

Chapter	Typical estate entities
7	Trustee[8]
9	Municipality
11	Debtor-in-possession; creditors' committee
12	Debtor-in-possession (family farmer); trustee
13	Debtor-in-possession (individual); trustee

---

shall include a copy of the instrument, if any, whereby the entity, committee, or indenture trustee is empowered to act on behalf of creditors or equity security holders. A supplemental statement shall be filed promptly, setting forth any material changes in the facts contained in the statement filed pursuant to this subdivision.

(b) Failure to comply; effect

On motion of any party in interest or on its own initiative, the court may (1) determine whether there has been a failure to comply with the provisions of subdivision (a) of this rule or with any other applicable law regulating the activities and personnel of any entity, committee, or indenture trustee or any other impropriety in connection with any solicitation and, if it so determines, the court may refuse to permit that entity, committee, or indenture trustee to be heard further or to intervene in the case; (2) examine any representation provision of a deposit agreement, proxy, trust mortgage, trust indenture, or deed of trust, or committee or other authorization, and any claim or interest acquired by any entity or committee in contemplation or in the course of a case under the Code and grant appropriate relief; and (3) hold invalid any authority, acceptance, rejection, or objection given, procured, or received by an entity or committee who has not complied with this rule or with § 1125(b) of the Code.

8. In a Chapter 7 case, the debtor doesn't take on the role of administering the estate.

In order to determine whether you can represent an estate entity, turn to § 327. Under § 327(a):

> Except as otherwise provided in this section, the trustee, with the court's approval, may employ one or more attorneys, accountants, appraisers, auctioneers, or other professional persons, *that do not hold or represent an interest adverse to the estate,* and that *are disinterested persons,* to represent or assist the trustee in carrying out the trustee's duties under this title.[9]

In Congress's Department of Redundancy Department of Drafting, § 327(a) refers to professionals who don't "hold or represent an interest adverse to the estate" and who are "disinterested persons." Section 101(14) defines "disinterested person" to include a person who:

> (A) is not a creditor, an equity security holder, or an insider;
> . . . and
> (E) does not have an interest materially adverse to the interest of the estate or of any class of creditors or equity security holders, by reason of any direct or indirect relationship to, connection with, or interest in, the debtor . . . or for any other reason . . . .

So, as long as you don't:

(1) hold or represent an adverse interest and
(2) have a materially adverse interest (!)

you're disinterested and may file an application to approve your appointment as a professional in the case. You'll also need to file a Rule 2014 statement.[10]

---

9. Emphasis added.
10. Rule 2014 says:
    Employment of Professional Persons
    (a) Application for an order of employment
    An order approving the employment of attorneys, accountants, appraisers, auctioneers, agents, or other professionals pursuant to § 327, § 1103, or § 1114 of the Code shall be made only on application of the trustee or committee. The application shall be filed and, unless the case is a chapter 9 municipality case, a copy of the application shall be transmitted by the applicant to the United States trustee. The application shall state the specific facts showing the necessity for the employment, the name of the person to be employed, the reasons for the selection, the professional services to be rendered, any proposed arrangement for compensation, and, to the best of the applicant's knowledge, all of the person's connections with the debtor, creditors, any other party in interest, their respective attorneys and accountants, the United States trustee, or any person employed in the office of the United States trustee. The application shall

Then, at intervals,[11] upon application, you'll be able to be paid from the estate.[12]

A Note About Limited Representation[13]

Some lawyers explain very well in their engagement letters that the initial fee covers only certain parts of the representation. For example, filing the petition and schedules and appearing at the § 341 meeting is covered, but defending an attack on the client's good faith in filing is not.

Will this work under state ethics rules (or under my take on how state ethics rules would be interpreted)?

- This unbundling of representation may work fine when the client is relatively sophisticated and can understand the ramifications of a carve-out of representation.

- For the less sophisticated client, though, an engagement letter that limits representation may not be enforceable. A court is likely to ask whether the client understood the engagement letter. The clearer the letter—in plain language and with several examples of what is and isn't covered—the better.

Don't forget that once a lawyer signs on to represent a client, the lawyer must actually represent the client. Leaving a client in the lurch—with or without a properly worded engagement letter—is only asking for trouble.

Some bankruptcy courts acknowledge that limited representation lowers the cost of filing bankruptcy and will enforce these agreements. Others rule that the lawyer is in for the entire case, regardless of the engagement letter.

---

be accompanied by a verified statement of the person to be employed setting forth the person's connections with the debtor, creditors, any other party in interest, their respective attorneys and accountants, the United States trustee, or any person employed in the office of the United States trustee. . . .

11. *See* Code § 330.

12. *See* Code § 329.

13. For more on this topic, see Chapter 6. For more information on engagement letters, see Chapters 10 and 11.

IV. *The Three Cs: Competency, Confidentiality, and Conflicts (Avoidance of)*

In order to represent a client well, a lawyer should remember the Three Cs:

- providing *competent* representation,
- keeping client *confidences,* and
- avoiding *conflicts* of interest.

Although there are many other ethics rules, a lawyer who is conscious of the Three Cs will likely stay on the straight and narrow.

A. Competency

Under Model Rule 1.1, "[a] lawyer shall provide competent representation to a client. Competent representation requires the legal knowledge, skill, thoroughness and preparation reasonably necessary for the representation." Woe befalls a lawyer who thinks that she can just start representing a debtor or creditor in a bankruptcy case without understanding the Bankruptcy Code. Bankruptcy is a specialty practice, and bankruptcy lawyer wanna-bes often find themselves in trouble because they don't understand various terms of art that more experienced bankruptcy practitioners use. Moreover, thanks to the BRA, there are countless new traps for the novice bankruptcy lawyer.[14] Your mantra: when in doubt, ask someone who knows bankruptcy law. Don't hurt your client—or yourself—by pretending that you know more than you do.

Competency issues are more likely in consumer cases, not because consumer bankruptcy lawyers aren't smart (they are), but because there tend to be fewer bankruptcy lawyer wanna-bes in high-stakes Chapter 11 cases.

B. Confidentiality

Under Model Rule 1.6:

(a) A lawyer shall not reveal information relating to the representation of a client unless the client gives informed consent, the disclosure is impliedly authorized in order to carry out the representation or the disclosure is permitted by paragraph (b).

---

14.   For specific issues that you will face if you represent a consumer debtor, *see, e.g.,* American Bar Association, Business Law Section's Ad Hoc Committee on Bankruptcy Court Structure and Insolvency Processes, Task Force on Attorney Discipline, *Report: Attorney Liability Under § 707(b)(4) of the Bankruptcy Abuse Prevention and Consumer Protection Act of 2005* (Oct. 6, 2005).

(b) A lawyer may reveal information relating to the representation of a client to the extent the lawyer reasonably believes necessary:

(1) to prevent reasonably certain death or substantial bodily harm;

(2) to prevent the client from committing a crime or fraud that is reasonably certain to result in substantial injury to the financial interests or property of another and in furtherance of which the client has used or is using the lawyer's services;

(3) to prevent, mitigate or rectify substantial injury to the financial interests or property of another that is reasonably certain to result or has resulted from the client's commission of a crime or fraud in furtherance of which the client has used the lawyer's services;

(4) to secure legal advice about the lawyer's compliance with these Rules;

(5) to establish a claim or defense on behalf of the lawyer in a controversy between the lawyer and the client, to establish a defense to a criminal charge or civil claim against the lawyer based upon conduct in which the client was involved, or to respond to allegations in any proceeding concerning the lawyer's representation of the client; or

(6) to comply with other law or a court order.

The *raison d'etre* of the confidentiality rule is to encourage a client to tell his lawyer everything, even embarrassing things, so that the lawyer can best represent the client. Will a client tell you everything? Probably not, especially if you don't ask the right questions (see competency discussion above).

C. Conflicts of Interest

This issue is explained more fully above.

My research indicates that different types of bankruptcy practice tend to implicate different ethics rules. Conflicts of interest are less likely in consumer cases (but beware of issues involving family and friends) than they are in business cases.

V. Money, Money, Money, Money—MONEY![15] (Reasonable Fees)

If you're planning on getting paid by any client, here are four things to keep in mind:

1. All attorneys must keep their fees *reasonable,* per each state's ethics rules. No matter how tempting "fees without work" might be (or any other arrangement), remember that all fees are bounded by reasonableness, whether or not the fees are being paid from estate funds.

---

15. This is an old O'Jays song. *See* http://primetimetv.about.com/cs/lyrics/a/theapprentice.htm.

2. Fees being paid from estate funds are, of course, also bounded by various provisions in the Bankruptcy Code, the Rules, and any local rules. These provisions include (a) court appointment of professionals (§ 327), and (b) compliance with guidelines set by the particular bankruptcy court, the U.S. Trustee's office, or the district court (if the bankruptcy court hasn't spoken).

3. Communication is key. If you get the sense that the court, the U.S. Trustee, the client, or a creditor just "ain't happy," then you should try to touch base with the appropriate people to get a feel for why there's a problem. Sometimes the unhappiness is caused when people don't understand how expensive it is to resolve problems via the legal system. Sometimes, though, it's because the lawyer really *did* do something wrong, for example, by charging too much for routine work, by missing an important deadline, by charging over the market price for expenses (like faxes or copying costs), or by not returning a client's phone calls in a timely manner. Ethics issues often get raised in the medium of fee disputes.

WARNING!! ▬

Courts can approve fee enhancements for extraordinary work, but courts can also approve fee *reductions* for poor work. Don't assume that any interim fees are equivalent to final fees—the court has the power to issue reductions in its final fee order.

VI. What the Heck Is "Bankruptcy Assistance," Anyway?

According to Code § 101(4A):

[t]he term 'bankruptcy assistance' means any goods or services sold or otherwise provided to an assisted person [itself a term of art, defined in § 101(3)] with the express or implied purpose of providing information, advice, counsel, document preparation, or filing, or attendance at a creditors' meeting or appearing in a case or proceeding on behalf of another or providing legal representation with respect to a case or proceeding under this title.[16]

---

16. Congress decided to use single quotation marks, instead of the more proper double quotation marks, in its definitions section. I'm sure that Lynne Truss, of *Eats, Shoots, and Leaves*, would not be amused.

That's a pretty expansive definition, so let's parse it in terms of seeing what counts as bankruptcy assistance under the BRA and what counts as legal advice under state law.

This issue is a tough one. Think of legal advice as a continuum. On one side of the continuum is technical legal advice, such as whether something is or is not a preference. On the other side is purely business advice, such as whether the font used in an advertisement looks good. Somewhere in the middle is legal advice embedded inside business advice ("you could do it, but it would be wrong").[17] Defining legal advice is "squishy," at best, but it probably involves using a lawyer's training in substantive law and in other, related areas, such as business, economics, sociology, and psychology, to come up with the best resolution of an issue.

"Bankruptcy assistance," thanks to Congress, is not nearly as "squishy" a concept. It's very broad:

- any goods or services sold or otherwise provided
- to an assisted person
- with the express or implied purpose of providing
  - information,
  - advice,
  - counsel,
  - document preparation, or
  - filing,
- or attendance at a creditors' meeting or
- appearing in a case or proceeding on behalf of another or
- providing legal representation with respect to a case or proceeding under this title.

The concepts of "legal advice" and "bankruptcy assistance" intersect without overlapping completely. If I teach a bankruptcy course to our students and speak to them about the nondischargeability of their student loans, I'm not giving them legal advice, because they have no expectation that I am representing them in a lawyer-client relationship—and that relationship is a necessary precursor to the provision of legal advice.[18] But because the definition of

---

17. No, I'm not trying to channel President Nixon's famous quote here. Another, better version is from former Secretary of State and Nobel Laureate Elihu Root: "The law lets you do it, but don't. . . . It's a rotten thing to do."

18. Don't sigh with relief about that "necessary precursor" business. The creation of a lawyer-client relationship is amazingly easy to do—if the client reasonably thinks that you are his lawyer and seeks your advice, you *are* his lawyer, even if you never asked him for money, never sent him an engagement letter, and never took any formal action to open his case. (It's a good thing that asking our advice at cocktail parties doesn't create a "reasonable" belief that a lawyer-client relationship has been created!)

bankruptcy assistance is so broad, and because most law students would qualify as assisted persons under § 101(3), my advice is "bankruptcy assistance" and I'm a "debt relief agency."[19] Does this result make sense? No. There should be arenas in which information given to consumers doesn't trigger the BRA. But in the meantime, I'm planning on telling our associate dean that I'll be sticking to the Professional Responsibility course that I currently teach, rather than moving back into the Basic Bankruptcy course.

Exhibit 7-4

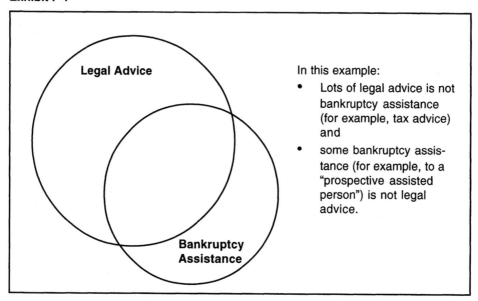

In this example:

- Lots of legal advice is not bankruptcy assistance (for example, tax advice) and

- some bankruptcy assistance (for example, to a "prospective assisted person") is not legal advice.

VII. The Pen Is Mightier Than the Sword: Rule 11 of the Federal Rules of Civil Procedure and Bankruptcy Rule 9011

One of the things that will get a lawyer into trouble quickly is failing to investigate an allegation properly before filing a pleading, motion, or other paper. Both Rule 11[20] and its bankruptcy equivalent, Rule 9011, essentially

---

19.   This issue is discussed at length in Chapter 4.
20.   Rule 11 provides:

Signing of Pleadings, Motions, and Other Papers; Representations to Court; Sanctions

. . . .

(b) Representations to Court. By presenting to the court (whether by signing, filing, submitting, or later advocating) a pleading, written motion, or other paper, an attorney or unrepresented party is certifying that to the best of the person's knowledge, information, and belief, formed after an inquiry reasonable under the circumstances,

require a lawyer's signature to be as good as (or, in cases of a bad lawyer, better than) her word. Both rules give the party whose filed document is being attacked up to 21 days to retract the document before the court may entertain a motion for sanctions.[21]

> (1) it is not being presented for any improper purpose, such as to harass or to cause unnecessary delay or needless increase in the cost of litigation;
> (2) the claims, defenses, and other legal contentions therein are warranted by existing law or by a nonfrivolous argument for the extension, modification, or reversal of existing law or the establishment of new law;
> (3) the allegations and other factual contentions have evidentiary support or, if specifically so identified, are likely to have evidentiary support after a reasonable opportunity for further investigation or discovery; and
> (4) the denials of factual contentions are warranted on the evidence or, if specifically so identified, are reasonably based on a lack of information or belief.
>
> (c) Sanctions. If, after notice and a reasonable opportunity to respond, the court determines that subdivision (b) has been violated, the court may, subject to the conditions stated below, impose an appropriate sanction upon the attorneys, law firms, or parties that have violated subdivision (b) or are responsible for the violation.
>
> > (1) How Initiated.
> >
> > (A) By Motion. A motion for sanctions under this rule shall be made separately from other motions or requests and shall describe the specific conduct alleged to violate subdivision (b). It shall be served as provided in Rule 5, but shall not be filed with or presented to the court unless, within 21 days after service of the motion (or such other period as the court may prescribe), the challenged paper, claim, defense, contention, allegation, or denial is not withdrawn or appropriately corrected. If warranted, the court may award to the party prevailing on the motion the reasonable expenses and attorney's fees incurred in presenting or opposing the motion. Absent exceptional circumstances, a law firm shall be held jointly responsible for violations committed by its partners, associates, and employees.
> >
> > (B) On Court's Initiative. On its own initiative, the court may enter an order describing the specific conduct that appears to violate subdivision (b) and directing an attorney, law firm, or party to show cause why it has not violated subdivision (b) with respect thereto. . . .

21.   Failure to wait the 21 days before filing the motion (already served) with the court will jeopardize the motion for sanctions. *See, e.g., In re* Kitchin, 327 B.R. 337, 360 (Bankr. N.D. Ill. 2005) ("Several Courts have found that failure to follow the safe harbor provision requires denial of a sanctions motion.") (citations omitted).

Note that, under the BRA, consumer lawyers must be extremely careful. For example, under new § 707(b)(4):

(C) The signature of an attorney on a petition, pleading, or written motion shall constitute a certification that the attorney has—
    (i) performed a *reasonable investigation* into the circumstances that gave rise to the petition, pleading, or written motion; and
    (ii) determined that the petition, pleading, or written motion—
        (I) is well grounded in fact; and
        (II) is warranted by existing law or a good faith argument for the extension, modification, or reversal of existing law and does not constitute an abuse under paragraph (1).
(D) The signature of an attorney on the petition shall constitute a *certification that the attorney has no knowledge after an inquiry* that the information in the schedules filed with such petition is incorrect.[22]

The italicized phrases above should strike fear into the heart of any consumer debtor's attorney, even though they look innocuous. There's no good case law yet that will give a lawyer a sense of comfort that her pre-filing discussions with the debtor will pass muster, but there is a great discussion in Chapter 13 on § 707(b). My advice: if something that the debtor tells you doesn't ring true, investigate further if at all possible. Failure to act as a reasonable bankruptcy lawyer would act will cost you.[23]

VIII. Just When You Thought It Was Safe to Go Back in the Water: You're a Debt-Relief Agency!

Lawyers representing consumer debtors are now, thanks to the BRA, "debt relief agencies."[24] Chapter 4 covers who actually fits the debt relief agency definition, and Chapters 9 and 11 include guidance on what debt relief agencies must, and may not, do. As a "debt relief agency," you must

---

22.   Emphasis added. Chapter 13 discusses these provisions in detail.

23.   *See, e.g., In re* Bailey, 321 B.R. 169 (Bankr. E.D. Pa. 2005) (client omitted several prior filings from her conversations with her attorney, and attorney found a "bar order" prohibiting more filings, yet continued to prepare a new filing); Grunewalt v. Mutual Life Ins. Co. (*In re* Coones Ranch), 7 F.3d 740 (8th Cir. 1993) (filing a Chapter 11 proceeding four days after debtor had incorporated was a suspicious circumstance that the lawyer should have investigated; filing was deemed to have been in bad faith).

24.   Section 101(12A) defines a "debt relief agency" as "any person who provides any bankruptcy assistance to an assisted person in return for the payment of money or other valuable consideration, or who is a bankruptcy petition preparer under section 110 [with some exceptions not relevant here]."

comply with §§ 526-528.[25] As such, under § 527, you must "Mirandize" your debtor client, in writing, informing him that:

- any information that he or she provides must be truthful;
- he or she must disclose all assets and liabilities;
- his or her current monthly income and disposable income need to be stated accurately; and
- his or her information can be audited.

Moreover, thanks to § 527(b), Congress has now given you new material to provide to your consumer clients in a clear and conspicuous writing,[26] and § 528 has provided you with an outline of what your engagement letter should say, including the following statement: "We are a debt relief agency. We help people file for bankruptcy relief under the Bankruptcy Code."[27]

IX. Am I My Client's Keeper? Reaffirmations under the BRA

The BRA changes the relationship between lawyer and client dramatically with a new provision that makes the lawyer essentially the guarantor of the client's reaffirmation agreement.[28] Under amended § 524(c):

> An agreement between a holder of a claim and the debtor, the consideration for which, in whole or in part, is based on a debt that is dischargeable in a case under this title is enforceable only to any extent enforceable under applicable nonbankruptcy law, whether or not discharge of such debt is waived, only if—
>
> . . . .
>
> (3) such agreement has been filed with the court and, if applicable, accompanied by a declaration or an *affidavit of the attorney that represented the debtor during the course of negotiating an agreement under this subsection,* which states that—
>
> (A) such agreement represents a fully informed and voluntary agreement by the debtor;

---

25. Even if you represent a creditor, you might be held to be a debt relief agency. See Chapters 4 and 15, and Catherine E. Vance & Corinne Cooper, *Nine Traps and One Slap: Attorney Liability Under the New Bankruptcy Law,* 79 Am. Bankr. L.J. 283, 295 (2005) ("Lawyers who do no more than fill out a proof of claim form on behalf of their consumer clients could get swept into the torture chamber Congress has created. 'Document preparation,' without more, appears to be enough to constitute 'bankruptcy assistance.'").

26. You can find a complete discussion of the new "notice" issues in Chapter 11.

27. BRA Section 229, adding Code § 528, especially subsection 528(d). See Chapter 9 for a discussion of this provision. Although there is an argument that the engagement letter does not need the "Scarlet Letter" language, it's a good idea to include it.

28. Reaffirmations are discussed in detail in Chapter 14.

(B) *such agreement does not impose an undue hardship on the debtor or a dependent of the debtor;* and

(C) the attorney fully advised the debtor of the legal effect and consequences of—

    (i)   an agreement of the kind specified in this subsection; and

    (ii) any default under such an agreement. . . .[29]

Lawyers have always had the obligation to think critically about the information that a client has given them and to investigate further if the information seems bogus. But lawyers have never had to act as the guarantors of a client's decision. Under Model Rule 1.2(a), "a lawyer shall abide by a client's decisions concerning the objectives of representation." So if your client decides—foolishly—to reaffirm a debt, and you don't withdraw from the representation (see below), now you're on the hook with a certification. Withdrawal might not be easy, but if you're not comfortable with the client's decision, don't sign anything that implies (let alone states) that you believe that your client's choice to reaffirm is a good idea.[30]

X. *The Final Word: Withdrawal*

What if, after reading this book, you decide to get out of the consumer bankruptcy business and enter a new, less stressful profession, such as air traffic control? Just remember one last thing: you can't abandon your clients once you've taken on their representation without withdrawing from that representation.[31] Until you withdraw, you must be diligent in representing them,[32] even at a high cost to (and a high risk of potential liability for) yourself. Thanks to the BRA, all of these new demands on lawyers—especially consumer bankruptcy lawyers—have added increased costs and stress. Depressed? Well, the only good news I can offer is that every consumer bankruptcy lawyer is going through the same feelings that you are.

Those who think that law is mostly a business would advise you right now to get out: if the profit margins (small enough, even before the BRA) have declined to the point where your income isn't sufficient to balance out your risks, don't stay in the business. If, however, law is more of a profession—a calling—then my guess is that you'll stay in "the biz," at least for now, hoping that the BRA pendulum eventually swings back to center.

---

29.   Emphasis added. *See also* Code § 524(k)(5) (attorney certifies that the debtor can make the payments).

30.   *See also* Chapter 14.

31.   *See* MODEL RULE OF PROF'L CONDUCT 1.16 for the rules concerning withdrawal.

32.   *See, e.g.,* MODEL RULE OF PROF'L CONDUCT 1.3 concerning diligence.

CHAPTER 8

Constitutionality of the
Attorney Liability Provisions
of the Bankruptcy Reform Act

by Erwin Chemerinsky and Barbara Glesner Fines

The attorney liability provisions of the Bankruptcy Abuse Prevention and Consumer Protection Act of 2005 (BRA)[1] will present many attorneys with a difficult choice if they decide to continue to advise clients about bankruptcy: either challenge these provisions or risk conceding important rights and professional independence. The constitutional implications of the BRA look like a table of contents in a constitutional law treatise:[2]

- First Amendment issues arise because of the ways in which attorneys must alter their advertising and the limitations on the advice they may give their clients;
- Privacy rights of clients may be infringed because of the debtor disclosure requirements;
- Equal protection questions are raised by the "means test"; and
- Separation of powers and Tenth Amendment limitations may invalidate the limits on certain judicial actions and the Act's regulation of attorneys.

This Chapter targets two specific First Amendment issues in the BRA's regulation of individual attorneys: the advertising requirements and the restrictions on attorney advice-giving. The Chapter suggests arguments and approaches to challenging these restrictions.

---

1. S. 256, Pub. L. No. 109-8, 119 Stat. 23 (2005). Unless otherwise indicated, citations to the Bankruptcy Code (the Code) are to 11 U.S.C. §§ 101 *et seq.*, as amended by the BRA.

2. For a more comprehensive analysis of all of these constitutional issues, *see* Erwin Chemerinsky, *Constitutional Issues Posed in the Bankruptcy Abuse Prevention and Consumer Protection Act of 2005*, 79 Am. BANKR. L.J. 571 (2005).

**Two Essential Cases for Challenging
Attorney Advertising Restrictions**

- *Zauderer v. Office of Disciplinary Counsel of Supreme Court*, 471 U.S. 626, 639 (1985), involved an Ohio attorney who was disciplined for advertising legal services for women injured by the Dalkon Shield IUD. The Court held that the advertisement was not false or deceptive because the attorney never promised litigation would be successful or that he had any special expertise in handling lawsuits involving the Dalkon Shield. The Court rejected the attorney's contention that state advertising disclosure requirements must use the least restrictive means in order to conform with the First Amendment. The Court held an attorney's rights as an advertiser are adequately protected as long as disclosure requirements are reasonably related to the state's interest in preventing the deception of consumers. The opinion emphasized, however, that unjustified or unduly burdensome disclosure requirements might offend the First Amendment by chilling protected commercial speech.

- In *In re R.M.J.*, 455 U.S. 191 (1982), the Supreme Court held that a state's disciplinary rule that limited the areas of practice an attorney could include in advertisements to one or more of a list of 23 and provided no flexibility in phrasing these practice areas was an invalid restriction upon speech. The attorney advertised using the terms "personal injury" and "real estate" instead of the required terms "tort law" and "property law," and he listed areas of practice, such as "contract" and "zoning & land use," that were not authorized by the regulation. The Court found the restrictions unconstitutional because the listing published by the attorney had not been shown to be misleading, and the committee of the state's highest court responsible for prosecuting attorney disciplinary proceedings had suggested no substantial state interest served by the rule's restriction.

I. BRA's Regulation of Attorney Advertising

Under Code §§ 526, 527, and 528, a lawyer who provides any "bankruptcy assistance"[3] to an "assisted person"[4] is deemed a "debt relief agency."[5]

---

3.   "Bankruptcy assistance" means any goods or services sold or otherwise provided to an assisted person with the express or implied purpose of providing information, advice, counsel, document preparation, or filing, or attendance at a creditors' meeting or appearing in a case or proceeding on behalf of another or providing legal representation with respect to a case or proceeding under this title. BRA Section 226(a)(2), adding Code § 101(4A).

4.   "The term 'assisted person' means any person whose debts consist primarily of consumer debts and the value of whose nonexempt property is less than $150,000." BRA Section 226(a)(1), adding Code § 101(3).

5.   Code § 101(12A), added by BRA Section 226(a)(3), defines a debt relief agency as

Because the BRA speaks of "persons" rather than "debtors," attorney interaction with a wide range of clients can bring them within the definition of a debt relief agency. Just about any middle- or low-income person who walks into your office could be an "assisted person." If their debt is mostly consumer debt and their assets are limited, they are likely to be "assisted persons." Give that person some assistance regarding bankruptcy—their own or someone else's—and you've become a "debt relief agency." The assisted person might be a landlord seeking advice about his rights in the bankruptcy case of a tenant, a family member seeking protection from claims that a bankruptcy debtor transferred property to her fraudulently, a domestic relations client being counseled to see a bankruptcy attorney in connection with a divorce, or even a creditor making a claim in a bankruptcy case.[6]

Having been transformed into a DRA, you now have certain restrictions on any advertisement of services related to bankruptcy, credit defaults, mortgage foreclosures, evictions, or debt problems. Regardless of what you actually do for your clients, you now must advertise that: "We are a debt relief agency. We help people file for bankruptcy relief under the Bankruptcy Code."[7]

Suppose you don't want to include that statement in your advertising. Suppose you think it is inaccurate, because in fact you represent creditors or you help parents collect child support. Suppose you do represent debtors, but you think people who are looking for a range of options for dealing with debt will be discouraged from seeking your assistance because they will think bankruptcy is the only option you provide. Or perhaps you think the average consumer who sees this statement will not understand that you are an attorney and may confuse you with document preparation services. You may decide to challenge the constitutionality of this advertising directive.

"any person who provides any bankruptcy assistance to an assisted person in return for the payment of money or other valuable consideration, or who is a bankruptcy petition preparer under section 110," subject to certain exclusions.

   6.   For a more detailed discussion of this problem, see Chapter 4.

   7.   BRA Section 229, adding Code § 528(a)(4) & (b)(2)(B).

The Alternative to a Constitutional Challenge:
Getting Out of the Bankruptcy Business

If your practice involves providing information about bankruptcy but you don't actually represent clients in bankruptcy actions, you may avoid the liability provisions of BRA by simply refusing to give any information on bankruptcy to your clients. To protect yourself from claims of negligence for failing to inform clients of their rights and obligations under bankruptcy law, you should specifically limit the scope of your representation in your representation agreement. You might state, for example:

> "You understand and agree that I will not be providing you with information or advice regarding any bankruptcy law, even if bankruptcy issues are relevant to this representation. If you want advice about how bankruptcy law affects your case, I will be happy to provide you with a list of attorneys who can provide this advice."

The First Amendment protects attorney advertising as commercial speech.[8] Commercial speech that is false or misleading may be freely regulated.[9] As with any other speech, reasonable restrictions on the time, place, and manner of lawyer advertising are permissible.[10] Content regulation, however, is unconstitutional unless it meets the commercial speech test of *Central Hudson Gas & Electric Corporation v. Public Service Commission of New York.*[11]

> In commercial speech cases, then, a four-part analysis has developed. At the outset, we must determine whether the expression is protected by the First Amendment. For commercial speech to come within that provision, it at least must concern lawful activity and not be misleading. Next, we ask whether the asserted governmental interest is substantial. If both inquiries yield positive answers, we must determine whether the regulation directly advances the governmental interest asserted, and whether it is not more extensive than is necessary to serve that interest.[12]

Attorney advertising of bankruptcy services is within the realm of protected commercial speech. It does not concern illegal activity, nor is it inherently misleading. Thus, the first task in applying the *Central Hudson* test

---

8.   Bates v. State Bar of Arizona, 433 U.S. 350, 356 (1977).

9.   "Advertising that is false, deceptive, or misleading of course is subject to restraint. Since the advertiser knows his product and has a commercial interest in its dissemination, we have little worry that regulation to assure truthfulness will discourage protected speech." *Id.* at 383 (citation omitted).

10.   *Id.* at 384.

11.   447 U.S. 557 (1980).

12.   *Id.* at 566.

becomes anticipating what governmental interest the restriction on advertising might be serving. The court must restrict its analysis to the interests identified by the government. If the court finds one of those proffered interests "substantial," that's enough to satisfy the first prong of the test.[13] In the context of attorney commercial speech, the Court has considered a very few state interests to be substantial. These are the interest in maintaining standards of licensed professionals,[14] in preserving the reputation of the legal profession,[15] and in protecting the privacy and decision making of consumers.[16]

The most common justification, however, is that restrictions are designed to prevent deception. In this context, the U.S. Supreme Court has held that misstatements that might be overlooked in other advertising may be especially harmful given the public's lack of sophistication regarding legal services.[17] While soap manufacturers may advertise that they are "powerful" or "best," attorneys may not. Claims as to the quality of services are not easily subject to measurement or verification, and therefore are more likely to be so misleading as to warrant restriction.[18] In cases involving required disclosures or disclaimers in attorney advertising, a number of disclaimer requirements have been upheld under the *Central Hudson* test, all justified as advancing a substantial governmental interest in preventing misleading, deceptive or predatory speech.[19] For example, most states require that direct mail advertising include a statement indicating that the material is an advertisement.[20]

---

13.   Fla. Bar v. Went For It, Inc., 515 U.S. 618, 624-25 (1995); *see also* Rubin v. Coors Brewing Co., 514 U.S. 476, 485 (1995) (deeming only one of the government's proffered interests "substantial").

14.   Ohralik v. Ohio State Bar Ass'n, 436 U.S. 447, 460 (1978); Fla. Bar v. Went For It, 515 U.S. 618, 624 (1995).

15.   *Id. But see* Zauderer v. Office of Disciplinary Counsel, 471 U.S. 626 (1985) (noting that the state has a substantial interest in ensuring dignified behavior in the courtroom, but that the state's interest in the protection of the dignity of the legal profession was not substantial enough to justify restricting free speech rights under the First Amendment).

16.   In contrast to advertising restrictions, restrictions on face-to-face solicitation are often justified on grounds that consumers are less likely to make informed choices and more likely to succumb to "fraud, undue influence, intimidation, overreaching, and other forms of 'vexatious conduct,' by attorneys soliciting employment." Ohralik v. Ohio State Bar Ass'n, 436 U.S. 447, 460 (1978); moreover, solicitation is usually private and therefore more difficult to police. These concerns have provided the basis for courts to approve more expansive regulation and even flat bans on this form of commercial speech. Fla. Bar v. Went For It, Inc., 515 U.S. 618, 624-25 (1995). The BRA's advertising restrictions do not appear to be directed toward in-person solicitation and its related governmental interests.

17.   *Bates* at 375.

18.   *Id.* at 384.

19.   *In re* R.M.J., 455 U.S. 191, 201 (1982).

20.   Leoni v. Cal. State Bar, 39 Cal. 3d 609, 704 P.2d 183, 217 Cal. Rptr. 423 (1985), *appeal dismissed*, 475 U.S. 1001 (1986).

It seems likely that the government would argue that the BRA's advertising directives are justified by an interest in reducing confusion or deception of consumers. Requiring that debt relief agencies expressly indicate that they provide bankruptcy assistance reduces the risk that consumers may be misled regarding the nature of the services the agencies provide. There is little doubt but that the courts would accept this interest as a substantial one.

However, no matter how substantial an interest is in the abstract, the restriction must directly and materially advance that interest and must be "narrowly drawn."[21] "The regulation may not be sustained if it provides only ineffective or remote support for the government's purpose."[22] In other words, the government may not justify a restriction on speech supported by "mere speculation or conjecture; rather, a governmental body seeking to sustain a restriction on commercial speech must demonstrate that the harms it recites are real and that its restriction will in fact alleviate them to a material degree."[23]

Thus, the question becomes whether the government can provide evidence that consumers are in fact being misled or deceived. There is no such evidence in the Congressional Record supporting the BRA. The little empirical evidence available on bankruptcy attorney advertising both supports and undermines this assumption. While it is true that many attorneys avoid using the term "bankruptcy" in their advertisements, research discloses that these attorneys are not trying to mislead consumers by luring them into their offices with the promise that there is an "easier out" than bankruptcy. Rather, consumer bankruptcy attorneys report that they avoid the term because consumers already have so many negative and false beliefs about bankruptcy that they are reluctant to seek it as a solution.[24] The risk that consumers would approach an attorney for assis-

---

21.   *See* R.M.J., 455 U.S. at 203 (holding that in order for a state to regulate non-misleading attorney advertising, the state must assert a substantial interest and the interference with speech must be in proportion to the interest served). The Court also noted that "[a]lthough the potential for deception and confusion is particularly strong in the context of advertising professional services, restrictions upon such advertising may be no broader than reasonably necessary to prevent the deception." *Id. See also* Zauderer v. Office of Disciplinary Counsel of Supreme Court of Ohio, 471 U.S. 626 (1985) (indicating that attorney advertising was covered by the doctrine that commercial speech that is not false or deceptive and does not concern unlawful activities may be restricted only in the service of a substantial governmental interest, and only through means that directly advance that interest); Shapero v. Ky. Bar Ass'n, 486 U.S. 466 (1988) (observing that state regulation of lawyer advertising may extend only as far as the interest such regulation serves).

22.   Central Hudson Gas & Electric Corp., 447 U.S. at 564.

23.   Edenfield v. Fane, 507 U.S. 761, 770-71 (1993), *citing* Zauderer v. Office of Disciplinary Counsel of Supreme Court of Ohio, 471 U.S. 626, 648-49 (1985).

24.   Jean Braucher, *Lawyers and Consumer Bankruptcy: One Code, Many Cultures,* 67 AM. BANKR. L.J. 501, 553-54 (1993) (noting that on balance, most clients come to bankruptcy attorneys with negative misinformation about bankruptcy, often conveyed to them by bill

tance with debt restructuring and be unaware that the attorney may, if appropriate, counsel bankruptcy seems a slim risk indeed.

Even if there are situations in which debtors may be confused or deceived about the nature of advertising offering assistance with debt relief, the Court has held that advertising restrictions must be "narrowly drawn"[25] to the proffered justification. For example, many states require disclaimers when an advertised specialization is not certified by the state bar. But at least one court has struck down as too broad a requirement that a lawyer advertising a limited practice must include a statement that he is not a certified specialist.[26]

If you challenge these restrictions, you might argue that the new "debt relief agency" provisions do not directly and materially advance the interest in protecting consumers. You may argue that the required advertising statements will actually create more confusion among debtors seeking assistance because there are many instances in which the required statement does not accurately describe the attorney's services. Because the overbreadth doctrine does not apply to commercial speech,[27] you cannot bring facial challenges to the regulation but must show that, in your practice, the regulation is not narrowly drawn to advance the government interest.

collectors. "Many clients come with 'foggy ideas,' as one lawyer put it, or with outright misinformation, most commonly obtained from creditors who have tried to scare debtors about bankruptcy.").

25. *See In re* R.M.J. 455 U.S. 191, 203 (1982) (holding that in order for a state to regulate non-misleading attorney advertising, the state must assert a substantial interest, and the interference with speech must be in proportion to the interest served). The Court also noted that "[a]lthough the potential for deception and confusion is particularly strong in the context of advertising professional services, restrictions upon such advertising may be no broader than reasonably necessary to prevent the deception." *Id. See also* Zauderer v. Office of Disciplinary Counsel of Supreme Court, 471 U.S. 626 (1985) (indicating that attorney advertising was covered by the doctrine that commercial speech that is not false or deceptive and does not concern unlawful activities may be restricted only in the service of a substantial governmental interest, and only through means that directly advance that interest); Shapero v. Ky. Bar Ass'n, 486 U.S. 466 (1988) (observing that state regulation of lawyer advertising may extend only as far as the interest such regulation serves).

26. Spencer v. Hon. Justices of the Sup. Ct. of Pa., 379 F. Supp. 880 (E.D. Pa. 1984). *See also* Lyon v. Ala. State Bar, 451 So. 2d 1367 (Ala. 1984), in which the Alabama Supreme Court reviewed the state requirement that attorneys include the following disclaimer in their advertising: "No representation is made about the quality of legal services to be performed or the expertise of the lawyer performing such services." The court upheld the constitutionality of this disclaimer as advancing a substantial interest in preventing the public from being misled. *Accord*, Mezrano v. Ala. State Bar, 434 So. 2d 732 (Ala. 1983). *See generally* 81:401 ABA/BNA LAWYERS MANUAL ON PROFESSIONAL CONDUCT, *Advertising and Solicitation, Restrictions and Disclaimers* (2003).

27. Village of Hoffman Estates v. Flipsides Hoffman Estates, Inc., 455 U.S. 489, 496-97 (1982) (overbreadth does not apply in commercial speech cases).

Some attorneys might argue that the regulation actually requires them to make inaccurate or confusing statements in their advertising. Entities that represent creditors might be deemed debt relief agencies under the broad language of the provisions. Clearly, these creditors' lawyers will have a strong argument that their First Amendment rights are violated when they have to make the false statement, "We are a debt relief agency. We help people file for bankruptcy." The statement would be obviously inaccurate for any attorneys who provide information about bankruptcy when representing clients in other matters—for example, divorce, property transactions or business advice. In light of the Supreme Court's decisions in other attorney advertising cases,[28] any compulsory disclosures are of questionable constitutionality, especially when the government is requiring false statements.

Any attorney might claim that the required "debt relief agency" label is inaccurate and confusing. The BRA fails to distinguish between attorneys and non-attorneys providing bankruptcy services. Yet under current law, only attorneys are permitted to give legal advice, file pleadings, or represent debtors in bankruptcy hearings. Also, unlike non-attorney bankruptcy petition preparers, only attorneys are licensed by the state in which they practice, bound by ethical requirements, and subject to discipline by the courts in which they practice. Finally, only communications between debtor and attorney are protected by the attorney-client privilege. As a result, the provisions are likely to confuse the public, since both attorneys and non-attorney bankruptcy petition preparers are required to use identical language to advertise themselves as "debt relief agencies."

WARNING!!

Attorneys should carefully examine their state's advertising regulations to determine whether advertising as a "debt relief agency" generates additional disclaimer requirements.

---

28.   See discussion of *R.M.J.*, above at note 21.

**Beware the Alternative to a Constitutional Challenge:
Advertising as a Debt Relief Agency**

Just exactly how will you advertise yourself as a "debt relief agency"?

- Some attorneys will use the language of the BRA verbatim.
- Some will include the required language and then provide explanations of the term.
- Others appear to be using the designation as a positive statement of specialization or certification. For example, attorneys might advertise, "We Are a Designated Debt Relief Agency Under Federal Law" or "The law office of X is a federally-designated debt relief agency pursuant to Title 11 of the U.S. Code."

While all these disclaimers clearly comply with the BRA, they may run afoul of state advertising restrictions. The ABA Model Rules of Professional Conduct allow attorneys to advertise that they practice in certain areas of law, but Rule 7.4(d) provides that "A lawyer shall not state or imply that a lawyer is certified as a specialist in a particular field of law, unless: (1) the lawyer has been certified as a specialist by an organization that has been approved by an appropriate state authority or that has been accredited by the American Bar Association; and (2) the name of the certifying organization is clearly identified in the communication."

Most states have additional requirements, including disclaimers whenever one advertises a specialization or limitation of practice areas. In Texas, for example, an attorney who advertises practice in a specific area of law must include the phrase "Not Certified by the Texas Board of Legal Specialization" in advertisements. Texas Disciplinary Rules of Professional Conduct Rule 7.04(b)(3) (2005).

Attorneys should carefully examine their state's advertising regulations to determine whether advertising as a debt relief agency generates additional disclaimer requirements.

II. BRA's Prohibitions on Attorney Advice

When counseling clients, the BRA requires you to make some statements and prohibits others. These restrictions on advice strike even closer to the core of an attorney's First Amendment rights than do the advertising regulations. New Code §§ 527 and 528 require disclosures and statements to be made by a debt relief agency.[29] Within three business days of first offering to provide bankruptcy advice to an "assisted person," the debt relief agency

---

29. For more information on the required and prohibited communications, see Chapters 9 and 11.

must provide a clear and conspicuous written notice of a number of things relating to a contemplated bankruptcy filing. However, as we've seen, you may be deemed a DRA even if you are simply advising individuals about bankruptcy in situations in which your client would not be filing bankruptcy. In these situations, the required disclosures are irrelevant and inaccurate at best, if not affirmatively misleading and confusing.[30]

Worse, Code § 526 imposes restrictions on the kind of advice you can provide. Much of this prohibits specific misrepresentations,[31] adding nothing to the constraints on attorney speech that already exist under the rules of professional conduct.[32]

One provision, however, specifically prohibits advice to a client that would be accurate, legal, and appropriate—indeed, this may be information that any competent attorney would consider essential to ensuring that the client is fully informed.[33] Code § 526(a)(4) forbids the attorney from advising a client to incur any debt in contemplation of the bankruptcy.[34] The prohibition directly regulates the content of speech by lawyers to their clients.

This prohibition is particularly troubling when it might be completely legal and even desirable for the client to incur this debt. Suppose your client wants to obtain a mortgage or refinance an existing mortgage to obtain a

---

30.   For example, the DRA must provide the assisted person with a clear and conspicuous written notice that all information required to be provided by the assisted person during a bankruptcy case must be complete, accurate, and truthful; that all assets and liabilities must be completely disclosed; that "the replacement value of each asset as defined in section 506 must be stated in those documents where requested after reasonable inquiry to establish such value"; that current monthly income and disposable income are required to be disclosed after reasonable inquiry; that information an assisted person provides during a case may be audited; and that failure to provide such information may result in dismissal of the case or criminal sanctions. BRA Section 228(a), adding Code § 527(a)(2).

31.   Code § 526(a)(1) prohibits a debt relief agency from failing to perform any service that it had informed the assisted person that it would provide in connection with a case or proceeding under Title 11. Section 526(a)(2) prohibits a debt relief agency from making any untrue or misleading statement, or advising any assisted person to make any such untrue or misleading statement. Section 526(a)(3) prohibits a debt relief agency from misrepresenting to any assisted person the services that the agency will provide or the benefits and risks from being a debtor in a bankruptcy case.

32.   Attorneys are prohibited from engaging in "conduct involving dishonesty, fraud, deceit or misrepresentation." ABA MODEL RULES OF PROF'L CONDUCT R. 8.4(c) (2005).

32.   An attorney is required by the rules of professional conduct to "explain a matter to the extent reasonably necessary to permit the client to make informed decisions regarding the representation." ABA MODEL RULES OF PROF'L CONDUCT R. 4.1(b) (2005).

34.   BRA Section 227(a), adding Code § 526(a)(4) (a debt relief agency shall not "advise an assisted person to incur more debt in contemplation of such person filing a case under this title or to pay an attorney or bankruptcy petition preparer fee or charge for services performed as part of preparing for or representing a debtor in a case under this title").

lower interest rate. Suppose your client intends to pay this debt, even if he files for bankruptcy. He may intend to keep all payments fully current and to reaffirm the debt once the case is filed. Under the BRA, you are arguably required to discourage the client from incurring this debt and clearly may not suggest this as a possible means of achieving the client's goals.

You can't even advise your client about ways to pay your fee. Most of an attorney's fee for handling a Chapter 13 case is paid over time through the Chapter 13 plan. But that means that at the time the case is filed, the client has incurred additional debt in contemplation of filing a bankruptcy case. Indeed, this debt was specifically incurred for the purpose of paying the fees of the attorney filing the case. Under the BRA, you are prohibited from advising a client to take this appropriate, legal, and helpful approach to paying for your fees.

If you seek to challenge these restrictions on your advice-giving, you will have sound First Amendment precedent and public policy arguments on your side. The Supreme Court has been very protective of the First Amendment rights of attorneys to advise and zealously represent their clients.[35] Unlike the regulation of advertising, these regulations on your advice to clients are content-based restrictions of speech that will be reviewed with strict scrutiny. In *Turner Broadcasting System v. FCC*,[36] Justice Kennedy, writing for the majority, noted that "[g]overnment action that stifles speech on account of its message, or that requires the utterance of a particular message favored by the Government, contravenes this essential [First Amendment] right."[37] Justice Kennedy explained, "For these reasons, the First Amendment, subject only to narrow and well-understood exceptions, does not countenance governmental control over the content of messages expressed by private individuals."[38]

The BRA restrictions prevent lawyers from giving important, lawful information to their clients; these restrictions cannot be reconciled with the First Amendment. However, while you may succeed in having a court declare this provision unconstitutional, it will likely be as the BRA is applied, rather than on its face. In recent years, the Court has not readily upheld facial challenges to the constitutionality of federal laws.[39] The Court has said that a facial challenge requires demonstrating that *all* applications of

---

35. Legal Servs. Corp. v. Velazquez, 531 U.S. 533, 548-49 (2001).
36. 512 U.S. 622 (1994).
37. *Id.* at 641.
38. *Id.*
39. Sabri v. United States, 541 U.S. 600, 124 S. Ct. 1941, 1948-49 (2004).

the law would be unconstitutional.[40] That is not likely with regard to these provisions of the BRA.

Instead, courts are likely to hold that it is unconstitutional to prohibit lawyers from giving truthful, lawful information to their clients, and that it is unconstitutional to require attorneys to put false information in their advertisements. Nonetheless, for most of your representations, that will provide the freedom you need to continue to competently represent your clients.

III. Conclusion

As the BRA is implemented and its provisions are litigated, a plethora of constitutional issues will be raised.[41] For attorneys, the liability provisions are clearly subject to constitutional challenge as a violation of the First Amendment. These liability provisions present grim choices: don't talk bankruptcy with your client and thus limit the information and representation you can provide; ignore the speech restrictions of the BRA and face a host of penalties; or challenge the act as unconstitutional. It seems that the shared interest of the profession would favor attorneys taking this last approach.

---

40.   United States v. Salerno, 481 U.S. 739 (1987) ("A facial challenge to a legislative Act is, of course, the most difficult challenge to mount successfully, since the challenger must establish that no set of circumstances exists under which the Act would be valid. . . . [W]e have not recognized an 'overbreadth' doctrine outside the limited context of the First Amendment.") (due process challenge to the Bail Reform Act).

41.   For discussion of the pending cases, see Chapter 9.

CHAPTER 9

Drop the Yellow Pages and Put Your Hands in the Air! The Perils of Advertising Under the BRA

by Corinne Cooper

Attorneys experienced in consumer bankruptcy cases may be shocked to learn that liability problems loom before a client walks in your office. You cannot even advertise your services without the BRA governing your behavior. Under the BRA, debtors' attorneys are required by law to make several "disclosures" beginning with their advertisements.[1]

I. The Provisions[2]

Any attorney who fits the definition of a debt relief agency under the BRA must comply with its regulation of advertisements. If the attorney's advertisement is directed to the general public and:

- includes a description of bankruptcy assistance,[3] or
- uses language that could lead a reasonable consumer to believe that debt counseling is being offered when in fact the services are directed to providing bankruptcy assistance, or
- offers assistance with credit defaults, mortgage foreclosures, or eviction, excessive debt, debt collection pressure, or an inability to pay any consumer debt,

---

1. See Chapter 11 for a complete discussion of the required disclosures.

2. This Chapter is based on Catherine E. Vance & Corinne Cooper, *Nine Traps and One Slap: Attorney Liability under the New Bankruptcy Law*, 79 Am. Bankr. L.J. 283, 298-305 (2005). However, the conclusions about the impact of the provisions, particularly Code § 526(c)(1), are different in this Chapter from those presented in the article.

3. Including assistance in connection with a Chapter 13 plan, whether or not Chapter 13 is specifically mentioned. BRA Section 229(a), adding Code § 528(b)(1).

then the attorney is required to disclose that the services relate to bankruptcy and include this statement clearly and conspicuously in the advertisement:

> We are a debt relief agency. We help people file for bankruptcy relief under the Bankruptcy Code.[4]

There are two separate, though nearly identical, provisions on advertising.[5] These are among the most confusing and convoluted in the BRA (and that is saying a lot). Section 528(a) says that a debt relief agency shall:

> (3) clearly and conspicuously disclose in any advertisement of bankruptcy assistance services or of the benefits of bankruptcy directed to the general public (whether in general media, seminars or specific mailings, telephonic or electronic messages, or otherwise) that the services or benefits are with respect to bankruptcy relief under this title; and
> (4) clearly and conspicuously use the following statement in such advertisement: 'We are a debt relief agency. We help people file for bankruptcy relief under the Bankruptcy Code.' or a substantially similar statement.[6]

Subsection 528(b) states:

> (1) An advertisement of bankruptcy assistance services or of the benefits of bankruptcy directed to the general public includes—
>> (A) descriptions of bankruptcy assistance in connection with a chapter 13 plan whether or not chapter 13 is specifically mentioned in such advertisement; and
>> (B) statements such as 'federally supervised repayment plan' or 'Federal debt restructuring help' or other similar statements that could lead a reasonable consumer to believe that debt counseling was being offered when in fact the services were directed to providing bankruptcy assistance with a chapter 13 plan or other form of bankruptcy relief under this title.
> (2) An advertisement, directed to the general public, indicating that the debt relief agency provides assistance with respect to credit defaults, mortgage foreclosures, eviction proceedings, excessive debt, debt collection pressure, or inability to pay any consumer debt shall—
>> (A) disclose clearly and conspicuously in such advertisement that the assistance may involve bankruptcy relief under this title; and
>> (B) include the following statement: 'We are a debt relief agency. We help people file for bankruptcy relief under the Bankruptcy Code.' or a substantially similar statement.[7]

---

4.   BRA Section 229(a), adding Code § 528(a)(3)-(4) and (b).
5.   Both are found in BRA Section 229, adding Code § 528.
6.   BRA Section 229(a), adding Code § 528(a)(3)-(4) and (b).
7.   *See id.*

This whole provision reminds me of *The Scarlet Letter*. According to Congress, sinful bankruptcy attorneys must be branded in order to warn society of their wicked ways.

There's a lot of substance to complain about as well. First, you don't have to be a constitutional scholar to wonder about First Amendment issues.[8] Expect constitutional challenges of this provision (and others) mandating or prohibiting attorney speech.[9] Second, I confess that it is not precisely clear how these two subsections interact. To assist in the analysis, I developed a six-color, four-column, side-by-side comparison chart, highlighting the similar language in the two provisions, and I still can't make sense of it. The chart (sans color) is shown on the following page.

As you can see, there is a lot of duplication in the language of the two provisions. Whether subsections (a) and (b) are to be read together or whether each is intended to address only the advertisements specifically described within that subsection is a mystery.

---

8.   See Chapter 8. Here's what the author, Professor Barbara Glesner Fines, previously wrote about this issue:

> One obvious question emerges from this discussion of the attorney liability provisions. Can the Congress regulate, to this degree, the attorney-client relationship, a field historically left to the states? And specifically, are these proposals constitutional under the First Amendment? This section attempts to analyze just one part of that question, specifically, whether the advertising provisions violate the First Amendment.
>
> …
>
> [R]estrictions on consumer bankruptcy advertising would be constitutional only if the restrictions:
>
> • are justified by a government interest in preventing the significant possibility of consumer deception;
> • advance that interest; and
> • are narrowly tailored. . . .
>
> Without some demonstration that there is a significant risk of deception of consumers by attorneys in this field, the regulations imposed by the BRA are overbroad and a court is likely to find that they represent unjustified restrictions on the First Amendment expression by attorneys.

Corinne Cooper, Catherine E. Vance & Barbara Glesner Fines, Attorney Liability in Bankruptcy 9 (program materials from Bankruptcy Update, ABA Annual Meeting (2003)) (citations omitted).

9.   At the time of publication, several constitutional challenges had already been filed. *See, e.g.,* Milavetz, Callop and Milavetz, P.A. v. United States, Civ. No. 05-CV-2626RHK/AJB (D. Minn. 2005), *available at* www.abiworld.org/pdfs/amendedcomplaint.pdf; and Geisenberger v. Gonzales, Civ. No. 2:05-CV-5460-JS (E.D. Pa. 2005), *available at* www.geiscoop.com/bapcpa.pdf. *See also* Hersh v. United States, Case No. 3-05-CV-2330N (N.D. Tex. 2005). One bankruptcy attorney identified suits pending in Georgia, Kentucky, Minnesota, Oklahoma, Pennsylvania, South Carolina, Texas, and Washington.

Cite	Provision	Cite	Provision
528(a)(3)	CLEARLY AND CONSPICUOUSLY disclose in ANY ADVERTISEMENT OF BANKRUPTCY ASSISTANCE SERVICES OR OF THE BENEFITS OF BANK-RUPTCY *DIRECTED TO THE GENERAL PUBLIC* *(whether in general media, seminars or specific mailings, telephonic or electronic messages, or otherwise)* **that the services or benefits are with respect to bankruptcy relief under this title**	528(b)(1)	AN ADVERTISEMENT OF BANKRUPTCY ASSISTANCE SERVICES OR OF THE BENEFITS OF BANKRUPTCY *DIRECTED TO THE GENERAL PUBLIC* includes—(A) descriptions of bankruptcy assistance in connection with a *chapter 13 plan whether or not chapter 13* is specifically mentioned in such advertisement; and (B) statements such as *'federally supervised repayment plan'* or *'Federal debt restructuring help'* or *other similar statements* that could lead a reasonable consumer to believe that debt counseling was being offered when in fact the **services were directed to providing bankruptcy assistance with a** *chapter 13 plan* **or other form of bankruptcy relief under this title.**
528(a)(4)	CLEARLY AND CONSPICUOUSLY use the following statement in such advertisement: '**We are a debt relief agency. We help people file for bankruptcy relief under the Bankruptcy Code.**' or a substantially similar statement.	528(b)(2)	AN ADVERTISEMENT, *DIRECTED TO THE GENERAL PUBLIC*, indicating that the debt relief agency provides assistance with respect to *credit defaults, mortgage foreclosures, eviction proceedings, excessive debt, debt collection pressure, or inability to pay any consumer debt* shall— (A) disclose CLEARLY AND CONSPICUOUSLY in such advertisement that **the assistance may involve bankruptcy relief under this title**; and (B) include the following statement: '**We are a debt relief agency. We help people file for bankruptcy relief under the Bankruptcy Code.**' or a substantially similar statement.
Key: Language in *italics* is definitional. SMALL CAPS identify the defined term. CAPITALIZED language describes how the disclosure must appear. Language in **bold** is required disclosure.			

Let's start with subsection (a)(3), which describes what I call an "Explicit Bankruptcy" ad. It requires that:

- any advertisement of
  - bankruptcy assistance services or
  - of the benefits of bankruptcy
- directed to the general public
- clearly and conspicuously disclose that the services or benefits are with respect to bankruptcy relief.

Subsection (a)(4) requires that Explicit Bankruptcy ads clearly and conspicuously include the "Scarlet Letter" disclosure:

> **We are a debt relief agency. We help people file for bankruptcy relief under the Bankruptcy Code.**

Subsection (b)(2)(A) describes another kind of ad, which I call a "Credit Assistance" ad. It requires that:

- any ad indicating that the DRA provides assistance with respect to
  - credit defaults,
  - mortgage foreclosures,
  - eviction proceedings,
  - excessive debt,
  - debt collection pressure or
  - inability to pay any consumer debt
- directed to the general public
- clearly and conspicuously disclose that the assistance may involve bankruptcy relief.

Subsection (b)(2)(B) requires that Credit Assistance ads include the Scarlet Letter disclosure.

As you can see, the difference between §§ 528(a) and 528(b)(2) is *only* in the description of the ads. In both cases, the mandated disclosure is the same:

1. You must mention "bankruptcy relief" under Title 11,
2. You must include the Scarlet Letter statement, and
3. The disclosure must be clear and conspicuous.[10]

Although § 528(b)(2)(B) doesn't require it to be disclosed "clearly and conspicuously," you wouldn't want to do otherwise.

Subsection (a)(3) includes a definition in the form of examples of what "directed to the general public" means. But it is unclear whether these examples also apply to the phrase as used in subsection (b).

Subsection 528(b)(1), although awkwardly constructed, is apparently an

---

10.   There is plenty of law on what "conspicuous" means. For example, it is a defined term under the Uniform Commercial Code. *See* U.C.C. § 1-201(b)(10) (2001). But what "clear" might have meant to the BRA's anonymous drafter is anyone's guess.

attempt to define the term, "advertisement of bankruptcy assistance services." Subparagraph (A) brings in Chapter 13 ads, whether they mention Chapter 13 or not. Subparagraph (B) includes ads that "could lead a reasonable consumer to believe that debt counseling was being offered," which I call "Debt Counseling" ads.

Again, it is not clear whether this definition applies only within § 528(b) or whether it also applies to the phrase as used in subsection (a)(3).[11]

Setting aside all the terrible drafting, if an ad by a DRA falls within one of these four categories, two clear and conspicuous disclosures are required:

- The Scarlet Letter language must be included, and
- The ad must disclose that the assistance may involve bankruptcy relief.

The Four Types of Bankruptcy Advertisements		
§ 528(a)(3)	*Explicit Bankruptcy ad*	an advertisement of • bankruptcy assistance or • the benefits of bankruptcy
§ 528(b)(1)(A)	*Chapter 13 ad*	an advertisement of bankruptcy assistance services or of the benefits of bankruptcy that includes Chapter 13, whether it is mentioned or not
§ 528(b)(1)(B)	*Debt Counseling ad*	an advertisement of a "federally supervised repayment plan" or similar statement that could lead a reasonable consumer to believe that debt counseling is being offered when in fact the services are directed to providing bankruptcy assistance, either under Chapter 13 or otherwise
§ 528(b)(2)	*Credit Assistance ad*	an advertisement indicating that the DRA provides assistance with • credit defaults, • mortgage foreclosures, • eviction, • excessive debt, • debt collection pressure or • inability to pay consumer debts

11.   *See* BRA Section 229(a), adding Code § 528(b)(1). The phrase defined, "An advertisement of bankruptcy assistance services or of the benefits of bankruptcy directed to the general public," appears in Code § 528(a)(3); in Code § 528(b)(2), the phrase used is "An advertisement, directed to the general public." But given the structure of the provisions and the duplication, it's impossible to tell with certainty what this definition defines!

What Is an "Advertisement of Bankruptcy Assistance"?

What qualifies as an "advertisement of bankruptcy assistance"? According to the statute, the mandatory disclosures apply to:

> any advertisement of bankruptcy assistance services or of the benefits of bankruptcy directed to the general public (whether in general media, seminars or specific mailings, telephonic or electronic messages, or otherwise) that the services or benefits are with respect to bankruptcy relief under this title . . . .

Let's take this apart:
1. The communication must be an advertisement of:
   - bankruptcy assistance services or
   - the benefits of bankruptcy.
2. It must be directed to the general public.
3. It includes communications in:
   - general media, which presumably include:
     - television, radio, newspapers, and magazines
     - billboards and other public displays
     - Yellow Pages ads
     - Web site ads
   - seminars
   - specific mailings, which presumably means:
     - mailings addressed to a recipient, and
     - might also include mass-mailed advertising supplements with no address
   - telephonic messages, presumably including:
     - automated outgoing calling services
     - pre-recorded messages advertising bankruptcy services played on hold for incoming calls, and
     - live telemarketing calls
   - electronic messages, presumably including:
     - mass e-mail messages
     - bulletin boards and listservs directed to the general public

The list ends with the all-encompassing "or otherwise."

Business Cards
- Does a business card that does not mention bankruptcy qualify as an "advertisement of bankruptcy assistance services"? No.
- What if your card includes your designation as a bankruptcy specialist permitted state law? While the disclosure requirements only apply to DRAs, the statute does not require that the ad identify you specifically as a consumer debtor's attorney. The answer boils down to two issues:
  - whether a business card is directed to the "general public" and
  - whether a card designating you as a specialist is an "advertisement of bankruptcy assistance services."

Letterhead
- As long as you are not mailing to the general public, your letterhead should not constitute an advertisement, even if it designates you or members of your firm as bankruptcy lawyers.[12]
- If you use your letterhead to make announcements or for other mass mailings, either delete the bankruptcy references or add the mandatory language.

E-mail
- Many people (including the author) use auto-signatures that describe their practices. If you include references to bankruptcy and you are a DRA, include the mandatory language to be safe.
- Postings to listservs should be safe if they are not open to the general public but are limited to lawyers and other professionals.

Web site
- Since your Web site is open to the world, include the mandatory language on the site, and also on any page that refers specifically to bankruptcy services.
- If you aren't a DRA, you don't need to include the language (but read Chapters 4 and 5 before you reach any conclusions!).
- If you post to bulletin boards or other sites open to the public and refer to bankruptcy or "the benefits of bankruptcy," include the language in your signature.

All of this is nonsensical and provides no protection to consumers, who are more likely to be misled by the mandatory language than by prior ads. The only point is to comply with the law and avoid challenges based upon your failure to do so.

---

12.   Chapter 7 suggests that you include the Scarlet Letter language even in your engagement agreement. I don't think it is necessary to do so, but it can't hurt.

II. The Penalties

What happens if you violate these rules? The BRA provides several means of enforcement.[13]

First, there is the argument that the assisted person (AP) can avoid any obligation to the attorney, based solely on a non-complying advertisement.[14] Section 526(c)(1) provides:

> Any contract for bankruptcy assistance between a debt relief agency and an assisted person that does not comply with the material requirements of . . . section 528 shall be void and may not be enforced by any Federal or State court by any other person, other than such assisted person.[15]

This provision appears to permit an assisted person who received competent and effective representation to walk away from any liability to the attorney solely because the attorney's ad failed to include the required disclosures. There is no express requirement that reliance be shown, nor even that the client prove she saw the ad.

WARNING!!

Since § 526 refers to the AP, it is not limited to attorneys representing debtors (as discussed in Chapter 4). For example, if you represent a creditor who fits the definition of an assisted person in a dischargeability action and win, you could also lose! You never thought of yourself as a DRA, so you have not complied with the requirements of § 528 other than to have a written retainer agreement. You're a DRA who hasn't complied with the Scarlet Letter requirement, and the contract may be unenforceable as a result.

What public policy can possibly be promoted by permitting the client to refuse to pay for legal services? Common sense and basic principles of fairness and equity—particularly in light of the remedies provided by § 526(c)(2) discussed below—should preclude interpreting § 526(c)(1) in a manner that permits the assisted person to escape paying the attorney solely because the attorney did not comply with an advertising requirement that caused no harm.

---

13. Both BRA Sections 227(a) and 229(a) are titled "Enforcement," but Section 229(a) doesn't contain any enforcement provisions.

14. The statute says "void" but it means "voidable." A void contract is a nullity—it can't be enforced by either party, but this provision permits the debtor to enforce it, at her option. That's a voidable contract.

15. BRA Section 227(a), adding Code § 526(c)(1).

Here is the counter-argument. There are two ways to read § 526(c)(1):

Any contract for bankruptcy assistance between a debt relief agency and an assisted person that does not comply with the material requirements of this section, section 527, or section 528 shall be void . . . .[16]

Interpretation I
- Any contract for
- bankruptcy assistance that does not comply with § 528
- shall be void.

In other words, if any aspect of the assistance provided by the DRA does not comply with §§ 526-528, the contract for bankruptcy assistance is void. That might support the argument that even a violation of the advertising provision would give the AP grounds to avoid the contract.

Interpretation II
- Any contract for bankruptcy assistance that does not comply with § 528
- shall be void.

This interpretation limits § 526(c)(1) to *a contract* that does not comply with the provisions of §§ 526-528; it does not void a contract because the attorney violated a *non-contractual* provision of §§ 526-528. The provisions of § 528 that specifically refer to the contract are contained in § 528(a)(1) (provide the written contract within 5 days, explain the services to be provided and the charges) and (a)(2) (provide the assisted person with a copy of the contract). The advertising requirements are noncontractual provisions. So only violations of § 528(a) would result in the contract being "void" under this interpretation of § 526(c).

This is clearly a more sensible argument, and one well-justified by the statutory language.[17]

The AP isn't left without a remedy by this argument. Section 526(c)(2) gives the AP several remedies for any violation of the advertising requirements. The AP may recover:

---

16.   *Id.* The references to § 527 in subsection (c) are confusing and add to the ambiguity, because Code § 527 contains no provision that pertains to the contract between the assisted person and the attorney.

17.   Thanks to Tom Yerbich for this argument. This issue is also discussed in Chapter 11.

- all fees and charges that the attorney received,
- actual damages, and
- attorney's fees and costs

if the client has been harmed by the attorney's intentional or negligent violation.[18] Unlike the voidability provision in subsection (c)(1), this section requires a causal relationship between the advertisement and the harm.[19] This bolsters Interpretation II as well.

Injunctions and other remedies are available to state officials on behalf of their citizens.[20]

Here's another problem with Interpretation I: As discussed in Chapter 11, the BRA prohibits the attorney from advising the debtor to incur debt in contemplation of filing, including incurring debt to pay the attorney's fee. [21] So if the debtor doesn't owe any fee to the attorney for filing the case, what obligation does the *debtor* have to the *attorney* after the petition is filed?[22]

This provision could refer to an obligation to pay fees for post-petition representation that is beyond the scope of the initial engagement. Although few consumer cases see any action beyond the § 341 meeting and reaffirmation negotiations, this language could be critical in those cases that do.

In jurisdictions where the courts do not permit the attorney to:

- withdraw from the main case or adversary proceedings for nonpayment, or
- exclude contested matters and adversary proceedings from the scope of representation,

---

18. There's also a provision applicable to a dismissed or converted case, but that applies to failure to file, not ads. BRA Section 227(a), adding Code § 526(c)(2)(B).

19. BRA Section 227(a), adding Code § 526(c)(2)(A). It's not clear from this provision if "intentionally or negligently failed to comply" modifies only the award of attorney's fees and costs or all the measures of damages. I believe it applies to all the measures, although a careful drafter would have placed a comma after "costs," since there are commas after each of the other two categories of damages.

20. BRA Section 227(a), adding Code § 526(c)(3).

21. Even before the BRA, attorneys who let their clients pay them after filing often found themselves holding nothing but a dischargeable debt. *See, e.g.*, Rittenhouse v. Eisen, 404 F.3d 395, 395-96 (6th Cir. 2005).

22. Actually, we thought of one: careful attorneys should be delineating in their engagement contracts exactly what documentation and cooperation the debtor is required to provide. This will be essential for the attorney's protection, since she cannot fail to provide promised services. *See* Chapters 10 and 11. So theoretically, if the attorney failed to comply with the advertising provision, this obligation of the debtor is discharged under Interpretation I.

this provision is not an issue.[23] The attorney remains in the case, period.

But in jurisdictions where the courts permit the attorney to withdraw or to narrow the scope of representation, this provision might prevent the attorney from enforcing the debtor's contractual obligation to pay fees for the additional post-petition representation.

If the court does not buy Interpretation II, things could get even worse. Section 526 appears to give any AP[24] a claim against the attorney for return of all fees—pre- and post-petition—and any other actual damages, including the attorneys' fees and costs expended to recover it. After all, if the contract is voidable (or, according to the statute, "void" at the option of the AP), then under contract law, the AP would be entitled to rescind the contract and demand that the money be returned. The attorney can't get his work back, but the AP may get the fee back.

And if a debtor doesn't ask for it, the trustee may. The advertising violation occurs before the bankruptcy is filed, so the debtor's cause of action against the attorney may be property of the estate.[25]

Finally, if the trustee can enforce the debtor's cause of action for violations of the advertising provisions, then the trustee also has that claim for other pre-petition violations of §§ 526, 527, and 528![26] While Interpretation II avoids this result for advertising violations, it still leaves the attorney in the soup for contract violations.

III. The Possibilities

Despite the messy language of the statute, compliance with the advertising provisions seems easy enough—say the services relate to bankruptcy and include the Scarlet Letter language.

---

23.   *See* Chapters 6 and 7 for discussion of the compensation for services issue.

24.   I use "AP" here because, as discussed above, the AP definition may apply to parties who are not debtors, including creditors. *See* Chapters 4 and 15. When talking about the trustee's rights, I use debtor, assuming that the debtor also qualifies as an AP.

25.   The battle between the trustee and the debtor over ownership of a pre-petition claim against a DRA is oversimplified here. Answering this question requires not just an analysis of the DRA provisions (which don't mention the trustee at all), but also a comparison of enforcement rights granted the trustee in the Code's closest analog, § 110 and bankruptcy petition preparers. In addition, the BRA's very specific use of "debtor" could even implicate the body of case law in Chapter 11 and 13 cases that addresses the corresponding question of whether the Code's use of "trustee" allows other parties, such as the debtor or a creditors' committee, to pursue remedies available under the Code.

26.   BRA Section 227(a), adding Code § 526(c)(2)(A). *See* Chapter 4 for the other DRA requirements.

Yet think about the nature of advertising. What do you do if the statute went into effect before your ad in the Yellow Pages renews? What if a potential client has retained an old firm brochure?

I don't have answers for these questions, but I'm willing to bet that bankruptcy judges will use their good sense.

This advice won't help the domestic relations attorney or tax lawyer whose legal advice brands her a DRA.[27] She won't be thinking about bankruptcy at all when she places ads, and won't have time to comply before the legal advice that constitutes "bankruptcy assistance" comes out of her mouth. In my opinion, that's a good reason not to apply the advertising requirements imposed on DRAs to non-bankruptcy lawyers.

For lawyers who represent consumer debtors (absent a successful constitutional challenge[28]), there's no avoiding the requirements. Although compliance isn't literally difficult, it can still be problematic.

For example, suppose you advertise in another language. Is translation permissible? Could it violate the law to translate the Scarlet Letter language? Can it qualify as "conspicuous" if the disclosure is in a language the reader does not understand? No answer—the statute does not require (or prohibit) translation.

Some lawyers are already adding subtle alteration, prettying up the language to make it look like a qualification. One Web site used this language:

> This law firm is a debt relief agency. In addition to other services we offer, we help people file for bankruptcy relief under the U.S. Bankruptcy Code.[29]

Does this comply with the requirements of the BRA? It contains the required language, adding only a clarification between the mandated disclosures. It should fit within the scope of "substantially similar."

What about this:

> This law firm is a federally-designated Debt Relief Agency, authorized to help people file for bankruptcy relief under the U.S. Bankruptcy Code.

This isn't a treatise on attorney advertising,[30] but even if this language passes muster under the BRA, it must also comply with applicable state regu-

---

27. *See* Chapter 4.

28. *See* note 9 and Chapter 8.

29. *See* http://www.jthomasblack.com/.

30. The ABA recently published KERRY RANDALL & ANDRU JOHNSON, THE LAWYER'S GUIDE TO EFFECTIVE YELLOW PAGES ADVERTISING, 2D ED. (2005), *available at* http://www.abanet.org/abastore/index.cfm?section=main&fm=Product.AddToCart&pid =5110538.

lations on attorney advertising.[31] In general, your description of the firm may not be misleading, and it cannot infer specialization where you have not qualified as a specialist.[32] Many states would frown on this description as violating both these guidelines.

IV. Conclusion

If you are a DRA, include the language on everything that falls within the description of "advertisement of bankruptcy assistance or the benefits of bankruptcy" (see sidebar: What Is an Advertisement?). It isn't painless, but it's sure to be less painful than defending your failure to comply with the law.

---

31.   See Chapter 7 for a discussion of this issue.

32.   *See* MODEL RULE 7.4(d). There is a short section on the ethics of lawyer branding and marketing in Corinne Cooper, HOW TO BUILD A LAW FIRM BRAND (ABA 2005), *available at* http://www.abanet.org/abastore/index.cfm?section=main&fm=Product.AddToCart&pid= 5150404PDF.

CHAPTER 10

Representation, Consultation, and Termination Agreements[1]

by Marc S. Stern and Joel Pelofsky

I. Consultation Agreement

A contract, by definition, presupposes that the parties have entered into an agreement to perform (or not to perform) an act. But suppose the potential client is just shopping for advice or price. We have all seen that occur. Section 528(a)(1) creates a real problem for attorneys in this situation because it says that the "debt relief agency" (DRA) attorney "shall" execute a written contract within five days from the first date the DRA "provides any bankruptcy assistance services" to the "assisted person" (AP). These concepts are all defined in § 101 and are discussed in detail in Chapter 4.

The consultation no doubt involves "bankruptcy assistance," even where it ends with a determination that a bankruptcy filing may not be appropriate, is better deferred until later, or with the prospective client simply saying, "I'll get back to you" and never calling again. Given the sweeping definition of bankruptcy assistance, if the initial consultation is for a fee, the BRA requires execution of the contract, but if the individual doesn't hire you, how can the contract possibly be executed?

To address this problem, we suggest that you have the individual execute a "Consultation Agreement." In the Consultation Agreement, you can make clear that the AP is not retaining you.

Whether you charge for the consultation makes a big difference in the content of the Consultation Agreement. If the consultation is free, the con-

---

1. This chapter is based upon material from MARC S. STERN & JOEL PELOFSKY, LETTERS FOR BANKRUPTCY LAWYERS (ABA Press 2005).

sideration element of the DRA definition is lacking, and no rights or duties arise under §§ 526, 527, or 528 between you and the prospective client. Charging any fee changes this, and even your Consultation Agreement must comply with certain DRA mandates. For example, § 526(b) commands:

> Any waiver by an assisted person of any protection or right provided under this section shall not be enforceable against the debtor by any Federal or State court or any other person, but may be enforced against a debt relief agency.

The phrase "under this section" means § 526, suggesting that you can include a waiver of any rights or duties under §§ 527 and 528. Even though you could include this waiver, you might not want to, especially of § 527. The notices required under that section have been the subject of much criticism, but as discussed in Chapter 11, if you draft them well (while remaining true to the spirit of § 527), these notices can actually provide you some protection in any disputes.

Don't forget that good old-fashioned contract law can protect you as well. If the reason you "violated" the contract execution requirement is that your client refused to sign it, you have the defense of impossibility.

Consultation Agreement

This Consultation Agreement is entered into on _____, 200__, by _____ (name of attorney) (referred to as "I," "me," or "my") and _____ (name of debtor) (referred to as "you or your").

Recitals

• You met with me today to review your financial situation and the alternatives available to you.

• Section 528 of the Bankruptcy Code requires us to sign a written contract for bankruptcy assistance services (as defined in § 101(4A)) within five (5) days of our first consultation.

• You are not ready to decide whether you want to enter into such a contract with me.

Agreement

• By signing this, you agree that you have not requested further services and, at this time, you decline to enter into a § 528(a) contract or otherwise retain my services.

[*Option 1, if there is no charge for the consultation:*]

• You understand that you have no rights arising out of the provisions of Sections 526, 527 and 528 of the Bankruptcy Code.

[*Option 2, if there is a charge for the consultation:*]

• For this meeting, you have paid me $_____ in full payment for the services I gave you today.

• You understand that you have no rights arising out of the provisions of Sections 527 and 528 of the Bankruptcy Code.

_____

• After this meeting [and payment of the agreed fee], neither of us shall have any obligation to the other. You are not obligated to employ me and I am not obligated to provide additional professional services to you relative to proceeding pursuant to the Bankruptcy Code.

• You understand that unless and until you retain me, I cannot fully inform you of the services I will provide to you, or of the benefits and risks that may result if you become a debtor in a case under the Bankruptcy Code.

Signed on the above date by:

_____ ATTORNEY

_____ By _____
ASSISTED PERSON(S)   DEBT RELIEF AGENCY

II. The Representation Agreement

In the ideal situation, every representation should be memorialized in writing. Now the Code requires a contract in writing, coupled with extensive disclosures, commitments regarding work to be done, and potential liability. Lawyers who do not comply with the statutory requirements or the scope of work described can be subject to sanctions and possible malpractice actions.

WARNING!! ━━━━━━━

The Code requires a contract in writing, coupled with extensive disclosures, commitments regarding work to be done, and potential liability. Lawyers who do not comply with the statutory requirements or the scope of work described can be subject to sanctions and possible malpractice actions.

This agreement is intended to address one part of those statutory requirements: that the contract be in writing and specify the work to be done and the fees to be charged. These forms are for your guidance and are not a substitute for your own independent determination of what is required for your relationship with your client.

DRAs must comply with the requirements of §§ 526, 527, and 528, which are extensive and expose lawyers to sanctions for noncompliance. They are discussed in detail in Chapter 11 and Chapter 9.

There are two critical deadlines relating to the Representation Agreement:

1. No later than three business days after the first date on which a DRA first offers to provide any bankruptcy assistance services to an AP, the agency must provide the § 342(b)(1) notice and other notices, if necessary, described in § 527(a)(2), and the "Important Information" notice described in § 527(b). These are discussed in detail in Chapter 11.
2. No later than five business days after the first date on which a DRA provides any bankruptcy assistance to an AP, but before filing, the DRA and the AP must execute a Representation Agreement containing the provisions described in § 528(a).

These time requirements may be impractical but suggest that the notices and execution of the agreement should occur at the first point when services are provided, even if that is only a free consultation. The definition of "bankruptcy assistance" in § 101(4A) talks about "goods or services sold or otherwise provided," and the definition of DRA in § 101(12A) says that bankruptcy assistance is provided to the AP by the DRA "for the payment of money or other valuable consideration," so a free consultation *alone* should not trigger these obligations. (See Chapter 4 for discussion of the consideration requirement.) But if the client retains the lawyer after the free consultation, then the lawyer becomes a DRA and the clock may already be running. To be safe, either the Consultation Agreement or the Representation Agreement must be signed at the end of the free consultation. If the latter, the clock begins running.

We recommend that you deliver all four required notices to the AP at the time of the execution of the Representation Agreement (or, if you charged for your initial consultation, at the time the Consultation Agreement is executed). Sample forms for all four notices are provided in Chapter 11. These forms are called the § 342(b) Notice, Mini-Miranda II, the Prescribed Language Notice, and the "How To" Notice.

Representation Agreement[2]

Date

Name
Company Name
Address 1
Address 2
City, State, Zip Code

Re:

Dear Client:

We appreciate the opportunity to assist in reviewing your financial situation. Since that review, you have concluded that the filing of a Chapter 7 bankruptcy case is your best course of action.

This letter will serve as an engagement agreement that will establish the terms of our relationship. When you sign it, it will become a contract between us.

In passing the Bankruptcy Abuse Prevention and Consumer Protection Act of 2005, the Congress imposed strict requirements upon attorneys representing debtors, requiring them to specify what duties they will perform and to make certain representations to clients. Those specific duties and representations are set out in this representation agreement.[3]

---

2. Based upon materials from Spencer Fane Britt & Browne LLP, Kansas City, Missouri; Kinny & Urban, Lancaster, Wisconsin; Mark J. Markus, Studio City, California, and used with permission.

3. These statements do not include all the matters set out in Code §§ 101 (12A), 526, 527, and 528. *See* Chapter 11 for additional disclosure requirements.

Please read this agreement carefully and be sure you understand it. If you have any questions, you should consult with me before signing. Once you are satisfied with the agreement, please sign and return a copy to me.

The following are the details of our proposed representation:

1. We will perform the following work on your behalf in connection with the filing of your Chapter 7 case:

   a. Meet with you to discuss your financial situation and possible solutions;

   b. Provide the § 342(b)(1) notice, which sets out the purpose, benefits, and costs of filing under Chapters 7, 11, 12 or 13, the types of services available from credit counseling agencies, and the penalties of committing certain bankruptcy crimes, and will explain the notice to you;

   c. Prepare the necessary bankruptcy petition, schedules, statement of affairs, and other documents, and review and file the bankruptcy case under the chapter you select;

   d. Prepare for and go with you to the § 341 first meeting of creditors;

   e. Assist in the amendments to the papers filed and the production of such documents as the trustee requests;

   f. Assist you in the negotiation and execution of reaffirmation agreements that are in your best interest and meet all requirements of the law. However, we will not approve any reaffirmation agreement if we cannot truthfully tell the court that it does not create an undue hardship and that you can make the payments. In this instance, we will file an appropriate motion and go to court with you so that the judge can decide whether approval is proper. We will appear as your attorney, but you must come to court and explain why you think that you can make the payments.

   g. There are some issues that we cannot predict before filing. For instance, if you miss the § 341 meeting or do not tell us about a creditor, we will have to reschedule and attend the meeting or file amended schedules. In this case, we will do what we believe is necessary to protect your rights, and we will bill you for the additional work and any costs that we advance.

2.   For this work, we will charge [*Select one*]:

[*Option 1*] Our usual hourly rates as listed here:

(names of attorneys, paralegals and rates)

[*Option 2*] A flat fee of $_____

[*Option 3*] A minimum fee of $_____

In addition, you agree to reimburse us for the filing fees and other costs which the court allows or, if no court order is required, which are incurred on your behalf and normally paid by our clients.

Upon execution of this agreement, and no later than the date of filing, you will provide us a retainer of $_____

[*Option 1*] against which we will charge fees as costs, as allowed by the court.

[*Option 2*] which will be earned when received.

3.   ANY OTHER SERVICES, SUCH AS DEFENSE OF A COMPLAINT TO DETERMINE DISCHARGEABILITY OF A DEBT OR OF A UNITED STATES TRUSTEE MOTION TO CONVERT THIS CASE OR DISMISS IT AS AN ABUSIVE FILING, ARE NOT INCLUDED IN THIS AGREEMENT AND WILL BE PROVIDED ONLY THROUGH A SEPARATE REPRESENTATION AGREEMENT.

4.   As a separate document, but included as part of this representation agreement, we are giving you notice of "Important Information About Bankruptcy Assistance Services From an Attorney" as required by § 527 of the Bankruptcy Code.

5.   You agree to furnish all information necessary to enable us to complete the papers that will be filed in your case and that such information will be complete, accurate, and truthful.

6.   If you fail to provide the full amount of the retainer, as set out herein, we may be relieved from the responsibility of performing any further work under this representation agreement.

7.   We may also be relieved of the responsibility to represent you if you fail to provide us information or documents in time and with sufficient adequacy to enable us to respond to any inquiry, or do not appear at any court hearing. If these failings on your part occur after we have filed your bankruptcy

case, we can only be relieved if the court allows our withdrawal. You will receive notice of any motion and hearing on our desire to withdraw.

8.   This representation agreement and the attached notices represent the complete agreement between the parties and may not be modified or replaced except by a subsequent written agreement executed by the parties.

9.   This representation shall be void if not executed by the parties no later than five (5) business days after the first date on which the agency provides any bankruptcy assistance services to an assisted person.

10.   This representation is terminated _____ days after execution if the client does not provide the information requested and proceed with filing. In that event, we will bill all time spent and costs incurred to date and refund any remaining balance. If, after _____ days, the client wants to pursue filing, a new agreement and new fee will be necessary.

Sincerely and agreed:

_____
Counsel for the Firm
A Debt Relief Agency[4]

Date:_____

Accepted this _____ day of _____, 200___.

_____
Debtor

_____
Debtor

---

4.   Although the BRA does not require you to include this designation in a letter to a client (see Chapter 9), it does no harm to include it (see Chapter 7).

III. Declining Representation

On some occasions you or the prospective client will decline representation. It has always been a good idea to memorialize, for your file and with the client, your intention not to represent her or vice versa. It is more important now.

Write the client a letter and state with particularity that you are declining representation. There two main reasons for this, especially if the decision not to represent the client is yours.[5]

First, most potential bankruptcy clients have several creditors pursuing them. They may already have one or more lawsuits filed against them. If you do not make it clear to a potential client that you are not representing her, she may assume that you are. This means that she might assume you are taking care of the collection letters, judgments, notices of garnishment, or other information she's received. If you have not memorialized that you are not going to represent potential clients, you could be a defendant in a lawsuit seeking damages for your failure to represent them in these matters.

Second, providing a letter declining representation makes a record that supports your statements that you were not representing the client and had no responsibility for the problems that he is experiencing. (This is true whether you declined to represent the client or she declined to hire you.)

A sample letter is provided. Obviously, you will tailor your letter to the specific circumstances with the prospective client.

---

5.   If the client signs the consultation agreement indicating that no further representation is contemplated, a separate letter declining representation is not necessary.

Declining Representation

Date
Name
Company Name
Address 1
Address 2
City, State, Zip Code

    Re:

Dear (name):

    On the ___ day of _____, 200__, you met with us to discuss your financial situation and possible future courses of action.

    At that time you declined to execute a consultation agreement memorializing our meeting and its purpose. You also indicated that you were not certain how you would proceed or whether you would retain this firm to assist you.

    During the meeting, at our request, you furnished us a summary list of your creditors. We have examined that list and determined that former and/or existing clients are included.

    In view of the possible conflicts that would prohibit our representation, we have concluded that we cannot enter into an agreement to represent you in this matter.

                    Sincerely,

_____
Counsel
A Debt Relief Agency

IV. Termination of Representation

There are those occasions when it is necessary to fire your client and a termination of representation letter is important for both of you. For your client, the letter serves as clear notice that you are no longer her lawyer, avoiding the same sorts of mistaken assumptions discussed with the letter declining representation. For you, the letter makes a record, providing you a defense against a malpractice claim for actions that take place after the termination.

You should have established in the Representation Agreement the grounds for refusing further representation to the extent they are foreseeable, such as a lack of cooperation or dishonesty.

If the client's bankruptcy case has already been filed, you have to withdraw formally, which may require court approval depending upon the local rules of your district. If you have laid the foundation and have recorded the events leading to the decision to withdraw, getting the court to approve may not be much of a problem. Send a copy of the Motion Authorizing Withdrawal to the client in the manner provided in your local rules. Usually this requires certified mail or a return receipt. Formally seeking withdrawal may require that notice be sent to the entire creditor list. Again, this is a matter of local rule. If feasible, couple the Motion to Withdraw with a Request for an Award of Final Fees.

In the order, you might include a finding that you competently represented the client, that appropriate notice of the motion was given, that fees are allowed in a certain amount, how they are to be paid, and a specific provision that exempts you from responding or doing anything with future notices that are sent to you by mistake.[6] After the court enters the order, you should send a copy to the client.

If you are in the prefiling stage, no order is necessary, making a termination letter even more important, because you don't have the protection a court order provides. The letter should set forth the reasons you are terminating the representation, making a record that you tried to represent the client and detailing the conduct that led to your decision. Where possible, cite to applicable provisions of the Representation Agreement.

The termination letter is critical because of BRA provisions that could put you on the hook for your client's behavior. You have to certify the correctness of the client's schedules, for example (see Chapter 13), and if you are a DRA, you could be liable to the client if he or she failed to provide a required document and the case ended up getting dismissed (see Chapter 12). The termina-

---

6. A finding of competence by the court may preclude a malpractice or other action by the client at a later time. *See, e.g., In re* Iannochino, 242 F.3d 36 (1st Cir. 2001) (award on fee application bars malpractice action against debtor's attorney). Similarly, an order exempting you from further work may come in handy if the client complains to the bar association or licensing authority concerning your lack of diligence in representing them.

tion letter protects you in these and other situations that may arise under the BRA. Send the termination letter with a "return receipt" request, so you can prove that it was delivered. This is better than registered mail, because the client may refuse to sign for it.

Termination of Representation Letter

Date
Name
Company Name
Address 1
Address 2
City, State, Zip Code

Re:

Dear (Client):

In the representation agreement that we signed, you agreed to cooperate with us in the preparing of your schedules so that we could file a bankruptcy on your behalf.

We have asked on several occasions for copies of your [*Example 1:* tax returns for the last two years. Being current on those filings is a condition to the filing of your bankruptcy. The trustee will want these documents to verify your income and some expenses.] Despite our requests, you have failed to deliver these documents.

[*Example 2:* Although required by the contract you signed, you have failed to pay the last installment on the agreed fee schedule.]

[*Example 3:* After reviewing the creditors' list that you provided, we have determined that there is a potential conflict of interest and we cannot ethically represent you. Consequently, we are returning your retainer and all documents to you. We will assist you in finding new counsel, and as you know, we are required to keep any information we received from you in the strictest confidence.]

We cannot fulfill our obligations to you or to the court without your cooperation. Therefore, we have concluded that we must withdraw from representing you unless by close of business on _____ you have

[*Example 1:* produced these documents].

[*Example 2:* paid the overdue amounts].

Sincerely,

_____
Counsel
A Debt Relief Agency

Complying with Debt Relief Agency Provisions: Notices, Prohibitions, and Enforcement

by Catherine E. Vance

This Chapter gets into the substance of the debt relief agency (DRA) provisions, which can be put into three general categories:

1. Required Disclosures
2. Prohibitions
3. Enforcement

Before you begin reading, however, you are strongly urged to have a bottle of aspirin (maybe even some tequila) nearby.

I. The Inevitable Conflict: Attorney Ethics and DRA Compliance

This Chapter details what "debt relief agencies" must do, what they may not do, and the penalties for failing to comply. Tension permeates this discussion—and many others throughout this book—because of the inevitable conflict attorneys will face in attempting to comply with the DRA mandates while serving the best interests of their "assisted person" (AP) clients.

What do you do when an actual conflict arises? There aren't many options. In some cases, you might be able to harmonize the conflict by advocating an interpretation of a given DRA provision that is in line with your client's needs. But there may be times when harmony is impossible, and here you have to keep in mind that your duty to your client overrides your own interest. You will have to give very thoughtful consideration to your options, including whether you are willing to be the test case that challenges the applicability, legality or constitutionality of a DRA provision as applied to your client. Above all else, protecting your client is the right choice and the one you swore you would make.

Admittedly, the DRA provisions put attorneys in a difficult situation, made worse by the fact that clients gain little by the "protections" the new rules are supposed to provide. Practice under the BRA for consumer debtors' attorneys isn't fair and won't be easy.

Samuel B. Fortenbaugh, Jr., an attorney, was faced with a similar choice and he refused to comply with the court's order to turn information over to his adversary. The court, in turn, held Mr. Fortenbaugh in contempt and ordered that he be confined in the Philadelphia County Prison until he complied. The matter ended up before the United States Supreme Court, and because of Mr. Fortenbaugh's refusal to comply with the order, even at the risk of serving time, all in service of his client's best interest, attorneys today enjoy the work-product privilege.[1]

The bright spot in all this is that in the worst-case scenario—you're called before a tribunal to answer for your actions—you are far better off explaining that your statutory violation occurred in service to your client.

And you've got the rest of this Chapter to help see you through!

II. Required Disclosures

Required Disclosure	Source of Authority	General Content
§ 342(b) Notice	§ 527(a)(1)	General description of costs and benefits under various chapters, types of services available from credit counselors, and Mini-Miranda I
Mini-Miranda II	§ 527(a)(2)	Warnings for and requirements of the debtor, all in Miranda fashion
Prescribed Language Notice	§ 527(b)	Language of notice must be that which is in the statute, or substantially similar; purports to be general information about filing a bankruptcy case, including representation
"How To" Notice	§ 527(c)	Reasonably sufficient information for the debtor on how to provide certain information
Contract	§ 528(a)(1)	Written contract executed by debtor

---

1. Many thanks to Professor Charlie Wilson for providing the details about Mr. Fortenbaugh's story. Professor Wilson's advice on privilege to his first-year Civil Procedure students was more succinct: Don't go to court without your toothbrush.

A. Time for Making Required Disclosures

Wow, is this ever a nightmare:

- Section 527 is silent as to when the attorney is supposed to provide the § 342(b) Notice. The only reference to time is in § 342(b) itself, which provides that *the clerk* must give the § 342(b) Notice to the debtor "before the commencement" of a bankruptcy case.
- Mini-Miranda II must be provided within three days after the first date on which the DRA *first offers to provide* any bankruptcy assistance.
- The Prescribed Language Notice must be given "at the same time as the *notices* required under subsection (a)(1)." But § 527(a)(1) only mentions the § 342(b) Notice, which, as mentioned above, doesn't say when the attorney must comply.
- The "How To" Notice suffers the same problem; it must be given along with the "notices" that subsection (a)(1) requires, but only one notice is required under that subsection and no time is given for compliance.
- The Contract, governed by Code § 528, is the only mandated disclosure in which the timing is clear. The DRA must give the client a written contract not later than five business days after the first date on which bankruptcy assistance is *provided*, but in all events before the bankruptcy petition is filed.

The DRA must retain a copy of the § 342(b) Notice and Mini-Miranda II for a period of two years after the date on which the notice was given. The BRA does not specify how long the other required documents must be retained.

B. Required Disclosures

1. *§ 342(b) Notice*

Code § 527(a)(1) imposes on DRA attorneys the duty to provide their clients with the notice required under Code § 342(b). The notice must be in writing and contain:

- A brief description of:
  - chapters 7, 11, 12, and 13 of the Code and the general purpose, benefits, and costs of proceeding under each of those chapters; and
  - the types of services available from credit counseling agencies.
- Statements specifying that:
  - a person who knowingly and fraudulently conceals assets or makes a false oath or statement under penalty of perjury in connection with a case under Title 11 shall be subject to fine, imprisonment or both; and

- all information supplied by a debtor in connection with a case under Title 11 is subject to examination by the Attorney General.

WARNING!! ━━━━━━━━━━━━━━━━

The § 342(b) Notice must be filed with the court by the 45th day after the bankruptcy case is commenced. Failure to file the Notice results in automatic dismissal of the case on day 46, unless certain exceptions apply.[2] (See Chapter 12 for a discussion of § 521 and automatic dismissal.)

If you read § 527(a)(1) carefully, you'll notice that it only requires some of the information that § 342(b) itself calls for.

- Section 527(c)(1) requires a DRA to provide "the written notice required under section 342(b)(1)," so the DRA's § 342(b) Notice technically requires only the brief description of relief under the various Code chapters and the types of services available from credit counselors.
- The Mini-Miranda I statements fall under § 342(b)(2), which § 527(c)(1) doesn't mention at all. However, under § 521(a)(1)(B)(iii), the debtor must file a certificate stating that the attorney provided the debtor the notice required under § 342(b), including both paragraphs (1) and (2).
- This suggests that § 527(a)(1) is a technical error and that Congress never intended for the DRA to provide only half of the § 342(b) Notice. The wise choice is to include both paragraphs (1) and (2) in the § 342(b) Notice, since your failure to give proper notice could cause your client's case to be dismissed.

Notice also that the § 521 filing requirement makes no distinction between consumer debtors' attorneys who are DRAs and those who are not. Every attorney who represents an individual debtor with primarily consumer debts must provide the § 342(b) Notice, irrespective of whether the debtor is an assisted person or the attorney is a DRA.

---

2.   As of this writing, Interim Bankruptcy Rule 1007 requires that certain § 521(a)(1) documents be filed within 15 days of the filing of the petition. If challenged, this rule would likely be struck down because it has the effect of diminishing a substantive right, that is, a 45-day period within which to file the necessary documents and avoid automatic dismissal. But see Code § 707(a)(3) (15-day filing period).

Director's Procedural Form B201: 342(b)—Modified
The author's changes in the official form are shown as underlined and strike-through text.

B 201 (10/05)

UNITED STATES BANKRUPTCY COURT
**NOTICE TO INDIVIDUAL CONSUMER DEBTOR UNDER § 342(b)
OF THE BANKRUPTCY CODE**

In accordance with § 342(b) of the Bankruptcy Code, this notice: (1) Describes briefly the services available from credit counseling services; (2) Describes briefly the purposes, benefits and costs of the four types of bankruptcy proceedings you may commence; and (3) Informs you about bankruptcy crimes and notifies you that the Attorney General may examine all information you supply in connection with a bankruptcy case. You are cautioned that bankruptcy law is complicated and not easily described. Thus, you may wish to seek the advice of an attorney to learn of your rights and responsibilities should you decide to file a petition. Court employees cannot give you legal advice.

1. Services Available from Credit Counseling Agencies
        With limited exceptions, § 109(h) of the Bankruptcy Code requires that all individual debtors who file for bankruptcy relief on or after October 17, 2005, receive a briefing that outlines the available opportunities for credit counseling and provides assistance in performing a budget analysis. The briefing must be given within 180 days **before** the bankruptcy filing. The briefing may be provided individually or in a group (including briefings conducted by telephone or on the Internet) and must be provided by a nonprofit budget and credit counseling agency approved by the United States trustee or bankruptcy administrator. The clerk of the bankruptcy court has a list that you may consult of the approved budget and credit counseling agencies. <u>Credit counselors may charge you for this briefing, but approved counselors must provide services without regard to ability to pay the fee.</u>

        In addition, after filing a bankruptcy case, an individual debtor generally must complete a financial management instructional course before he or she can receive a discharge. The clerk also has a list of approved financial management instructional courses.

**2. The Four Chapters of the Bankruptcy Code Available to
        Individual Consumer Debtors**

        Chapter 7: Liquidation ($220 filing fee, $39 administrative fee, $15 trustee surcharge: Total fee $274)

        1. Chapter 7 is designed for debtors in financial difficulty who do not have the ability to pay their existing debts. Debtors whose debts are primarily con-

sumer debts are subject to a "means test" designed to determine whether the case should be permitted to proceed under chapter 7. If your income is greater than the median income for your state of residence and family size, the trustee, creditors, and other parties may ~~in some cases, creditors~~ have the right to file a motion requesting that the court dismiss your case under § 707(b) of the Code. It is up to the court to decide whether the case should be dismissed.

2. Under chapter 7, you may claim certain of your property as exempt under governing law. A trustee may have the right to take possession of and sell the remaining property that is not exempt and use the sale proceeds to pay your creditors.

3. The purpose of filing a chapter 7 case is to obtain a discharge of your existing debts. If, however, you are found to have committed certain kinds of improper conduct described in the Bankruptcy Code, the court may deny your discharge and, if it does, the purpose for which you filed the bankruptcy petition will be defeated.

4. Even if you receive a general discharge, some particular debts are not discharged under the law. Therefore, you may still be responsible for most taxes and student loans; debts incurred to pay nondischargeable taxes; domestic support and property settlement obligations; most fines, penalties, forfeitures, and criminal restitution obligations; certain debts which are not properly listed in your bankruptcy papers; and debts for death or personal injury caused by operating a motor vehicle, vessel, or aircraft while intoxicated from alcohol or drugs. Also, if a creditor can prove that a debt arose from fraud, breach of fiduciary duty, or theft, or from a willful and malicious injury, the bankruptcy court may determine that the debt is not discharged.

Chapter 13: Repayment of All or Part of the Debts of an Individual with Regular Income ($150 filing fee, $39 administrative fee: Total fee $189)

1. Chapter 13 is designed for individuals with regular income who would like to pay all or part of their debts in installments over a period of time and to retain property that might be surrendered in a chapter 7 case. You are only eligible for chapter 13 if your debts do not exceed certain dollar amounts set forth in the Bankruptcy Code.

2. Under chapter 13, you must file with the court a plan to repay your creditors all or part of the money that you owe them, using your future earnings. The period allowed by the court to repay your debts may be three years or five years, depending upon your income and other factors. The court must approve your plan before it can take effect.

3. After completing the payments under your plan, your debts are generally discharged except for domestic support obligations; most student loans; certain taxes; most criminal fines and restitution obligations; certain debts which are not properly listed in your bankruptcy papers; certain debts for acts that caused death or personal injury; and certain long term secured obligations.

Chapter 11: Reorganization ($1,000 filing fee, $39 administrative fee: Total fee $1,039)

Chapter 11 is designed for the reorganization of a business but is also available to consumer debtors. Its provisions are quite complicated, and any decision by an individual to file a chapter 11 petition should be reviewed with an attorney.

Chapter 12: Family Farmer or Fisherman ($200 filing fee, $39 administrative fee: Total fee $239)

Chapter 12 is designed to permit family farmers and fishermen to repay their debts over a period of time from future earnings and is similar to chapter 13. The eligibility requirements are restrictive, limiting its use to those whose income arises primarily from a family-owned farm or commercial fishing operation.

3. Bankruptcy Crimes and Availability of Bankruptcy Papers to Law Enforcement Officials

A person who knowingly and fraudulently conceals assets or makes a false oath or statement under penalty of perjury, either orally or in writing, in connection with a bankruptcy case is subject to a fine, imprisonment, or both. All information supplied by a debtor in connection with a bankruptcy case is subject to examination by the Attorney General acting through the Office of the United States Trustee, the Office of the United States Attorney, and other components and employees of the Department of Justice.

WARNING: Section 521(a)(1) of the Bankruptcy Code requires that you promptly file detailed information regarding your creditors, assets, liabilities, income, expenses, and general financial condition. Your bankruptcy case may be dismissed if this information is not filed with the court within the time deadlines set by the Bankruptcy Code, the Bankruptcy Rules, and the local rules of the court.

Certificate of [Non-Attorney] Bankruptcy Petition Preparer

I, the [non-attorney] bankruptcy petition preparer signing the debtor's petition, hereby certify that I delivered to the debtor this notice required by § 342(b) of the Bankruptcy Code.

Printed name and title, if any, of Bankruptcy Petition Preparer	Social Security number (If the bankruptcy petition preparer is not an individual, state the Social Security number of the officer, principal, responsible person, or partner of the bankruptcy petition preparer.) (Required by 11 U.S.C. § 110.)

Address:

_____

_____

X_____
Signature of Bankruptcy Petition Preparer or officer, principal, responsible person, or partner whose Social Security number is provided above.

Certificate of the Debtor

I (We), the debtor(s), affirm that I (we) have received and read this notice.

_____   X_____
Printed Name(s) of Debtor(s)   Signature of Debtor   Date

Case No. (if known) _____   X_____
                                                 Signature of Joint Debtor (if any) Date

---

The new Director's Procedural Forms, created in response to the enactment of the BRA, include Form B 201, which is the § 342(b) Notice. Although you will want to use this official form, note that it is not completely accurate. The form includes this:

> Chapter 7 is designed for debtors in financial difficulty who do not have the ability to pay their existing debts. Debtors whose debts are primarily consumer debts are subject to a "means test" designed to determine whether the case should be permitted to proceed under chapter 7. ***If your income is greater than the median income for your state of residence and family size, in some cases, creditors have the right to file a motion requesting that the court dismiss your case under § 707(b) of the Code***. It is up to the court to decide whether the case should be dismissed. (Emphasis added.)

The highlighted language fails to give the debtor complete information about the means test because it states that only creditors have the right to move for dismissal under § 707(b). It omits the United States Trustee's duty to:

- review the materials filed by the debtor,
- file a statement with the court regarding whether the debtor's case is presumed to be an abuse, and,
- if there is a presumption of abuse, file either a motion to dismiss or a statement indicating why such a motion would be inappropriate.

Note also that the filing fees may not be correct. As of this writing, a fee increase is pending in Congress as a part of S.1932, the Budget Reconciliation Bill.

2. *Mini-Miranda II*

Notice to Assisted Persons
This Notice Is Required by Section 527(a)(2) of the Bankruptcy Code

If you file a bankruptcy case:

   1.   All information that you are required to provide with your bankruptcy petition and throughout your bankruptcy case is required to be complete, accurate and truthful.

   2.   All of your assets and liabilities are required to be completely and accurately disclosed in the documents filed to commence the case, and the "replacement value" (as defined in Section 506 of the Bankruptcy Code) of assets, if applicable, must be stated in those documents where requested after reasonable inquiry to establish such value.

   3.   You will be required to state, after a reasonable inquiry, your "current monthly income," amounts specified in Section 707(b)(2) of the Bankruptcy Code, which generally concern certain of your expenses, and, if your case is being filed under Chapter 13, your "disposable income," which is determined under Section 707(b)(2) of the Bankruptcy Code.

   4.   Information that you provide during your bankruptcy case may be audited and your failure to provide such information may result in dismissal of your bankruptcy case or other sanction, including a criminal sanction.

I/we have read and understand the foregoing and understand that only attorneys can give legal advice regarding my/our compliance with the duties stated in the foregoing.

_____   Date:_____
Debtor
_____   Date:_____
Co-debtor

Mini-Miranda II[3] neatly captures the distrust of consumer debtors reflected in the BRA. Mini-Miranda II tells AP clients that they have to be honest and comply with the law, and that a failure to do so will bring nasty results. Specifically, the disclosure must advise the AP that:

- All information that the AP is required to provide with the petition and thereafter during the bankruptcy case is required to be complete, accurate, and truthful.
- All assets and liabilities are required to be completely and accurately disclosed in the documents filed to commence the case, and the replacement value of each asset as defined in § 506 must be stated in those documents where requested, after reasonable inquiry to establish such value.
- Current monthly income, the amounts specified in § 707(b)(2) and, if the case is filed under Chapter 13, disposable income (determined in accordance with § 707(b)(2)) are required to be stated after reasonable inquiry.
- Information that an AP provides during his or her case may be audited, and failure to provide the information may result in dismissal of the bankruptcy case or other sanction, including a criminal sanction.

Mini-Miranda II requires these disclosures only "to the extent not covered in" the § 342(b) Notice, suggesting the two might be combined. But the better course is to keep these disclosures separate and allow them to overlap if the same information ends up in each. There are three reasons for this:

1. Although both must be in writing, only Mini-Miranda II has a "clear and conspicuous" requirement.
2. Of the two documents, only the § 342(b) Notice must be filed with the court.
3. The statute does not clearly permit combining the notices. Doing so is an unnecessary risk that attorneys should avoid, given the many inherent risks presented in the DRA provisions.

Section 527(a)(2) strongly implies that the statutory language, changed so that it is directed at the AP, is all that's required. In other words, as long as you get the four required points across in your notice, it appears that you don't have to actually explain what they mean.

You will, however, have to explain the definition of "replacement value" because what Mini-Miranda II requires you to say isn't consistent with the law. Under Mini-Miranda II, you have to tell your client:

---

3.   Mini-Miranda I is in the § 342(b) Notice.

All assets and liabilities are required to be completely and accurately disclosed in the documents filed to commence the case, and the replacement value of each asset as defined in § 506 must be stated in those documents where requested after reasonable inquiry to establish such value.

The problem is that § 506 concerns only specific property. As added by the BRA, § 506(a)(2) provides:

If the debtor is an individual in a case under chapter 7 or 13, such value with respect to personal property securing an allowed claim shall be determined based on the replacement value of such property as of the date of the filing of the petition without deduction for costs of sale or marketing. With respect to property acquired for personal, family, or household purposes, replacement value shall mean the price a retail merchant would charge for property of that kind considering the age and condition of the property at the time value is determined.

Section 506 plainly applies only to assets securing an allowed claim. No other provision of the Code expands application of the § 506 "replacement value" definition to include all assets.

This is one of those inevitable conflicts between your ethical duties and DRA compliance discussed at the beginning of this Chapter. In the sample Mini-Miranda II provided in the sidebar, you'll notice that the "replacement value" statement has been qualified, so that the replacement value of assets must be stated only if § 506 is applicable. This is a minor deviation from the statute, but a necessary one for both you and your client. If replacement value is used for all assets, your client might not be able to exempt some property, and you will have knowledge that the information in the debtor's schedules is incorrect.[4]

3. *Prescribed Language Notice*

Complying with the Prescribed Language Notice, required by § 527(b), is relatively easy because the statute dictates the content of the notice and comes close to stating when it must be given (see the discussion above on timing). The problem is how the DRA attorney complies and gives good legal advice at the same time.

Most glaring, the Prescribed Language Notice creates the impression that attorneys and bankruptcy petition preparers are on par with each other.[5] Here's how this Notice must begin:

---

4. This could put you at risk of violating the Schedules Certification of Code § 707(b)(4)(D), which is discussed in Chapter 13.

5. See Chapter 3 on the History of the BRA, particularly the proposed amendment to this section.

IMPORTANT INFORMATION ABOUT BANKRUPTCY
ASSISTANCE SERVICES FROM AN ATTORNEY
OR BANKRUPTCY PETITION PREPARER.

If you decide to seek bankruptcy relief, you can represent yourself, you can hire an attorney to represent you, or you can get help in some localities from a bankruptcy petition preparer who is not an attorney. THE LAW REQUIRES AN ATTORNEY OR BANKRUPTCY PETITION PREPARER TO GIVE YOU A WRITTEN CONTRACT SPECIFYING WHAT THE ATTORNEY OR BANK-RUPTCY PETITION PREPARER WILL DO FOR YOU AND HOW MUCH IT WILL COST. Ask to see the contract before you hire anyone.

Not until the very last paragraph does the Prescribed Language Notice tell the AP client the critical distinction between an attorney and a bankruptcy petition preparer:

> Your bankruptcy case may also involve litigation. You are generally permitted to represent yourself in litigation in bankruptcy court, but only attorneys, not bankruptcy petition preparers, can give you legal advice.

Even this fails to inform the AP client fully about the very limited range of services a bankruptcy petition preparer is permitted to provide. By tying the fact that preparers can't give legal advice to the possibility of post-petition litigation rather than the preparation of the petition itself, the Prescribed Language Notice comes perilously close to endorsing the use of bankruptcy petition preparers as a comparable alternative to the services of attorney.

There are other problems with the Prescribed Language Notice. For example:

- It says that the debtor will have to pay a fee without mentioning that the fee can be waived in some circumstances.
- Its statement that "most cases are routine" suggests to the debtor that her own case is likely to be routine and ignores the fact that, from the debtor's perspective, the case is probably anything but routine.[6]
- Chapter 13 payments are described as "what you can afford" without any mention of the income and expense calculations of the new § 707(b) means test and their application in Chapter 13.

This creates another conflict: Can the DRA attorney correct these inaccuracies in the Prescribed Language Notice? More important, must she? The answer to the second question is "absolutely." To the first question, the response is "quite possibly, but you have to try."

---

6.   Here's another thought: If you use a statement that suggests to the debtor that her case will likely be "routine," you might have misrepresented "the benefits and risks that may result" if she becomes a bankruptcy debtor, which would violate Code § 526(a)(3)(B).

The changes in the BRA text are shown as underlined and strike-through text.

Notice to Assisted Persons
This Notice Is Required by Section 527(b) of the Bankruptcy Code

IMPORTANT INFORMATION ABOUT BANKRUPTCY ASSISTANCE SERVICES FROM AN ATTORNEY OR BANKRUPTCY PETITION PREPARER.

If you decide to seek bankruptcy relief, you can represent yourself, you can hire an attorney to represent you, or you can get help in some localities from a bankruptcy petition preparer who is not an attorney. THE LAW REQUIRES AN ATTORNEY OR BANKRUPTCY PETITION PREPARER TO GIVE YOU A WRITTEN CONTRACT SPECIFYING WHAT THE ATTORNEY OR BANKRUPTCY PETITION PREPARER WILL DO FOR YOU AND HOW MUCH IT WILL COST. Ask to see the contract before you hire anyone.

Only attorneys can give you legal advice. Bankruptcy petition preparers are not attorneys; they are prohibited by law from giving you legal advice.

The following information helps you understand some of the things that what must be done in a routine bankruptcy case to help you evaluate how much service you need. Although bankruptcy can be complex, many cases are routine. You should not assume that your case is routine.

Before filing a bankruptcy case, either you or your attorney should analyze your eligibility for different forms of debt relief available under the Bankruptcy Code and which form of relief is most likely to be beneficial for you. Be sure you understand the relief you can obtain and its limitations.

To file a bankruptcy case, documents called a Petition, Schedules and Statement of Financial Affairs, as well as in some cases a Statement of Intention need to be prepared correctly and filed with the bankruptcy court. Other documents will also be required. You will have to pay a filing fee to the bankruptcy court (although the law does allow a waiver of the fee in some circumstances). Once your case starts, you will have to attend the required first meeting of creditors where you may be questioned by a court official called a "trustee" and by creditors.

If you choose to file a chapter 7 case, you may be asked by a creditor to reaffirm a debt. You may want help deciding whether to do so. A creditor is not permitted to coerce you into reaffirming your debts.

If you choose to file a chapter 13 case in which you repay your creditors <u>a monthly amount approved by the court</u> ~~what you can afford~~ over 3 to 5 years, you may also want help with preparing your chapter 13 plan and with the confirmation hearing on your plan which will be before a bankruptcy judge <u>and where your creditors may appear</u>.

If you select another type of relief under the Bankruptcy Code other than chapter 7 or chapter 13, you will want to find out what should be done from someone familiar with that type of relief.

Your bankruptcy case may also involve litigation. You are generally permitted to represent yourself in litigation in bankruptcy court, but only attorneys, not bankruptcy petition preparers, can give you legal advice.

<u>I/we have read and understand the foregoing and understand that only attorneys can give legal advice regarding my/our bankruptcy case.</u>

_____   Date:_____
Debtor

_____   Date:_____
Co-debtor

Because you can use language "substantially similar" to that set out in § 527(b), you may alter the Prescribed Language Notice. For example, you can insert the following sentence as its own paragraph after the end of the first: "Only attorneys, not bankruptcy petition preparers, can give you legal advice." This language is not contrary to that Congress prescribed because it copies verbatim the last sentence of the Notice. A sample form with this and other changes is provided in the sidebar, with suggested changes highlighted.

The risk is that a court will find that your changes to the Prescribed Language Notice render it not substantially similar to the language Congress demands. This isn't likely as long as the changes are modest and do, in fact, correct inaccurate and misleading statements.

Your duty to your client requires that you give accurate information. Changing the Prescribed Language Notice (or supplementing it with additional information in a separate accompanying document) puts you at risk of liability for a statutory violation. But the alternative is to give your client less than accurate information.

4. The "How To" Notice

**Filing a Bankruptcy Case: Things You Need to Know
[Adapted § 527(c) Notice]**

This Notice is intended to provide you with reasonably sufficient information about your bankruptcy case and the information you have to provide. Be sure to ask your attorney if you have any questions.

Some Basics about Bankruptcy
In addition to the general information you were given in the notice entitled, "Notice to Individual Consumer Debtor under § 342(b) of the Bankruptcy Code," there are some things you need to know about bankruptcy.

The goal in filing a bankruptcy case is to get a "discharge" of your debts. The "discharge" is a court order that prevents your creditors from collecting the amounts you owed before you filed for bankruptcy. Some of your debts, like child support or student loans, might not be discharged. You and your lawyer will talk about any of your debts that might not be discharged.

The most important thing for you to understand is what is expected of you when you file for bankruptcy. In exchange for getting rid of your debts, you must make "full disclosure." This means you must give complete and accurate information about everything you own and everything you owe. Do not leave anything out.

Most people who file for bankruptcy are not dishonest and they don't plan on not telling the complete truth to the trustee and the bankruptcy court. What's more common is for people to fail to disclose all the required information because they don't want certain people to know they're filing for bankruptcy, because they want to protect a friend or family member by "keeping them out of the bankruptcy," or for similar reasons.

But it doesn't matter if your intentions are good. THE LAW DOES NOT ALLOW YOU TO MAKE EXCEPTIONS.

It's also common for people to think they file bankruptcy "against" their creditors, and that they can choose to leave certain creditors out. This is not true. All of your creditors are included in your bankruptcy, whether you want them to be or not. If you don't provide information about your creditors so that they get notice of your bankruptcy, your debts to them might not be discharged. Worse, keeping creditors in the dark may lead to the denial of your discharge. In other words, all of your creditors can still collect what you owe them after the bankruptcy.

You also need to be sure you understand what "property" means before you begin compiling information for your attorney. Many people think "property" means only tangible goods, like furniture, a house, or a car. But "property" means much more, including:

- Money that anyone owes you, even the tax refund you expect to get next year
- Deposits, such as those held by landlords or utilities
- Your right to sue anyone for any reason (for example, if someone hurt you or damaged your property, or if someone didn't honor the promises they made in a contract with you)
- Repossessed property
- Interests in certain insurance policies, annuities and retirement accounts
- Rights in licenses, patents, copyrights, and other, similar items
- Animals
- Farm subsidies

Differences in state laws, the availability of exemptions, and other matters will determine what property you get to keep, and your attorney can help you with that.

What's important is for you to be sure you aren't leaving out information that the bankruptcy court expects you to disclose. People sometimes leave out information because they don't think of something as being "property" or because they think the property "isn't worth anything." Failure to list everything can hurt your chances of getting your bankruptcy discharge. It could also affect your own legal rights to property, meaning you might lose property that you could have kept if it was disclosed.

Remember, your duty is to disclose everything and cooperate with the trustee. The value is not as important as the fact that the item is listed. If you aren't sure whether anything in particular needs to be included, just ask your attorney.

Information Needed to Prepare the Official Bankruptcy Forms
In order for your attorney to prepare all of your Official Forms completely and accurately, you need to provide the following information and, wherever possible, provide documentation relating to the information. For some of the items below, documentation is required. Indicate whether any of these documents are unavailable and provide a brief explanation why they are unavailable. Keep in mind that your attorney will ask you for other information, as needed.

1. Information about Creditors
You must provide the name and address for *all* of your creditors. If you have it, provide the account number as well.

The amount you owe each creditor must be stated in your bankruptcy papers. You can usually get this figure from your most recent bill or statement. Bring those bills and statements when you meet with your attorney.

You must provide statements, bills, collection letters or similar correspondence that includes the account number received from *each* of your creditors in the last 90 days. This might seem like a lot, but it is necessary so that your attorney has the right address to give your creditors notice of your bankruptcy. Your creditors have more rights against you if the notice of your bankruptcy is sent to the wrong address. If you don't have letters or statements going back 90 days, give your attorney whatever you have.

2. Information about Your Property
All of your property must be disclosed. Some types of property can be grouped into a single category, such as your clothing, which can be generally listed as "wearing apparel." Any particular item within that group that has a value that is unusual for that category must be listed separately. For example, you can group together all of your records and CDs, but if you have a copy of the Beatles "Abbey Road" autographed by John Lennon, it has to be separated from the group and listed on its own.

Some of your property might serve as "collateral" for a debt you owe. This is true for many people's cars, for example. While you are still making payments, the creditor has a "lien" on the car (the collateral), which allows the creditor to repossess the car if payments aren't made. A creditor in this situation is called a "secured creditor." For any of your property that is "collateral," you must provide a copy of the contract or other documents relating to your loan. You must also provide a copy of your registration showing who the legal owner of the car is.

Also make note of any of your property that you bought with a store credit card rather than a general credit card like Visa, MasterCard or Discover. The store might claim a lien on that property and may be a secured creditor.

The value of all of your property (meaning what your property is worth) must also be disclosed. For property that is *not* collateral, you can determine the value in different ways, but you must make a good-faith estimate. One method is to imagine you are going to replace a piece of property by buying it at someone else's garage sale. What would you pay for it? That is the value that needs to be listed. For some kinds of property there are guides available that provide estimated value, and some of these are available on the Internet.

The rules are very different if your property is collateral. The Bankruptcy Code requires that you value this kind of property at "replacement value." For property you acquired for personal, family, or household purposes, this means "the price a retail merchant would charge for property of that kind considering the age and condition of the property at the time value is determined."

Here's an example. Suppose you bought a computer on credit. You still owe the financing company for the computer and they can repossess it if you don't pay. Your computer is "collateral" and you need to find out what its "replacement value" is. You can't use the garage sale example because that's not a "retail merchant." You need to know what a store would charge you for property that's like yours. That doesn't mean you have to find out what a *new* computer would cost. Instead, you need to know what a store like the Salvation Army or [for-profit, used-goods merchant][7] would charge you for a computer that's about the same age, and in about the same shape, as your computer.

3.   Information about Your Income and Expenses

Recent changes to the Bankruptcy Code have made income and expense disclosures very complicated. In addition to providing information about your actual income, you must also provide what's called your "current monthly income," which is, roughly speaking, an average of all the money you received in the last six months. "Current monthly income" isn't just what you earned at work, but amounts received from virtually any source, like interest on savings accounts or child support payments.

Expenses are just as complicated. Again because of the changes to the Bankruptcy Code, what you actually spend for things like housing, transportation, or food is not relevant because the new law uses guidelines developed by the IRS to determine what these expenses are for you.

Your attorney will prepare your income and expenses schedules, which will have to be filed with the bankruptcy court. Your part is to be sure you provide all of the information your attorney asks you for.

Documents Required by the Court

Your attorney will let you know what documents you have to file with the bankruptcy court to file your case and, depending on the circumstances, to deal with matters that come up after the case has started. You WILL have to provide the following documents:

---

7.   Attorneys will need to provide the name of a for-profit, used-goods merchant known in the area of practice.

• The certificate you received from the credit counseling agency that provided your mandatory counseling session and any budget plan or analysis the agency gave you

• Copies of all of your pay stubs or other evidence of payment you received in the 60 days before your bankruptcy is filed

• A statement that describes any increase in your income or expenses that you expect will occur over the 12 months after you file for bankruptcy

• A copy of the tax return you filed with the IRS that was due last April 15

If you don't provide these documents (and others that your attorney tells you about) you could face serious trouble, including the chance that your case will be automatically dismissed – without you getting your discharge.

I/we have read and understand this Notice and agree to cooperate with my/our attorney and to comply with my/our duties in the bankruptcy case.

_____   Date:_____
Debtor

_____   Date:_____
Co-debtor

Section 527(c) requires you to give your AP clients what I've termed the "How To" Notice, which is a confusing notice with respect to both its content[8] and its point. Here's what it requires:

> Except to the extent the debt relief agency provides the required information itself after reasonably diligent inquiry of the assisted person or others so as to obtain such information reasonably accurately for inclusion on the petition, schedules or statement of financial affairs, a debt relief agency providing bankruptcy assistance to an assisted person, to the extent permitted by nonbankruptcy law, shall provide each assisted person at the time required for the notice required under subsection (a)(1) reasonably sufficient information (which shall be provided in a clear and conspicuous writing) to the assisted person on how to provide all the information the assisted person is required to provide under this title pursuant to section 521, including—
>
> (1)   how to value assets at replacement value, determine current monthly income, the amounts specified in section 707(b)(2) and, in a chapter 13 case, how to determine disposable income in accordance with section 707(b)(2) and related calculations;
>
> (2)   how to complete the list of creditors, including how to determine what amount is owed and what address for the creditor should be shown; and
>
> (3)   how to determine what property is exempt and how to value exempt property at replacement value as defined in section 506.

In other words, § 527(c) means that:

- A DRA providing bankruptcy assistance to an assisted person[9] shall provide
  - to the AP
  - at the same time the § 342(b) Notice must be provided
  - in a clear and conspicuous writing
  - "reasonably sufficient information" on how to provide all the information the AP must provide under Code § 521
- except to the extent
  - the DRA provides the information on the AP's behalf
  - after reasonably diligent inquiry of the AP or others
  - to obtain reasonably accurate information for inclusion on the petition, schedules, or statement of affairs, or
  - nonbankruptcy law does not permit the DRA to give the "reasonably sufficient information" to the AP.

---

8.   Its quirkiest feature is in the technical requirement that the DRA "shall provide each assisted person . . . to the assisted person."

9.   Notice the redundancy: a DRA, by definition, is providing bankruptcy assistance to an AP.

Before getting into the "How To" Notice in detail, two points are worth raising:

- the statute's exceptions, and
- the scope of "all the information the assisted person is required to provide under" Code § 521.

First, the exceptions: A BPP, or any other non-attorney DRA, is probably exempt from having to provide the "How To" Notice at all. The "to the extent permitted by nonbankruptcy law" would preclude anyone other than an attorney from complying with this notice requirement because the information required constitutes the practice of law. This is especially true if the DRA is a bankruptcy petition preparer. Section 110 expressly forbids a BPP from offering any legal advice, and the courts have sanctioned BPPs for providing precisely the sort of information that's supposed to be included in a "How To" Notice.

The exception for attorneys is somewhat ambiguous but critically important. The exception speaks to specific information required under § 521(a)(1)—information needed to produce and file an accurate petition, schedules, and statement of financial affairs. But in describing the "How To" Notice, § 527(c) refers generally to § 521 and the "information" required under that section. The question is, does the "How To" Notice's reference to "information" required by "§ 521" actually mean just that governed by § 521(a)(1)?

Look at what § 521 requires. Most of § 521 deals with documents and duties. For example, § 521(a)(2) and (6) detail the debtor's duties with respect to the statement of intention, while § 521(e)(2) requires debtors to produce copies of their pre-petition tax returns.

Section 521(a)(1) is different because it mostly deals with the creation of new documents, which are essential to the filing of the case and created by assembling "information" from a variety of disparate sources. Language within § 527(c) suggests that the "How To" Notice is concerned only with the § 521(a)(1) documents and the information needed to produce them. Section 527(c) specifically expects the "How To" Notice to include "reasonably sufficient information" so that the debtor is able to:

- value assets, including exempt property, at replacement value
- determine current monthly income
- determine the amounts specified in § 707(b)(2)
- if the case is a Chapter 13 case, determine disposable income in accordance with § 707(b)(2) and related calculations
- complete the list of creditors, including how to determine what amount is owed and what address for the creditor should be shown
- determine what property is exempt.

Almost all of these tasks are expressly included in § 521(a)(1). The only exceptions are the references to § 707(b)(2), but this is of little importance because § 707(b) itself brings this information back into § 521(a)(1):

> As part of the schedule of current income and expenditures required under section 521, the debtor shall include a statement of the debtor's current monthly income, and the calculations that determine whether a presumption arises under subparagraph (A)(i), that who how each such amount is calculated.[10]

This "schedule of current monthly income and expenditures" is required under § 521(a)(1)(B)(ii). Thus, the "information" in the "How To" Notice is limited to what's required under § 521(a)(1).

Why is all this important? If the "How To" Notice encompasses just the information required under § 521(a)(1), then the attorney exception applies to the whole notice. The lawyer can get back to practicing law, the client won't get confused by the notice, and the courts won't be bogged down in disputes over the meaning of "reasonably sufficient information," a term that is crying out for litigation.

To be clear: I am not arguing that this is a means of *evasion* for attorneys. I'm arguing that the exception to giving the notice for the DRA who "provides the required information itself after reasonably diligent inquiry . . . " applies to the entire "How To" Notice. And there is a sound policy justification: attorneys must have the flexibility to give their clients the information genuinely needed to commence a bankruptcy case. The biggest failing of the "How To" Notice is that it tries to tell an AP how to accomplish the tasks that the lawyer should perform, such as figuring out the appropriate address for notice to a creditor under new, convoluted language in § 342, or determining which assets are subject to the new "replacement value" definition in § 506.

What the client really needs from the attorney is:

- information on what to expect in filing and through the course of the bankruptcy,
- the duties the Code imposes on the debtor, and
- information that helps the attorney to provide the best possible representation.

The "How To" Notice is useful to both attorney and client if it includes this kind of information. A suggested template for the "How To" Notice is provided in the sidebar. Will you violate § 527(c) if you follow this template? Probably not. In the first place, you have the argument that you fit within the exception,

---

10.   Code § 707(b)(2)(C).

meaning you don't have to provide the notice at all. More important, it's difficult to imagine any court finding you in violation of a statute when you provided better, more clearly stated information than the statute itself requires.

5. *The Contract*

You have to look at both §§ 526 and 528 to get the full range of statutory requirements for the contract (and there's a sample contract for you in Chapter 10). Section 528(a) states that a debt relief agency shall:

(1) Not later than 5 business days after the first date on which such agency provides any bankruptcy assistance services to an assisted person, but prior to such assisted person's petition under this title being filed, execute a written contract with such assisted person that explains clearly and conspicuously:
   (A) the services such agency will provide to such assisted person; and
   (B) the fees or charges for such services, and the terms of payment.
(2) Provide the assisted person with a copy of the fully executed and completed contract.

All attorneys should provide a written contract to clients.[11] Under the BRA, the contract must take account of these specifics:

- The services you will provide and the fees and terms of payment must be clearly and conspicuously explained.
- The contract must be executed no more than five days after you first provide bankruptcy assistance, but before the petition actually gets filed.

If your contract waives any of the DRA provisions, it has no effect because § 526(b) provides:

---

11.   *See* MODEL RULES OF PROF'L CONDUCT R. 1.5(b), which provides:

The scope of the representation and the basis or rate of the fee and expenses for which the client will be responsible shall be communicated to the client, preferably in writing, before or within a reasonable time after commencing the representation, except when the lawyer will charge a regularly represented client on the same basis or rate. Any changes in the basis or rate of the fee or expense shall also be communicated to the client.

See also Chapter 7. See Chapter 10 for a representation agreement.

> Any waiver by any assisted person of any protection or right provided under this section shall not be enforceable against the debtor by any Federal or State court or any other person, but may be enforced against a debt relief agency.

The waiver provision refers to "this section," which is § 526, and not all of the debt relief agency provisions. A strict reading of the waiver restriction suggests that the client *may* waive receipt of the various notices required under § 527. Before drafting a waiver, keep in mind that the § 342(b) Notice will still have to be provided, and a certificate that you did so must be filed with the court. More generally, a waiver is likely to increase a court's scrutiny of your contract, and it's not worth the risk that the contract will be deemed unenforceable under § 526(c)(1).

Speaking of which, § 526(c)(1) says this:

> Any contract for bankruptcy assistance between a debt relief agency and an assisted person that does not comply with the material requirements of this section, section 527, or section 528 shall be void and may not be enforced by any Federal or State court or by any person, other than such assisted person.

This requirement is quite odd. It's not the *contract* that has to comply with most of §§ 526-529, but the *debt relief agency*. A significant number of these new provisions are restrictions or prohibitions on attorney conduct, some of which make no sense in reference to the contract.[12] DRA advertisements, discussed in Chapter 9, are a prime example.

And then there's the "void, but enforceable" description. This is obviously a drafting error. A "void" contract is a nullity, incapable of enforcement at all. "Voidable at the option of the assisted person" would be the correct language.

The enforceability language raises an interesting question for trustees. Elsewhere in the book, we've suggested[13] that if the attorney's violation of a DRA provision occurs before the petition is filed, the debtor's rights against the attorney pass into the bankruptcy estate. The "may not be enforced . . . by any

---

12.   There is an argument that Code § 526(c)(1) need not be read so expansively. It voids *a contract that does not comply* with the provisions of § 528; it does not void a contract because the attorney violated a noncontractual provision of § 528. You can argue that provisions of § 528 that specifically refer to the contract are contained in § 528(a)(1) (provide the written contract within five days, explain the services to be provided and the charges) and (a)(2) (provide the assisted person with a copy of the contract). This is discussed in more detail in the discussion of the Third Commandment, below. See also Chapter 9.

13.   See Chapter 9.

person, other than such assisted person" language could be interpreted to preclude even the trustee from asserting a right that, if it arises under the contract, belongs to the estate and not the debtor. The trustee's argument is, of course, that she merely steps into the debtor's shoes and would be enforcing the contract as if she were the AP.[14]

III. Debt Relief Agency Prohibitions: The Five Commandments

Consumer bankruptcy attorneys have always been required to perform according to their retainer agreements, by both contract law and ethics rules. The BRA turns a natural and normal part of the attorney-client relations— "You pay, I perform"—into a draconian series of duties and penalties destined (and surely intended) to snag debtors' attorneys.

Section 526 is the "sadistic" provision of the BRA. It will tie you up in knots and then punish you for any failure to perform exactly as instructed. Section 526(a) addresses specific restrictions, providing that a debt relief agency shall not:

(1) fail to perform any service that such agency informed an assisted person or prospective assisted person it would provide in connection with a case or proceeding under this title;

(2) make any statement or counsel or advise any assisted person or prospective assisted person to make a statement in a document filed in a case or proceeding under this title, that is untrue and misleading, or that upon the exercise of reasonable care, should have been known by such agency to be untrue or misleading;

(3) misrepresent to any assisted person or prospective assisted person, directly or indirectly, affirmatively or by material omission, with respect to—

(A) the services that such agency will provide to such person; or

(B) the benefits and risks that may result if such person becomes a debtor in a case under this title; or

(4) advise an assisted person or prospective assisted person to incur more debt in contemplation of such person filing a case under this title or to pay an attorney or bankruptcy petition preparer fee or charge for ser-

---

14. The battle between the trustee and the debtor over ownership of a pre-petition claim against a DRA is oversimplified here. Answering this question requires not just an analysis of the DRA provisions (which don't mention the trustee at all), but also a comparison of enforcement rights granted the trustee in the Code's closest analog, § 110 and bankruptcy petition preparers. In addition, the BRA's very specific use of "debtor" could even implicate the body of case law in Chapter 11 and 13 cases that address the corresponding question of whether the Code's use of "trustee" allows other parties, such as the debtor or a creditors' committee, to pursue remedies available under the Code.

vices performed as part of preparing for or representing a debtor in a case under this title.[15]

Before discussing each of these prohibitions ("Commandments"), it's important to point out that they apply not just to clients, but also *prospective* clients, because each uses "assisted person or prospective assisted person" (PAAP) when describing the prohibited conduct.[16]

The good news is that in the enforcement provisions, discussed below, the PAAP disappears; enforcement rights are granted only to the AP.[17]

A. The First Commandment

A debt relief agency shall not fail to perform any service that such agency informed an assisted person or prospective assisted person it would provide in connection with a case or proceeding under this title.

Nothing about the DRA provisions is easy. The critical word here is "informed." The DRA does not have to "promise" or "contract" or otherwise be legally or even morally obligated to perform the service in order to violate this prohibition. No casual statement appears to be excluded. Yellow Pages ads would seem to fall within its scope. Absence of consideration or reliance offers no obvious defense because prospective clients are included. And, finally, the client's failure to cooperate with the attorney does not seem to be an excuse.

So, for example, if you say, "I'll pick you up on my way to court" and your car breaks down, or you miss the § 341 meeting of creditors because you're being rushed to the hospital after a heart attack, you could be in violation of the First Commandment.

Courts can, and should, limit this provision to the contract. Section 528(a)(1)(A) requires that that the contract clearly and conspicuously describe the services the DRA will provide to the AP.

B. The Second Commandment

A debt relief agency shall not make any statement or counsel or advise any assisted person or prospective assisted person to make a statement in a document filed in a case or proceeding under this title, that is untrue and

---

15.   Code § 526(a)(4).

16.   There is an argument to be made that there's no such thing as a "prospective assisted person." The definition of "debt relief agency" requires consideration. So, unless you charge anyone who calls your office with general questions or who corners you at the neighborhood barbeque, you're not a debt relief agency and, consequently, not bound by the § 526 prohibitions.

17.   And state officials, the court, and the United States Trustee.

misleading, or that upon the exercise of reasonable care, should have been known by such agency to be untrue or misleading.

On its face, this Commandment seems benign; when is an attorney ever allowed to advise a client to mislead or deceive? But look carefully at the language. It seems to say that "the attorney should have known, upon the exercise of reasonable care, that the debtor's statement in the document was untrue or misleading."

Where did "reasonable care" come from? Sloppy drafting most likely gave us this standard, adding to the list the new and undefined terms the BRA uses as the threshold for acceptable attorney inquiry.[18]

"Reasonable care" is a term defined in contexts outside bankruptcy. *Black's* provides the following definitions:

- That degree of care which a person of ordinary prudence would exercise in the same or similar circumstances.
- That degree of care which ordinarily prudent and competent person engaged in same line of business or endeavor should exercise under similar circumstances.
- Due care, or ordinary care, under all the circumstances.[19]

Black's adds: "Failure to exercise such care is ordinary negligence."[20] That "negligence," in turn, triggers DRA liability, because a negligent failure to comply with the DRA provisions is specifically defined as a violation.

The Second Commandment doesn't refer to statements generally, but to statements in *documents*, which include the petition, schedules, and statement of financial affairs. But for these documents, § 527(c) speaks of the attorney's "reasonably diligent inquiry of the assisted person or others so as to obtain such information reasonably accurately for inclusion on the petition, schedules or statement of financial affairs."

These two standards may be the same in many respects.[21] But the failure to perform a "reasonably diligent inquiry," which will probably be measured under the same or a similar standard as under Rule 9011, is not per se negligent.

The best reconciliation is to interpret the "reasonably diligent inquiry" as supplying the meaning and standard for "reasonable care." This resolves any

---

18. A chart describing the various standards of conduct is provided in Chapter 13.
19. BLACK'S LAW DICTIONARY 1265 (6th ed. 1990).
20. *Id.*
21. See Chapter 13, which discusses the BRA's use of different standards in the new § 707(b)(4) certifications. The conclusions of that Chapter, that Rule 9011 should control, can and should apply to the "reasonably diligent inquiry" and "reasonable care."

conflict between the two regarding the standard expected of attorneys with respect to the veracity of the debtors' documents.[22]

C. The Third Commandment

A debt relief agency shall not misrepresent to any assisted person or prospective assisted person, directly or indirectly, affirmatively or by material omission, with respect to the services that such agency will provide to such person; or . . . .

Breaking this Commandment down to its component parts, you are in violation if you:

- misrepresent to a PAAP
  - directly or indirectly
  - affirmatively or by material omission
- the services you will provide.

This requirement is in addition to the First Commandment obligation to perform all the services you inform the AP that you will perform. Here, you are liable for "misrepresentation," a term not defined in the statute.[23] The misrepresentation does not need to be material; "material" modifies only the "omission" provision.[24]

The potential for missteps based on the language of the Commandment appears limitless.[25] The example above about offering to give the debtor a lift to the § 341 meeting could apply here, with the attorney violating the prohibition against misrepresenting that a service would be offered, when in fact it wasn't provided.

The attorney could say, for example, "We should have your documents ready to file by the end of the week," and be in violation if they ended up being delayed until early the next week. If the debtor's house is set for foreclosure sale first thing Monday morning, then the "end of the week" assurance is critical, but without that sort of time constraint, it's difficult to justify punishing the attorney for a short delay.

---

22.   This resolution also brings the competing DRA standards in line with the "inquiry" under Code § 707(b)(4)(D), as explained in Chapter 13.

23.   There is, however, a large body of case law on "misrepresentation" including from the Code itself, under § 523(a)(2).

24.   *See* Code § 526(a)(3).

25.   Even more examples of the "parade of horribles" under both the Third and Fourth Commandments are given in Catherine E. Vance & Corinne Cooper, *Nine Traps and One Slap: Attorney Liability under the New Bankruptcy Law*, 79 Am. Bankr. L.J. 283 (2005).

The attorney could also be found to have violated the Third Commandment if she understates the services that she will provide. Suppose your client pulled a disappearing act and a deadline is fast approaching. To protect your client, you call the trustee to arrange an extension and prepare and file an agreed order to that effect. You've upheld your duty as an attorney, but failed as a DRA if you didn't tell your client you'd perform such a service. We hope the courts would find the statement is not a "misrepresentation" or, perhaps, an omission that isn't material.

The language of the Third Commandment (and the First, for that matter) does not seem to admit the possibility of correction based on new facts, as in:

- "I told you we would file a Chapter 7, but that was before I discovered that your wife earned $28,000 last year as a teacher's aide, putting you over the median income. I know she lost her job in a school cutback but when we met, you described her as unemployed, which is correct but not for this purpose."
- "Yes, I told you that we would represent you in bankruptcy, but before we filed, your check for our retainer bounced."
- "Yes, we agreed that we would file your petition and your schedules for you, but the information you provided has turned out to be, after inquiry, totally fraudulent and you won't give us the real figures."[26]

Although the examples presented here seem to fit squarely within the Third Commandment, it is doubtful courts will give the statute such sweeping effect. Nor do they have to. Let's look again at the exact language of the prohibition, which applies to:

the services that such agency will provide to such person

Compare that to what a DRA is required to disclose in the contract:

the services such agency will provide to such assisted person

A logical interpretation is that the "services" in both phrases mean the same thing. As a result, the prohibition will only apply to misrepresentations or material omissions in the contract or, with respect to prospective assisted persons, services that could reasonably be expected to be included in the contract.

---

26. This scenario is made more plausible because of the certification requirement for the schedules under Code § 707(b)(4)(D), which is discussed in Chapter 13. There is a double whammy if the failure to file the schedules results in dismissal, an express condition for DRA liability. See Chapter 12.

D. The Fourth Commandment

A debt relief agency shall not misrepresent to any assisted person or prospective assisted person, directly or indirectly, affirmatively or by material omission, with respect to the benefits and risks that may result if such person becomes a debtor in a case under this title.

The breakdown for this prohibition is the same as for the previous one. You are in violation if you:

- misrepresent to a PAAP
  - directly or indirectly
  - affirmatively or by material omission
- the benefits and risks that may result by filing bankruptcy.

As with the Third Commandment, this language could lead to a parade of horribles. You could, for example, run afoul of this provision if your prospective client dissolves in a pool of tears and you say to the sobbing debtor, "Everything will be okay" when you know that everything is a mess and might continue to be even after filing. This statement is made by a DRA to a PAAP and directly and affirmatively misrepresents the benefits that may result by filing. It also indirectly and materially omits certain disclosures, like the loss of non-exempt property or the possibility of being hounded into the grave by creditors if you fail to make payments in your Chapter 13.

Like the Third Commandment, it is doubtful the courts will give this prohibition broad effect, penalizing attorneys for every technical violation. Unlike the Third Commandment, however, there isn't a document like the contract that provides the natural limits of the prohibition. But there is a statutory constraint: the enforcement provisions require that an attorney's failure to comply with the DRA provisions be intentional or negligent. An attorney's innocent misrepresentation would not be actionable.[27]

The required disclosures can also insulate attorneys from DRA liability. The Director's § 342(b) Notice explains, for example, that the "trustee may have the right to take possession of and sell the remaining property that is not exempt and use the sale proceeds to pay your creditors." The "How To" Notice provides a useful means to convey additional information that would limit liability under this section by explaining, for example, the debtor's duty of full disclosure, the limits of the discharge, or that some property might be lost to the trustee or creditors.

---

27. The content of innocent, negligent, and intentional misrepresentation will be supplied by the common law. *See* Field v. Mans, 516 U.S. 59, 69 (1995) ("Where Congress uses terms that have settled meaning under . . . the common law, a court must infer, unless the statute dictates otherwise dictates, that Congress means to incorporate the established meaning of those terms.") (citations omitted).

E. The Fifth Commandment

A debt relief agency shall not advise an assisted person or prospective assisted person to incur more debt in contemplation of such person filing a case under this title or to pay an attorney or bankruptcy petition preparer fee or charge for services performed as part of preparing for or representing a debtor in a case under this title.

Not only does this provision raise First Amendment issues, it also creates two conflicts. One is between two provisions of the Code; the second is between you and your client. It also creates a morass of possible interpretations.

Four different interpretations of this language are possible, each presenting a different description of what the DRA is prohibited from doing. The sidebar below breaks down the statutory language and the use of "or."[28]

The Meaning of "Or"

Interpretation 1
A debt relief agency shall not advise an assisted person or prospective assisted person

- to incur more debt
  - in contemplation of such person filing a case

or

  - to pay an attorney fee or charge for services performed as part of preparing for or representing a debtor in a case under this title.

Translation: A debt relief agency shall not advise the PAAP:

1. to incur more debt in contemplation of filing a case; or
2. to incur more debt to pay an attorney fee or charge for services performed as part of preparing for or representing a debtor in a case.

Interpretation 2
A debt relief agency shall not advise a PAAP

- to incur more debt in contemplation of bankruptcy

or

- to pay an attorney fee or charge for services performed as part of preparing for or representing a debtor in a case under this title.

Translation: A debt relief agency shall not advise the PAAP:

---

28.   This section has more "ors" than the Olympic rowing team!

1. to incur more debt in contemplation of bankruptcy; or
2. to pay an attorney fee or charge for services performed as part of preparing for or representing a debtor in a case.

Interpretation 3
A debt relief agency shall not
- advise a PAAP
  - to incur more debt in contemplation of bankruptcy

or
  - to pay an attorney fee

or
- charge for services performed as part of preparing for or representing a debtor in a case under this title.

Translation: A debt relief agency shall not

1. advise a PAAP to incur more debt in contemplation of bankruptcy
2. advise a PAAP to pay an attorney fee
3. charge for services performed as part of preparing for or representing a debtor in a bankruptcy case

Interpretation 4
A debt relief agency shall not

- advise a PAAP
  - to incur more debt
    - in contemplation of bankruptcy

  or
    - to pay an attorney fee

or
- charge for services performed as part of preparing for or representing a debtor in a bankruptcy case.

Translation: A debt relief agency shall not:

1. Advise a PAAP to incur more debt in contemplation of bankruptcy.
2. Advise a PAAP to incur more to pay an attorney fee.
3. Charge for services performed as part of preparing for or representing a debtor in a bankruptcy case.

The correct interpretation is the first one: Congress doesn't want debtors borrowing when they know they're going to file for bankruptcy, not even to pay the attorney. Let's forget for a moment how unlikely it is that the attorney will get paid otherwise. What this means is that debtors' attorneys can no longer do three things:

1. They can no longer take credit cards.[29] (They can take debit cards, but as with a check, they shouldn't file the petition until they are sure the amount has arrived in their account.)
2. They can't suggest that the debtor borrow the money from a family member or a friend.
3. They cannot *answer* if the debtor asks whether borrowing money to pay the attorney's fee is an option.

F. Conflict over Fees

Even if the intent of the statute is not to deny debtors' attorneys all payment or to prohibit them from charging for their services, but only to prohibit payment obtained by incurring debt, what more does this mean for debtors' attorneys? Can they acquire unencumbered assets of the debtor to pay their fees (however unlikely it is that the debtor has unencumbered assets)? Probably yes, so you can drain the debtor's bank account or take his chickens, but not his promise to pay.

Under this prohibition, can attorneys barter for future goods or services from the debtor—say, eggs, or labor? Probably not, as this contractual obligation would not only be dischargeable in bankruptcy, it would create an impermissible debt.

The bottom line is that attorneys representing debtors will have to document carefully how their fees are paid or risk falling afoul of this prohibition.

G. Conflict over Other Issues

It's also important to remember that the debt prohibition doesn't just apply to the attorney's fee. Under this provision, counsel can't advise the debtor to incur additional debt for any purpose, even if it's in the best interest of the client to do so.[30]

Suppose you properly instruct your client in your first meeting not to use her credit card or incur any other debt. Between the initial consultation and the filing of the petition, your client calls and says, "My son is sick and he has

---

29. For an article on small firms accepting credit cards, *see* Dan Hudson, *Accepting Credit Card Payments: A Primer*, GP/SOLO, Apr./May 2005, at 10.

30. It's also important to remember that this is not a prohibition on the debtor incurring debt but a prohibition against the attorney *advising* the debtor to do so.

to go to the doctor. I don't have insurance or any money to pay for the doctor or for my son's medicine. Can I put it on my Visa?"

What is the attorney to do? The attorney has given the required advice at the initial meeting, and the client has scrupulously followed it. Because a bankruptcy is in the works for the client, the Visa charge would be a debt incurred in contemplation of filing, so § 526(a)(4) requires the attorney to say, "No, you can't use your Visa." This is true even though nothing else in the law makes this type of debt improper; it's certainly not enough to warrant a dischargeability complaint for fraud, and the client isn't gaming the system in an effort to take advantage of her creditors.[31]

The attorney can avoid this conundrum by following the lead of generations of criminal lawyers. At the initial meeting, the attorney can give the required advice ("I must advise you not to use your credit cards anymore.") and follow up later with a warning ("Don't tell me if you did it."). This protects the lawyer from giving the prohibited advice, and it will protect the right of the client to incur additional debt in emergency situations. Of course, it's terrible lawyering, but it's the only real option for the attorney.

IV. Enforcement

Enforcement of the DRA provisions is dealt with in § 526(c)(2), (3), and (5).[32] These can be categorized in terms of who has the right to take action against the DRA:

1. Assisted Persons
2. State Officials
3. Courts, the United States Trustee, and Debtors

Let's look at each of these categories. If you went through the bottle of aspirin you were advised to have on hand at the outset of this Chapter, replenish the supply. The news here is not good.

---

31.   There's another trap lurking in the "shall not advise" prohibition. If the attorney complies with Code § 526 and tells the client she can't incur the debt, it is reasonably foreseeable that she will forgo the doctor's visit for her son because she can't pay for it and he will become sicker, making an emergency room visit necessary. The public policy consequences here are obvious, but what's more relevant for the attorney is that he might face tort liability if his "advice" is the proximate cause of the child's worsened condition. Can it be a tort (or malpractice) to do what a bad statute requires you to do? We sincerely hope not.

32.   Paragraph (4) provides that the state and federal courts share concurrent jurisdiction over actions for injunctive and other relief by state officials, such as the attorney general.

A. Actions by the Assisted Person

Section 526(c) provides:

(2) Any debt relief agency shall be liable to an assisted person in the amount of any fees or charges in connection with providing bankruptcy assistance to such person that such debt relief agency has received, for actual damages, and for reasonable attorneys' fees and costs if such agency is found, after notice and a hearing, to have –
(A) intentionally or negligently failed to comply with any provision of this section, section 527, or section 528 with respect to a case or proceeding under this title for such assisted person;
(B) provided bankruptcy assistance to an assisted person in a case or proceeding under this title that is dismissed or converted to a case under another chapter of this title because of such agency's intentional or negligent failure to file any required document including those specified in section 521; or
(C) intentionally or negligently disregarded the material requirements of this title or the Federal Rules of Bankruptcy Procedure applicable to such agency.

The AP's recovery comes in three forms:

- The DRA's fees and charges
- Actual damages
- Reasonable attorneys' fees and costs

Notice that these awards are all preceded by the phrase "shall be liable." The court seems to have no discretion to limit the award in appropriate circumstances, even where the debtor can prove no harm as a result of the violation (although the lack of harm will mean there are no "actual damages").

It might look like good news that all the violations require negligence or an intentional act. In some respects, that's true because no attorney—DRA or not—should face stiff penalties for technical or inadvertent violations, especially when dealing with new, burdensome, and poorly drafted laws.

A negligence standard, by itself, isn't necessarily bad. But in ordinary negligence suits, the defendant has to pay an amount commensurate with the harm, and the plaintiff's own negligence, as well as intervening and supervening events, will be factored into any award against the defendant.

By contrast, the DRA is punished to a degree that could be out of proportion to any harm the client suffered.

Suppose, for example, a court issues a decision about one of the required notices that details what content it requires. A couple of months later, you give a client all the required disclosures, but, through negligence, you use your old form—the one you handed out before the court provided its guidance. The form is close, but not completely in compliance with the court's directive. You otherwise navigate your client through the bankruptcy successfully.

That one simple mistake puts you at risk of extraordinary liability. A similar misstep in getting all the required documents filed will produce the same result if the case is dismissed or converted, which Chapter 12 talks about in more detail. Worse, the BRA sweeps the entire Code and all of the rules into the reach of § 526(c)(2).

The "intentional" aspect could be even worse. It's easy to assume this refers to the bad actors, attorneys who harm their clients and the system by flaunting the Code and rules that everyone else follows.

But think about this: bankruptcy's best lawyers will be forced into situations that may *require* an intentional violation because of the attorney's overriding duty to the client's best interest. Some examples were presented in the discussion of the required disclosures earlier in this Chapter. You must, for example, tell your client that all her assets, including exempt property, are to be valued at "replacement value" as defined in § 506. Because that isn't what the law requires, and could lead to bad results for the client, you have to violate your DRA obligation.

Your reward for doing what's right: disgorgement of what your client paid, any actual damage the client suffered, and a bill for what it cost your client in litigating your DRA violation.

B. Actions by State Officials

(3) In addition to such other remedies as are provided under State law, whenever the chief law enforcement officer of a State, or an official or agency designated by a State, has reason to believe that any person has violated or is violating this section, the State —

   (A) may bring an action to enjoin such violation;

   (B) may bring an action on behalf of its residents to recover the actual damages of assisted persons arising from such violation, including any liability under paragraph (2); and

   (C) in the case of any successful action under subparagraph (A) or (B), shall be awarded the costs of the action and reasonable attorneys' fees as determined by the court.

This paragraph speaks for itself. Attorneys, already governed by ethics rules and subject to disciplinary proceedings, now face the possibility of actions by the state attorney general, head of consumer protection, and who knows what other state officials, based on nothing more than a "reason to believe" that the attorney violated or is violating the DRA provisions, or intentionally or negligently disregarding any provision of the Code or the rules.

Let's assume, and hope, that officials use this power sparingly and only where the public interest demands it, or that there won't be a politically ambitious official looking to make headlines or with an ax to grind. Remember also that you will lay claim to higher ground than these officials if your statutory violation is based on your ethical obligations to your clients.

C. Actions by the Court, United States Trustee or the Debtor

(5) Notwithstanding any other provision of Federal law and in addition to any other remedy provided under Federal or State law, if the court, on its own motion or on the motion of the United States trustee or the debtor, finds that a person intentionally violated this section, or engaged in a clear and consistent pattern or practice of violating this section the court may –

(A) enjoin the violation of such section; or

(B) impose an appropriate civil penalty against such person.

Again, there are no tricks or traps here; the language speaks for itself. The most striking feature about this paragraph is that it includes the debtor as a party authorized to initiate action against the attorney, alleging the attorney "engaged in a clear and consistent pattern or practice of violating" § 526. Private attorney general actions are hardly new to the law. What's surprising is that debtors, described time and again by supporters of the BRA as irresponsible schemers, are among those to whom the integrity of the bankruptcy system is entrusted.

CHAPTER 12

Attorney Liability and § 521: Dismissal for Failure to File Required Documents

by Catherine E. Vance

Among the many new Bankruptcy Code provisions regulating attorneys as "debt relief agencies" is § 526(c)(2)(B), under which a debt relief agency (DRA) *shall* be liable to an assisted person if the DRA is found to have:

> provided bankruptcy assistance to an assisted person in a case or proceeding under this title that is dismissed or converted to a case under another chapter of this title because of such agency's intentional or negligent failure to file any required document including those specified in section 521.

The biggest (but by no means the only) threat is that § 521 provides for *automatic* dismissal of a bankruptcy case where certain documents are not filed in a timely manner. Even where dismissal is not automatic, the risk of liability is high.[1]

I. What Does § 521 Require?

Three categories of documents are addressed by the relevant provisions of § 521:

- General documents relating to the commencement of the case
- Pre-petition tax documents
- Post-petition tax documents.

---

1. Code § 521, as amended, merits its own book because the BRA turned it into a complicated and confusing statute. Because the focus of this Chapter is the attorney's liability for a case that was dismissed or converted, a lot of § 521's tricks and traps aren't discussed here.

II. General Documents

The first category, general documents relating to the commencement of the case, is governed by §§ 521(a) and 521(i). Section 521(i) provides at paragraph (1):

> Subject to paragraphs (2) and (4) and notwithstanding section 707(a),[2] if an individual debtor in a voluntary case under chapter 7 or 13 fails to file all the information required under subsection (a)(1) within 45 days after the date of the filing of the petition, the case shall be automatically dismissed effective on the 46th day after the date of the filing of the petition.

Section 521(a) tells us what documents § 521(i) is concerned with:

- a list of creditors
- a schedule of assets and liabilities
- a statement of financial affairs
- if § 342(b) applies, the certificate of the attorney whose name is on the petition as the attorney for the debtor indicating that the attorney delivered to the debtor the notice required by § 342(b)[3]
- copies of all payment advices and other evidence of payment received by the debtor from any employer within 60 days prior to the petition
- a statement of the amount of monthly net income, itemized to show how the amount is calculated
- a statement disclosing any reasonably anticipated increase[4] in income or expenditures over the 12-month period following the date of the filing of the petition

---

2. Code § 707(a) says:

    The court may dismiss a case under this chapter only after notice and a hearing and only for cause, including –
    (1) unreasonable delay by the debtor that is prejudicial to creditors;
    (2) nonpayment of any fees or charges required under chapter 123 of title 28; and
    (3) failure of the debtor in a voluntary case to file, within fifteen days or such additional time as the court may allow after the filing of the petition commencing such case, the information required of paragraph (1) of section 521, but only on a motion by the United States trustee.

3. The § 342(b) notice requirement is broader than set forth here, addressing petition preparers and *pro se* filers.

4. Why the statute isn't also interested in anticipated *decreases* in income or expenditures is a mystery.

If *any* of these documents is not filed by the end of the 45th day after the date the petition is filed, then the case is *automatically dismissed* on the 46th day. Section 521 offers two express exceptions; two others are suggested but not clearly permitted by the language.

A. Express Exceptions to Automatic Dismissal

On motion of the *debtor*, the court can *extend the time* within which the debtor must comply by up to 45 days. The debtor's motion for the extension must be filed before the 45-day period expires and the court must find "justification" for the extension. The statute is silent about whether the case is automatically dismissed if the debtor fails to file the various documents by the end of the extended period, but that is the presumed result.

Second, the *trustee* can ask the court to *decline to dismiss* the debtor's case. The trustee's motion must be filed before the end of the initial 45-day period or, if granted to the debtor, the extension of that period. The section also says that the trustee can make the motion before the expiration of the five-day period after dismissal, during which "any party in interest may request the court to enter an order dismissing the case." Because this five-day period is confusing, it's discussed in greater detail in section B, below.

The court can grant the trustee's motion and decline to dismiss the debtor's case if it finds that:

- The best interests of the creditors would be served by administration of the case; and
- The debtor attempted in good faith to file copies of all payment advices or other evidence of payment received within 60 days before the date of the filing of the petition by the debtor from any employer of the debtor.

The second finding seems odd at first glance because it excuses a failure to file only one of several required documents. But it does make some sense in the context of all the documents required under § 521(a)(1). Evidence of payment from employers is the one filing requirement that is generally out of the debtor's control. For any number of reasons, many having to do with the employer, the debtor may simply be unable to comply.

What is odd is that the debtor's good faith in trying to file her pay stubs is worthless unless the trustee wants to retain the case. Without a motion by the trustee, the debtor faces dismissal of the case despite even extraordinary efforts to acquire and file the required information. It's difficult to see why a few missing pay stubs should lead to dismissal where the trustee has proven the first element of this exception, that administering the case is in the best interests of the creditors. It's even harder to understand why a debtor who acts in good faith should have her case dismissed, which is the result if the trustee doesn't take any action to keep the case.

B. Implied Exceptions

Two additional exceptions are implied under § 521. First, the "unless the court orders otherwise" language of § 521(a)(1)(B) qualifies the debtor's duty to file all the § 521(a) documents listed above except the list of creditors. This language predates the BRA and could be interpreted as continuing to grant the courts the same discretion as they had before the amendment to order that a particular document need not be provided at all, such as where it is impossible for the debtor to comply.

Another interpretation is that the "unless the court orders otherwise" language is now limited to the two express exceptions to the document filing requirement: orders granting the debtor's request for additional time, or the trustee's motion to not dismiss the case—the express exceptions found in amended § 521. Under this interpretation, the courts could (as some have) order that the debtor's pay stubs be provided to the trustee instead of filed with the court, but they could not dispense with the pay stub requirement in its entirety.

The second implied exception to automatic dismissal comes from § 521(i)(2), which provides:

> Subject to paragraph (4) [the exception to dismissal on motion of the trustee] and with respect to a case described in paragraph (1), any party in interest may request the court to enter an order dismissing the case. If requested, the court shall enter an order of dismissal not later than 5 days after such request.

By itself, this language creates no exception, but provisions within § 521(i) treat paragraph (2) as if it does provide for an additional exception:

- Paragraph (1), which mandates automatic dismissal on the 46th day, is made expressly "subject to" paragraph (2).
- The trustee's motion requesting that the case not be dismissed may be made before the end of paragraph (2)'s five-day period, even though the case is, technically speaking, already dismissed.

In other words, the plain language of paragraph (1) regarding automatic dismissal ("the case shall be automatically dismissed") is in direct conflict with the "subject to" language of paragraph (1), and with paragraph (4)'s allowance for a motion by the trustee on or after day 46 but before the end of the five-day period. This could be interpreted to mean that the dismissal is not effective *unless and until* a party makes a request and the order of dismissal is entered.

No attorney should rely solely upon the implied exceptions created by the poorly constructed language of paragraph (2), or the general "unless the court orders otherwise" language. However, either could prove useful for an attorney facing liability or any ethical obligation the attorney has to her client to challenge a statute that puts a debtor in a position where compliance is impossible.

III. Pre-petition Tax Documents

Pre-petition tax documents are governed by § 521(e)(2), which requires the debtor to provide a copy of the most recent federal income tax return (or, at the election of the debtor, a transcript of that return) to the trustee and any creditor that requests a copy of the return or transcript.[5] The pre-petition tax return must be provided (but not filed with the court) at least seven days prior to the first date *set* for the § 341 meeting of creditors.

If the debtor fails to provide the return, then "the court shall dismiss the case unless the debtor demonstrates that the failure to so comply is due to circumstances beyond the control of the debtor."

Dismissal in this situation does not appear to be automatic. Section 521(e)(2) makes no explicit reference to an automatic dismissal, as does § 521(i). The section also seems to contemplate notice and a hearing because of the "unless" clause, under which the debtor may seek to be excused for the compliance failure. On the other hand, the court has very limited discretion: the only way to avoid dismissal is if circumstances beyond the debtor's control prevented the debtor from complying.

IV. Post-petition Tax Documents

The debtor's duty regarding post-petition tax documents, and the potential for dismissal of the case if the debtor fails to comply, is outlined in new § 521, subsections (f) and (j). Let's look at § 521(j), the easier of the two, first. That subsection provides:

(1) Notwithstanding any other provision of this title, if the debtor fails to file a tax return that becomes due after the commencement of the case or to properly obtain an extension of the due date for filing such return, the taxing authority may request that the court enter an order converting or dismissing the case.

(2) If the debtor does not file the required return or obtain the extension referred to in paragraph (1) within 90 days after a request is filed by the taxing authority under that paragraph, the court shall convert or dismiss the case, whichever is in the best interests of creditors and the estate.

---

5.   The duty to creditors is stated twice in new § 521(e)(2): once in § 521(e)(2)(A)(ii) and again in § 521(e)(2)(C). The first qualifies the creditor's request with "timely," but the second does not.

Of the § 521 dismissals triggered by a failure to file documents, the duty to file post-petition tax returns is the most straightforward.[6] Section 521(j) creates no new obligations; it just imposes an additional penalty for the failure to file tax returns.

Notice also that § 521(j) does not require the filing of any particular document *with the court*. Although some may argue ambiguity, it appears clear that "file" in paragraph (1) refers to the annual ritual of filing with the IRS. In addition, § 521(j) is not automatic, and the attorney will have 90 days from the date the IRS requests that the debtor's case be dismissed or converted to insist on her client's compliance with his duties under the tax code.

Section 521(f) is more complicated. If "requested" by the court, United States trustee, or any party in interest, the debtor must file with the bankruptcy court all tax returns (or transcripts) filed with taxing authorities during the pendency of the bankruptcy case. This includes tax returns that come due as the case progresses and any tax returns that should have been filed in the three years preceding the petition, but weren't actually filed until after the bankruptcy case was under way. Amendments to any of these tax documents must be provided as well.[7]

What § 521(f) doesn't mention is whether a debtor's failure to comply will result in conversion or dismissal of the case. Neither does the Code—but the BRA does. Not codified anywhere, BRA Section 1228 provides:

(a) Chapter 7 Cases—The court shall not grant a discharge in the case of an individual who is a debtor in a case under chapter 7 of title 11, United

---

6.   "Most straightforward" is a relative term. Virtually nothing about amended § 521 is straightforward. Section 521(j) is just less confusing than its companion subsections.

7.   I've obviously simplified the statute. Code § 521(f) specifically provides:

At the request of the court, the United States trustee, or any party in interest in a case under chapter 7, 11, or 13, a debtor who is an individual shall file with the court—

(1) at the same time filed with the taxing authority, a copy of each Federal income tax return required under applicable law (or at the election of the debtor, a transcript of such tax return) with respect to each tax year of the debtor ending while the case is pending under such chapter;

(2) at the same time filed with the taxing authority, each Federal income tax return required under applicable law (or at the election of the debtor, a transcript of such tax return) that had not been filed with such authority as of the date of the commencement of the case and that was subsequently filed for any tax year of the debtor ending in the 3-year period ending on the date of the commencement of the case;

(3) a copy of each amendment to any Federal income tax return or transcript filed with the court under paragraph (1) or (2)[.]

There's also a paragraph (4), but it's not relevant here.

> States Code, unless requested tax documents have been provided to the court.
>
> (b) Chapter 11 and Chapter 13 Cases—The court shall not confirm a plan of reorganization in the case of an individual under chapter 11 or 13 of title 11, United States Code, unless requested tax documents have been filed with the court.

The barrier to confirmation created by this uncodified provision constitutes cause to dismiss or convert the case under both Chapter 11[8] and Chapter 13.[9] So, although the route is less direct, the failure to file post-petition tax documents leads to the same result as the other documents discussed in this Chapter: dismissal or conversion of the case.

The outcome in Chapter 7 is less clear and quite complicated.[10] But it is clear that no dismissal or conversion of the case will result simply because the court does not enter a discharge. Dismissal or conversion of a Chapter 7 case is dealt with extensively in amended § 707(b), with its means test and good faith filing requirement; it's the opening bell, while the discharge is the final round.

And remember, this Chapter is concerned only with dismissal or conversion. It's not a "how to" for getting your client through a bankruptcy case, but rather for avoiding liability under § 526(c)(2)(B) for your failure to file required documents and the resulting dismissal or conversion of the case.

V. Attorney Liability for Dismissal or Conversion

What happens to the attorney who fits the definition of a debt relief agency when the debtor's case is dismissed or converted because a document has not been filed, served, or provided as required under § 521?

Because of new § 526(c)(2)(B), liability to the client is *mandatory* as long as it is shown that:

---

8. Code § 1112(b)(4)(J).

9. Code § 1307(c)(5).

10. Here's the rub: BRA Section 1228(a) could ultimately lead to a denial of the debtor's discharge, but that's a subject governed by Code § 727(a). Section 727(a) provides that the court shall grant the discharge "unless" one of the enumerated exceptions applies. BRA Section 1228(a) can only be harmonized with Code § 727(a) if it is read as an addition to those exceptions, albeit in a poorly drafter manner. Some procedural issues come into play at this point, including the necessity of an adversary proceeding filed against the debtor to deny the discharge, and the Rule 4004(a) requirement that the adversary proceeding be commenced within 60 days from the first date set for the § 341 meeting of creditors. Interim Rule 4004(c)(1)(K) adds another layer of complexity, creating for parties requesting the debtor's tax information a right to file a motion to "delay" the debtor's discharge.

- the dismissal or conversion resulted from the *attorney's* failure to file the required document, and
- that failure was intentional or negligent.

WARNING!! ━━━━━━━━━━━━━━━━━━━━━━━━━━━━━━━━

Keep in mind that if the debtor refiles within a year, the automatic stay is restricted because the debtor is treated as a serial filer. Blaming the attorney for the prior case's dismissal is one of the few ways the debtor can convince the court to lift the restrictions and give the automatic stay full effect.

Because Code § 526(c)(2)(B) requires that the attorney act intentionally or negligently in order to be liable, diligent attention to the § 521 filing requirements is in the best interest of not only the debtor but the attorney as well. The best way to avoid liability is to implement strict procedures for requesting, obtaining or completing, and filing the required documents and an effective calendar system to ensure compliance.[11] Attorneys should also make clear to their clients—in writing—what the Code requires of them and the consequences that could follow a failure to comply.

Here is a timeline form to help you comply with these deadlines.

---

11.   *See* Catherine E. Vance & Corinne Cooper, *Nine Traps and One Slap: Attorney Liability under the New Bankruptcy Law*, 79 Am. Bankr. L.J. 283, 323-25 (2005).

Timeline Form

Client Name:_____   File No. _____

Date of Initial Consultation:_____   Fee Received $_____

The attorney should initial and date the timeline when   Date/Initials
each step is completed.

   Mini Miranda Notice (§ 527(a)(2)) given?   Yes   No ____/____

     If no, due by _____ (3 days from initial consultation)

   § 342(b) Notice (§ 527(a)(1)) given?   Yes   No ____/____

     If no, due prior to filing petition

   Prescribed Language Notice (§ 527(b)) given?   Yes   No ____/____

     If no, due when § 342(b) Notice given

   How To Notice (§ 527(c)) given?   Yes   No ____/____

     If no, due when § 342(b) Notice given

   Written Contract executed?   Yes   No ____/____

   If no, due by _____ (5 days from consultation but before petition)

   Or, Consultation Agreement executed?   Yes   No ____/____

Date of Mandatory Pre-petition Counseling:_____
   (Must be within 180 days of the petition)

   Certificate received?   Yes   No   None prepared by counselor
   Budget Plan received?   Yes   No   None prepared by counselor

Petition Date:_____

   § 521(a)(1) documents filed with petition?   Yes   No ____/____

     If no, due by: _____ (45 days from petition date per Code)

     _____ (15 days from petition per Rule 1007)

§ 341 Meeting Date:_____

   Tax return due by_____ (7 days before § 341 meeting) ____/____

CHAPTER 13

Section 707(b)(4):
New Certifications, New Sanctions

by Catherine E. Vance

You've heard about it and labored under it for some time already; here is Code § 707(b)(4) in all its glory:

(A) The court, on its own initiative or on the motion of a party in interest, in accordance with the procedures described in rule 9011 of the Federal Rules of Bankruptcy Procedure, may order the attorney for the debtor to reimburse the trustee for all reasonable costs in prosecuting a motion filed under section 707(b), including reasonable attorneys' fees, if—
  (i) a trustee files a motion for dismissal or conversion under this subsection; and
  (ii) the court—
    (I) grants such motion; and
    (II) finds that the action of the attorney for the debtor in filing a case under this chapter violated rule 9011 of the Federal Rules of Bankruptcy Procedure.
(B) If the court finds that the attorney for the debtor violated rule 9011 of the Federal Rules of Bankruptcy Procedure, the court, on its own initiative or on the motion of a party in interest, in accordance with such procedures, may order—
  (i) the assessment of an appropriate civil penalty against the attorney for the debtor; and
  (ii) the payment of such civil penalty to the trustee, the United States trustee (or the bankruptcy administrator, if any).

(C) The signature of an attorney on a petition, pleading, or written motion shall constitute a certification that the attorney has—
   (i) performed a reasonable investigation into the circumstances that gave rise to the petition, pleading, or written motion; and
   (ii) determined that the petition, pleading, or written motion—
      (I) is well grounded in fact; and
      (II) is warranted by existing law or a good faith argument for the extension, modification, or reversal of existing law and does not constitute an abuse under paragraph (1).

(D) The signature of an attorney on the petition shall constitute a certification that the attorney has no knowledge after an inquiry that the information in the schedules filed with such petition is incorrect.

Talking about these provisions by describing their place in the statute (e.g., "subparagraph (B) provides this, while subsection (b)(4)(D) provides that") tends to bog down the discussion, so this Chapter will refer to these four provisions as follows:

§ 707(b)(4)(A)	"Trustee Sanctions"	Collectively,
§ 707(b)(4)(B)	"Civil Penalty"	"Sanctions" provisions
§ 707(b)(4)(C)	"Petition Certification"	Collectively,
§ 707(b)(4)(D)	"Schedules Certification"	"Certification" provisions

This Chapter will look at all these provisions. Specific sections will discuss:

- the scope of § 707(b)(4),
- the Petition Certification,
- the Schedules Certification, and
- the Sanctions provisions.

You'll notice that the various subparagraphs of § 707(b)(4) are not discussed in order. The Certification provisions are discussed before the Sanctions provisions because you should know what's required of you before you get to any penalties for not living up to those standards.[1]

On with the show.

---

1.   *See also* Catherine E. Vance, *Attorneys and the Bankruptcy Reform Act of 2001: Understanding the Imposition of Sanctions Against Debtors' Counsel*, 106 Com. L.J. 241, 245 (2001). The critical distinction between Code § 707(b)(4) when I wrote this article and as the new paragraph was enacted is that sanctions were mandatory in 2001. In a subsequent version of the BRA, Congress changed this to a discretionary standard. See Chapter 3.

I. Scope of § 707(b)(4)[2]

Despite the seemingly broad language used in § 707(b)(4), its scope is limited to a specific set of cases: consumer debtors seeking relief under Chapter 7 of the Bankruptcy Code subject to the new "abuse" standard adopted by the BRA, which is reflected in the means test and the good faith requirement.

Section 103(b) makes clear that new § 707(b)(4) applies only in Chapter 7 cases. That section, which the BRA does not amend, plainly states that "Subchapters I and II of chapter 7 apply only in cases under such chapter."

The language and placement within § 707(b) of new § 707(b)(4) further restrict the paragraph's application. The Trustee Sanctions and Petition Certification provisions expressly relate to "abuse" as defined in § 707(b), which, in turn, applies only to consumer debtors. Thus, it is only two provisions of § 707(b)(4), the Civil Penalty and Schedules Certification, that are capable of broad application to all Chapter 7 debtors' attorneys or to any attorney after the petition has been filed.

However, applying the Civil Penalty and Schedules Certification provisions broadly in the face of the statute's specific limitations is not consistent with well-accepted principles of statutory construction. As I explained in my previous article on § 707(b)(4):

> Applying the maxims of *ejusdem generis* (general terms should be understood in context of specific ones) and *noscitur a sociis* (a term is known by the company it keeps), courts have applied narrow definitions to otherwise broad words, phrases, or subparts of various statutes, recognizing that to do otherwise would create anomalous results, create broader applicability than legislatively intended, or both.[3]

Although few would doubt that Congress meant to tighten judicial oversight with respect to debtors' counsel, nothing in the BRA or its legislative history suggests that this intent was directed at any attorneys other than those representing consumer debtors. In addition to congressional intent, § 707(b)(4) is preceded by the means test and the good faith filing requirement and suc-

---

2. The Certification provisions sections of this Chapter incorporate a good deal of discussion from an ABA Task Force on Attorney Discipline report, *Attorney Liability under § 707(b)(4) of the Bankruptcy Abuse Prevention and Consumer Protection Act of 2005.* I am co-reporter for the Task Force and a principal author of the report, but credit is due to my co-author, Jimmy Dahu, and the report's contributing authors, Nancy Rapoport, Jan Ostrovsky, and Marc Stern. This section is largely a reiteration of the § 707(b)(4) Report at 10-12. This Chapter also relies heavily, as does the Task Force report, on a previous article I wrote on § 707(b)(4). *See* Vance, note 1.

3. *See* Vance, note 1 at 245.

ceeded by a paragraph (5),[4] which provides for sanctions against creditors relating to improper motions to dismiss a debtor's petition as an abuse.

Furthermore, the language of § 707(b)(4) limits its application to the attorney's pre-filing conduct.[5] The Petition Certification's "reasonable investigation" requirement is expressly directed at "the circumstances that gave rise to the petition, pleading, or written motion." Similarly, the Schedules Certification applies only to "the schedules filed with such petition," which would exclude any post-petition amendments.

In addition, as discussed above, § 707(b)(4) is limited to "abusive" filings. A motion alleging abuse must be filed in short order; Rule 1017(e)(1)[6] requires that a § 707(b) motion to dismiss be filed no later than 60 days from the first date set for the § 341 meeting of creditors. The BRA, moreover, requires the United States Trustee to file a statement within 10 days of the meeting of creditors as to whether the debtor's case would be presumed to be an abuse and, not more than 30 days later, file either a motion to dismiss or a statement indicating why no motion will be filed.[7] This restricted time frame regarding whether the debtor's case will be challenged as "abusive" leaves no room for § 707(b)(4) to encompass the attorney's post-petition activities.

Therefore, § 707(b)(4) is limited to the pre-filing conduct of attorneys representing consumer debtors in Chapter 7 cases to ensure that the debtor's case is not an "abuse" under the means test and is not filed other than in good faith.

II. § 707(b)(4)(C): The Petition Certifications

One of two new certification requirements is the Petition Certification, codified at § 707(b)(4)(C), which provides, with important words and phrases highlighted, as follows:

(C) The signature of an attorney on a **petition, pleading, or written motion** shall constitute a certification that the attorney has—
   (i) performed a **reasonable investigation** into the **circumstances that gave rise to the petition**, pleading, or written motion; and
   (ii) determined that the petition, pleading, or written motion—
      (I) is **well grounded in fact**; and

---

4.   Code § 707(b)(5). This new subsection is discussed at length in Chapter 15.

5.   So-called "short filings," where the debtor files only the petition and list of creditors to commence the case, with schedules and other required documents filed shortly thereafter, would be considered within what is generally described as "pre-petition" conduct in this discussion.

6.   FED. R. BANKR. P. 1017(e)(1).

7.   Code § 704(b).

(II) is ***warranted by existing law or a good faith argument for the extension, modification, or reversal of existing law*** and ***does not constitute an abuse*** under paragraph (1).

A. Petition, Pleading, or Written Motion

The use of the phrase "petition, pleading, or written motion" in the Petition Certification is Sloppy Drafting 101. It is a basic rule of construction that when you construe a statute, every word should be given operative effect. This is possible only for "petition," the real object of the Petition Certification, but nearly impossible for "pleading" and "written motion."

To be sure, attorneys commonly use the term "pleading" to refer to any document filed in a case, including motions. Regardless of the shorthand use, "pleading" and "motion" each mean something different.

"Pleading" is defined by reference to the Federal Rules of Civil Procedure. Rule 7(a) instructs that pleadings are complaints, answers, replies to counterclaims, answers to cross-claims, third-party complaints, and third-party answers. Courts have been unwilling to approach Rule 7(a) with liberality. Both in bankruptcy and federal civil litigation generally, the courts construe other documents as pleadings only in exceptional circumstances.

This limited construction of a pleading applies in bankruptcy whenever an adversary proceeding is commenced or, if the court directs, in contested matters under Rule 9014. Conversion or dismissal under § 707(b) is governed by Rule 1017(e), which, unlike adversary proceedings or Rule 9014 contested matters, seems to make no allowance for the filing of any pleadings. If courts are hesitant to expand the application of Rule 7(a)'s construction of "pleading" in adversary proceedings or nonbankruptcy litigation, surely they would not import that term into Rule 1017(e) when there is no textual authority to do so.

Like a pleading, the definition of "motion" is not without limitation; it is a request for an order. Because of Rule 1017(e), motions are certainly going to be filed in § 707(b) disputes, but it is difficult to imagine when the debtor will be the movant. In practice, the trustee, a creditor, or some other entity will file a motion to dismiss or convert under § 707(b), and the debtor will file a response. Oddly enough, under a strict reading of the Petition Certification, that response *is not* included because it's not a pleading or a motion.

If anything saves the Petition Certification from superfluity, it must be the mere possibility that some pleading or written motion could be filed by the debtor in a § 707(b) dispute. The debtor could, for example, request that the court determine whether a particular debt is entitled to priority, the answer to which could alter the income and expense ratio under the means test. Such scenarios are difficult to imagine and not likely to arise, but the prospect that the debtor might file a pleading or written motion bearing on a finding of abuse allows the Petition Certification's "pleading or written motion" language to be construed in a way that each of its terms is given operative effect.

Note that neither "pleading" nor "written motion" is given operative effect in the remainder of this Chapter. The Petition Certification is actually directed at the petition, not litigation documents, and it will be treated as such here.

B. The Attorney's Reasonable Investigation[8]

The use of the phrase "reasonable investigation" in the Petition Certification is just one of many ways the BRA departs from standards to which attorneys and courts are accustomed and replaces them with all sorts of new standards. See Exhibit 13-1.

Here we deal with "reasonable investigation," which, despite the difference in language, should be equated with Rule 9011's reasonable inquiry and governed by the case law developed under the rule.

The reason is simple: there is no discernible difference between an "investigation" and an "inquiry." A brief review of the authorities attorneys rely on shows that these two terms are commonly used interchangeably or to define each other.

Here's just one example from the case law:

> Rule 11 requires an attorney to make a **reasonable inquiry** into the factual and legal basis for the claims asserted. The failure of an attorney to make an objectively **reasonable investigation** of the facts underlying a claim or the applicable law justifies the imposition of Rule 11 sanctions.[9]

And one from a treatise:

> Rule 11 places an affirmative duty on attorneys and litigants to make a **reasonable investigation** (under the circumstances) of the facts and the law before signing and submitting any pleading, motion, or other paper.... The scope of **reasonable inquiry** in any given factual setting may be subject to dispute.[10]

And from *Webster's:*

> **Investigate.** To observe or study by close examination and systematic **inquiry**; to make systematic investigation; to conduct an official **inquiry**.[11]

---

8.   This discussion incorporates discussion from the § 707(b)(4) Report, note 2 above at 12-17.

9.   *In re* Ronco, Inc., 838 F.2d 212, 217 (7th Cir. 1988) (emphasis added).

10.   2 JAMES W. MOORE ET AL., MOORE'S FEDERAL PRACTICE ¶ 11.11[2] (3d ed.).

11.   WEBSTER'S DICTIONARY 624 (9th Collegiate Ed. 1988).

Standards for Determining Accuracy and Veracity of Documents in a Bankruptcy Case

Source	Standard	Object	Comment
Rule 9011	Inquiry that is reasonable under the circumstances	Any petition, pleading, written motion, or other paper presented to the court, except schedules and statement of financial affairs	Exception for schedules eliminated in consumer Chapter 7 cases by § 707(b)(4)(D).
§ 707(b)(4)(C)	Reasonable investigation	Debtor's petition, pleading or written motion	See Section II of this Chapter for complete discussion.
§ 707(b)(4)(D)	Inquiry	Schedules	See Section III of this Chapter for complete discussion.
§ 707(b)(5)	Reasonable investigation	Creditor's petition, pleading or written motion	See Chapter 15 for complete discussion.
§ 526(a)(2)	Reasonable care	Untrue or misleading statements in documents filed in bankruptcy cases or proceedings	Debt relief agencies may not make, or counsel or advise an assisted person to make, statements known to be untrue or misleading in documents filed in bankruptcy cases or proceedings. Reasonable care is the standard for statements the debt relief agency should have known were untrue or misleading.

Standards for Determining Accuracy and Veracity of Documents in a Bankruptcy Case *(continued)*

Source	Standard	Object	Comment
§ 527(a)(2)(B)	Reasonable inquiry	Replacement value of assets and liabilities	Included in notice to an assisted person and may impose standard on the assisted person rather than the attorney. See generally Chapter 11 on notices.
§ 527(a)(2)(C)	Reasonable inquiry	Current monthly income, amounts specified in § 707(b)(2) and, in Chapter 13 cases, disposable income determined in accordance with § 707(b)(2)	Included in notice to an assisted person and may impose standard on the assisted person rather than the attorney. See generally Chapter 11 on notices.
§ 527(c)	Reasonably diligent inquiry for reasonably accurate inclusion	Petition, schedules, and statement of affairs	Applies only if debtor is assisted person. In a Chapter 7 case, this standard must be reconciled with § 707(b)(4)(D). See Section III of this Chapter for more complete discussion of reconciliation.

Inquiry. A request for information; a systematic *investigation* often of a matter of public interest.[12]

And from *Black's Law Dictionary*:

Investigate. To follow up step by step by patient *inquiry* or observation. To trace or track; to search into; to examine and *inquire* into with care and accuracy; to find out by careful inquisition; examination; the taking of evidence; a legal *inquiry*.[13]

Investigation. The process of *inquiring* into or tracking down through *inquiry*.[14]

Black's doesn't define "inquiry," but says that "inquiry notice" means:

Information which is charged to a person where a duty is imposed upon him by law to make a reasonable *investigation*; the information which such *investigation* would have revealed is imputed to such person.[15]

The body of Rule 9011 (and Rule 11) case law is too extensive to detail here, and the ABA Task Force Report has a lot of useful annotations on the reasonable inquiry and other aspects of the Petition and Schedules Certifications. But by way of example, the following case summarizes nicely what is expected of attorneys at the pre-filing stage:

The duty of reasonable inquiry imposed upon an attorney by Rule 11 and by virtue of the attorney's status as an officer of the court owing a duty to the integrity of the system requires that the attorney (1) explain the requirement of full, complete, accurate, and honest disclosure of all information required of a debtor; (2) ask probing and pertinent questions designed to elicit full, complete, accurate, and honest disclosure of all information required of a debtor; (3) check the debtor's responses in the petition and Schedules to assure they are internally and externally consistent; (4) demand of the debtor full, complete, accurate, and honest disclosure of all information required before the attorney signs and files the petition; and (5) seek relief from the court in the event that the attorney learns that he or she may have been misled by a debtor.[16]

What's interesting is that new statutory mandates may well lead to satisfaction of these considerations in some respects, especially if the attorney is also a "debt relief agency."

---

12. *Id.* at 636 (emphasis added).
13. BLACK'S LAW DICTIONARY 825 (6th ed. 1990) (emphasis added).
14. *Id.* (emphasis added).
15. BLACK'S LAW DICTIONARY 792 (6th ed. 1990) (emphasis added).
16. *In re* Robinson, 198 B.R. 1017, 1024 (Bankr. N.D. Ga. 1996); *In re* Armwood, 175 B.R. 779, 789 (Bankr. N.D. Ga. 1994); *In re* Matthews, 154 B.R. 673, 680 (Bankr. W.D. Tex. 1993).

For example, in all consumer cases, much of the factual support for the petition must be filed with the court or provided to the trustee, including detailed statements of net monthly income, payment advices, and tax returns.

Attorneys who are debt relief agencies must give the debtor and file with the court the required § 342(b) notice, which includes a statement that debtors who make false statements under penalty of perjury are subject to fine or imprisonment and that information the debtor provides is subject to Attorney General review. The DRA attorney must also provide written notice to the debtor that:

- all information that the debtor is required to provide with a petition and thereafter during the case is required to be complete, accurate, and truthful;[17]
- all assets and liabilities are to be completely and accurately disclosed in the documents filed to commence the case; and[18]
- information that the debtor provides during the case may be audited, and failure to provide such information may result in dismissal of the case or other sanction, including a criminal sanction.[19]

Compliance with these new filing and disclosure requirements would presumably satisfy some of the attorney's reasonable inquiry duties.

Beyond these statutory requirements, attorneys should satisfy their reasonable investigation duty by complying with the law as set out under Rule 9011. However, they should perform this investigation with a cautionary reminder always present in their minds: there will be people out there wanting to scrutinize how well the attorney did her job.

WARNING!! ━━━━
The new provisions of § 707(b)(4) apply to *all* consumer debtors' attorneys, whether or not they are DRAs.

---

17.   Code § 527(a)(2).
18.   *Id.*
19.   *Id.*

C. The Object of the Reasonable Investigation: The Circumstances That Gave Rise to the Petition

A rather strange component in the Petition Certification is the object of the attorney's reasonable investigation: "the circumstances that gave rise to the petition." The "gave rise to" language suggests causation, meaning the circumstances that led to the debtor's financial distress and the consequent determination that bankruptcy relief was in order.

For the most part, the reason why a debtor files for bankruptcy is irrelevant; indeed, not even insolvency is required in voluntary cases. Neither before nor after the BRA has the Code been all that concerned with the particular misfortune that has befallen the debtor, and eligibility does not turn on normative value judgments. There are exceptions, of course, but as a general rule, the pre-petition circumstances that propelled the debtor into bankruptcy bear little on whether the debtor is eligible for bankruptcy relief.

Indeed, in many respects the means test has nothing at all to do with the debtor's actual circumstances. It doesn't matter, for example, what the debtor actually spent on housing, transportation, clothing, and other expenses before filing because the means test allows the debtor to deduct only the amounts the IRS says she *should* have spent. Neither does it matter what the debtor is earning every month because the means test uses "current monthly income," which averages what the debtor received in the six months before the petition, not just in wages or salary, but from virtually any source. So a debtor who lost her job four months before the bankruptcy would have two months of income from that job factored into the average. The same is true if the debtor caught a lucky break on a scratch-off lottery ticket and won $600 three months before filing; the winnings are counted as "current monthly income" even though it was a one-time shot.

There's more. Because of the manner in which the means test accounts for indebtedness, the debtor who still drives a 1990 Toyota Corolla, is current with his child support, and pays his taxes on time might have a harder time getting Chapter 7 relief than his counterpart with a payment for a brand new Hummer, child support arrearages, and back taxes due. These debtors' "circumstances," however, would suggest that the latter is closer to the abusive bankruptcy petitioner.

In short, the debtor's prepetition circumstances have precious little to do with the means test and vice versa.

But this does not render meaningless the attorney's duty to investigate the "circumstances that gave rise to the petition" because abuse is also defined in terms of the debtor's good faith under § 707(b)(3). If the debtor is seeking bankruptcy protection with inappropriate motives, the circumstances that gave rise to the petition become relevant, and the attorney who aids in the filing of a bad faith petition, or one in which the totality of the circumstances demon-strates abuse, will have violated the Petition Certification (and, before the BRA, Rule 9011).

Good Faith Filing: A Primer

The BRA's "abuse" standard does not end with the means test, but, rather, represents the first of a two-part inquiry. While the means test purports to ascertain a debtor's *need* for Chapter 7 relief, § 707(b)(3) focuses on whether the debtor has the right *motive* for filing.

Section 707(b)(3) commands:

> In considering under paragraph (1) whether the granting of relief would be an abuse of the provisions of this chapter in a case in which the presumption in subparagraph (A)(i) of such paragraph does not arise or is rebutted, the court shall consider—
> (A) whether the debtor filed the petition in bad faith; or
> (B) [whether] the totality of the circumstances (including whether the debtor seeks to reject a personal services contract and the financial need for such rejection as sought by the debtor) of the debtor's financial situation demonstrates abuse.

Attorneys might be on the hook if the motive proves unacceptable. The Petition Certification includes certifying that the debtor's petition "is not an abuse," which includes the new good faith requirement. This is because of the lead-in language: "In considering under paragraph (1) whether the granting of relief would be an abuse"—language that pulls § 707(b)(3) into the Petition Certification.

The scope of § 707(b)(3) will be set by the courts because the statute isn't clear regarding whether debtors who *aren't* means-tested are subject to the good faith test. The answer depends on the phrase "in a case in which the presumption in subparagraph (A)(i) . . . does not arise." There are two possi-bilities:
- The presumption of abuse "does not arise" because the debtor has "passed" the means test; or
- The presumption of abuse "does not arise" because *either* the debtor has "passed" the means test *or* is exempt from it.

There is good news: Because Congress used "bad faith" and "totality of the circumstances" as the standards for determining § 707(b)(3) abuse, there is a body of specific, pre-BRA case law on which to rely. These phrases repre-sent tests developed under the "dismissal for cause" language of § 707(a), which the BRA does not amend, and the "substantial abuse" standard of § 707(b) that the BRA supplants. There's an Appendix at the end of this Chap-ter that gives you the factors you should consider.

This limited application of the attorney's "reasonable investigation into the circumstances that gave rise to the petition" to only the debtor's good faith and not eligibility under the means test was no doubt unintentional. But under the prevailing plain language regime, what was intended is irrelevant as long as the statutory language is unambiguous. There is nothing ambiguous in the phrase "circumstances that gave rise to the petition"; it has nothing to do with the means test and everything to do with the debtor's good faith.

D. The Petition is Well Grounded in Fact[20]

The Petition Certification includes the attorney's certification that the petition is "well grounded in fact." The problem with the use of this phrase is that it resurrects language used in Rule 9011 before the rule was amended in December 1997. This may be the product of congressional oversight: the earliest versions of the BRA were introduced prior to the effective date of the rule amendment.[21] Even if true, the oversight is of no moment because it is the language of the statute that matters.

The courts have two options. The first is to apply those Rule 9011 cases decided after the 1997 amendment, treating the "well grounded in fact" language as largely synonymous with the rule's current requirement that "allegations and other factual contentions have evidentiary support or, if specifically so identified, are likely to have evidentiary support after a reasonable opportunity for further investigation or discovery."[22]

Despite the different treatment of factual allegations under the Petition Certification and Rule 9011, it is doubtful that there will be any significant practical effect. Except in cases involving very close calls, the distinction between the two is slight. Moreover, many of the facts that support the bankruptcy petition will need to be filed with the court, including detailed statements of net monthly income, payment advices, tax returns, and other information that bears on means test eligibility. Thus, much of the factual support will be provided along with the petition, or shortly thereafter.

Alternatively, the courts might be constrained to rely on case law decided under the pre-amendment Rule 9011. Although the difference between the statute and the rule is not significant, it is possible that Congress, which is presumed to have knowledge of this rule change, intended to revert to the pre-amendment version. The most important consequence of reverting to the cases interpreting the pre-amendment rule is that such a reversion will necessarily cause an increase in disputes over whether the attorney should be sanctioned.

20.   This discussion is largely a reiteration of the § 707(b)(4) Report, note 2 above at 17-18.

21.   *See e.g.,* S. 1301, introduced Oct. 21, 1997.

22.   Fed. R. Bankr. P. 9011(b)(3).

E. The Petition Is Warranted by Law or a Good Faith Argument for the Extension, Modification or Reversal of Existing Law[23]

As with factual support, the Petition Certification reverts to the language of Rule 9011 before its 1997 amendment, which replaced "good faith" with "nonfrivolous" in an effort to forestall the "empty head, pure heart" type of argument.

Again, the difference is slight. Like the factual distinction, the difference here is one of degree rather than kind, and the two can easily become blurred. Prior to the rule's amendment, courts examined objective good faith by looking, in part, at whether the argument was frivolous. Post-amendment, determining whether an argument is not frivolous seems to involve at least some measure of good faith.

The likely effect of the statute, then, is that courts will apply current Rule 9011 standards, with the possible addition of defenses associated with the term "good faith."

F. The Petition Is "Not an Abuse under Paragraph (1)"

Abuse under paragraph (1) means that either the debtor "failed" the means test under § 707(b)(2) or, under § 707(b)(3), the debtor's petition is filed in bad faith or the totality of the circumstances demonstrates abuse. As discussed above regarding the "circumstances that gave rise to the petition," an abuse as determined under the means test appears to be removed from the Petition Certification.

The most important point to be made here involves the scope of the Petition Certification (and the Schedules Certification as well), discussed above. The courts' review of whether the attorney appropriately determined that the petition is not an abuse must be confined to the attorney's pre-petition activity. Otherwise, the statute would bring a new, radical element to legal practice: liability for losing. This would not only be an untenable and unprecedented result, it would dramatically chill effective representation of clients. Because the Petition Certification expressly includes the attorney's assertion of good-faith arguments for the extension, modification or reversal of existing law, the Petition Certification does not lend itself to such a draconian result.

Moreover, the means test is riddled with litigable words and phrases whose meaning won't be known with much precision until after the courts have had the opportunity to review them in actual cases. For example:

---

23.   This discussion is largely a reiteration of the § 707(b)(4) Report, note 2 above at 18-19.

- The debtor's expenses will include amounts "reasonably necessary" for health and disability insurance, health savings accounts, and "to maintain the safety of the debtor and the family of the debtor."[24]
- It is unclear what income will be excluded from "current monthly income" as a benefit received under the Social Security Act.[25]
- Housing and utility expenses may exceed the IRS guidelines based on the actual expenses for home energy costs if the "actual expenses are reasonable and necessary."[26]
- If the presumption of abuse arises, it may be rebutted only by "demonstrating special circumstances . . . that justify additional expenses or adjustments of current monthly income for which there is no reasonable alternative."[27]

Even after decisions emerge on these and other issues, certainty will still be lacking. Consider the devastatingly tragic example Mother Nature gave us on the eve of the BRA's effective date: Hurricane Katrina. Few would doubt that residents of New Orleans, many of whom lost everything, would be able to demonstrate "special circumstances" to rebut the means test presumption. But that event wouldn't *define* "special circumstances," leaving open the opportunity to make the argument in other circumstances, including those that have nothing to do with natural disasters and that involve just the individual filer, rather than a whole community.

In the end, the "not an abuse" provision of the Petition Certification can have fair and practical meaning only if it is confined to the attorney's conduct with respect to the preparation of the petition, schedules, and other documents necessary in commencing the debtor's case. To be sure, attorneys will be charged with the facts and circumstances about which they knew or should have known (such as the pre-BRA case law interpreting "bad faith" and "totality of the circumstances," the two phrases used in the § 707(b)(3) good faith requirement). But any broader application is simply not supported by the statute or long-standing legal precedent.

III. § 707(b)(4)(D): The Schedules Certification[28]

Attorney liability for the information on the schedules is new, at least as an explicit statement in the law. The Schedules Certification provides:

---

24. Code § 707(b)(2)(A)(ii)(I).
25. Code § 101(10A)(B).
26. Code § 707(b)(2)(A)(ii)(V).
27. Code § 707(b)(2)(B)(ii).
28. This discussion incorporates much of the § 707(b)(4) Report, note 2 above at 21-26.

(D) The signature of an attorney on the petition shall constitute a certification that the attorney has no knowledge after an inquiry that the information in the schedules filed with such petition is incorrect.[29]

Rule 9011 expressly excludes schedules from the signature requirement as it pertains to counsel,[30] and some courts interpreted this exception to mean that attorneys could not be sanctioned under the rule when the documents at issue are the debtor's schedules. Even if inapplicable, however, the courts have been naturally unwilling to allow a culpable attorney to escape liability by simply claiming that the rule does not apply, with other sources, such as Code § 105 or the court's inherent authority, supplying the authority to impose sanctions.

The standard for imposing sanctions has differed, however. Rule 9011 looks to objective reasonableness, while other sources of sanctions typically require bad faith. In expressly applying a certification requirement with respect to the schedules, the Schedules Certification has struck fear into the heart of debtors' attorneys, who see the change as swinging the pendulum too far in the opposite direction and holding counsel accountable for even minor technical errors or omissions in the schedules.

A careful reading and reasoned analysis of the Schedules Certification does not require such a frightening conclusion. We simply need to find the answer to a single question: what is the scope of the required inquiry?

Defining the scope of the required inquiry is the most important part of the analysis because, once defined, it helps supply the meaning for determining whether the information is "incorrect" and when the attorney has "knowledge" of the incorrectness. And the best possible scope is to require that the "inquiry" be a "reasonable inquiry."

A reasonableness standard would resolve the conflict between the wildly divergent alternatives under a plain inquiry. It is possible that the use of the word *inquiry*, without more, requires counsel to conduct an exhaustive investigation of the debtor's assets, liabilities, and every other bit of information disclosed in the schedules. This would include acquisition of bank statements,

---

29.   Code § 707(b)(4).

30.   Rule 9011(a) provides:

Every petition, pleading, written motion, and other paper, except a list, schedule, or statement, or amendments thereto, shall be signed by at least one attorney of record in the attorney's individual name. A party who is not represented by an attorney shall sign all papers. Each paper shall state the signer's address and telephone number, if any. An unsigned paper shall be stricken unless omission of the signature is corrected promptly after being called to the attention of the attorney or party.

appraisal of household goods, title checks, and a host of other activities that would be far too costly for most, if not all, consumer debtor practices to afford. As a practical matter, it is highly unlikely that courts would give the Schedules Certification such an onerous effect. To do so would be to impose a level of exactitude that the nature of the schedules itself renders impossible.

Moreover, courts have long recognized that attorneys may be dependent upon the information supplied by the client, and that independent corroboration of the information might not be possible. The client may be in a better position to conduct an inquiry, or simply disorganized. Pertinent information may be unavailable for any number of reasons. And not all clients are fully candid with their attorneys; when this happens, the courts have been reluctant to sanction attorneys who have been misled or deceived by their clients. Interpreting the Schedule Certification's "inquiry" as encompassing absolute verification under such difficult, if not impossible, circumstances is draconian and imposes a virtually insurmountable task.

Although "inquiry" must mean something less than a search for exactitude, it is equally improbable that a bare inquiry would be sufficient to satisfy the Schedules Certification. Simply asking the debtor for the information needed, even when red flags appear, is too low a threshold for courts to accept or for attorneys, as learned professionals, to expect.

Reasonableness resolves this disparity, requiring attorneys to do their job and verify information when the circumstances warrant, but allowing them to rely on their clients when it is difficult or impossible to do otherwise.

Reasonableness is also critical in reconciling otherwise different standards for attorneys who are also "debt relief agencies." New § 527(c) requires that DRA attorneys give their clients a written notice with "reasonably sufficient information" on how the debtor is to provide the required information, value assets, and other information. That section is qualified, however, with the following:

> Except to the extent the debt relief agency provides the required information itself after ***reasonably diligent inquiry*** of the assisted person or others ***so as to obtain such information reasonably accurately for inclusion on the petition, schedules or statement of financial affairs***, a debt relief agency providing bankruptcy assistance to an assisted person, to the extent permitted by nonbankruptcy law, shall provide . . . .

If the Schedules Certification's inquiry means something other than a reasonable inquiry, two different standards will exist in consumer Chapter 7 cases: § 527(c) will supply the standard where the debt relief agency provisions apply, while the Schedules Certification will apply to everyone else. This is, obviously, a silly result.

It's clear that defining the Schedule Certification's inquiry as a reasonable inquiry is sensible and in the best interests of everyone involved because it standardizes what the attorney must do within § 707(b)(4) and in relation to the debt relief agency provisions.

Of course there's a catch to this. How do you insert into a statute a word that has been omitted?

Normally you can't because of one oft-cited principle of statutory construction: where Congress includes a particular word in one provision of a statute but omits it from a similar provision, the omission is intentional and must be given effect. Congress used "reasonable" to qualify the Petition Certification investigation and so, the reasoning goes, it intended a different meaning in the Schedules Certification. In addition, the inquiry in the Schedules Certification also differs from Rule 9011, which requires an inquiry that is reasonable under the circumstances.

Despite the language differences and the rule of construction that usually guides resolution, it actually *is* possible to bring the Schedules Certification's "inquiry" into the realm of reasonableness.

Code § 523(a)(2) presents an analogous situation. Section 523(a)(2)(B) provides that a debt obtained by the debtor's use of a materially false statement in a written financial statement, on which the creditor reasonably relied, is nondischargeable. Subparagraph (A) of that section renders debts incurred through the debtor's misrepresentation, false pretenses, or actual fraud nondischargeable without reference to reliance. The question arose regarding the level of reliance, if any, that § 523(a)(2)(A) required.

The disparity was resolved in *Field v. Mans*,[31] in which the Supreme Court held that the inclusion of "reasonable" in § 523(a)(2)(B), but not § 523(a)(2)(A), meant that the latter required something different, which the Court determined to be the more lenient standard of justifiable reliance.

The level of inquiry required in the Schedules Certification, then, may be gleaned in part from *Field v. Mans*, in which the Court stated:

It is only where, under the circumstances, the facts should be apparent to one of his knowledge and intelligence from a cursory glance, or he has discovered something which should serve as a warning that he is being deceived, that he is required to make an investigation of his own.

To continue the analogy between the reasoning of *Field v. Mans* and the language of the Schedules Certification, an "inquiry," which need not be "reasonable" or "reasonable under the circumstances," is required when information given by the client appears incorrect on its face or serves as a warning of

---

31.   519 U.S. 59 (1995).

an inaccuracy. Although this interpretation lessens the inquiry requirement under Rule 9011, which is arguably inconsistent with what Congress wanted to do, the case law supports this reading of the actual language of the Schedules Certification.

If we take this reasoning one step further, the ironic conclusion is that the standard departs little, if at all, from what Rule 9011 requires, save for the clarification that schedules are no longer an exception to the attorney's signature certification. *Field v. Mans* discusses justifiable reliance from the standpoint of "one of [the person's] own knowledge and intelligence," which, here, would be debtors' counsel generally. Thus, something very close to reasonableness emerges. The analysis would not be one that is purely subjective; instead, the courts would examine counsel's conduct in light of that of a knowledgeable and intelligent attorney who represents Chapter 7 debtors.

Voila! The Schedules Certification requires a reasonable inquiry.

Once the inquiry is set at the point of reasonableness, the meaning of "knowledge" and "incorrect" will fall naturally into place.

As to knowledge, a reasonable inquiry will mean that the Schedules Certification encompasses what the attorney knew or should have known. Without reasonableness, the Schedules Certification is open to an actual knowledge standard. Such a low knowledge threshold is no doubt contrary to what Congress intended, but more important, it is below what the courts will likely demand. If "knowledge" could mean only actual knowledge, courts are likely to draw on Rule 9011 to capture those attorneys who should have known of schedules problems.

Reasonableness also helps confine "incorrect" to a useful place. Litigation over technical, no-harm/no-foul errors serves the interests of no one, including courts and parties in other cases who will experience delay. There will *always* be imperfections in the schedules, and debtors have the right to amend their schedules after the bankruptcy case is under way. Examination of whether the schedules are incorrect should be directed at information bearing on whether the debtor's case is an abuse and ensuring that the attorney did all that was reasonably possible to arrive at correct figures for means testing and in ensuring that the debtor is not manipulating asset, liability, income or other information in a way that implicates her good faith in seeking Chapter 7 relief.

IV. § 707(b)(4)(A) and (B): The Sanctions Provisions

Subparagraphs (A) and (B) of § 707(b)(4), which I've termed the Trustee Sanctions and the Civil Penalty provisions, are the new law's punishment provisions for attorneys whose clients are found to have filed "abusive" Chapter 7 cases. These two subparagraphs provide:

(A)   The court, on its own initiative or on the motion of a party in interest, in accordance with the procedures described in rule 9011 of the Federal Rules of Bankruptcy Procedure, may order the attorney for the debtor to reimburse the trustee for all reasonable costs in prosecuting a motion filed under section 707(b), including reasonable attorneys' fees, if—

    (i)   a trustee files a motion for dismissal or conversion under this subsection; and

    (ii) the court—

        (I)   grants such motion; and

        (II) finds that the action of the attorney for the debtor in filing a case under this chapter violated rule 9011 of the Federal Rules of Bankruptcy Procedure.

(B)   If the court finds that the attorney for the debtor violated rule 9011 of the Federal Rules of Bankruptcy Procedure, the court, on its own initiative or on the motion of a party in interest, in accordance with such procedures, may order—

    (i)   the assessment of an appropriate civil penalty against the attorney for the debtor; and

    (ii) the payment of such civil penalty to the trustee, the United States trustee (or the bankruptcy administrator, if any).

Skim through these two provisions once and they seem easy to understand. Read them a few more times and you'll begin to lose the clarity of your first impression. Study them carefully and you'll see all sorts of disputable issues.

A. When Do the Sanctions Provisions Apply?

The answer to this question with respect to the Trustee Sanctions provision is easy: it applies when the trustee moves to dismiss or convert the debtor's case as an "abuse" of the provisions of Chapter 7. (By the way, this is the *only* aspect of all of § 707(b)(4) that is clear and easy to understand.)

The Civil Penalty is a different matter, and its most striking feature is its structure. Reading the Civil Penalty provision without the benefit of the Trustee Sanctions provision leads to the impression that that this is a general sanctions provision; any debtor's attorney who violates Rule 9011 is subject to the assessment of a civil penalty payable to the trustee, United States Trustee, or the bankruptcy administrator.

But the Civil Penalty provision does not stand alone. It follows a very specific provision that allows the court to order the debtor's attorney to pay the trustee's costs in successfully prosecuting a motion to dismiss if the attorney violated Rule 9011. Because of the Trustee Sanctions provision, it is entirely reasonable to interpret the Civil Penalty provision as applying only when the conditions set forth in the Trustee Sanctions provision are met. That is, the

Civil Penalty provision exists only as an *additional* or *alternative* sanction the court may impose on the debtor's attorney where the trustee moved for dismissal, won the case, and proved that counsel violated Rule 9011.

Notice how the Trustee Sanctions provision proceeds:

- The court may order sanctions *if*
  - the trustee successfully moves to convert or dismiss; and
  - the court finds that counsel violated Rule 9011.

The Civil Penalty provision, by contrast, proceeds as follows:

- *If* the court finds that counsel violated Rule 9011,
- *then* the court, on its own initiative or on motion, may order the assessment of the civil penalty.

See Chart on the following page.

In other words, the finding of a Rule 9011 violation is a condition precedent to the motion or show cause order for "the assessment of an appropriate civil penalty against the attorney for the debtor." The Rule 9011 violation itself cannot be found without a motion or show cause order, and the only means within either of the Sanctions provisions for such a motion or order arises under the Trustee Sanctions provision.

The Civil Penalty provision's dependence on the Trustee Sanctions provision is also evidenced by the need to reference the latter in order to give full effect to the Civil Penalty. The Trustee Sanctions provision states that the motion must conform to "the procedures described in rule 9011," while the Civil Penalty provision requires conformity with "such procedures," requiring reference to Trustee Sanctions to determine that "such procedures" means "the procedures described in rule 9011." Without the introductory "if" clause in the Civil Penalty provision, this reference might not mean much. But the combined effect of the "if" clause and the Civil Penalty's statutory dependence on the Trustee Sanctions provision leads to the conclusion that the Civil Penalty is applicable only where the Trustee Sanctions provision has been satisfied.

B. What's the Point of the Sanctions Provisions?

Distilled to their essence, the Sanctions provisions allow the court to order the debtor's attorney to pay the trustee's costs of prosecuting a motion to dismiss, and to assess a civil penalty against counsel, if the motion is successful and the attorney violated Rule 9011.

So what? Attorneys who violate Rule 9011 have always been subject to sanctions, the range of which includes civil penalties and payment of the

Trustee Sanctions Provision	Civil Penalty Provision

• **The court,**
  • **on its own initiative or**
  • **on the motion of a party in interest,**
• **in accordance with the procedures described in rule 9011 of the Federal Rules of Bankruptcy Procedure,**
• may order
• *the attorney for the debtor to reimburse the trustee for all reasonable costs in prosecuting a motion filed under 707(b), including reasonable attorneys' fees,*
 	
IF —
 	
(I) A TRUSTEE FILES A MOTION FOR DISMISSAL OR CONVERSION UNDER THIS SUBSECTION;
 	
AND
 	
(II) THE COURT —
  (I) GRANTS SUCH MOTION; **AND**
  (II) FINDS THAT THE ACTION OF THE ATTORNEY FOR THE DEBTOR IN FILING A CASE UNDER THIS CHAPTER VIOLATED RULE 9011 OF THE FEDERAL RULES OF BANKRUPTCY PROCEDURE.
	• IF THE COURT
	• FINDS THAT THE ATTORNEY FOR THE DEBTOR VIOLATED RULE 9011 OF THE FEDERAL RULES OF BANKRUPTCY PROCEDURE,
	• **the court,**
	  • **on its own initiative or**
	  • **on the motion of a party in interest,**
	• **in accordance with such procedures,**
	• may order —
	  (i) *the assessment of an appropriate civil penalty against the attorney for the debtor;* **and**
	  (ii) *the payment of such civil penalty to the trustee, the United States trustee (or the bankruptcy administrator, if any).*

Key: LANGUAGE IN SMALL CAPS IDENTIFIES PREREQUISITE EVENTS.
Language in italics identifies the penalty.
Language in Bold identifies the procedural requirements.

adversary's legal bill. In this respect, the Sanctions provisions add little to existing law.

But there are differences:

- The Sanctions provisions limit the range of punishment available against a miscreant attorney, which under the rule encompasses everything from a private reprimand to suspension or disbarment.
- The range of sanctions is expanded in one respect: costs and attorneys fees are permitted only on motion under Rule 9011; the Trustee Sanctions provision permits them on the court's initiative.
- Court discretion to determine the type of penalty that would best serve to deter similar misconduct by the offending attorney and others is likewise diminished. This is a double-edged sword. Some attorneys will face a stiffer penalty than the circumstances warrant, while others, including those who behave egregiously, may get off relatively easy.
- There is an express requirement in the Trustee Sanctions provision that the court grant the motion to dismiss before any Rule 9011 sanctions can be imposed,[32] making the section more of a fee-shifting statute than is Rule 9011.
- The attorney can't bill the client for defending against sanctions because only the attorney, not the client, is at risk of being sanctioned.
- The client is removed from the sanctions scenario. Under the rule and case law from the nation's highest court, there has always been discretion to mete out punishment proportionately between attorney and client based on their relative contribution to the wrongdoing.

Some of these differences are discussed in more detail below, but the last point deserves some more discussion because of the old maxim it implicates: *expressio unius est exclusion alterius.* The expression of one thing is the exclusion of others.

Suppose the debtor is to blame for the dismissal or conversion that will result from the trustee's motion. The new statute expressly provides for sanctions against counsel, but only if the attorney violated Rule 9011. An attorney who's been duped by her client isn't in violation of the rule, making sanctions inappropriate. Because the BRA expressly provides for sanctions only insofar as the attorney is concerned, then our old maxim tells us that sanctions against the debtor are precluded.

---

32. Courts won't likely require that the trustee actually "win" the motion, but will also consider cases where the debtor seeks voluntary dismissal or conversion after the trustee has filed the motion. Indeed, this approach is required if the case is converted because conversion requires the debtor's consent.

Of course, dismissal of the case could be described as the punishment the debtor suffers. But let's face it: debtors who set out to deceive even their own lawyers are usually up to no good. The means test challenge could, for example, provide the debtor sufficient time under the protection of the automatic stay to achieve a mischievous purpose or to commit some other, dare I say it, "abuse" of the bankruptcy process.

By the same reasoning, the BRA seems to preclude an award of sanctions in favor of a *creditor* who successfully prosecutes the motion to dismiss. Creditors are not at all likely to undertake means testing challenges against debtors because new § 704(b) provides that the U.S. Trustee or the panel trustee assigned to the case will do so. Creditors might move under § 707(b)(3), which expands "abuse" beyond the means test to also include bad faith filings and those where the totality of the circumstances demonstrate abuse.[33]

Here again, the conduct of the debtor, whether with the complicity of an attorney or not, is demonstrably worse than his means-tested counterpart, who suffered the simple misfortune of having a few too many presumed dollars left over each month. Yet, the creditor that ferrets out the misconduct won't be reimbursed; the statute expressly allows the trustee to recover, and so, by implication, the creditor cannot.

C. Who Can Move the Court for Sanctions Against the Debtor's Attorney?

Both Sanctions provisions refer to "the motion of a party in interest," suggesting that any party to the bankruptcy case has standing to seek punishment of debtor's counsel. The Constitution, however, compels a contrary result.

In short, Congress cannot cross the threshold described as "the irreducible minimum" of standing under the Constitution. This requires that the aggrieved party "demonstrate that he has suffered 'injury in fact,' that the injury is 'fairly traceable' to the actions of the defendant, and that the injury will likely be redressed by a favorable decision."[34]

In the broadest sense, every party suffers some harm when a debtor files an abusive bankruptcy case (or, for that matter, any bankruptcy case). If nothing else, the automatic stay has frozen creditors in place for a period of time. The courts have dealt with this notion of generalized harm in the context of bankruptcy appeals, refining and limiting standing to appeal to only those parties with a direct pecuniary stake in the outcome. An analogous approach should—and likely will—be utilized to interpret standing under the Sanctions provisions.

---

33.   *See* the sidebar on Good Faith Filing.

34.   O'Halloran v. First Union Nat'l Bank of Fla., 350 F.3d 1197, 1202 (11th Cir. 2003), *quoting* Bennett v. Spear, 520 U.S. 154, 162 (1997).

More important, where is the redress? With respect to the Trustee Sanctions, the argument amounts to this: "Your Honor, I was harmed by the debtor's abusive bankruptcy filing. To redress my injury, I respectfully request that you make the debtor's attorney pay the trustee's costs and attorney's fees incurred in getting this case dismissed."

The argument is virtually the same for the Civil Penalty, but with a small measure of redress in the form of vindication for the party requesting sanctions. But vindication is not only insufficient for standing purposes; any creditor who affirmatively seeks the assessment of the civil penalty without having participated in proving the debtor's case was an abuse had better be prepared to answer whether its own motion for sanctions was filed for an improper purpose under Rule 9011.

And under both of the Sanctions provisions, harm and redress disappear completely for parties if the case is *converted* rather than dismissed because the debtor and all the creditors' claims remain in bankruptcy.

D. What's the Relationship Between the Sanctions Provisions and Rule 9011?

Any examination of the relationship between the Sanctions provisions and Rule 9011 is premised on an indisputable rule: any conflict between § 707(b)(4) and Rule 9011 must be resolved in favor of the statute.

The Sanctions provisions mandate that the "procedures described in" Rule 9011 will govern proceedings under both Trustee Sanctions and the Civil Penalty, but the statutory reference to the Rule 9011 procedures likely refers only to Rule 9011(c), because that is the part of the rule that governs the actual procedural, rather than substantive, aspects of Rule 9011.[35]

Here is Rule 9011(c), with the words and phrases that are important in relation to the statute highlighted:

> (c) Sanctions. If, after notice and a reasonable opportunity to respond, the court determines that *subdivision (b)* has been violated, the court may, subject to the conditions stated below, impose *an appropriate sanction* upon the attorneys, law firms, *or parties* that have violated *subdivision (b)* or are *responsible for the violation*.
> (1) *How initiated.*
> (A) By motion. A motion for sanctions under this rule shall be made separately from other motions or requests and shall describe the specific conduct alleged to violate *subdivision (b)*. It shall be served as provided in Rule 7004. The motion for sanctions

---

35. Rule 9011(a) is the signature requirement; subsection (b) describes the conduct the rule is intended to proscribe; Rule 9011(d) removes the rule from the discovery process; and subdivisions (e) and (f) deal with verification of documents.

may not be filed with or presented to the court unless, within 21 days after service of the motion (or such other period as the court may prescribe), the challenged paper, claim, defense, contention, allegation, or denial is not withdrawn or appropriately corrected, except that this limitation shall not apply if the conduct alleged is the filing of a petition in violation of *subdivision (b)*. If warranted, *the court may award to the party prevailing on the motion the reasonable expenses and attorney's fees incurred in presenting or opposing the motion*. Absent exceptional circumstances, a law firm shall be held jointly responsible for violations committed by its partners, associates, and employees.

(B) On court's initiative. On its own initiative, the court may enter an order describing the specific conduct that appears to violate *subdivision (b)* and directing an attorney, law firm, *or party* to show cause why it has not violated *subdivision (b)* with respect thereto.

(2) *Nature of sanction; limitations.* A sanction imposed for violation of this rule *shall be limited to what is sufficient to deter repetition of such conduct or comparable conduct by others similarly situated*. Subject to the limitations in subparagraphs (A) and (B), *the sanction may consist of, or include, directives of a nonmonetary nature*, an order to pay a penalty into court, or, *if imposed on motion and warranted for effective deterrence, an order directing payment to the movant of some or all of the reasonable attorneys' fees and other expenses incurred as a direct result of the violation*.

(A) Monetary sanctions may not be awarded against a represented party for a violation of subdivision (b)(2).

(B) Monetary sanctions may not be awarded on the court's initiative *unless the court issues its order to show cause before a voluntary dismissal or settlement* of the claims made by or against the party which is, or whose attorneys are, to be sanctioned.

(3) *Order.* When imposing sanctions, the court shall describe the conduct determined to constitute a violation of this rule and explain the basis for the sanction imposed.

It appears clear that these aspects of Rule 9011 apply to the Sanctions provisions:

- A motion for sanctions must be made separately from the motion to dismiss or other requests for sanctions.
- The motion or show cause order must describe the specific misconduct alleged against the attorney.
- Notice and a reasonable opportunity to respond are required.

- The attorney's firm will be jointly liable for any sanctions imposed.
- If sanctions are imposed, the court must describe the sanctionable conduct and explain the basis for the sanction imposed.

Because the statute and the rule conflict in certain respects, the following aspects of Rule 9011 *do not* apply:

- The court's consideration of what sanction is appropriate is limited to reimbursement of the trustee's reasonable costs in prosecuting the motion and/or a civil penalty payable to the trustee or United States Trustee.
- As discussed above, the court may not consider who is actually responsible for the violation, only whether the attorney's conduct warrants sanctions.
- The statute permits an award of costs and attorney's fees when the court acts on its own initiative. Under Rule 9011, such an award is allowed only when a party moves for sanctions.

There is tension between the statute and Rule 9011 that is not so easily resolved.

- Rule 9011 permits the court to award the prevailing party its costs and attorney's fees incurred in prosecuting the sanctions motion (as opposed to the motion to dismiss the debtor's case). The plain language of the Trustee Sanctions provision, combined with the maxim that the expression of one thing is the exclusion of the other, seems to preclude such an award if the trustee prevails, but the debtor's attorney may recover for successfully opposing the motion for sanctions.[36]
- Bankruptcy petitions are expressly excluded from Rule 9011's safe harbor, but the statute raises questions about the continued viability of the exclusion. The Trustee Sanctions provision makes *granting the motion* a condition for imposing sanctions. Except for a provision that prohibits a court from imposing monetary sanctions if a show cause order is issued after voluntary dismissal or settlement, the rule is silent as to whether success on the merits is a condition precedent to a sanctions award. Moreover, the courts generally *do not* impose such a condition because victory does not eviscerate otherwise sanctionable conduct.[37]
- The role of deterrence as a guiding principle in determining what sanction is appropriate is certainly diminished under the statute, but it may not be fully eradicated. For example, whether to impose sanctions is discretionary, so the court could render a "warning decision," one that

---

36. Section 707(b)(5) precludes an award to the debtor for costs in opposing the motion to dismiss.

37. *See* note 32, above.

puts the bar on notice that the described conduct will lead to sanctions in future cases, but without ordering the attorney to pay the trustee's costs or a civil penalty in the present case. The court may also have the discretion to choose between reimbursement of the trustee's costs and the civil penalty or, in more egregious cases, to require both.

But by far the most mysterious conflict between the statute and Rule 9011(c) is the statute's complete disregard for the language of the Certification provisions, which differs from that in Rule 9011. The Sanctions provisions are expressly conditioned on a violation of Rule 9011, and the rule's procedures, which the statute mandates must be followed, repeatedly refer not to the Rule 9011(a) Certification provision, but the prohibited conduct laid out in Rule 9011(b). Rule 9011(b) provides:

> Representations to the court. By presenting to the court (whether by signing, filing, submitting, or later advocating) a petition, pleading, written motion, or other paper, an attorney or unrepresented party is certifying that to the best of the person's knowledge, information, and belief, formed after an inquiry reasonable under the circumstances—
> (1) it is not being presented for any improper purpose, such as to harass or to cause unnecessary delay or needless increase in the cost of litigation;
> (2) the claims, defenses, and other legal contentions therein are warranted by existing law or by a nonfrivolous argument for the extension, modification, or reversal of existing law or the establishment of new law;
> (3) the allegations and other factual contentions have evidentiary support or, if specifically so identified, are likely to have evidentiary support after a reasonable opportunity for further investigation or discovery; and
> (4) the denials of factual contentions are warranted on the evidence or, if specifically so identified, are reasonably based on a lack of information or belief.

Where do the Petition and Schedules Certifications fit into the Sanctions provisions? This is one of the hardest questions to arise under the BRA, and the answer is far from clear.

On the one hand, we can make a good guess of what Congress intended. The Petition and Schedules Certifications would supplant the Rule 9011 certification and, therefore, a violation of Rule 9011 under the Sanctions provisions would be measured under the statutory Certifications provisions standards. Under this reasoning, the Sanctions provisions would be triggered where:

- The petition is
  - not well grounded in fact;
  - not warranted by existing law or a good faith argument for the extension, modification, or reversal of existing law; and

- an abuse under § 707(b)(1); or
- the information in the schedules is incorrect and the attorney knew or should have known of the errors.

The trick is that irrespective of legislative intent, this scenario is not what the statute actually *says*. The statute's plain language directs the court and the parties to Rule 9011 with no mention whatsoever of the Petition or Schedules Certification, save for the single reference to "abuse" in both the Trustee Sanctions and Petition Certification provisions. Under a plain language interpretation, therefore, the Certification provisions are irrelevant in evaluating whether sanctions will be imposed.

The plain language interpretation, however, is just as problematic as the legislative intent interpretation, but for different reasons. The plain language interpretation:

- violates the interpretive rule against superfluity because the Certification provisions would have no meaning at all; or
- if superfluity is to be avoided, opens the door for all sorts of attacks against the attorney based solely on the Certification provisions.

Still more issues emerge under the plain language interpretation. The Certification provisions probably cannot be interpreted as allowing any party to seek sanctions against the debtor's attorney for alleged violations for several reasons, including:

- The Petition Certification's reference to "abuse" would be governed by the Trustee Sanctions provision. As discussed above, because the Trustee Sanctions provision allows only the trustee to recover from the attorney if the petition is proved to be abusive, no other party can do so. By implication, sanctions based on the "warranted by law" and "well grounded in fact" requirements are similarly precluded.
- Neither the Petition nor the Schedules Certification provides a means for enforcement or for a remedy. In other words, no one has been granted any right to move for any sanctions under the Certification provisions.
- A party's standing to allege violations of the Certification provisions is questionable. The irreducible minimum for standing—required not by statute but as a constitutional principal—is a demonstration of harm and the possibility of redress for that harm.

As a practical matter, the courts would likely frown on parties who, feeling statutorily emboldened, act aggressively under any authority they perceive the Certification provisions grant them. This would be especially true

for the Schedules Certification because most debtors' schedules will have degrees of inaccuracy simply because precision is difficult in some respects and
impossible in others. In response, there is little doubt that courts will entertain,
and approve, motions by *debtors'* counsel under Rule 9011, sanctioning parties that put the Certification provisions to uses disapproved under the rule.

V. Conclusion

To summarize, §707(b)(4) is riddled with conflict, and resolution is not
easy. My recommendation is to allow both the Certification provisions and
Rule 9011 to have meaning in the determination of whether an attorney should
be sanctioned under the Sanctions provisions. Here's why:

- Choosing between the Certification provisions and Rule 9011 as the
  appropriate measure of misconduct is, as detailed above, virtually impossible and leads to unacceptable results either way.
- Using both helps the courts to resolve the subtle differences regarding
  the factual and legal support for the petition that arise from the statute's
  use of Rule 9011 language prior to the 1997 clarifying amendment.
- Rule 9011(b)(1), which proscribes filing a petition "for any improper
  purpose, such as to harass or to cause unnecessary delay or needless
  increase in the cost of litigation," is an appropriate standard when
  "abuse" is found not under the means test, but the good faith requirement of § 707(b)(3).
- Sanctions are entirely appropriate when false information is included
  in the schedules, or information is omitted, in order to create the appearance that an ineligible debtor is able to proceed under Chapter 7.
  Before enactment of the Schedules Certification, some courts held they
  had no authority to order sanctions in a situation like this.
- Incorporating the Certification provisions into the Sanctions provisions ensures that the attorney is afforded notice and an opportunity to
  be heard.

Of course, there needs to be a sound legal basis for following my recommendation. It can be found in the Petition Certification, under which the attorney for the debtor certifies that the petition "is not an abuse." The Trustee
Sanctions provision, you'll recall, is triggered by a successful motion to convert or dismiss the debtor's case as abusive. This finding of abuse, in turn,
triggers the Petition Certification and, by implication, the Schedules Certification. Following the statute in this manner, and bearing in mind that § 707(b)(4)
applies only to the attorney's pre-petition conduct, allows the court to incorporate in its sanctions analysis whether the attorney truly did know that a
Chapter 7 filing would be inappropriate in individual cases and gives sensible
meaning to all of § 707(b)(4) in all cases.

Appendix
§ 707(b)(3) and the Good Faith Filing Requirement
Factors for Consideration of "Bad Faith" and "Totality of the Circumstances"

The BRA's new § 707(b)(3) codifies a good faith filing requirement for Chapter 7 debtors. The good news is that because Congress used "bad faith" and "totality of the circumstances" as the standards for determining § 707(b)(3) abuse, there is a body of specific, pre-BRA case law on which attorneys may rely. These phrases represent tests developed under the "dismissal for cause" language of § 707(a), which the BRA does not amend, and the "substantial abuse" standard of § 707(b) that BRA supplants. Below are some factors, complete with case citations, you will want to consider.

One case cited below warrants special mention. Judge Cohen's opinion in *In re Attanasio*[1] is extraordinary. *Attanasio* is a treasure trove of analysis and case citations on various issues discussed under former § 707(b), most of which will remain relevant even after the BRA's replacement of the "substantial abuse" standard. More important, Judge Cohen, through *Attanasio*, raises important policy questions reflected in the Code and decisions interpreting it. For example, he cites cases finding indications of abuse based on debtors' decisions to leave jobs or reduce overtime for health or family reasons, which resulted in reductions in income, but reminds the reader: "Wage and hour laws contemplate that a person works 40 hours per week. Section 707(b) neither provides nor even suggests that a debtor must work beyond that amount for the benefit of creditors."[2]

Attanasio could prove important not just in terms of the bad faith and totality of the circumstances standards, but in giving meaning to many of the new Code provisions.

I. Bad Faith
- Concealment or misrepresentation of assets or sources of income[3]
- Excessive continued expenditures[4]
- Maintenance of lavish lifestyle despite financial circumstances[5]

---

1. 218 B.R. 180 (Bankr. N.D. Ala. 1998).
2. *Id.* at 215.
3. *In re* Zick, 931 F.2d 1124 (6th Cir. 1991).
4. *Id.*
5. *Id.*; McDow v. Smith, 295 B.R. 69 (E.D. Va. 2003). For a discussion of "luxury purchases," *see* United States v. Lacrosse (*In re* Lacrosse), 244 B.R. 583 (Bankr. M.D. Pa. 1999).

- Intent to avoid a single, large debt or manipulation of debt to direct consequences of filing at a particular creditor[6]
- Conduct akin to fraud, misconduct or gross negligence[7]
- Using bankruptcy as a "scorched earth" tactic against a diligent creditor[8] or using bankruptcy as a deliberate and persistent pattern of evading a creditor[9]
- Having a frivolous, non-economic motive for filing or a sinister or unworthy purpose[10]
- Attempting to collaterally attack a creditor's state court judgment or forestall the inevitable consequences of the judgment[11]
- Multiple filings or other procedural gymnastics[12]
- Systematic and deliberate misstatements or omissions in the schedules[13]
- Giving knowingly false testimony at the meeting of creditors or a court hearing[14]
- Intentional acts to hinder the trustee's administration of the estate[15]
- Unfair or unconscionable use of Chapter 7[16]
- Payment of debt to insiders[17]
- Failure to make candid and full disclosure[18]
- Lack of attempt to pay creditors[19]

II. Totality of the Circumstances
- The reason for the bankruptcy, including whether the petition was filed because of sudden illness, calamity, disability or unemployment[20]

---

6. *In re* Zick, 931 F.2d 1124 (6th Cir. 1991); *In re* Spagnolia, 199 B.R. 362, 365 (Bankr. W.D. Ky. 1995).

7. *In re* Zick, 931 F.2d 1124 (6th Cir. 1991).

8. Huckfeldt v. Huckfeldt (*In re* Huckfeldt), 39 F.3d 829 (8th Cir. 1994).

9. McDow v. Smith, 295 B.R. 69 (E.D. Va. 2003).

10. Huckfeldt v. Huckfeldt (*In re* Huckfeldt), 39 F.3d 829 (8th Cir. 1994, *quoting* 4 COLLIER ON BANKRUPTCY P 707.03, at 707 to 710-11 (15th ed. 1992).

11. Blumenberg v. Yihye (*In re* Blumenberg), 263 B.R. 704 (Bankr. E.D.N.Y. 2001).

12. *In re* Spagnolia, 199 B.R. 362, 365 (Bankr. W.D. Ky. 1995).

13. *In re* Kahn, 172 B.R. 613, 625 n.23 (Bankr. D. Minn. 1994).

14. *Id.*

15. *Id.*

16. *In re* Zick, 931 F.2d 1124 (6th Cir. 1991); Deglin v. Keobapha (*In re* Keobapha), 279 B.R. 49, 53 (Bankr. D. Conn. 2002).

17. *In re* Spagnolia, 199 B.R. 362, 365 (Bankr. W.D. Ky. 1995).

18. *Id.*

19. McDow v. Smith, 295 B.R. 69 (E.D. Va. 2003).

20. Office of the United States Trustee v. Mottilla (*In re* Mottilla), 306 B.R. 782 (Bankr. M.D. Pa. 2004), citing *In re* Attanasio, 218 B.R. 180 (Bankr. N.D. Ala. 1998).

- Consumer purchases far in excess of ability to repay[21] or made on the "eve of bankruptcy"[22]
- An excessive or unreasonable proposed family budget[23]
- The debtor's age, health, dependents, and other family responsibilities[24]
- The degree to which the schedules and statements of current income and expenditures reasonably and accurately reflect the debtor's true financial condition[25]
- The bankruptcy petition was filed in bad faith[26]
- The existence of state remedies with the potential to ease the debtor's financial predicament[27]
- The degree of relief obtainable through private negotiations with creditors[28]
- The debtor's lifestyle in relation to income, expenses, and debt[29]
- Whether the debtor's standard of living substantially improved as a result of filing bankruptcy or essentially remained the same[30]

---

21. Office of the United States Trustee v. Mottilla (*In re* Mottilla), 306 B.R. 782 (Bankr. M.D. Pa. 2004).

22. *In re* Krohn, 886 F.2d 123 (6th Cir. 1988).

23. Office of the United States Trustee v. Mottilla (*In re* Mottilla), 306 B.R. 782 (Bankr. M.D. Pa. 2004), citing *In re* Attanasio, 218 B.R. 180 (Bankr. N.D. Ala. 1998).

24. Turner v. Johnson (*In re* Johnson), 318 B.R. 907 (Bankr. N.D. Ga. 2005), citing *In re* Brown, 301 B.R. 607 (Bankr. M.D. Fla. 2003); *In re* Degross, 272 B.R. 309 (Bankr. M.D. Fla. 2001), citing *In re* Green, 934 F.2d 568 (4th Cir. 1991); *In re* Krohn, 886 F.2d 123 (6th Cir. 1988).

25. Office of the United States Trustee v. Mottilla (*In re* Mottilla), 306 B.R. 782 (Bankr. M.D. Pa. 2004), citing *In re* Attanasio, 218 B.R. 180 (Bankr. N.D. Ala. 1998); Turner v. Johnson (*In re* Johnson), 318 B.R. 907 (Bankr. N.D. Ga. 2005), citing *In re* Brown, 301 B.R. 607 (Bankr. M.D. Fla. 2003); *In re* Degross, 272 B.R. 309 (Bankr. M.D. Fla. 2001) (citing *In re* Green, 934 F.2d 568 (4th Cir. 1991)); and *In re* Krohn, 886 F.2d 123 (6th Cir. 1988).

26. Office of the United States Trustee v. Mottilla (*In re* Mottilla), 306 B.R. 782 (Bankr. M.D. Pa. 2004), citing *In re* Attanasio, 218 B.R. 180 (Bankr. N.D. Ala. 1998).

27. *In re* Krohn, 886 F.2d 123 (6th Cir. 1988). *But see In re* Attanasio, 218 B.R. 180 (Bankr. N.D. Ala. 1998) (non-bankruptcy alternatives offer little to the truly needy and are available, as a practical matter, only to those with high monthly incomes).

28. *In re* Krohn, 886 F.2d 123 (6th Cir. 1988).

29. *See In re* Attanasio, 218 B.R. 180 (Bankr. N.D. Ala. 1998).

30. Turner v. Johnson (*In re* Johnson), 318 B.R. 907 (Bankr. N.D. Ga. 2005), citing *In re* Brown, 301 B.R. 607 (Bankr. M.D. Fla. 2003); *In re* Degross, 272 B.R. 309 (Bankr. M.D. Fla. 2001), citing *In re* Green, 934 F.2d 568 (4th Cir. 1991); *In re* Krohn, 886 F.2d 123 (6th Cir. 1988).

- The debtor's prospective earning capacity[31]
- Intent to pay select creditors and discharge the remainder[32]
- The availability of exempt property that could be voluntarily liquidated in satisfaction of creditor claims[33]

---

31.   *In re* Attanasio, 218 B.R. 180 (Bankr. N.D. Ala. 1998).
32.   *Id.*
33.   *Id.*

CHAPTER 14

Reaffirming Debt after Bankruptcy

by Catherine E. Vance[1]

The BRA's reaffirmation amendments are unlike any other discussed in this book. Most Chapters deal with brand-new law. Reaffirmation is different. In some respects, the amendments are a radical departure from prior law, most notably in the new standardized content of the agreement set out in the statute. But in other ways, the BRA has retained pre-amendment law, including the requirement that the debtor's attorney approve of the agreement and make affirmative representations to the court. This Chapter will explore this curious mix of old and new and will attempt to ferret out the traps lurking in the amendment.

I. A History of Reaffirmation

The notion of formally "reaffirming" a dischargeable debt is a relatively new phenomenon in bankruptcy law. Under the Bankruptcy Act of 1898, when bankruptcy became a permanent fixture in the law,[2] it was generally understood that a debtor could waive the discharge with respect to a particular debt, and the courts would enforce the promise to pay despite the lack of new consideration.[3]

Over the years, it became apparent that some creditors were taking unfair advantage of debtors' voluntary attempts to repay discharged debts, undermining the "fresh start" that bankruptcy promises. In 1973, the Commission on the Bankruptcy Laws of the United States, in its recommendations to Congress, identified the problems with reaffirmation practices in bankruptcy:

---

1. Thanks to Marc S. Stern, Joel Pelofsky, Corinne Cooper, Michelle Branigan, and others for much-needed assistance with the preparation of this Chapter.

2. Congress enacted bankruptcy laws on three occasions before the Bankruptcy Act of 1898, but each was short lived. For a history of bankruptcy in the United States, *see* DAVID A. SKEEL, JR., DEBT'S DOMINION: A HISTORY OF BANKRUPTCY LAW IN AMERICA (2001).

3. *In re* Melendez, 224 B.R. 252 (Bankr. D. Mass. 1998) (hereinafter Melendez I). Much of the history presented in this Chapter is drawn from the Melendez I decision.

Substantial evidence of the use of reaffirmation to nullify discharges has come to the Commission's attention. To the extent reaffirmations are enforceable, the "fresh start" goal of the discharge provision is frustrated. Reaffirmations are often obtained by improper methods or result from the desire of the discharged debtor to obtain additional credit or continue to own property securing a discharged debt.[4]

The 1973 Bankruptcy Commission recommended that Congress enact a statutory reaffirmation process limited to secured debt.[5] Congress obliged, but without the limitation. Instead, it required court approval of any reaffirmation agreement.[6]

Problems soon emerged. The courts were overwhelmed. A hearing was necessary for every reaffirmation agreement. Debtors were burdened by attendance at an additional hearing,[7] which meant more missed work. The process was unworkable and needed to be changed.

In the Bankruptcy Amendments and Federal Judgeship Act of 1984,[8] Congress shifted the approval burden from the courts to debtors' counsel. Under the amendment, attorneys were required to sign an affidavit attesting that the agreement "represents a fully informed and voluntary agreement of the debtor" and that it "does not impose an undue hardship on the debtor or a dependent of the debtor."[9] Court approval was required only where the debtor was appearing *pro se*.[10]

---

4. *Id.* at 254, quoting Report of the Commission on the Bankruptcy Laws of the United States, H.R. Doc. No. 93-137, 93d Cong., 1st Sess. (1973) (pt. I, ch. 7, § C.3).

5. This recommendation would resurface 25 years later in the National Bankruptcy Review Commission Report. Report of the National Bankruptcy Review Commission, Oct. 20, 1997, Vol. 1.

6. As enacted in the 1978 Code, § 524(c) provided, in relevant part:
    (4) in a case concerning an individual, to the extent that such debt is a consumer debt that is not secured by real property of the debtor, the court approves such agreement as—
    (A)(i) not imposing an undue hardship on the debtor or a dependent of the debtor; and
    (ii) in the best interest of the debtor; or
    (B)(i) entered into in good faith; and
    (ii) in settlement of litigation under section 523 of this title, or providing for redemption under section 722 of this title.

7. The statute required a § 341 meeting of creditors and a discharge hearing. If there was a reaffirmation, a separate hearing might be held for that as well. This practice differed from district to district.

8. Bankruptcy Amendments and Federal Judgeship Act of 1984, Pub. L. No. 98-353, 98 Stat. 353 (1984).

9. Melendez I, 224 B.R. at 257.

10. *Id.* Despite language limiting hearings to pro se debtors, courts have held that they have the authority to review reaffirmation agreements even where the debtor was represented by counsel. *See, e.g., In re* Vargas, 257 B.R. 157, 166 (Bankr. D. N.J. 2001).

Thus was born the entire basis for attorney liability in the current reaffirmation process.

Requiring the attorney to approve the agreement created a conflict between the debtor and his attorney. The attorney was required to exercise independent business judgment in determining whether to approve the reaffirmation. It was not enough simply to explain the law and the consequences of reaffirming a debt, leaving to the debtor the decision about whether to reaffirm.

Notwithstanding the requirement, too many attorneys routinely approved reaffirmation agreements. Section 524(c) was again revised under the Bankruptcy Reform Act of 1994[11] to remedy this problem. Under the 1994 amendment, two new requirements were added to § 524(c):

- Subsection (c)(2)(B) provided that any reaffirmation agreement filed with the court include "a clear and conspicuous statement that such agreement is not required under this title, under non-bankruptcy law, or under any agreement not in accordance with the provisions of this subsection."

- Subsection (c)(3)(C) incorporated the debtor's counsel's heightened accountability, requiring that the affidavit of an attorney representing the debtor state explicitly that "the attorney fully advised the debtor of the legal effects and consequences of a reaffirmation and any default under such an agreement."

The next major event in the history of reaffirmation agreements came not from Congress but from the courts. A Massachusetts bankruptcy judge noticed some problems in Sears' handling of its reaffirmations with debtors. The court discovered a pattern of noncompliance on Sears' part that landed the retailer in serious hot water; it was on the receiving end of a class action and had to pay millions of dollars in damages and civil fines.[12]

But the judge discovered another problem: many of the problems with the Sears agreements could and should have been discovered by the debtors' attorneys, who should never have filed the declarations or approved of the agreements because they were burdensome, contained onerous terms, or were generally not in the debtors' best interests. The court began to issue show cause orders as to why these attorneys should not be sanctioned under Rule 9011. The result was *In re Melendez*,[13] and, in many bankruptcy courts, a heightened degree of

---

11.   Bankruptcy Reform Act of 1994, Pub. L. No. 103-394.

12.   This little synopsis doesn't even begin to describe the magnitude of the Sears debacle, where just about everything that could be done wrong *was* done wrong, save for the bankruptcy judges who brought the spotlight of attention to the problems. For a more complete discussion of the Sears tale, start with *In re* Latanowich, 207 B.R. 326 (Bankr. D. Mass. 1997).

13.   Melendez I, *supra* n.3.

scrutiny of the terms of reaffirmation agreements and attorney declarations. Ironically, some courts have gone full circle to 1978, holding hearings on all reaffirmation agreements, including those where the debtor is represented by counsel.[14]

II. Introduction to the BRA Reaffirmation Process

The BRA marks the fourth attempt to implement a reaffirmation process that allows debtors to maintain relationships with pre-petition creditors without denying them the fresh start afforded by the bankruptcy discharge. Here's a general assessment of the BRA's reaffirmation amendments:

- **The Good**: Disclosure dominates the amendment. As the case law developed, courts have imposed specific requirements about the sort of information debtors must be given before reaffirming a debt.[15] The BRA codifies much of this case law, and debtors are now statutorily entitled to much more specific information than the Code has previously required. For example, reaffirmation agreements must provide specific information with respect to:
  - the amount reaffirmed;
  - the annual percentage rate;
  - any security interest and a list of all collateral and the original purchase price of each item; and
  - repayment schedule information.[16]

- **The Bad**: The attorney declaration—which hasn't worked well in the past—is not only retained, but expanded to include (in certain circumstances explained below) an attorney certification that the debtor can afford to pay the reaffirmed debt. For debtors' attorneys, the amendment means the BRA will:
  - exacerbate the tension over the appropriate role for the attorney in the reaffirmation process and the conflicting duties that result, and
  - potentially create a new plaintiff for reaffirmation liability claims: creditors.

---

14.   *See, e.g., In re* Izzo, 197 B.R. 11 n.2 (Bankr. D.R.I. 1996) ("[W]e feel compelled to and will resume the practice of reviewing *all* such agreements, since the current procedure does not appear to be operating as intended by Congress.").

15.   *See, e.g., In re* Bruzzese, 214 B.R. 444, 452-53 (Bankr. E.D.N.Y. 1997).

16.   *See generally* David B. Wheeler & Douglas E. Wedge, *A Fully-Informed Decision: Reaffirmation, Disclosure and the Bankruptcy Abuse Prevention and Consumer Protection Act of 2005*, 79 Am. Bankr. L.J. 789 (2005), which provides an extensive discussion of reaffirmation agreements under the BRA.

- **The Ugly**: The BRA undermines its own efforts to improve on the reaffirmation process by creating a good faith "out" for creditors and allowing them to keep payments the debtor makes under an agreement that is later disapproved by the court. This point, however, is a policy issue and better left for another day.

This Chapter will focus mainly on "The Bad," and will examine the attorney certifications from three perspectives:

- what the certifications are supposed to say,
- what the certifications are supposed to mean, and
- the potential liability for the attorney arising from the certifications.

We'll also take a look at how creditors' lawyers might be affected in the brave new world of reaffirmation agreements under the BRA.

III. The Reaffirmation Certifications: What Must They Say?

Let's start with the language of the certifications. The attorney's signature on a reaffirmation agreement confirms three specific representations:

- The agreement represents a voluntary, fully informed agreement by the debtor.
- The attorney has advised the debtor of the legal effect and consequences of entering into a reaffirmation agreement and of defaulting on such an agreement.
- The agreement does not impose an undue hardship.

If the presumption of undue hardship arises, there is a fourth representation:

- The debtor can make the payments.

Most of this is not new, as discussed in the brief history above. But the BRA does add a new certification where the agreement is presumed to be an undue hardship. An undue hardship is presumed if:

the debtor's monthly income less the debtor's monthly expenses as shown on the *debtor's* completed and signed statement in support of such agreement required under subsection (k)(6)(A) is less than the scheduled payments on the reaffirmed debt.[17]

If an undue hardship is *not* presumed, the attorney must sign a declaration certifying that:

---

17. Code § 524(m)(1). Under Code § 524(m)(2), the undue hardship certification requirement does not apply if the creditor is a credit union.

- the agreement represents a fully informed and voluntary agreement by the debtor;
- the agreement does not impose an undue hardship on the debtor or any dependent of the debtor; and
- the attorney fully advised the debtor of the legal effect and consequences of the agreement and any default under the agreement.

Certification Forms

Certification where there is no presumption of undue hardship

Part C: Certification by Debtor's Attorney (If Any).

I hereby certify that
(1) this agreement represents a fully informed and voluntary agreement by the debtor;
(2) this agreement does not impose an undue hardship on the debtor or any dependent of the debtor; and
(3) I have fully advised the debtor of the legal effect and consequences of this agreement and any default under this agreement.

Signature of Debtor's Attorney: Date:

_____   _____

Certification where there is a presumption of undue hardship

Part C: Certification by Debtor's Attorney (If Any).

I hereby certify that
(1) this agreement represents a fully informed and voluntary agreement by the debtor;
(2) this agreement does not impose an undue hardship on any dependent of the debtor; and
(3) I have fully advised the debtor of the legal effect and consequences of this agreement and any default under this agreement; and
(4) in my opinion, the debtor is able to make the payment.

Signature of Debtor's Attorney: Date:

_____   _____

If undue hardship is presumed, the attorney must certify that "in the opinion of the attorney, the debtor is able to make the payment."[18]

The form that this "ability to pay" certification should take is not clear, yet it is incredibly important. The statute creates three possibilities. As we discuss the possibilities, we assume that the content is true (the next section is dedicated to ensuring the truth of the content).

Alternative I

A language problem caused us to consider this alternative:

- The presumption provision asks whether the agreement is an undue hardship *on the debtor*, but
- The attorney must certify that there's no undue hardship on *the debtor and the debtor's dependents*.

This is almost certainly a drafting error,[19] and this intepretation would create a big problem for the attorney, who represents the debtor, not the debtor's dependents. But it's what the statute says. In this interpretation, the certification might state:

I hereby certify that
   (1) this agreement represents a fully informed and voluntary agreement by the debtor;
   (2) this agreement does not impose an undue hardship on any dependent of the debtor;
   (3) I have fully advised the debtor of the legal effect and consequences of this agreement and any default under this agreement; and
   (4) this agreement imposes an undue hardship as defined in § 524(m)(1) on the debtor, but, in my opinion, the debtor is able to make the payment.

Alternative II

Under this interpretation, the "ability to pay" certification simply replaces the "no undue hardship" certification:

I hereby certify that
   (1) this agreement represents a fully informed and voluntary agreement by the debtor;

---

18.   Code § 524(k)(5)(B).
19.   In Part D of the reaffirmation agreement, the Debtor's Statement in Support of Reaffirmation, the debtor is supposed to state, "I believe this reaffirmation agreement will not impose an undue hardship on my dependents or me." *See* Code § 524(k)(6)(A). This bolsters the conclusion that the omission of "dependents" in the statute's definition of the undue hardship presumption was unintentional.

(2) this agreement imposes an undue hardship on the debtor as defined in § 524(m)(1), but, in my opinion, based upon information I
have received from the debtor, the debtor is able to make the payment;

(3) I have fully advised the debtor of the legal effect and consequences
of this agreement and any default under this agreement.

Alternative III

This certification form is all-encompassing; it ignores the drafting error
that presumes an undue hardship on the debtor but not the debtor's dependents, and acknowledges that an undue hardship presumption can arise even
if the debtor has the ability to pay the reaffirmed debt. This form would state:

I hereby certify that
(1) this agreement represents a fully informed and voluntary agreement
by the debtor;

(2) this agreement does not impose an undue hardship on the debtor or
any dependent of the debtor;

(3) I have fully advised the debtor of the legal effect and consequences
of this agreement and any default under this agreement; and

(4) this agreement imposes an undue hardship as defined in § 524(m)(1)
on the debtor, but, in my opinion, the debtor is able to make the payment.

Why is all this important? Remember the history of reaffirmation agreements: in too many cases, debtors were victimized not just by overreaching
creditors but by their own attorneys, who too often treated the reaffirmation
declaration as a routine exercise.

Because you're reading this book, we think you want to get your certification right. That means you have to be on guard against adopting a form that
looks like a shortcut, a way out of the standards we think the courts will continue to expect of you.

The moral of this story: don't lose sight of the forest of court expectations
by concentrating too much on the statutory trees!

Rebutting the presumption of undue hardship is a perfect example. The
debtor can overcome the presumption if she has a mere $10 left over each
month, and you can factually certify that the debtor is able to make the payment. But you still face the possibility that the court will find the arrangement
actually does impose an undue hardship (not under the presumption but as a
matter of fact), particularly if the collateral is an unnecessary item, or when
considering the debtor's dependents.

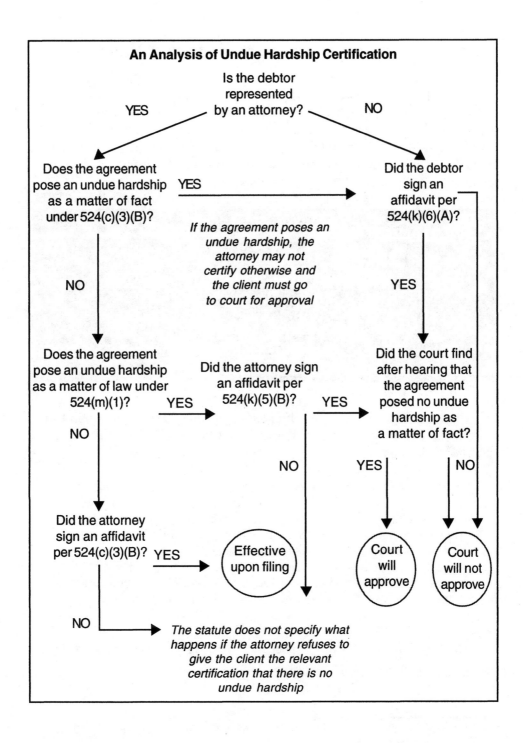

IV. What Do the Attorney's Certifications Mean?

The attorney's reaffirmation certifications are not boilerplate contract language; they are representations to the court governed by Rule 9011.[20] Rule 9011 expressly and unambiguously imposes an affirmative duty on the attorney to conduct a reasonable inquiry into the validity of the facts that she is certifying are true. If the attorney certifies that the agreement doesn't impose an undue hardship, then it better not impose an undue hardship! (More on this below.)

WARNING!! ━━━

Rule 9011 governs *everyone's* participation in a reaffirmation agreement—debtor's counsel, the creditor and its lawyer, and the debtor. As one court quipped in frustration with a particular agreement: "Clearly, something is wrong with either the schedules, the attorney's certification, the seriousness with which reaffirmation agreements are being treated by creditors, debtors, and their attorneys, *or* this Court's ability to read."[21]

There are also two important limitations in Rule 9011's application to reaffirmation agreements and the attorney's certification. The first comes from the following language:

(b) *Representations to the Court.* By presenting to the court (whether by signing, filing, submitting, or later advocating) a petition, pleading, written motion, or other paper, an attorney or unrepresented party is certifying that to the best of the person's knowledge, information, and belief, formed after an inquiry reasonable under the circumstances,—
    (3) the allegations and other factual contentions have evidentiary support or, if specifically so identified, are likely to have evidentiary support after a reasonable opportunity for further investigation or discovery. . . .[22]

This "evidentiary support" aspect of Rule 9011 does not apply to the attorney certifications. As one court explained:

---

20.   *See, e.g., In re* Vargas, 257 B.R. at 165, *citing In re* Melendez, 235 B.R. 173 (Bankr. D. Mass. 1999) (Melendez II).
21.   *In re* Izzo, 197 B.R. 11 (Bankr. D. R.I. 1966).
22.   Fed. R. Bankr. P. 9011.

Here, the challenged representations are that the respective debtors have been *fully informed* as to the legal consequences of their reaffirmation agreements, and that the reaffirmation of the referenced consumer debt will *not constitute an undue hardship* for them or their dependents. These conclusive statements can not (sic) be made merely by having some evidence as to their truth. . . . Only if an attorney undertakes an appropriate investigation and considers the totality of the surrounding circumstances will the attorney have complied with Rule 9011 in making the § 524(c)(3) declaration.[23]

This means that the attorney's declaration cannot encompass any statements that are "likely to have evidentiary support after a reasonable opportunity for further investigation or discovery," as is normally allowed under Rule 9011. This makes sense because the attorney's declaration is an end-point of the reaffirmation process; once filed, there is no further investigation or discovery.

The second limitation is that Rule 9011's safe harbor doesn't apply. The parties don't usually raise problems with reaffirmation agreements. Instead, the court gets involved *sua sponte*, issuing a "show cause" order to the creditor, debtor, or debtor's attorneys after detecting trouble. By this point it is too late to withdraw the attorney declaration (or the agreement itself) in order to avoid sanctions.

Except for the new "ability to pay" certification (required only when the presumption of undue hardship arises), virtually everything attorneys need to know to avoid liability has already been decided by the courts and is discussed in this Chapter. Where provisions of the BRA complicate the prior analysis, they are discussed below.

A. "A Fully Informed and Voluntary Agreement by the Debtor"

The requirement that the reaffirmation be a voluntary agreement of the debtor generally means that the attorney must ensure that the reaffirmation is not the product of coercion or threats by the creditor.[24]

Most common is the debtor's fear that collateral securing the debt will be repossessed, in which case the attorney must determine certain facts. The courts have articulated specific requirements for attorneys in this regard,[25] which are set out in the following sidebar.

---

23. Melendez II, 235 B.R. at 194-95.

24. *See, e.g., id.* at 200.

25. *See, e.g., In re* Claflin, 249 B.R. 840, 847 (1st Cir. B.A.P. 2000), *citing* BankBoston, N.A. v. Nanton, 239 B.R. 419, 425 (D. Mass. 1999); *In re* Vargas, 257 B.R. at 165-66; Melendez II, 235 B.R. at 199-200.

Reaffirmation Questions

Debtors commonly want to reaffirm debts in order to keep the collateral that secures the debt. Before approving of the agreement, attorneys must ask the following questions:

- Does the creditor in fact have a valid security interest in property?
- Is the lien securing the property avoidable?
- What is the creditor's actual intent with respect to repossessing the collateral?
- What is the value of the collateral, independent of any value provided by the creditor?
- Has the creditor properly credited all payments the debtor has made?
- Is redemption a viable alternative to reaffirmation?
- Is the debtor better off converting the case to Chapter 13 and using a payment plan to retain collateral?
- Does the debtor still have possession of the collateral?

On the question regarding value, the attorney now has to take account of the new statutory definition of "replacement value." New Code § 506(a)(2) provides:

> If the debtor is an individual in a case under chapter 7 or 13, such value with respect to personal property securing an allowed claim shall be determined based on the replacement value of such property as of the date of the filing of the petition without deduction for costs of sale or marketing. With respect to property acquired for personal, family, or household purposes, replacement value shall mean the price a retail merchant would charge for property of that kind considering the age and condition of the property at the time value is determined.

This new "replacement value" definition is likely to drive up the cost of retaining property (arguably codifying the "hostage" value for items that have no real worth to anyone but the debtor) as well as the likelihood that the agreement will impose an undue hardship on the debtor.[26]

---

26.   A form for determining value is included in MARC S. STERN & JOEL PELOFSKY, LETTERS FOR BANKRUPTCY LAWYERS (2005).

If the debtor wants to reaffirm a wholly unsecured debt—usually out of a desire to maintain a line of credit after bankruptcy—the attorney must ensure that better options aren't available.[27]

The BRA's reaffirmation amendments add a new dynamic to this certification (and the others). For the first time, the statute requires disclosure of specific information, including:

- a summary of the agreement;
- the amount reaffirmed;
- the annual percentage rate;
- disclosure of any security interest and a list of all collateral and its original purchase price; and
- repayment schedule information.

In addition, the agreement has to give the debtor various "warnings" about reaffirmation, such as the following:

Are you required to enter into a reaffirmation agreement by any law? No, you are not required to reaffirm a debt by any law. Only agree to reaffirm a debt if it is in your best interest. Be sure you can afford the payments you agree to make.[28]

By definition, these disclosures enhance the likelihood that the debtor is making a voluntary, fully informed decision. But what does this mean for the debtor's attorney?

The answer to this question depends, in part, on who drafts the agreement. Despite the extensive nature of the BRA reaffirmation amendments, nowhere does it identify the drafter. In practice, the creditor (through its lawyer) will likely take charge of the task. In that case, the courts probably won't allow debtors' counsel to take the creditors at their word, and will expect the attorney to make a reasonable inquiry into the veracity of the information the creditor provides.

B. "I Have Fully Advised the Debtor of the Legal Effect and Consequences of This Agreement and Any Default"

This is a straightforward requirement. Attorneys must ensure that their clients understand that they will not have the discharge protection for reaffirmed debts. If the debt is secured, debtors need to understand that they will be personally liable if they default, not just for the value of the collateral, but

---

27. *See, e.g., In re* Bruzzese, 214 B.R. 444, 449 (Bankr. E.D.N.Y. 1997).
28. Code § 524(k)(3)(J)(*i*).

for any deficiency as well. In addition, the debtor must be advised of the right to rescind the agreement and the time restrictions for doing so.[29]

But just as with the "voluntary, fully informed" certification, the BRA mandates that many of the legal consequences of reaffirmation be detailed in the agreement. For example:

> Your right to rescind (cancel) your reaffirmation agreement. You may rescind (cancel) your reaffirmation agreement at any time before the bankruptcy court enters a discharge order, or before the expiration of the 60-day period that begins on the date your reaffirmation agreement is filed with the court, whichever occurs later. To rescind (cancel) your reaffirmation agreement, you must notify the creditor that your reaffirmation agreement is rescinded (or canceled).
>
> What are your obligations if you reaffirm the debt? A reaffirmed debt remains your personal legal obligation. It is not discharged in your bankruptcy case. That means that if you default on your reaffirmed debt after your bankruptcy case is over, your creditor may be able to take your property or your wages. Otherwise, your obligations will be determined by the reaffirmation agreement, which may have changed the terms of the original agreement. For example, if you are reaffirming an open-end credit agreement, the creditor may be permitted by that agreement or applicable law to change the terms of that agreement in the future under certain conditions.[30]

Again, it is doubtful that any court will allow the attorney to provide the statutory certifications, justified only by the presence of these and similar disclosures in the agreement. The attorney will have to explain to the debtor what these disclosures mean, particularly where terms like "open end credit agreement" are used.

But the presence of these and similar disclosures in the agreement might assist the attorney in proving that the debtor was fully informed and knew the consequences of signing the reaffirmation agreement. It might be helpful to view the certification as a representation upon which the court will rely in its decision to permit the reaffirmation. If those representations aren't factual, the reliance may be misplaced.

C. "The Agreement Does Not Impose an Undue Hardship"

Remember that "undue hardship" is now a two-step process as far as the certifications go. The attorney must determine whether an undue hardship is imposed either as a matter fact or presumption under the statute, and, if the latter, whether the debtor can nevertheless pay the debt.

---

29.   *See, e.g., In re* Vargas, 257 B.R. at 165.
30.   Code § 524(k)(3)(J)(i).

Prior to the BRA, the Code did not specifically define "undue hardship." Even as amended, § 524 doesn't provide a specific definition, but there is an explanation of when a presumption of undue hardship arises. New Code § 524(m)(1) provides, in part:

[I]t shall be presumed that such agreement is an undue hardship on the debtor if the debtor's monthly income less the debtor's expenses as shown on the debtor's completed and signed statement in support of such agreement required under subsection (k)(6)(A) is less than the scheduled payments on the reaffirmed debt.[31]

Courts have also used an income-less-expenses analysis of undue hardship, but they've also looked beyond this measure to examine the effect of the agreement. One court stated that an undue hardship will exist if the reaffirmation agreement "would result in a significant, but otherwise avoidable, obstacle to the attainment or retention of necessaries by the debtor or the debtor's dependents." [32] Notice that the court, unlike the BRA, looked at the hardship visited on the debtor's *dependents*; the statute's presumption of undue hardship speaks only of the *debtor*.[33]

The BRA does not seem to preclude the courts from applying a broader definition of undue hardship. The BRA addresses only the presumption, and just because the debtor is able to rebut the presumption does not lead to the automatic (or mandatory) conclusion that undue hardship will not result if the debtor reaffirms the debt. Moreover, the attorney must certify that the agreement "does not impose an undue hardship on the debtor or any dependent of the debtor," which is separate from (and differently worded than) language relating to the presumption of undue hardship. Finally, in cases where the presumption does not apply, the attorney still has the previously existing obligation to certify that there is no hardship.

What is required before an attorney can properly certify that the reaffirmation agreement does not impose an undue hardship? One court summarized the attorney's duty this way:

In order to be satisfied that reaffirmation would not cause a debtor undue hardship, an attorney must be fully conversant with the financial circumstances of both the debtor and the debtor's dependents. An attorney should analyze the income and expenses of the debtor's household, including a review and update of the information contained in the debtor's Schedules I

---

31.   Code § 524(m)(1).

32.   *In re* Melendez II, 235 B.R. at 197, quoting Melendez I, 224 B.R. at 261.

33.   As discussed above, the omission of "dependents" from the undue hardship presumption is probably a drafting error.

and J. If it appears that the debtor's expenses will exceed his or her postpetition income, and if reaffirmation of the debt is not necessary to retain an item which the debtor or his or her dependents require for their well-being—or if the item itself is not necessary—then payment of the reaffirmed debt in addition to the debtor's existing expenses would clearly jeopardize the debtor's ability to pay for necessary living expenses and impose an undue hardship.[34]

We think the courts will continue to take a broad approach to "undue hardship" rather than confining their inquiry into the simplified income-less-expenses analysis called for under the presumption. Bankruptcy courts, as courts of equity, generally prefer to look at the substance of transactions over their form. With reaffirmation agreements, this means the courts will prefer to determine what really matters: whether the agreement will actually impose an undue burden.

D. "Ability to Pay" Certification Where Undue Hardship Is Presumed

If undue hardship is presumed, then the attorney's certification must include a statement that "in the opinion of the *attorney*, the *debtor* is able to make the payment."[35] Keep in mind that this certification seems to apply only where the statutory presumption arises—that is, where the debtor's income, less expenses, isn't sufficient to satisfy the reaffirmation payment terms. If the agreement imposes an undue hardship under the guidelines set by the courts, then the ability to pay certification doesn't seem to be required.

It's also hard to see the relevance of the ability to pay certification. Let's take another look at Code § 524(m)(1), this time in full:

[I]t shall be presumed that such agreement is an undue hardship on the debtor if the debtor's monthly income less the debtor's expenses as shown on the debtor's completed and signed statement in support of such agreement required under subsection (k)(6)(A) is less than the scheduled payments on the reaffirmed debt. This presumption shall be reviewed by the court. The presumption may be rebutted in writing by the debtor if the statement includes an explanation that identifies additional sources of funds to make the payments as agreed upon under the terms of such agreement. If the presumption is not rebutted to the satisfaction of the court, the court may disapprove such agreement. No agreement shall be disapproved without notice and a hearing to the debtor and creditor, and such hearing shall be concluded before the entry of the debtor's discharge.[36]

---

34.   *See, e.g.*, Melendez II, 235 B.R. at 197.
35.   Code § 524(k)(5)(B) (emphasis added).
36.   Code § 524(m)(1).

Here's the important information this statute gives us:

- When the presumption arises and where to find the applicable income and expense information;
- That court review is required if the presumption arises;[37]
- How *the debtor* may rebut the presumption; and
- If the court isn't satisfied with the debtor's rebuttal evidence, it can disapprove the agreement.

But it doesn't tell us anything about where the ability to pay certification fits into this process. A court hearing doesn't depend on the absence of the certification, and the court isn't required to approve the agreement if the certification is provided. Its only purpose seems to be as additional evidence for the debtor to give the court in rebuttal of the presumption and to satisfy the § 524(k)(5)(B) demand for it.

The meaningful part of the attorney's participation has less to do with the certification than with the Debtor's Statement in Support of Reaffirmation, on which the presumption depends. Provided for in Part D of the agreement, the Statement in Support provides in part:

> I believe this reaffirmation agreement will not impose an undue hardship on my dependents or me. I can afford to make the payments on the reaffirmed debt because my monthly income (take home pay plus any other income received) is $_____, and my actual current monthly expenses including monthly payments on post-bankruptcy debt and other reaffirmation agreements total $_____, leaving $_____ to make the required payments on this reaffirmed debt. I understand that if my income less my monthly expenses does not leave enough to make the payments, this reaffirmation agreement is presumed to be an undue hardship on me and must be reviewed by the court. However, this presumption may be overcome if I explain to the satisfaction of the court how I can afford to make the payments here:_____.[38]

Remembering the lessons of the pre-BRA case law, we can give meaning to the ability to pay certification if we see it as a reflection of an accurate Statement in Support. That is, the debtor's attorney should ensure that the debtor understands:

---

37. No court hearing is required if the creditor is a credit union, because the undue hardship presumption and the requirement of a hearing when the presumption arises are not applicable to credit unions. Code § 524(m)(2).

38. Code § 524(k)(3)(J)(i). The statute really does provide a line less than an inch long for the debtor to explain how she can afford to make the payment.

- what the Statement in Support means, and
- that she must provide complete and accurate information regarding
  - her income and expenses, and,
    - if needed, the explanation of how the debtor will perform if there is a presumption of undue hardship.[39]

This approach actually affords the debtor's attorney a measure of protection. For one thing, you run the risk that the agreement isn't "fully informed" if you leave the debtor on her own to complete the Statement in Support. More important, the debtor waves a big red flag if she provides information in the Statement that is inconsistent with the income and expense information in the schedules and statements she filed when her case began. This might trigger scrutiny not just of the reaffirmation agreement, but also of the schedules—which the attorney certified as being correct.

Remember: the attorney isn't required to provide any certification,[40] and providing one that isn't true is and always has been the basis for liability.

---

39.   The extent to which the creditor can rely on the Statement in Support, irrespective of whether the debtor is represented, depends on whether that reliance was reasonable (or, perhaps, justifiable). This issue is discussed in more detail below, but creditors must keep in mind that information in a reaffirmation agreement isn't provided in a vacuum, but in a context where the creditor can get its hands on all sorts of financial information about the debtor that might not otherwise be available.

40.   *See, e.g., In re* Vargas, 257 B.R. at 163 ("Debtor's attorneys have a choice to make when presented with their clients' reaffirmation agreements. They may remain strictly advocates and decline to sign the requisite declaration attached to the reaffirmation agreement.").

Reaffirmation and the Debtor's Attorney's Conflicts

Ever since Congress first shifted reaffirmation approval from the courts to debtors' attorneys, those attorneys have faced a conflict in serving their clients. The client, not the lawyer, has the ultimate authority to decide to reaffirm a debt, no matter how ill-advised the reaffirmation might be. Attorneys are advocates and legal representatives; controlling the client's conduct (so long as it is not illegal) is not the attorney's duty or right.

There are any number of reasons why a debtor might be tempted to reaffirm—to retain collateral, maintain a relationship with a creditor, or settle dischargeability litigation, to name a few—despite the undue hardship that might result.

But the attorney's declaration must be meaningful, not a means to achieve the client's end. Courts have insisted that attorneys exercise independent judgment, declining to approve any reaffirmation the attorney believes will impose an undue hardship. No less will be expected under the BRA.

Indeed, as officers of the court, attorneys are forbidden from representing that reaffirming a debt imposes no undue hardship if it isn't so.

An attorney's refusal to provide the required certification is not the death knell for the client's reaffirmation. It simply triggers a hearing and review by the court.

It's true that the law of reaffirmation creates a conflict in the attorney's role of advocate, requiring attorney approval of decisions that belong to the client. But the law simply doesn't allow you to acquiesce to your client's wishes any more than it permits you to abdicate your responsibilities to the court in all cases by adopting a policy of blanket refusal to provide the certifications.

In the final analysis, the reaffirmation certifications involve the same analysis as any other paper presented to the court: sign and file only if you can do so with candor.

V. *Liability Traps: Debtors' Attorneys*

There are a number of ways an attorney could find himself facing liability in the reaffirmation context.

Let's start with the most obvious, Rule 9011. The attorney's certifications are representations to the court. If the attorney fails to conduct a reasonable inquiry, or presents the certifications for a purpose the rule forbids, then the court can impose sanctions. Here are five scary scenes for you to contemplate before you sign that certification.

1. Suppose you receive a nearly complete agreement from a creditor, flag for your client where she needs to provide information, and for-

ward it to her. When you get it back, you sign the certification and file the agreement with the court.

This is the "rubber-stamp" example. You've represented to the court that you've analyzed the agreement and provided appropriate legal advice to your client when you've done nothing of the sort. You could face Rule 9011 sanctions, but the court also has Code § 329 at its disposal. If your client paid you for this service, she probably didn't get her money's worth and you might have to disgorge your fee.

You've also created a risk of malpractice. By signing the certifications, you've signaled to the client that the reaffirmation is not, in fact, an undue hardship. If she ends up defaulting on the agreement, then she may claim that she wouldn't have entered into the agreement without your imprimatur. This risk is heightened if the agreement likely wouldn't have passed judicial muster had a hearing been required.

2. Now suppose that you actually review the agreement after the client sends it back to you. You check the Debtor's Statement to see if undue hardship is presumed, but it shows sufficient income to cover expenses and the reaffirmed debt. So, you sign and file the agreement. You find out later (probably after a default) that your client used the income and expense amounts from your means test analysis, not what she actually earns and spends.

Are you in trouble? You could be, because your client wasn't "fully informed" about the income and expense information required in the reaffirmation agreement. With the new filing requirements, it's not unlikely that debtors will be confused in this regard, but it is reasonable for them to refer to their filing documents for the necessary information.

3. A modest change in facts opens a new door to liability. Your client provides income and expense information that is not consistent with what was provided at the time of filing, and the court suspects the numbers have been manipulated. If it turns out that it's the schedules that are wrong, you could be on the hook under new Code § 707(b)(4)(D) because you certified that, after an inquiry, you had no knowledge that the information was incorrect.[41]

4. What if you do everything exactly right and you're stuck with the conclusion that you cannot provide the attorney certifications and the court disapproves the agreement? If you're a debt relief agency, you could be in trouble here, too, if your contract isn't constructed in a way that allows for this possibility. If the contract simply states that

---

41.   For more information about the schedules certification, see Chapter 13.

you will "assist with reaffirmation agreements," for example, your client can claim that you failed to provide a service you informed her you would provide!

5. *Now brace yourself for the scary part*—You might even be challenged by the *creditor* if you certify that the debtor can pay the reaffirmed debt when the presumption of abuse arises.

The BRA's most radical departure from prior law is the risk that attorneys could be considered guarantors of their clients' reaffirmed debts.

The certification that the debtor has the ability to make the payment puts the attorney for the debtor at risk to the creditor for the first time. As a general rule, attorneys have no duty to non-clients.[42] An exception to this is the case in which the attorney took an action or made a representation with the expectation that a third party would rely on it, and the third party did rely upon that action or representation.[43]

The creditor can be expected to argue something like this against the attorney: "You certified that the debtor could make the payments. I would not have entered into this agreement but for your certification that she could. I relied upon that certification. But the debtor failed to perform. I have been damaged and you are the cause."

Is the attorney liable to the creditor as the guarantor of the debtor's reaffirmation agreement? We don't think so. There are enough waffle words in the statute that a clever attorney (one hired by the malpractice carrier, for example) can construct a defense. "It was his opinion; there were facts not disclosed; there was a change in circumstances that he could not reasonably foresee" are some that come to mind.

What's more, the creditor will have a hard time convincing a court that its reliance was reasonable or even justifiable. There is an enormous body of case law discussing reliance under Code §§ 523(a)(2)(A) and (B), which the courts can apply in the reaffirmation context. But here creditors face an additional hurdle: they are entitled to a wealth of information about the debtor's finances under various new provisions of the Code.[44] The courts can and should view the creditor's reliance on the attorney's certification—or any other representation in a reaffirmation agreement, for that matter—in the context of what the credi-

---

42. *See, e.g.,* Bon v. Cody, 119 Wn. 2d 357, 832 P.2d 357 (1992) (no duty to non-client unless special relationship present).

43. *See, e.g.,* Chesswell, Inc. v. Premier Homes and Land Corp., 319 F. Supp. 2d 144 (D. Mass. 2004); Tackling v. Shinerman, 42 Conn. Supp. 517, 630 A.2d 1381 (Conn. Super. 1993).

44. *See, e.g.,* Code § 521.

tor knew or should have known based on readily available information.

Another problem for creditors is the requirement of a hearing when undue hardship is presumed. The court has to be satisfied that the debtor actually can make the payment on the reaffirmed debt despite the presumption before it can approve the agreement. If it does, the creditor's argument of reliance on the attorney's certification loses a good deal of its force.

In short, a win for the creditor is not likely.

The attorney's best protection comes before the reaffirmation agreement is filed. Before the BRA, the courts were clear that an attorney should not sign the required declaration if its contents aren't true. That is, if the agreement isn't voluntary and fully informed, or it presents an undue hardship, the attorney shouldn't certify to the contrary. In all likelihood, the case law will apply equally to the ability to pay certification.

VI. Liability Traps, Part 2: Creditors' Lawyers

It's no secret that courts can sanction creditors for improper conduct in the reaffirmation process. Just ask Sears. But that's not what we're talking about here. What matters are the much less obvious liability traps.

Let's start with Rule 9011. In the reaffirmation agreement, the creditor—probably through its attorney—makes representations to the court. And remember, the thrust of the BRA is disclosure, so a lot of information must be specifically stated in the agreement. So it better be right, after a reasonable inquiry.

Suppose you're dealing with a debtor who isn't represented by counsel. Did you know you might be a bankruptcy petition preparer? A more complete discussion is in Chapter 15, but be forewarned that if you draft the reaffirmation agreement, which must be filed, and you're compensated for it, you might just fit the statutory "bankruptcy petition preparer" definition.

One last note for creditors' attorneys: don't count on using the new Chapter 7 filing requirements as a means of getting your debt reaffirmed. New Code § 707(b)(5), which is discussed in Chapter 15, is designed for just that purpose, and you could find yourself getting sanctioned.

VII. Conclusion

Attorneys might be able to avoid the whole reaffirmation issue by limiting representation and excluding any matters relating to reaffirming debts. Chapter 6 discusses this possibility in much greater detail. At a minimum, the retainer agreement should give the attorney the flexibility to decline to sign the declarations if, in the attorney's own judgment, he cannot do so truthfully. If the client is an "assisted person," there are specific requirements for retainer agreements. Retainer agreements are discussed in Chapter 10, and the liabilities that flow from being a debt relief agency are discussed in Chapter 11.

Keep in mind that, despite the seemingly extensive changes, the old adage that "the more things change, the more they stay the same" applies to the law of reaffirmations. In the end, reaffirmation agreements, including the certifications, involve the same analysis as any other paper presented to the court: sign and file, if you can do so with candor.

A checklist for Reaffirmation Transactions follows.

Checklist For Reaffirmation Transactions

Prior to the BRA, the process of reaffirmation established by § 524 was fairly well settled and relatively straightforward. Although the amendments to § 524 do not overturn precedent, they do require that information be provided to the debtor, primarily from the creditor or its counsel, and expand the duties of the debtor and the debtor's attorney concerning certification of the debtor's ability to make payments.

Because the transaction is more complicated, it is important for counsel to maintain records of the advice given, and debtor's acknowledgement that s/he received and understood the advice.

The following checklist tracks the statutory requirements and will assist you in making sure that the reaffirmation documents and processes meet the requirements of the law.

Initials

_____ Property listed with intention to retain:
_____ Amount of debt:
_____ Value of property:
_____ Terms of original obligation:
_____ Balance due:
_____ Amount of default, if any:
_____ Interest rate: _____%
_____ Security interest perfected (if necessary):

§ 524(k) disclosures:

_____   a. Total amount of debt to be reaffirmed:
_____   b. Total of fees and costs accrued:
_____   c. § 103 Truth in Lending open end credit extension amount:
_____   d. § 127(b) Truth in Lending ¶¶ (5) and (6) interest rate: _____%
_____   e. Simple interest rate applicable to reaffirmed debt: _____%
_____   f. If not open end extension, § 128(a)(4) Truth in Lending rate: _____%
_____   g. Simple interest rate applicable under this loan: _____%
_____   h. Variable rate notice (§ 524(k)(3)(F)), if applicable:
_____   i. Perfection of security interest, purchase price of items that constitute collateral
_____   j. Disclosures required by § 524(3)(J) included
_____   k. Reaffirmation agreement follows form
_____   l. Debtor's attorney certification:
_____   1. Not an undue hardship
_____   2. Presumption of undue hardship
_____   m. Motion for court approval required
_____   n. 60-day period expires on: _____
_____   o. Agreement returned to creditor on: _____
_____   p. Agreement filed by creditor on: _____
         Received on: _____ .

Thanks to Joel Pelofsky for providing this form.

CHAPTER 15

Creditors' Lawyers and Other White Meat

by Catherine E. Vance and Corinne Cooper

Most of the Chapters in this book talk about attorney liability from the perspective of attorneys representing consumer debtors. We focus on them for a good reason: most of the BRA's provisions affecting lawyers and the practice of law are directed at consumer debtor practice.

But there are provisions—some traps, if you will—into which other attorneys may stumble.[1] This Chapter points out some provisions that will eat you alive if you aren't aware of them.

I. Poof! You're a Bankruptcy Petition Preparer

The legislation that became the BRA was around for a long time, and through its journey from being just a lonely bill sitting up there on Capitol Hill[2] to becoming part of the Code, some surprising changes were made.

Among these changes is an amendment to the definition of "bankruptcy petition preparer" that is important because it has the potential to apply well beyond what Congress intended:

Old BPP: "a person, other than an attorney or an employee of an attorney, who prepares for compensation a document for filing."

New BPP: "a person, other than the attorney *for the debtor* or an employee of *such attorney under the direct supervision of such attorney*, who prepares for compensation a document for filing."[3]

---

1. This Chapter is largely based upon Catherine E. Vance & Corinne Cooper, *Nine Traps and One Slap: Attorney Liability under the New Bankruptcy Law,* 79 Am. Bankr. L.J. 283, 325-27 (2005).

2. Yes, that's the old Schoolhouse Rock song. Search for "Best of Schoolhouse Rock" on Amazon and you can listen to it for yourself.

3. A "document for filing" is "a petition or any other document prepared for filing by a debtor in a United States bankruptcy court or a United States district court in connection with" a bankruptcy case. Code § 110(a)(2).

Whether intended or not, this change has at least one very significant effect: attorneys who are retained by bankruptcy petition preparers to provide general—but not specific—client-directed advice to otherwise *pro se* bankruptcy debtors may fall within the ambit of the BPP definition. Many of these attorneys have long evaded the ethical and legal obligations imposed on attorneys because they do not have an attorney-client relationship with the individuals with whom they speak, and they limit any "advice" they give to providing general answers to debtors' questions, even though the debtors likely need specific information. The rewritten BPP definition curbs this activity by regulating the supervising attorneys as bankruptcy petition preparers.

But there's more. Under Code § 110(a)(1), as amended, an attorney who, for compensation, prepares *any* document for *any* debtor for filing with the court in connection with a proceeding under *any* chapter of the Code falls within one of two categories: an attorney for the debtor or a bankruptcy petition preparer.

Imagine this situation: You represent Acme Motor Sales, which sold a car, retaining a PMSI, to an individual who later became a *pro se* debtor in bankruptcy. At the request of Acme, you draft a reaffirmation agreement that fulfills the requirements of Code § 524(k), obtain the necessary information from Acme to complete Parts A and B, and have an authorized officer of Acme sign Part B. You then send the reaffirmation agreement to the debtor to sign Part B and complete Parts D and E, and to file the agreement with the court.

Are you a bankruptcy petition preparer? The "plain language" of Code § 110(a) creates a distinct possibility that you are. You are not the attorney for the debtor, and if the debtor files the reaffirmation agreement you prepared, it fits within the plain language of Code § 110(a)(2)—"document prepared for filing by a debtor."

Being cautious, you instruct the debtor in your cover letter to return the completed agreement to you for filing. (Most creditors will want to control filing to make sure it is timely filed and they have a valid reaffirmation agreement.) But here's the rub: because the debtor is *pro se*, a hearing is required, on motion of the debtor, which is Part E of the reaffirmation. The language of the Part E motion is set out in the statute and is clearly a motion by the debtor. So, even if the physical act of filing is not by the debtor, it is still the debtor's document.

Faced with this prospective problem, you prepare only Parts A and B, leaving it to the debtor to provide Parts D and E. Oops—the debtor is *pro se*, and doesn't have the foggiest idea of what to do next. Acme really wants this reaffirmation because the car is under water and Acme doesn't want it back. Because the debtor doesn't know what to do, you don't have much choice but to prepare Parts D and E for the debtor and to assist the debtor in completing them. This seems to fall squarely within the § 110(a) definition and, what's more, makes you a debt relief agency as well.[4]

---

4.   Unless a specific exception applies, all BPPs are debt relief agencies.

These results may seem ludicrous and are most certainly not what Congress intended in amending the "bankruptcy petition preparer" definition. But they are possible under the "plain meaning" of § 110(a).[5]

You are not without arguments against applying § 110(a) in these situations. In the first place, § 110(a) speaks of documents filed "by" the debtor. Read plainly, that probably doesn't mean a document you file "for" the debtor. There's also a question of consideration; the debtor probably isn't paying you to do any of this work. But your client is.

Should this issue ever come before a court, the "plain meaning" rule will collide head-on with common sense and what we presume is congressional intent,[6] and the court will determine the outcome. If courts find that these facts produce absurd results, or that the plain language is demonstrably at odds with the intent of the drafters,[7] they can rule that § 110(a) doesn't apply.[8]

II. Tax Return Preparers, Beware! Are You a BPP? A DRA?

Imagine another set of facts. Suppose Cathy Consumer comes to Joe, the neighborhood bankruptcy attorney, because she needs to file bankruptcy. In going over the means test checklist with Cathy, Joe asks for tax returns and Cathy confesses that she hasn't filed them in several years. So Joe sends Cathy to Robert, a tax attorney, who often works with Joe.[9] Robert prepares and files the back tax returns, but without making payment of back taxes because Cathy has no money (duh), and sends Cathy back to Joe. The newly calculated tax liability is properly listed on the schedules, and Joe copies the tax returns for use in the bankruptcy case.

Does Robert, as the return preparer, have any duties under the BRA? This seems like a pristine example of the kind of conduct the BRA intended to encourage. But there are two potentials traps lurking in this seemingly innocent conduct.

---

5.   "The fact that Congress may not have foreseen all of the consequences of a statutory enactment is not sufficient reason for refusing to give effect to its plain meaning." Union Bank v. Wolas, 502 U.S. 151, 158 (1991).

6.   There is no indication why Congress changed the definition of "bankruptcy petition preparer" in the way that it did. But the only other changes the BRA made to Code § 110 were in its penalties, which were strengthened. The courts can also look to the legislative history of the original enactment of § 110—which was clearly aimed at unregulated "service" providers who were taking advantage of financially strapped consumers—and the decade of case law interpreting § 110 in line with this intent.

7.   *See* United States v. Ron Pair Enters., Inc., 489 U.S. 235, 242 (1989).

8.   Ambiguity, the other route around the plain language rule, doesn't help here because the language of § 110(a) is not at all ambiguous.

9.   Thanks to Robert Nadler, a tax attorney in Nashville, for bringing this hypothetical to our attention.

Let's go back to the amended definition in § 110(a)(1):

a person, other than the attorney *for the debtor* or an employee of *such attorney under the direct supervision of such attorney*, who prepares for compensation a document for filing.

Oh no! Is Robert a BPP because he prepared the tax returns for Cathy in conjunction with the filing of her bankruptcy? Let's go through the definition step by step:

- Robert is a person.
- He is not the attorney for the debtor; he is the attorney for Cathy, who, from Robert's perspective, is a taxpayer; *Joe* is the attorney for the debtor.
- If Robert *is* considered the attorney for the debtor, he's not a BPP; he's a DRA (we'll get to this in a minute.)
- He isn't an employee of Joe working under Joe's direct supervision.
- He has received compensation for creating the returns.
- He has prepared a document for filing.

On the face of it, Robert seems to qualify as a BPP. But the words "for filing in connection with a case under this title" in this definition mean "for filing in the bankruptcy case" according to § 110(a)(2) and not "for filing in any place for any purpose." Even if the debtor were not in bankruptcy, the law still requires the tax returns to be filed.

So Robert has escaped the first trap.

Or has he? The tax returns in this case are being created for the purpose of complying with the requirements of the Bankruptcy Code. Doesn't that mean that they are being prepared for filing in the bankruptcy as well as with the IRS?

Not precisely. Under Code § 521(b)(2)(A), the tax returns aren't actually filed with the bankruptcy court; instead, copies are provided to the trustee and to any creditor who has timely requested a copy. A court looking carefully at the plain language will find that the tax return preparer is not a BPP.

But what about returns that are prepared post-petition, which *are* required to be filed with the court under Code §§ 521(f)(1) and (2)? In that case, if the debtor chooses to file the return (and not the transcript, an alternative permitted by the statute), and if the tax preparer knows of the bankruptcy at the time the returns are prepared, it is harder to argue that Robert is not a BPP. The same is true of amendments filed post-petition under Code § 521(f)(3), or in

Chapter 13 cases, under Code § 521(f)(4).[10] It's not the right result, but it's one possible interpretation of the statutory language.

On to the second trap. Even if Robert is not a BPP, is a tax lawyer a DRA? We think not, but this analysis is tricky as well. Code § 101(12A) defines a DRA as:

> any person who provides any bankruptcy assistance to an assisted person in return for the payment of money or other valuable consideration. . . .

Is Robert a DRA? Let's work through the definition:

- Again, he's a person.
- We assume that Cathy qualifies as an assisted person.[11]
- Robert received money for preparing the returns.
- Is he providing bankruptcy assistance?
  - Bankruptcy assistance includes services sold to the assisted person with the express or implied purpose of providing:
    - advice or counsel
    - document preparation or filing
    - legal representation with respect to a case or proceeding in bankruptcy.
  - Since at a minimum, Robert is preparing a document for filing, his services probably qualify as "bankruptcy assistance.

Since Robert seems to meet all the requirements, he looks like a DRA.[12] But remember that there is a list of exceptions in this definition, and the first excludes anyone who is an agent of a person who provides bankruptcy assistance. Here, *if* the relationship between Joe and Robert qualifies as an agency relationship, then Robert may get a pass out of this trap.[13]

Logically, Robert should get a pass. Clearly, these exclusions are intended to protect not only Joe's secretary, but also other professionals whom Joe might hire in order to represent Cathy. Robert should structure his relationship so that he is Joe's agent, rather than Cathy's attorney.[14] If so, he may avoid DRA liabil-

---

10. For more on the distinction between pre- and post-petition tax filings, *see* Chapter 12.

11. An assisted person must have primarily consumer debts and non-exempt property worth less than $150,000. For more on this definition, *see* Chapter 4.

12. For more discussion of this issue than you could ever reasonably want, *see* Chapters 4 and 5.

13. We note without expressing an opinion that there may be fee-sharing ethics issues if Joe pays Robert part of his fee to do the tax return.

14. In *United States v. Boyle*, 469 U.S. 241 (1984), the Supreme Court distinguished between reliance on an attorney to file a return and reliance on the attorney's legal advice.

ity. If Robert is Joe's employee, then he is clearly protected from BPP status under the language of § 110, and from DRA status by the exception to § 101(12A).

What if Joe sends Cathy not to a tax attorney, but to an accountant or bookkeeper who prepares tax returns? The result should be the same. Non-attorney tax return preparers sound more like BPPs, but after the amendment to § 110(a)(1), all tax preparers will be treated the same, whether or not they are attorneys. They aren't preparing documents for filing, and they should be exempt from complying with the DRA provisions.[15]

III. Employees and Agents: In or Out?

If you were paying attention to the last discussion, you're probably wondering why we even mention this. But there's an important flaw in the statutory language that we need to point out here.

The definition of BPP excludes only debtors' attorneys and employees under the debtor's attorney's direct supervision. As noted in Section I, this is a change from prior law, which excluded all attorneys. After this change, it gets harder to argue that Congress intended to exclude *other* attorneys.

For employees and agents of the debtor's attorney, a little circular interpretation problem arises:

- Under § 101(12A)(A), *employees and agents of the debtor's attorney* are excluded from the definition of DRA if the debtor's attorney is a DRA.
- But under § 110(a)(1), only *employees under the direct supervision of the debtor's attorney* are excluded from the definition of BPP.
- Since BPPs are included in the definition of DRAs, if you are a BPP, you are also a DRA.

The issue in *Boyle* was whether a penalty for a delinquent estate tax return could be imposed upon an executor. The executor had hired an attorney to prepare the estate tax return, but the attorney failed to file the return on time. In holding that the executor was liable for the penalty, despite his reliance on the attorney to file the return, the Supreme Court noted that the executor had a non-delegable duty to file the return in a timely fashion, and could not use his reliance upon an agent to avoid liability. The Court stated: " . . . That the *attorney, as the executor's agent,* was expected to attend to the matter does not relieve the principal of his duty to comply with the statute." *Id.* at 250 (emphasis added). Some cases hold that tax return preparation is not legal work; this makes sense, since non-lawyers also prepare tax returns. This distinction can also affect whether there is an attorney-client privilege.

15.   Again, this is only true as to pre-petition tax preparation, the most common type. Post-petition tax returns and amendments, as discussed above, are filed with the court and may reach a different result.

So which is it? If you are an employee or agent of the debtor's attorney (but not under his direct supervision) who prepares a document for filing, you are not a DRA under the exception to that definition, but you sure look like a BPP.

Independent appraisers, bookkeepers, and others who prepare documents for filing in the case should be concerned. But we take the position that the employee/agent exception in § 110(12A)(A) trumps the language of § 110(a)(1). There is no reason at all that these kinds of professionals should be subject to the BPP provisions, and it's doubtful that Congress intended this result. Unlike true BPPs, there is no history that suggests they need regulation in bankruptcy, and the debtor's attorney provides a check on their behavior. No benefit is gained by treating them like petition preparers when they are doing something that improves the quality of the information provided by the debtor—a stated intent of the BRA.

IV. Trustees Seeking Sanctions against Debtors' Counsel in Abusive Chapter 7 Cases

Chapter 13 briefly touched on an issue that's important to trustees who successfully move to convert or dismiss a consumer debtor's Chapter 7 petition as an abuse.

Section 707(b)(4)(A) allows a trustee in this situation to move for sanctions against the debtor's attorney in the form of reimbursement of the trustee's reasonable costs and attorney's fees in prosecuting the § 707(b) motion to dismiss, as well as a civil penalty.

Section 707(b)(5) prevents the debtor from recovering anything from the trustee if the trustee loses the motion to dismiss.[16] But nowhere does § 707(b) address the trustee's liability to the debtor's *attorney* if the court *declines to impose sanctions*.

Rule 9011 does, however, address this situation, and both the Trustee Sanctions and the Civil Penalty provisions discussed in Chapter 13 are required to comply with the procedures of Rule 9011. Rule 9011(c)(1)(A) provides, in relevant part:

> If warranted, the court may award to the party prevailing on the motion the reasonable expenses and attorney's fees incurred in presenting or opposing the motion.

Thus, trustees seeking sanctions against debtors' attorneys do so with some degree of peril, which is not evident from the language of § 707(b). The trustee's conduct can, and should, be scrutinized under Rule 9011, with debtor's counsel able to recover where the trustee wanders astray of that rule.

---

16. The language of § 707(b)(5) is not airtight and a court can work its way out of the statute's restrictions if a trustee behaves improperly in seeking to dismiss or convert the debtor's case.

V. *Trustees' Attorneys in Cases with Support Claims*

Supporters of the BRA took particular delight in emphasizing how favorable the new law would be to women and children, especially the amendment to § 507(a) that moved support obligations from seventh to first priority. Senator Hatch's statement in the 106th Congress was typical:

> This bill also protects our children. . . . Under my provisions, the obligation to pay child support and alimony is moved to a first-priority status, as opposed to its current place at seventh in line, behind attorney's fees and other special interests. If you really want to know the truth, my measures make improvements over current law in this area that are too numerous to mention here at this time, but they work to facilitate the collection of child support and alimony and effectively prevent deadbeats from getting their obligations discharged.[17]

The phrase "attorney's fees and other special interests" was meant to be derisive, and for a time this priority trumped even administrative expenses.

In near unanimity, commentators decried the change because of its practical effect: if trustees and their professionals—including attorneys—couldn't get paid, they wouldn't administer assets and support creditors would get nothing, leaving them worse off than they were before the change.[18] Congress agreed and further amended the support priority to provide the following carve-out:

> [T]he administrative expenses of the trustee . . . shall be paid before payment of claims under subparagraphs (A) and (B), *to the extent that the trustee administers assets that are otherwise available for the payment of such claims.*[19]

The trap here is that, rather than facing sanctions or otherwise being punished for some statutory violation, attorneys and other professionals may find themselves rendering services on behalf of the trustee on a volunteer basis. The highlighted language is ambiguous, and courts might interpret it as limiting the trustee's administrative expenses to property that the support creditor could have reached had the bankruptcy never been filed.

---

17. 146 CONG. REC. S50 (daily ed. Jan. 26, 2000) (statement of Sen. Hatch).

18. Bankruptcy experts also recognized that the priority elevation of support debts was largely cosmetic. Only in the rarest of bankruptcy cases in which there was a distribution to creditors did support obligations compete with any claimants, other than those with administrative claims, who were higher on the § 507(a) priority list. Even in those rare cases, the "special interests" to which Senator Hatch referred include workers who are owed back wages and consumers who paid a deposit but didn't get their goods before the company filed for bankruptcy.

19. BRA Section 212(9), amending Code § 507(a)(1) (emphasis added).

A bankruptcy trustee's powers exceed those of any creditor, even the justifiably favored support creditor. If "assets that are otherwise available" is interpreted to mean only those assets that a support creditor could pursue under non-bankruptcy law, the carve-out may not apply to assets administered through powers available only to the trustee in bankruptcy.

Here's an example. A fraudulent transfer can be avoided by a support creditor under a state law, and the trustee enjoys the same right in a bankruptcy case. The trustee's expenses for avoiding the transfer would be covered by the carve-out because the action is one that is "otherwise available" to the support creditor.

Suppose that, instead of a fraudulent transfer, the asset to be administered is a personal injury claim the debtor has arising out of an automobile accident. Upon the filing of a bankruptcy petition, this claim becomes property of the estate, and the trustee becomes the real party in interest with the exclusive right to prosecute the personal-injury action. A support creditor generally has no right to step into the debtor's shoes and sue another person for the debtor's right to damages. In other words, the personal-injury claim may not be an asset "otherwise available" to the support creditor, and as a result, the trustee's expenses in prosecuting the claim in bankruptcy might fall outside of the carve-out.[20]

When seeking compensation, the trustee's professionals will contend that the support creditor is entitled to the unencumbered proceeds of every action the trustee undertakes, and so the "assets otherwise available" language presents a facial, but not an actual, limitation. The problem with that argument is that the new administrative carve-out does not expressly include proceeds of administered assets. In other sections of the Code, such as § 541,[21] proceeds are specifically mentioned, so Congress knows how to include proceeds, but declined in the case of the support priority carve-out.

We acknowledge that the analysis may become murkier when the priority debt at issue is for child support, which is the subject of myriad state and federal statutes. Child support creditors are armed with pretty powerful weapons, and in some respects their power approaches that of a bankruptcy trustee.[22] But this only expands the category of assets that are "otherwise available" to

---

20.   Why wouldn't the debtor have pursued a personal-injury claim? Several reasons. First, it might be hard to find an attorney who will pursue a claim on a contingent-fee basis if a looming bankruptcy could deliver all the proceeds to the support creditor. Or the claim might be against a family member or friend. And there is no incentive for the debtor to pursue a claim if all the proceeds will go to his creditors, including his ex-wife.

21.   Code § 541 (2000).

22.   The child support creditor possesses a power of intimidation that appears to be unmatched in the law, except perhaps in the Internal Revenue Code. A recalcitrant child support obligor can, for example, be threatened with the loss of a professional license or even with jail time.

the support creditor, not the ability of the trustee to be paid for administering other assets that the support creditor has no non-bankruptcy right to pursue.

As written, the expense carve-out doesn't fix the problem. The trustee won't be able to hire professionals to administer an asset if there's no assurance of payment. This is hardly the super-priority for support creditors trumpeted by the bill's sponsors. In fact, because professionals will be disinclined to represent the trustee on a voluntary basis, it becomes less likely that assets will be administered, leaving support creditors where they were before the carve-out in some instances—first in line to collect nothing.

VI. Creditors' Attorneys and Abusive § 707(b) Motions

Although sanctions provisions against debtors' attorneys are a well-known part of the BRA, creditors and their attorneys aren't completely off the hook. Buried deep under § 707(b)'s layers of expense allowances and income reductions is a little-noticed provision that would allow courts to punish creditors and their lawyers who abuse the abuse provisions of § 707(b). Here it is, in full:

> (A) Except as provided in subparagraph (B) and subject to paragraph (6), the court, on its own initiative or on the motion of a party in interest, in accordance with the procedures described in rule 9011 of the Federal Rules of Bankruptcy Procedure, may award a debtor all reasonable costs (including reasonable attorneys' fees) in contesting a motion filed by a party in interest (other than a trustee or United States trustee (or bankruptcy administrator, if any)) under this subsection if—
>   (i) the court does not grant the motion; and
>   (ii) the court finds that –
>   (I) the position of the party that filed the motion violated rule 9011 of the Federal Rules of Bankruptcy Procedure; or
>   (II) the attorney (if any) who filed the motion did not comply with the requirements of clauses (i) and (ii) of paragraph (4)(C), and the motion was made solely for the purpose of coercing the debtor into waiving a right guaranteed to the debtor under this title.[23]

Let's take the statute one provision at a time.

---

23.   BRA Section 102(a)(2)(C), adding Code § 707(b)(5)(A). We want to keep attention focused on the application and interplay of clauses (i) and (ii) of this new Code section, but its exceptions deserve some explanation. The "subparagraph (B)" reference in subparagraph (A) creates an exception from sanctions for small-business creditors, defined by reference to the number of people the creditor employs full-time and a claim aggregating less than $1,000. Attorneys for these creditors will still have their conduct scrutinized. "Paragraph (6)," also mentioned in subparagraph (A), generally prohibits most parties in interest from moving to dismiss or convert a case where the debtor's income is below the statutory threshold.

Liability under § 707(b)(5)(A) for Filing a Motion

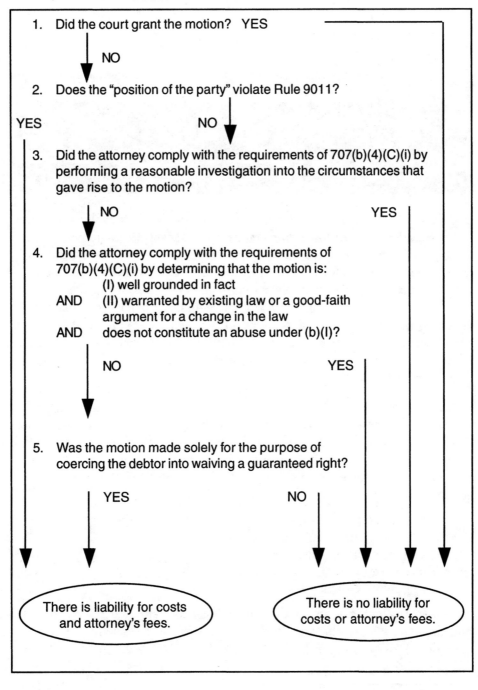

1. Did the court grant the motion?   YES

   NO

2. Does the "position of the party" violate Rule 9011?

   YES   NO

3. Did the attorney comply with the requirements of 707(b)(4)(C)(i) by performing a reasonable investigation into the circumstances that gave rise to the motion?

   NO   YES

4. Did the attorney comply with the requirements of 707(b)(4)(C)(i) by determining that the motion is:
   - (I) well grounded in fact
   - AND (II) warranted by existing law or a good-faith argument for a change in the law
   - AND does not constitute an abuse under (b)(I)?

   NO   YES

5. Was the motion made solely for the purpose of coercing the debtor into waiving a guaranteed right?

   YES   NO

There is liability for costs and attorney's fees.

There is no liability for costs or attorney's fees.

1. The court does not grant the motion.

Neither the creditor nor its attorney will be liable to the debtor if the motion to dismiss or convert the case as an abuse is successful. That much is obvious from the Section's language.

> **WARNING!!**
> Buried deep under § 707(b)'s layers of expense allowances and income reductions is a little-noticed provision that would allow courts to punish creditors and their lawyers who abuse the abuse provisions of § 707(b).

The case that gets litigated all the way to a decision on the merits, however, is the exception, so the phrase "the court does not grant the motion" takes on a shade of ambiguity. Does it mean that the debtor must prevail on the merits in order to recover or that sanctions are precluded only when the court actually orders dismissal (or, with the debtor's consent, conversion) of the case?

We don't think this ambiguity will cause much problem. The main point of § 707(b)(5) is to punish misconduct. Faced with a creditor that settles or withdraws a motion that should never have been made, courts aren't likely to focus on the debtor's lack of success on the merits but on enforcing the remainder of the statute.

2. The position of the party that filed the motion violated Rule 9011.

This language seems to state the obvious because sanctions are allowed any time a motion violates Rule 9011. But if you compare this language with other sections of the Code directed at misbehaving creditors, the language makes sense and is not redundant. It's just another check on creditor behavior, which are common in the Code:

- If a creditor alleges fraud in a dischargeability complaint, its position must be "substantially justified."[24]
- Violations of the automatic stay require "willfulness."[25]
- Involuntary petitions have to be in "bad faith" if the debtor wants actual and punitive damages.[26]

Viewed in context, the "position of the party violated Rule 9011" requirement is simply the standard Congress chose to measure whether a creditor's § 707(b) motion is improper. Rule 9011 remains in full force and effect.

---

24. *See* Code § 523(d).
25. *See* Code § 362(k) (Code § 362(h) prior to the BRA).
26. Code § 303(i)(2).

There is an important difference, however, between Rule 9011 as a standard in § 707(b)(5) and the rule itself. The rule is tied to documents filed with the court, which would be the motion to dismiss. The "position of the party" language goes beyond the document, looking to the party's overall conduct, including what it did (or should have done) before making any filing with the court.

3. The attorney who filed the motion did not comply with the requirements of clauses (i) and (ii) of paragraph (4)(c).

The phrase "the requirement of clauses (i) and (ii) of paragraph (4)(C)" means that when you sign your creditor client's motion to dismiss the debtor's case as an abuse, you are certifying that you have:

(i)   performed a reasonable investigation into the circumstances that gave rise to the petition, pleading, or written motion; and

(ii) determined that the petition, pleading, or written motion –

    (I)   is well grounded in fact; and

    (II) is warranted by existing law or a good faith argument for the extension, modification, or reversal of existing law and does not constitute an abuse under paragraph (1).[27]

"Paragraph (1)," of course, was the rallying point of the BRA for supporters and opponents alike; it commands the dismissal or conversion of abusive Chapter 7 consumer cases through the means testing and good faith provisions.[28]

But what could it possibly mean to say that a motion filed by the *creditor*—the whole purpose of which is to dismiss the debtor's case as an abuse of Chapter 7—"does not constitute an abuse under paragraph (1)?"

Consider the two possible interpretations of the plain language:

- The creditor's attorney must certify that the motion to dismiss is not an abuse of the provisions of Chapter 7 as defined by the means test or good-faith standard; or

- The creditor's attorney must certify that, notwithstanding the motion to dismiss, the debtor's case in which the motion was filed is not abusive.

---

27.   BRA Section 102(a)(2)(C), adding Code § 707(b)(4)(C)(i) and (ii).

28.   Specifically, amended § 707(b)(1) says the court "may dismiss a case filed by an individual debtor under this chapter whose debts are primarily consumer debts . . . if it finds that the granting of relief would be an abuse of the provisions of this chapter." The means test, codified at § 707(b)(2), creates a presumption of abuse that may be rebutted only by "demonstrating special circumstances, such as a serious medical condition or a call or order to active duty in the Armed Forces, to the extent such special circumstances that (sic) justify additional expenses or adjustments of current monthly income for which there is no reasonable alternative." *See* Code § 707(b)(2)(B)(i). If the means test presumption does not arise or has been rebutted, § 707(b)(3) requires that the court to consider whether the debtor filed the petition in bad faith or whether the totality of the circumstances of the debtor's financial situation demonstrates abuse.

The second interpretation puts the motion at odds with itself and the attorney between the proverbial rock and the hard place. Given the overall tilt of the BRA in favor of creditors (despite its lofty-sounding official title), it's hard to imagine that Congress meant to put creditors' lawyers in such an impossible situation. So the first interpretation must be the correct one, right?

Wrong. The first interpretation of the "paragraph (1)" language is just as problematic, but for a different reason. The first interpretation comes closer to what we think Congress meant to do: punish creditors, and their lawyers, for filing abusive motions. But instead of making compliance impossible, the first interpretation makes it meaningless.

All of the provisions that are relevant to the "not an abuse under paragraph (1)" language—paragraphs (1), (2), and (3) of § 707(b)—are expressly tied to the *debtor's* finances or conduct, and they cannot be read in a way that allows for sensible application to a creditor's motion to dismiss. How can the court apply them to determine if the creditor's motion is an abusive filing? It can't. The result is a standard empty of meaning.

There is a third possibility: Congress made a mistake—not just any mistake, but one that produces an absurd result. If a court draws this conclusion, then it would be free to implement the intent behind the language—discouraging creditor abuse and giving the debtor a remedy when a creditor crosses the line—rather than being limited to enforcing the language strictly according to its terms.

4. The motion was made solely for the purpose of coercing a debtor into waiving a right guaranteed to the debtor under Title 11.

The "solely to coerce" language is very problematic. Read literally, the language means that a creditor's attorney is relieved of nearly all the standards of conduct that govern other lawyers and all parties. We know from court decisions that "solely" means "only" and not "mostly," "materially" or "substantially."[29] So if an attorney signs a motion to dismiss that has any purpose other than coercion, no matter how slight, the attorney gets a free pass for certification violations under § 707(b)(5).

Less clear but equally important is figuring out how the "solely to coerce" language can be read harmoniously with the general "position of the party violated rule 9011" provision. Coercion most assuredly is an "improper purpose" under the rule, but for that very reason, the statute runs into a superfluity problem. That is, a violation of the certification and solely to coerce provision, by definition, triggers sanctions under its more general "position of the party" counterpart, causing the latter to swallow the former whole.

---

29. *See, e.g.,* White v. Kentuckiana Livestock Mkt., Inc., 397 F.3d 420, 425-26 (6th Cir. 2005).

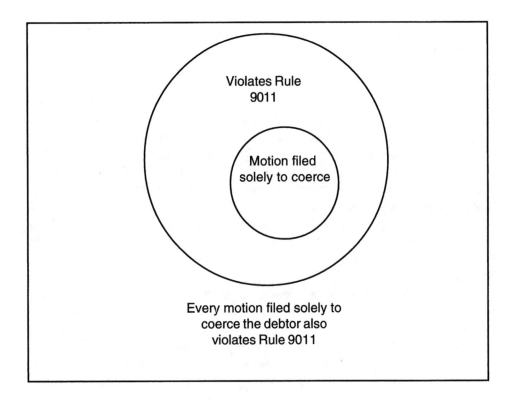

Adding even more confusion is the manner in which Congress has separated "the party" in subclause (I) from "the attorney" in subclause (II). As we stated above, this could mean that the attorney is completely off the hook unless the motion is made solely to coerce the debtor. But it could also mean that in *any* case in which the creditor is represented by counsel, the "position of the party" standard will not apply at all, leaving a very narrow range of circumstances in which the debtor could actually recover after defeating a motion to dismiss.

None of this is logical because it leads to results that thwart the apparent intent of the section: to discourage abusive creditor motions and to punish creditors who abuse their right to seek dismissal or conversion of the debtor's case.

We offer one plausible solution, a reading of the section's language that gives meaning to all of its parts, clarifies the confusion, and effectuates the legislative intent. We think the "solely to coerce" provision applies only to rogue attorneys whose actions in the bankruptcy case are made with neither the knowledge of their creditor clients nor a due regard for the law. That is, the language should be limited to extraordinary cases where the attorney's conduct does not represent "the position of the" creditor client.

Consider the facts of a case decided in a Texas bankruptcy court.[30] Myers & Porter represented creditors in a number of dischargeability complaints filed in consumer cases that alleged fraud. In these cases, the attorneys failed to serve the complaint on the debtor, who often learned of the complaint only after the attorneys moved for default judgment. The complaints generally failed to plead fraud with particularity, and supporting documents, like the contract or payment records, were not attached. The proposed order accompanying the motion for default judgment ordered the debtor to pay attorney's fees, but no evidence was offered to prove that the debtor was liable for those fees.[31]

In one case, the debtor's lawyer received a letter threatening dischargeability litigation unless the debtor reaffirmed a substantial portion of the debt. Debtor's counsel filed an answer and served interrogatories, which were never answered. When this case was called for trial, neither the creditor nor Myers & Porter appeared, as was common in proceedings on these dischargeability complaints.[32]

After handling a few of these cases, the court noticed a pattern and issued a notice to show cause to the creditors and the law firm's principals, Ms. Myers and Mr. Porter. Through evidence and court filings, the court learned that Myers & Porter was engaged by the creditors' national counsel and that, despite the written contract, Myers & Porter had acted without informing national counsel or the creditors, and without obtaining any requisite consent.[33]

The court made an express finding that the creditors and their national counsel "were not responsible for the problems caused by Myers & Porter."[34] The Myers & Porter attorneys, on the other hand, were dealt with severely: each was suspended from practicing in the United States Bankruptcy Court for the Northern District of Texas for a period of not less than four years.[35]

As unusual as it is to distinguish between the conduct of the creditor and its agent, the attorney, the Texas court did the right thing; the lawyers in that case truly were rogue attorneys, and they victimized not just debtors but the court, the system, and even their own clients.

Section 707(b)(5)(A)(ii)(II), with the attorney certification and the "solely to coerce" standard, can be read as codifying the case of the rogue attorney, and doing so resolves most of the interpretive problems with § 707(b)(5).

30.　Household Credit Servs., Inc. v. Dragoo (*In re* Dragoo), 219 B.R. 460 (Bankr. N.D. Tex. 1998).

31.　*Id.* at 461-64.

32.　*Id.* at 461-62.

33.　*Id.* at 464-65.

34.　*Id.* at 466.

35.　*Id.* at 467.

First, the rogue attorney interpretation allows subclauses (I) and (II)—which refer to both the party and the party's attorney—each to have an independent meaning and application. Subclause (I) would apply to cases that follow the usual course of a party asserting a position through the attorney who serves as the party's agent. That is, a creditor's motion that violates Rule 9011 triggers sanctions, which the court can apportion between attorney and client as the situation warrants, just as the courts have traditionally done.

Second, subclause (II) would be limited to the exceptional cases, like that presented in Texas, where an attorney files motions to dismiss or convert without the creditor's knowledge or consent, with the sole intent of coercing the debtor into waiving a right.

The rogue attorney interpretation also avoids the problem of superfluity that arises when interpreting the "solely to coerce" provision and the general violation of Rule 9011.

Finally, and most important, this interpretation avoids the disastrous result that the class of attorneys who represent creditors in consumer cases would be somehow exempt from the requirements of Rule 9011 that are intended to keep the process honest, orderly, and respectable.

CHAPTER 16

Criminal Liability
for the Bankruptcy Practitioner

by Ronald R. Peterson

John Gellene was a bright, rising bankruptcy star in the firmament above Bankruptcy World. He was a partner in one of Wall Street's most prestigious firms. On December 2, 1994, the 37-year-old Gellene had persuaded the United States Bankruptcy Court for the Eastern District of Wisconsin to confirm his embattled plan of reorganization for Bucyrus-Erie in less than one year.[1] For John Gellene, it was the greatest accomplishment of his legal career. He led Bucyrus-Erie from the brink of financial extinction through the gauntlet of angry creditors to the promised land of prosperity and growth. Bucyrus-Erie's creditors celebrated a larger recovery than many thought possible. By any measure the case was an unqualified success.

Two years later, John Gellene's star began to sink. In December 1996, Jackson National Life (JNL), one of Bucyrus-Erie's largest creditors, filed a motion in the bankruptcy court to compel his firm to disgorge millions of dollars in fees that Gellene and his firm had earned in saving the company. On September 25, 1997, Bucyrus-Erie sued Gellene's firm for over $35 million in damages arising from Gellene's representation.[2] Ultimately, his firm would return millions of dollars of fees that it had earned.

It got worse. On November 1, 1997, the law firm fired Gellene. Then, on December 9, 1997, a federal grand jury sitting in Milwaukee indicted Gellene on two counts of bankruptcy fraud and one count of perjury.[3] On March 3, 1998, after three hours of deliberation, a jury found John Gellene guilty on all

---

1. *In re* Bucyrus-Erie Co., Case No. 94-20787 (Bank. E.D. Wis.).
2. Bucyrus Int'l Inc., et al. v. Milbank Tweed, et al., Case No. 97-01051 (E.D. Wis.). The case was ultimately remanded to the Circuit Court of Milwaukee County.
3. United States v. Gellene, Case No. 97-00221 (E.D. Wis.).

three counts. On July 28, 1998, in the very courthouse where he had achieved his greatest success, John Gellene was sentenced to 15 months in prison at Fort Dix, New Jersey, a $15,300 fine and two years probation. Gellene's conviction was affirmed by the court of appeals in *United States v. Gellene*.[4] As a result, John Gellene was disbarred, and his career and life were totally ruined.

His rising star had become a fiery shooting star. How could something that seemed so right wind up so wrong? Gellene was the first lawyer in the United States convicted of executing a faulty Bankruptcy Rule 2014 affidavit.[5] Cynics would say that he was a victim of geography. Only north of the Cheddar Curtain would somebody dream of charging a bankruptcy lawyer with such a crime. Or, as some suggest, was it the culmination of a perfect bankruptcy storm?

Despite Mr. Gellene's fall from grace, very few bankruptcy professionals are charged with bankruptcy crimes in the United States. Research indicates that John Gellene is the only lawyer ever charged, criminally, with making a materially false Bankruptcy Rule 2014 affidavit. This phenomenon reflects not only the general integrity of the bankruptcy bar, but the fact that bankruptcy crimes are very hard to prove. In addition, the civil remedies—which include disgorgement or denial of fees, disqualification from a particular case, or a general bar from representing any debtor in any case—are used instead by bankruptcy courts to police the system; in many instances they have a greater deterrent effect. Bankruptcy crime is also underreported because prosecutors prefer to indict and accept pleas from defendants for crimes that are easier to prove, such as tax evasion, ERISA fraud, or garden-variety *malum in se*[6] offenses. Consequently, bankruptcy criminal prosecutions are show trials by an overworked Justice Department designed to keep the system honest by making examples out of some poor unfortunate. What evoked a civil penalty in one case, *Leslie Fay* (discussed below), became a criminal one in *Gellene*.

This Chapter will first explore what constitutes a bankruptcy crime. Next, it will show how these statutes were applied in a precedent-breaking way to Mr. Gellene. The Chapter will then review the areas where the professional may be skating on thin ice; finally, it will explore emerging areas of criminal exposure.

---

4.   182 F.3d 578 (7th Cir. 1999).

5.   *See* FED. R. BANK. P. 2014, requiring a verified statement of the professional to be engaged by the debtor setting forth the professional's connections with the debtor, creditors, any other party in interest, their respective attorneys and accountants, the United States Trustee, or any person employed in the office of the United States Trustee.

6.   *Malum in se* literally means "wrong in itself." An offense is "malum in se" if it is inherently evil, such as murder or theft.

I. The Crime

The following charts show the traditional bankruptcy crimes and the ancillary offenses that most often attach to bankruptcy related indictments.

Chart 1

18 U.S.C. § 152	General prohibition against sin: concealment of assets; false oaths and claims; bribery
18 U.S.C. § 153	Embezzlement against estate
18 U.S.C. § 154	Adverse interest and conduct of officers: Trustees buying property from their own estates
18 U.S.C. § 155	Borah Act: fixing of professional fees
18 U.S.C. § 156	Knowing disregard of bankruptcy law or rule by a Bankruptcy Petition Preparer
18 U.S.C. § 157	Bankruptcy fraud
18 U.S.C. § 158	Designation of United States attorneys and agents of the F.B.I. to address abusive reaffirmations of debt and materially fraudulent statements in bankruptcy schedules
18 U.S.C. § 3057	Bankruptcy investigations: Requirement that Judges, Trustees, and Receivers report to the U.S. Attorney any pre- or post-petition violations of bankruptcy or non-bankruptcy criminal statutes

In addition to these crimes, most bankruptcy indictments include indictments for the offenses listed on Chart 2.

Chart 2

18 U.S.C. § 2	Aiding and abetting
18 U.S.C. § 3	Accessory after the fact
18 U.S.C. § 4	Misprision of felony
18 U.S.C. § 371	Conspiracy to commit bankruptcy fraud
18 U.S.C. § 1001	Fraud and false statements
18 U.S.C. §§ 1341, 1343 & 1344	Mail fraud, wire fraud and bank fraud
18 U.S.C. § 1503	Obstruction of justice
18 U.S.C. §§ 1621 through 1623	Perjury
26 U.S.C. § 7201 et seq.	Tax evasion and fraud and willful failure to file

II. The General Prohibition Against Sin

The starting point for a lawyer's criminal liability for a bankruptcy crime is 18 U.S.C. § 152, the general prohibition against sin (set out in the sidebar).

---

§ 152 provides:

A person who —

(1) knowingly and fraudulently conceals from a custodian, trustee, marshal, or other officer of the court charged with the control or custody of property, or, in connection with a case under title 11, from creditors or the United States Trustee, any property belonging to the estate of a debtor;

(2) knowingly and fraudulently makes a false oath or account in or in relation to any case under title 11;

(3) knowingly and fraudulently makes a false declaration certificate, verification or statement under penalty of perjury as permitted under section 1746 of title 28, in or in relation to any case under title 11;

(4) knowingly and fraudulently presents any false claims for proof against the estate of a debtor, or uses any such claim in any case under title 11, in a personal capacity or as or through an agent, proxy or attorney;

(5) knowingly and fraudulently receives any material amount of property from a debtor after the filing of a case under title 11, with the intent to defeat the provisions of title 11;

(6) knowingly and fraudulently gives, offers, receives or attempts to obtain any money or property, remuneration, compensation, reward, advantage, or promise thereof for acting or forbearing to act in any case under title 11;

(7) in a personal capacity or as an agent or officer of any person or corporation, in contemplation of a case under title 11 by or against the person or any other person or corporation, or with intent to defeat the provisions of title 11, knowingly and fraudulently transfers or conceals any of his property or the property of such other person or corporation;

(8) after the filing of a case under title 11 or in contemplation thereof, knowingly and fraudulently conceals, destroys, mutilates, falsifies, or makes a false entry in any recorded information (including books, documents, records and papers) relating to the property or financial affairs of a debtor; or

(9) after the filing of a case under title 11, knowingly and fraudulently withholds from a custodian, trustee, marshal, or other officer of the court or a United States Trustee entitled to its possession, any recorded information (including books, documents, records, and papers) relating to the property or financial affairs of a debtor

shall be fined under this title, imprisoned not more than 5 years, or both.[7]

---

7.   18 U.S.C. § 3571(b)(3) provides that the fine for a felony is up to $250,000 for individuals and $500,000 for an organization. In addition, 18 U.S.C. § 3571(d)(3) increases

The statute contains the seven deadly sins of bankruptcy:

1. Concealment of estate property
2. False oaths and certifications
3. False claims
4. Improper receipt of estate property
5. Bribery
6. Destruction or falsification of records
7. Withholding information from the trustee

In addition, there is an implied requirement that the fraud relate to some material matter.[8] While these acts are fairly well understood, the most critical portions of this statute are the adverbs: knowingly and fraudulently.

A. Knowingly

An act is done knowingly if it is done voluntarily and intentionally, and not because of accident, mistake or other innocent reason.[9] The Seventh Circuit held that "[A]n action taken in good faith is on the other side of an action taken knowingly."[10] An action can also be taken knowingly if the defendant merely turned a blind eye to obvious facts.[11]

As one authority explained, "Examples of willful blindness might include signing the required statements and schedules without reviewing them, keeping sloppy books and records when circumstances would indicate that proper accounting would disclose adverse information or participating in a scheme in which there is ample reason to suspect skullduggery, but continuing to participate in the scheme despite these reasons."[12]

A debtor's lawyer is also skating on thin ice when she files a case without ever meeting her client. What is important to remember is that, unlike Sgt. Schultz of "Hogan's Heroes" fame, the "I know nothing" defense will not necessarily work in a criminal prosecution.

---

the fine to twice the pecuniary gain or loss involved in a crime. *See also* Sentencing Guidelines.

8.　1 E. DEVITT & C. BLACKMAN, FEDERAL JURY PRACTICE AND INSTRUCTIONS §14.04 (1977); *see also* United States v. Nichols, 808 F.2d 660, 663 (8th Cir. 1987).

9.　United States v. Shadduck, 112 F.3d. 523 (1st Cir. 1997); United States v. Zehbrach, 47 F.3d 1252 (3d Cir. 1995); United States v. Defazio, 899 F.2d 626, 635 (7th Cir. 1990); United States v. Lewis, 718 F.2d 883 (8th Cir. 1983).

10.　United States v. Koster, 163 F.3d 1008, 1012 (7th Cir. 1998).

11.　*See* United States v. Yasser, 114 F.2d 558 (3d Cir. 1940).

12.　COLLIER ON BANKRUPTCY (15th rev. ed.), 97.02[1](a), 7-32.

B. Fraudulently

A statement is fraudulent if it was made, or caused to be made, with the intent to deceive.[13] Fraud means that the perpetrator acts with the intent to deceive or to cheat parties affected by the bankruptcy case.[14] Fraud includes both misstatements and actions. As the Seventh Circuit explained in *McClellan v. Cantrell*:[15]

> Fraud is a generic term, which embraces all the multifarious means which human ingenuity can devise and which are resorted to by one individual to gain an advantage over another by false suggestions or by the suppression of truth. No definite and invariable rule can be laid down as to a general proposition defining fraud, and it includes all surprise, trick, cunning, dissembling, and any unfair way by which another is cheated.[16]

In *McClellan*, no one accused the perpetrators of communicating anything. The case dealt with actions rather than words.

Gellene appealed his conviction for bankruptcy fraud, arguing that in addition to proving that he acted knowingly and fraudulently, the government had to prove materiality. Because creditors did not suffer any loss (and quite possibly obtained a premium), Gellene argued "no harm, no foul." While that argument might work in basketball, the court of appeals in the *Gellene* case held that a statement is made fraudulently for purposes of § 152 if it is made with an "intent to deceive," and rejected Gellene's argument that § 152 is limited to false statements that deprive the debtor of his property or the bankruptcy estate of its assets.[17] The materiality requirement is satisfied because Gellene's conduct challenged the integrity of the bankruptcy system.

In *United States v. Sabbeth*, the court of appeals adopted the *Gellene* rule.[18] The court concluded: "We held long ago that section 152 is 'essentially equivalent to a perjury statute' and that 'only the basic requirements of perjury need be proved.'"[19]

In addition to the general prohibition against sin, Congress recently enacted 18 U.S.C. § 157 as a companion to § 152.

18 U.S.C. § 157 provides:

---

13.   BLACK'S LAW DICTIONARY 662 (6th ed. 1990).
14.   United States v. Sabbeth, 262 F.3d 207 (2d Cir. 2001).
15.   217 F.3d 890 (7th Cir. 2000).
16.   *Id.* at 893, *quoting* Stapleton v. Holt, 207 Okla. 443, 250 P.2d 451, 453-54 (Okla. 1952).
17.   United States v. Gellene, 182 F.3d 578, 586-87 (7th Cir. 1999).
18.   262 F.3d 207 (2d Cir. 2001).
19.   *Id.* at 217, *quoting In re* Robinson, 506 F.2d 1184, 1189 (2d Cir. 1974).

A person who, having devised or intending to devise a scheme or artifice to defraud and for the purpose of executing or concealing such a scheme or artifice or attempting to do so—

(1) files a petition under title 11, *including a fraudulent involuntary bankruptcy petition under section 303 of such title;*[20]
(2) files a document in a proceeding under title 11:
(3) makes a false or fraudulent representation, claim, or promise concerning or in relation to a proceeding under title 11, at any time before or after the filing of the petition, or in relation to a proceeding falsely asserted to be pending under such title,

shall be fined under this title, imprisoned not more than 5 years or both.

In addition, the fines for a violation of § 157 can cumulate up to $250,000. Section 157 has two fundamental requirements:

- There must be an artifice or scheme to defraud or an intent to devise a scheme or artifice to defraud; and
- That artifice or scheme must be made in contemplation of the filing of a bankruptcy case, the filing of a document in that case, or a representation made to the court in the case.

A fraudulent activity prior to bankruptcy, but not in contemplation that a bankruptcy would be filed, would probably not lead to a conviction under § 157.

Many wonder what this statute adds that is not already covered by § 152. Its most important contribution is that it follows very closely the language of the federal mail fraud statute.[21] There are over 133 years of judicial precedent behind the mail fraud statute that can be applied by analogy to bankruptcy fraud cases. Section 157 adds another arrow in the prosecutor's quiver. As a result, it is not unusual to see indictments for the same set of facts under both §§ 152 and 157.

III. In Search of Full Disclosure

The *Gellene* case gives an excellent example of how the prosecution established the elements of "knowingly" and "fraudulently."

The cause of Gellene's demise was two sworn statements that he executed in order to represent the debtor. These are the same type of sworn statements

---

20. It is not clear from the amendment whether the italicized language added by the BRA is intended to be added only in subsection (1) or in subsections (2) and (3) as well. One version of the amended Code shows it in all three places; another only in subsection (1). Both note the confusion.

21. 18 U.S.C. § 1341.

that bankruptcy lawyers provide by the hundreds to federal courts every day. When a lawyer is retained to act as counsel for the Chapter 11 debtor, for a creditors' committee, or for a trustee, that application must comply with Bankruptcy Code § 327. Section 327(a) requires the lawyer to swear that he does not represent an interest adverse to the estate, and that he is a disinterested person. "Disinterestedness" is defined in Code § 101(14), as amended by the BRA, to mean a person who:

(A) is not a creditor, an equity security holder, or an insider;
(B) is not and was not, within 2 years before the date of the filing of the petition, a director, officer, or employee of the debtor; and
(C) does not have an interest materially adverse to the interest of the estate or of any class of creditors or equity security holders, by reason of any direct or indirect relationship to, connection with, or interest in, the debtor, or for any other reason.[22]

To aid the court in determining whether the adverse interest and disinterested tests are met, Bankruptcy Rule 2014 was promulgated to compel full disclosure. It provides that:

... The application [for retention] shall be accompanied by a verified statement of the person to be employed setting forth the person's connections with the debtor, creditors, or any other party in interest, their respective attorneys and accountants, the United States trustee, or any person employed in the office of the United States trustee.[23]

Rule 2014 is a minefield for even the most skilled and experienced professional. Most courts hold that the lawyer is not to act as an editor and may not decide that some connections are too trivial to be disclosed. That is for the United States Trustee to raise and the courts to decide. On the other hand, if a lawyer were to disclose every conceivable connection with a case, he might as well attach a copy of the U.S. census and an encyclopedia of business entities authorized to do business in the United States as an exhibit to the affidavit.

The compromise is a set of best practices that has evolved. Professionals are expected to make conflicts sweeps, with the use of a computer and an independent conflicts analyst, to determine which of the firm's clients are creditors, and which clients are potential or existing targets of litigation by the debtor.[24] Lawyers are expected not only to look at their specific corporate

---

22.   The BRA deleted all references to investment bankers as not disinterested. Otherwise, new Code § 101(14) is the same definition confronted by Gellene prior to the BRA.

23.   FED. R. BANKR. P. 2014(a).

24.   See Chapter 7, which discusses bankruptcy conflicts in detail.

clients, but also to run a corporate family search to replicate the same search for corporate siblings, children, and parents. Lawyers are also generally expected to determine whether any partner or associate was a director, shareholder or officer of the debtor. They should determine whether they, themselves, are a target of a wrathful debtor for voidable preferences or just good old-fashioned malpractice. The latter is particularly true if the firm advised the debtor in a leveraged buyout, stock redemption, spinoff, split-up, or a deal that just went south. Worse yet, lawyers must determine whether the firm or a member of the firm had a piece of a deal with the debtor. Lawyers should check to determine whether another firm client is a strident competitor in an oligopolistic market. Finally, lawyers should circulate a memo to all professionals in the firm asking for a subjective response as to whether the firm has adverse interests or connections that would lead to a finding of lack of disinterest.

On the other hand, probably no one would expect the firm to inquire as to whether the firm janitor owns a mutual fund that invests in stock in the debtor or whether the paralegal's girlfriend is an employee of the debtor. Nevertheless, the lawyer runs the risk that if he is too parsimonious in his disclosure, he will face the consequences.

Regardless, the attorney has a duty to supplement his affidavit when confronted with competing interests within his firm.

IV. The Gellene *Case*

Gellene and his firm represented Bucyrus-Erie, a Midwest rust-belt manufacturer of mining machinery headquartered in Milwaukee, Wisconsin.[25] In late 1985, Becor Western Corporation (Becor), Bucyrus-Erie's earlier name, faced a serious financial crisis. Becor retained Goldman Sachs and its rising star, Mikael Salovaara, to act as its investment banker and help Becor fund a leveraged buyout and exchange offer. Salovaara was to act as the debtor's advisor. When the dust settled, the management directors owned 100 percent of the common stock, while Goldman Sachs and its affiliates owned 100 percent of the preferred convertible stock. Unfortunately, Becor now was the obligor of $177 million in high-interest debt. As a consolation prize, Becor had a new name, Bucyrus-Erie.

The lawyer who negotiated and documented this transaction was Lawrence Lederman of the leading firm of Wachtell, Lipton. Subsequently, Lederman migrated to Milbank Tweed, Hadley & McCloy, where Lederman met Gellene.

In the early 1990s, Bucyrus-Erie entered into additional financial transactions with Salovaara's new company, South Street Funds, including a sale/

---

25. *See* MILTON C. REGAN, JR., EAT WHAT YOU KILL (2004), for a detailed history of not only Bucyrus-Erie, but of the trial of John Gellene.

leaseback transaction, which allegedly impaired Bucyrus-Erie's unsecured creditors. JNL was Bucyrus-Erie's largest unsecured creditor and felt severely prejudiced by the deal. It was so angry that it demanded that Bucyrus-Erie sue Salovaara over the deal.[26]

As Bucyrus-Erie's financial condition worsened, crippled by a declining world market for its products and high interest rates, Lederman turned to Gellene to serve as Bucyrus-Erie's restructuring counsel. Gellene would spend the next year negotiating a prepackaged bankruptcy plan of reorganization that was approved by almost every creditor constituency except JNL.

On February 18, 1994, Bucyrus-Erie and its parent, B-E Holdings, filed a voluntary petition under Chapter 11 in the bankruptcy court in Milwaukee. Filed along with the petition were a plan of reorganization, disclosure statement, and ballots supporting the plan from all but JNL.

Gellene wanted the court to approve his pre-petition disclosure statement and move rapidly to a hearing on confirmation of the plan, which provided for releases for Salovaara, South Street, and Goldman Sachs. However, JNL wanted a new disclosure statement that would reveal that Bucyrus-Erie had significant causes of action against Salovaara, South Street, and Goldman Sachs.

Gellene, like all bankruptcy lawyers, filed his application for retention with the court along with a Rule 2014 affidavit. This certificate disclosed that Gellene's firm had represented the original investment banker, Goldman Sachs, but did not disclose any relationships between Gellene's firm and Salovaara or South Street. (Strike One.) The affidavit, as many do, declared that neither Gellene nor anyone at his firm was aware of any other connection with Bucyrus-Erie companies, their creditors, or any other party in interest. As would come out much later in the case, Gellene was simultaneously representing South Street in another transaction. In addition, Gellene's firm was representing Salovaara in a dispute with his partner at South Street. The affidavit also failed to disclose that Lederman had social relationships with Salovaara.

JNL objected to Gellene's retention, arguing that his law firm was not disinterested and held an adverse interest. First, Gellene's partner, Lederman, had drafted and negotiated the financial documents related to transactions that allegedly torpedoed Bucyrus-Erie. If the leveraged buyout was avoidable as a fraudulent transfer, then the lawyers who put together the deal had to be concerned that they, too, would be sued as aiders and abettors, co-conspirators, or for malpractice. In addition, the plan contained releases for Gellene's other clients. How could he advise Bucyrus-Erie to walk away from allegedly valuable causes of action while representing other clients in the case?

After a rancorous hearing on his retention, Gellene filed a supplemental affidavit that was as deficient as the first one. While it gave more detail as to

---

26. *Id.* at 92.

the Goldman Sachs engagements than the prior affidavit, it did not disclose any relationship with Salovaara or his companies. (Strike Two.)

In the meantime, Gellene was subject to a frontal assault by JNL, which challenged the adequacy of Gellene's disclosure statement. The debtors, the creditors' committee, and JNL spent over $1 million in professional fees over whether Bucyrus-Erie had to disclose the possibility of these actions against Goldman Sachs, Salovaara, and South Street. In June 1994, the court conducted a trial and denied approval of Gellene's disclosure statement[27] for failure to address in detail the legal issues that arose from these pre-bankruptcy refinancing and potential defendants, including Salovaara and South Street.

Ultimately the combatants reached a deal in which the fraudulent conveyance claims that Bucyrus-Erie might have had against Salovaara and South Street were assigned to JNL. JNL and the other creditors (except Salovaara and South Street) received substantially all of the stock of the company. Subsequently, the plan was confirmed.

However, peace was short-lived. In the spring of 1995, Gellene applied for over $1.96 million in compensation, as well as expense reimbursement for $370,000. At trial on the fee application, Gellene testified that the Rule 2014 verifications that he had filed were truthful. (Strike Three.)

The prosecutors in the case had to establish that Gellene's oversight was not an innocent mistake. They had to prove that on three separate occasions, Gellene knowingly failed to make accurate disclosures and did so with fraudulent intent. The following facts show a pattern of knowing behavior and intent to deceive. These facts came to haunt Gellene at the trial:

- At the fee hearing, Gellene was asked by Bankruptcy Judge Eisenberg about a certain disbursement to the Lotus Cab Company (Lotus). Judge Eisenberg asked Gellene if his firm owned Lotus, and Gellene answered no. Then Judge Eisenberg asked whether any of Gellene's partners owned Lotus and Gellene answered yes. The judge wondered why Gellene had not disclosed the relationship either in his fee application or in the motion for retention. Further, while Gellene's initial answer was technically correct, it was not totally candid.
- Gellene had practiced law in New York without a license for a number of years. He had passed the bar exam but failed to process the paperwork.

---

27. A disclosure statement requires "adequate information," which, before it was amended by the BRA, was defined as: "information of a kind, and in sufficient detail, as far as reasonably practicable in light of the nature and history of the debtor and the condition of the debtor's books and records . . . that would enable . . . a hypothetical reasonable investor of the relevant class to make an informed judgment about the plan. . . ." Former Code § 1125(a)(1).

- In Gellene's application to be retained as counsel in Bucyrus-Erie, he lied about being a member of the bar of the U.S. District Court for the Southern District of New York. He was not.
- Gellene got caught lying about work he did for South Street. He misrepresented to the Colorado bankruptcy trustee his failure to respond timely to a claim objection.
- Gellene had disclosed in his verification that his firm had involvement with other clients that had a relationship with Bucyrus-Erie, proving he knew how to disclose when he wanted to. This established knowledge.
- Gellene failed to disclose the JNL fee objection to his own partners and then altered the pleadings when he did turn them over to his partners. This showed a pattern of prior fraudulent conduct.
- Gellene had published articles on bankruptcy ethics. Together with his substantial experience as a bankruptcy practitioner, this showed that he knew the rules of engagement.
- Gellene knew that his firm had represented both Salovaara and South Street in other matters, as he had worked on them himself.
- Gellene had forced the estate to expend substantial funds defending a disclosure statement that failed to disclose alleged causes of action against Salovaara and South Street.

These facts gave the prosecutors the ammunition to bring the indictment. They showed a course of conduct where Gellene lied and that Gellene knew what he was doing. John Gellene was charged with two counts of bankruptcy fraud under 18 U.S.C. § 152, and one count of a fraudulent declaration before a court under 18 U.S.C. § 1863.

V. Foolish Consistency Is the Hobgoblin of Little Minds[28]

While John Gellene went to jail, similar cases with hauntingly similar facts have not resulted in any criminal charge. In fact, the conduct of the debtor's counsel in *Leslie Fay*[29] may have been more problematic than Gellene's. In that case, the debtor's counsel originally represented the debtor's audit committee. The audit committee issued a report exonerating the debtor's board of directors. However, the audit committee was composed of individuals who were themselves, or who worked for institutions that were, clients of the debtor's law firm. In addition, the accounting firm that was sued by angry shareholders of the company was also a client of the firm. The debtor's law firm did not disclose these connections when it was retained. Unlike the *Bucyrus-Erie* case,

---

28.   Ralph Waldo Emerson, SELF-RELIANCE (1841).
29.   175 B.R. 525 (Bankr. S.D. N.Y. 1994)

Leslie Fay was a financial scandal that did not have a successful reorganization. Nevertheless, the bankruptcy court permitted the debtor's counsel to continue and directed the parties to agree to a proper disgorgement of some of its fees to cover the costs suffered by the creditors' committee and an examiner in bringing this conduct to light. However, no one was indicted and nobody went to jail. One man's felony is—depending on the time and location—another man's civil penalty.

VI. What's Hot

While the *Gellene* case represents the high-water mark in what is criminal, most bankruptcy crime is far less extreme.

For example, Rule 2014 affidavits are not the only sworn statements that bankruptcy lawyers must make. Bankruptcy Rule 2016 provides:

> Every attorney for a debtor, whether or not the attorney applies for compensation, shall file and transmit to the United States Trustee within 15 days after the order for relief or at another time as the court may direct, the statement required by § 329 of the Code including whether the attorney has shared or agreed to share the compensation with any other entity. The statement shall include the particulars of any such sharing or agreement to share by the attorney, but the details of any agreement for the sharing of the compensation with a member or regular associate of the attorney's law firm shall not be required. A supplemental statement shall be filed and transmitted to the United States Trustee within 15 days after any payment or agreement not previously disclosed.

There are few reported criminal cases dealing with fraudulent Rule 2016 statements, although the same standards as in the *Gellene* case would apply. The most notorious is *United States v. Martin*.[30] Erik Martin was a licensed consumer bankruptcy attorney who routinely filed Chapter 13 petitions for his clients. Consequently, he also routinely filed Bankruptcy Rule 2016 affidavits. In addition, in the Northern District of Illinois, Martin was required to file a Local Rule 39 affidavit stating that he did not improperly solicit his clients or receive an improper referral.

Martin became associated with Christopher Claxton, the host of a religious radio program broadcast in the Chicago area. Claxton was also the president and owner of Equinox Financial, Inc., a real property financing and brokerage house. Beginning in 1995, Claxton offered assistance to debtors concerning the management of their debts during the "business ministry" portion of the radio program. Claxton promised, among other things, to assist debtors through a

---

30.   1 CR 470 (N.D. Ill).

debt-consolidation program. As a result of Claxton's debt-consolidation program, he referred over 900 cases to Martin. In exchange for these referrals,
Martin wrote checks to Claxton for almost $200,000. Martin's Rule 2016 affi-
davits neglected to disclose the referral payments to Claxton. As a result of the
fraudulent Rule 2016 affidavits and the Local Rule 39 affidavits, Martin was
indicted for violating 18 U.S.C. § 157(3). The U.S. attorney was not impressed,
and Martin ultimately pled guilty and was sentenced to five years' probation
and a $5,000 fine. Despite the *Martin* prosecution, the remedy of choice for
most violations of Bankruptcy Rule 2016 is civil and not criminal.[31]

VII. *You Scratch My Back, I'll Scratch Yours*

When it comes to fee applications, it is a red-letter day when parties object
to one another's applications. That phenomenon occurred in the case of former
Senator Borah of Idaho. As a result, in 1937, he drafted 18 U.S.C. § 155,
known today as the Borah Act. This provides:

> Whoever, being a party in interest, whether as a debtor, creditor, receiver,
> trustee or representative of any of them, or attorney for any such party in
> interest, in any receivership or case under title 11 in any United States court
> or under its supervision, knowingly and fraudulently enters into any agree-
> ment, express or implied, with another such party in interest or attorney for
> another such party in interest, for the purpose of fixing the fees or other
> compensation to be paid to any party in interest or to any attorney for any
> party in interest for services rendered in connection therewith, from the as-
> sets of the estate.

Violation of this statute is a Class A misdemeanor, carrying a penalty of
not more than one year in prison or a fine of $200,000, or both. The elements
of this offense include:

1. the existence of an agreement, which can be written or a handshake
2. between the attorneys for parties or, in rare cases, the parties themselves
3. in a bankruptcy
4. for the purpose of fixing compensation paid to any professional[32]
5. the compensation must come from assets of the estate, and
6. the agreements must have been made fraudulently and knowingly.

A review of case law and secondary sources does not reveal any criminal
prosecutions for a violation of the Borah Act. The absence of criminal prosecu-

---

31.   *See* Law Offices of Nicholas A. Franke v. Tiffany, 113 F.3d 1040 (9th Cir. 1997);
Neben & Starrett, Inc. v. Chartwell Financial Corp., 63 F.3d 877 (9th Cir. 1995).

32.   Including designated haircuts.

tions may be because many fee applications are granted without objection. Could all these applications be perfect? What happens when the U.S. Trustee directs the parties to meet and confer and agree to a percentage haircut?

The only protection for the practitioner is to make sure that any agreement is exposed to the healing light of day, with full disclosure to the Bankruptcy Court. There can be no deceit if the court is properly advised.

VIII. Sales

Some commentators have remarked that the Bankruptcy Code has become a "National Foreclosure" statute. If that is true, the high point of a foreclosure action is the sale. The sale is the primary mechanism by which creditors receive any money. If the sale is public, fair, and open, the theory is that the market will provide the highest prices for creditors.

What happens when the process is not fair, and the parties collude to prevent the highest bid?

Jules Bagdan was a respected trustee in South Florida. He was chosen to be the Chapter 7 Trustee for Southeast Bank Corp., one of the largest Chapter 7 cases ever filed in Florida. In December 1991, he asked the bankruptcy court for authority to sell a corporate jet at a public sale. One bidder, Maxfly Aviation, Inc. of Naples (Maxfly), raised its offer to $1.9 million. The other bidder, Gestiones y Transportes de Burgos S.A. from Spain (Gestiones), topped the bid by $50,000. Maxfly asked for a five-minute recess. During that time, Gestiones purportedly gave Maxfly $20,000 and Maxfly stopped bidding. The payment of the $20,000 was not disclosed to the bankruptcy court until March 1992. Both bidders were clients of the trustee's accounting firm. According to newspaper reports, at least one of the trustee's employees helped with the translation. At some point, the trustee obtained knowledge of what had happened but did not report it to the court in a timely fashion.

The U.S. attorney opened an investigation to determine whether Bagdan should be indicted. There were further fears that the U.S. attorney might indict his entire Big Eight accounting firm, although that would not become fashionable until Enron. Since 18 U.S.C. § 152(6) makes it illegal to knowingly give or receive money for acting or forbearing to act in a bankruptcy case, the U.S. attorney ultimately indicted the two bidders, but spared the trustee. Later, a court examiner recommended against prosecution of the trustee. However, the trustee's accounting firm fired him, he was removed from what would have been the most profitable case of his career, he was forced to resign from the panel of trustees, and his career was ruined.

The first lesson from this case is that knowledge of someone *else's* bankruptcy crime may implicate the trustee, even though he was not a participant in the scheme. The second lesson is that the bankruptcy professional does not have to be indicted to feel the deadly sting of a bankruptcy crime.

IX. *Where the Action Is*

The following cases involve attorneys and accountants who have recently been indicted or convicted of bankruptcy crimes. These cases are generally of the *malum in se* variety. This list should provide good clues as to the types of conduct that make attractive prosecutions for the U.S. attorney.

- Shannon Clark, a bankruptcy attorney, was indicted in the Eastern District of Tennessee on seven counts of mail fraud, money laundering, bankruptcy fraud, and false statements arising from her own Chapter 7 case, her representation of debtors, and a scheme with her husband involving credit card applications. She subsequently pled guilty. *United States v. Clark,* 04 CR 00057 (E.D. Tenn.).

- Patricia Anne O'Kane, a consumer bankruptcy lawyer, was charged with four counts each of wire fraud and bankruptcy fraud in the Southern District of Texas. O'Kane allegedly made unauthorized charges on clients' credit card accounts and used collateral intended by her clients to be surrendered to secured creditors. She subsequently pled guilty and was sentenced to 30 months in prison and five years' probation based upon her guilty plea to wire fraud and bankruptcy fraud. *United States v. O'Kane,* 03 CR 00364 (S.D. Tex.).

- Timothy Naegele, a lawyer and Chapter 7 debtor, was indicted on April 28, 2005, in the District of Columbia on 11 counts of bankruptcy fraud (18 U.S.C. §§ 152 and 157). The defendant allegedly failed to list several assets, including a case in which he represented a party with a potentially lucrative contingency-fee agreement. *United States v. Naegele,* 05 CR 00151 (D. C.).

- On May 11, 2005, Brian J. Almengual and his wife, Suzanne C. Warner-Almengual, both of whom are lawyers, were indicted in the Middle District of Florida on charges arising from their joint bankruptcy filing. The couple allegedly concealed property and gave false sworn testimony during their bankruptcy case. *United States v. Almengual, et al.,* 05 CR 00196 (M.D. Fla.).

- William Grabscheid pled guilty on April 11, 2005, to one count each of bankruptcy fraud and willful failure to file a tax return, admitting to diverting fiduciary-held funds totaling approximately $35,000, including $7,466 from accounts in cases where he served as bankruptcy trustee. *United States v. Grabscheid,* 05 CR 00035 (N.D. Ill.).

- Attorney Robert Suzenski pled guilty to one count of embezzlement of public money in the District of Arizona. Suzenski received debtors' funds into his trust account for payment of creditors and U.S. Trustee quarterly fees. He embezzled $74,500 in funds intended for quarterly fee payments. He was sentenced to 21 months in prison and three years' supervised release, and ordered to pay more than $76,000 in restitution, based on his guilty plea to one count of bankruptcy fraud. *United States v. Suzenski,* 03 CR 00502 (D. Ariz.).

• Disbarred attorney Bridgette Harris pleaded guilty to four counts of bankruptcy fraud in the District of Maryland. Harris solicited clients offering "foreclosure assistance" and filed bankruptcy petitions on their behalf using her home address and listing her employer, an attorney, as counsel of record without the attorney's knowledge or consent; and she filed bankruptcy in the Eastern District of New York, misrepresenting numerous facts and transferring her real property to relatives with the intent to hinder delay and defraud her creditors. She was sentenced to 18 months in prison and ordered to pay $8,785 in restitution. *United States v. Harris,* 03 CR 00047 (D. Md.).

• Steven A. Dayton pled guilty to making false statements and creating false bankruptcy court documents, including a forged bankruptcy court order purporting to discharge the debts of two former clients. Dayton made the statements and created the false documents to conceal a scheme to defraud the former clients, from whom he had accepted a fee to file a bankruptcy case he never filed. He was sentenced to three years' probation and fined $1,000 in the Central District of California based on his plea of guilty to one count of bankruptcy fraud (18 U.S.C. § 157(3)). *United States v. Dayton,* 03 CR 00057 (C.D. Cal.).

• Dean Bozzano was sentenced on October 24, 2003, in the District of Massachusetts to five years in prison and three years' supervised release, and ordered to pay $1.06 million in restitution, after pleading guilty to bankruptcy fraud and embezzlement. Bozzano embezzled $1.06 million from the estate of Chapter 11 debtor Maurice Corp. after the bankruptcy court appointed him as plan administrator, pursuant to a liquidating plan of reorganization, to oversee distribution of the estate assets. *United States v. Bozzano,* 02 CR 40007 (D. Mass.).

• Tax attorney Jeffrey A. Sherman was sentenced to 32 months in prison and ordered to pay $598,381 in restitution for conspiring to commit bankruptcy fraud and aiding and abetting tax evasion. Sherman, a prebankruptcy tax-planning specialist who formerly worked for the IRS, participated in a scheme with lawyer Robert V. Beaudry to help clients hide their wealth and then discharge federal and state tax liabilities in bankruptcy. Clients John and Letantia Bussell made false statements and concealed assets to discharge more than $4 million in liabilities, including a tax debt to the IRS of more than $1 million, and client Robert Grant fraudulently discharged an $11 million tax debt to the IRS. Beaudry, Grant, and the Bussells were also prosecuted. *United States v. Bussell,* 00 CR 00485, 01 CR 00056.

- Former panel trustee Robert Dennis Pryce pled guilty in the Central District of California to 17 counts relating to public corruption and 32 counts arising from a separate indictment alleging abuse of his role as a bankruptcy trustee. Pryce pleaded guilty to conspiracy, mail fraud, extortion, bribery, and money laundering in connection with his role in brokering a deal to bribe public officials for approving a waste-hauling contract in Carson County, California. The bankruptcy counts alleged that Pryce took kickbacks from a real estate agent and contractor in exchange for hiring them in his Chapter 7 trustee cases. He also made false entries on official trustee records and court submissions and laundered the kickback proceeds through bank accounts in his daughter's name. *United States v. Pryce*, 02 CR 1206, 02 CR 1207 (C.D. Cal.).
- Daniel Gates was indicted in the Western District of Pennsylvania on charges of mail fraud, bank fraud, money laundering, and bankruptcy fraud for embezzling at least $3.6 million from clients, including non-bankruptcy clients. *United States v. Gates,* 03 CR 00200 (W.D. Penn.).
- Los Angeles bankruptcy attorney Lloyd Segal was sentenced to 18 months in prison and three years' supervised release and ordered to pay $118,825 in restitution. Segal previously pleaded guilty in the Central District of California to providing false Social Security numbers, a false name, and other false information in his own bankruptcy filings. *United States v. Segal,* 03 CR 00159 (C.D. Cal.).
- Suspended attorney Allen Robert Thayer was sentenced in the Northern District of Indiana to 27 months in prison following his conviction for bankruptcy fraud and perjury. Before filing a Chapter 7 bankruptcy, Thayer transferred his stock in a family farm corporation into an irrevocable trust and backdated the trust document, as well as certain mortgages, to keep the property from creditors. On his bankruptcy documents, he stated the false date and falsely listed his son as trust beneficiary. *United States v. Thayer,* 01 CR 00182 (N.D. Ind.).
- Robert Burrick was sentenced in the District of New Jersey to 18 months' incarceration and ordered to pay $48,000 in restitution, based on his guilty plea to mail fraud and interstate transportation of securities and money obtained by fraud under 18 U.S.C. §§ 1341 and 2314. Burrick was charged with the embezzlement of more than $100,000 from clients' trust accounts and the diversion of $17,000 in funds from the Milburn Youth Soccer Club. One trust account held funds to be disbursed to creditors of Chapter 11 debtor Syntrex, Inc., for which Burrick served as post-confirmation distribution agent. *United States v. Burrick,* 002 CR 0081 (D.N.J.).
- On February 10, former consumer bankruptcy attorney Delbert Edwin Bartell of Ft. Worth, Texas, was sentenced in the Northern District of

Texas to six months in federal prison based on his November 2002 guilty plea to making a false declaration in his bankruptcy case. In almost 10 years, Bartell filed six bankruptcy petitions to forestall Internal Revenue Service collection activities. *United States v. Bartell*, 02 CR 00168 (N.D. Tex.).

- Richmond City Councilman Sa'ad El-Amin and his wife, Beverly D. Crawford, both disbarred lawyers, were indicted in the Eastern District of Virginia on charges of bankruptcy fraud, tax fraud, mail fraud, wire fraud, bank fraud, and embezzlement. The indictment alleged that El-Amin, Crawford, and their former law firms owed the IRS more than $700,000 in delinquent taxes, penalties, and interest for assessments and liens dating back to 1986; money from the couple's law firm trust account was used to pay $114,000 in personal expenses; and the couple filed bankruptcy six times to impair IRS collection efforts. *United States v. El-Amin, et al.*, 03 CR 00055 (E.D. Va.).

- Gregory Wayne Ginn and Waylon E. McCullen were indicted on August 24, 2004, in the Northern District of Texas on charges including concealment and transfer of assets, aiding and abetting, false statement, and conspiracy to commit bankruptcy fraud. Ginn, a certified public accountant, was appointed to carry out the reorganization plan of a company in Chapter 11 bankruptcy. The indictment alleged that Ginn transferred $300,000 of the company's assets to his friend and local lawyer McCullen to cover a check unrelated to the bankruptcy, and then concealed that transfer. Ginn and McCullen returned the money to the bankruptcy estate but allegedly tried to cover up the true purpose of the transaction. *United States v. Ginn & McCullen*, 04 CR 00282 (N.D. Tex.).

- Michael Roberts was indicted in the Northern District of Illinois in 2002 for bankruptcy fraud, wire fraud, and mail fraud. He pleaded guilty on March 24, 2005, to the bankruptcy fraud charge. Roberts admitted that he defrauded 35 clients he filed bankruptcy cases for by creating bogus garnishment orders and forging the signatures of eight bankruptcy judges on those orders. Roberts admitted he submitted those orders to his clients' employers to collect additional fees. He was sentenced in August 2005. *United States v. Roberts*, 02 CR 00675 (N.D. Ill.).

- Ronald A. Arthur and his wife, Mary K. Arthur, were convicted of bankruptcy fraud and money laundering on November 7, 2005. Mr. Arthur was a real estate lawyer and consultant, and Mrs. Arthur was a nursing home administrator and former district attorney. The indictment charged the defendants with conspiring to conceal assets and engaging in money-laundering financial transactions with the concealed property. Mr. Arthur was also charged with making false statements under oath by failing to disclose more than $237,000 in assets. They each face a maximum penalty of 20 years in prison, $500,000 in fines, and three years of supervised release. *United States v. Arthur, et al.,* 04 CR 00122 (E.D. Wis.).

- A former attorney and Chapter 7 trustee, Greg Hamilton, pled guilty to one count of embezzlement in the District of Rhode Island. Hamilton took $7,500 from a bankruptcy estate and paid his home mortgage with some of the proceeds. *United States v. Hamilton,* 04 CR 00041 (D.R.I.).
- William DeJesus Gutierrez pled guilty in the Eastern District of Pennsylvania to one count of making a false statement (18 U.S.C. § 1001). The indictment alleged Gutierrez used a fraudulent Social Security number on his Chapter 7 petition filed in the Eastern District of Pennsylvania. *United States v. Gutierrez,* 03 CR 00821 (E.D. Penn.).
- Chapter 11 debtor's counsel Laurence Y. Solarsh was indicted in the Southern District of New York on February 27, 2004, on one count of embezzlement (18 U.S.C. § 153(a)) of approximately $101,048 from the debtor's estate. *United States v. Solarsh,* 04 CR 00404 (S.D.N.Y.).
- Attorney Leland Jones III of Greenwood, Mississippi, was sentenced in the Northern District of Mississippi to five years' probation and ordered to pay a $10,000 fine and $8,681 in restitution to the estate, based on his guilty plea to concealing assets in a client's bankruptcy case (18 U.S.C. § 152(1)). *United States v. Jones,* 03 CR 00139 (N.D. Miss.).
- William S. Boyd III of Gulfport, Mississippi, pled guilty in the Southern District of Mississippi to embezzlement in connection with his representation of debtors. Boyd embezzled approximately $163,500 in at least two bankruptcy cases. He was sentenced to 26 months in prison followed by three years' supervised release, and ordered to pay $395,000 in restitution. *United States v. Boyd,* 03 CR 00005 (S.D. Miss.).
- Attorney John Eleazarian was indicted on October 27, 2005, for allegedly forging a bankruptcy judge's order. If Eleazarian is found guilty, the charge carries a maximum of five years in prison and/or a $250,000 fine. *United States v. Eleazarian,* 05 CR 00428 (E.D. Cal.).

X. Where's the Next Gellene Case?

There are two areas where criminal liability may increase under the BRA:

1. the attorney's responsibility to attest to the debtor's schedules and statement of affairs and
2. reaffirmation agreements.

In an address to the Central States Regional Meeting of the American Bankruptcy Institute, Bankruptcy Judge Stephen Rhodes of the U.S. Bankruptcy

Court for the Eastern District of Michigan revealed that he had conducted a survey of schedules and statements of affairs being filed in his courthouse.[33] He discovered that 198 out of 200 schedules and statements of affairs in the sampling contained errors, some significant.[34] Judge Rhodes opined that:

1. there is a general lack of care and understanding by debtors and their attorneys in fulfilling the disclosure requirements;
2. the official forms do not adequately communicate the disclosure requirements; and
3. in some ways, the disclosure requirements are unrealistic and unnecessary, and serve only to make knaves of otherwise honest debtors and their attorneys.[35]

Partly in light of Judge Rhodes's findings, Congress enacted § 319 of the BRA, which states that it is the "sense of Congress that Federal Rule of Bankruptcy Procedure 9011 be amended to provide that all documents, including schedules, submitted to the court or to a trustee by pro se debtors and represented debtors be submitted only after reasonable inquiry to verify that the information in the documents is well grounded in fact and warranted by existing law or a good faith argument for the extension or reversal of existing law."

It may take several years under the rule-making process before Rule 9011 is amended.

With respect to the reaffirmation abuse problem, the BRA also amended Code § 524(k) to require the attorney to execute a certificate in cases where there is a presumption of undue hardship. This is discussed in detail in Chapter 14. Just how an attorney is even supposed to know some of the facts to which he or she is certifying remains a mystery.[36]

What is not a mystery is what Congress intends to do about the problem of reaffirmation abuse. Congress has enacted 18 U.S.C. § 1958. This section provides:

> In General—The Attorney General of the United States shall designate the individuals described in subsection (b) to have primary responsibility in carrying out enforcement activities in addressing violations of section 152 or 157 relating to abusive reaffirmations of debt. In addition to addressing the violations referred to in the preceding sentence, the individuals described under subsection (b) shall address violations of section 152 and 157 relat-

---

33. Hon. Steven W. Rhodes, *An Empirical Study of Consumer Bankruptcy Papers*, 73 AM. BANKR. L.J. 653 (1999).

34. *Id.* at 678.

35. *Id.* at 653.

36. See Chapter 14.

ing to materially fraudulent statements in bankruptcy schedules that are intentionally false or intentionally misleading.

The statute goes on to require the U.S. attorney and the FBI to delegate one individual from each agency to be primarily responsible for investigating and prosecuting violations of §§ 152 and 157 related to schedules, statements of affairs, and reaffirmations.

XI. The New Bankruptcy Crime[37]

The BRA also creates a new bankruptcy crime: fraudulent involuntary petitions. In most jurisdictions, attorneys have always been on the hook for participating in improper involuntary bankruptcies through the sanctions provided for in Code § 303. The BRA does not affect these sanctions provisions, but it significantly increases the punishment: participating in an involuntary petition that is found to be fraudulent is now a crime. As amended, § 157 provides:

> A person who, having devised or intending to devise a scheme or artifice to defraud and for the purpose of executing or concealing such a scheme or artifice or attempting to do so -
> (1) files a petition under title 11, *including a fraudulent involuntary bankruptcy petition under section 303 of such title*;
> (2) files a document in a proceeding under title 11, *including a fraudulent bankruptcy petition under section 303 of such title*; or
> (3) makes a false or fraudulent representation, claim, or promise concerning or in relation to a proceeding under title 11, *including a fraudulent involuntary bankruptcy petition under section 303 of such title*, at any time before or after the filing of the petition, or in relation to a proceeding falsely asserted to be pending under such title
> shall be fined under this title, imprisoned not more than 5 years, or both.

As discussed above, it's not clear whether the highlighted language is added only to subsection (1) or to all three subsections.[38]

The BRA's tendency toward bad drafting creates some interpretive problems, most notably the lack of definition for "a fraudulent involuntary bankruptcy petition under" Code § 303 in either that section or amended 18 U.S.C. § 157. The logical interpretation is "an involuntary bankruptcy petition under § 303 that is fraudulent."

However, another BRA section amended Code § 303 in a way that raises questions about the correctness of this suggested interpretation. New Code § 303(l)(1) provides that if:

---

37. Thanks to Catherine E. Vance for contributing this discussion.
38. See discussion accompanying note 20 above.

- the petition under Code § 303 is false or contains any false, fictitious, or fraudulent statement;
- the debtor is an individual; and
- the court dismisses the petition,

then "the court, upon the motion of the debtor, shall seal all the records of the court relating to such petition, and all references to such petition."

Both this amendment and the inclusion of involuntary petitions in the criminal statute concern fraud, but the Code § 303 amendment is clearly directed only at cases commenced against individuals. So, it is possible that the new criminal statute applies only to individual cases as well.

It is beyond the scope of this discussion to resolve the question whether the new criminal provisions apply only in individual cases or to any involuntary petition, including in business cases, that is fraudulent. Therefore, the prudent approach for attorneys is to assume that, despite the possible limitation arising from the amendments to § 303, criminal liability attaches in both individual and business cases.

The more important question for our purposes is whether the new criminal provisions will apply to attorneys. We think the answer is "yes" for two reasons.

- Courts commonly mete out sanctions between the offending parties and their attorneys under § 303(i) and other provisions of the Code and rules as the circumstances warrant.
- Attorneys may not actively participate with their clients in perpetuating a fraud in any event.

Moreover, as discussed in this Chapter, prosecutors have gone after attorneys under § 157 successfully and with devastating consequences to the offending lawyer.

My recommendation to the bar is that, in addition to reading Chapter 13, which thoroughly explores the new attorney certifications, consumer bankruptcy practitioners adopt a best-practice guide to ensure that a reasonable inquiry into the client's assets and liabilities is conducted by the lawyer prior to filing. These tests may include a Choice Point or Lexis review on the Internet and ordering up a title search, car title search, a *Kelley Blue Book* review, or requiring the client to fill out a detailed questionnaire.

This procedure imposes two new burdens on an attorney. First, if the attorney fails to conduct any inquiry at all and the schedules or statement of affairs are materially false and the falsity could have easily been detected, will the U.S. attorney take the position that the attorney acted knowingly by burying his head in the sand? Will the Sgt. Schultz defense have any further vitality?

Second, if the attorney, through her new best business practices, discovers inaccuracies in the schedules or statement of affairs but files them anyway, she may be dead meat in a future criminal prosecution. Will the prosecutor wait for a set of egregious facts and bring an indictment against a bankruptcy lawyer, just to make her an example?

With respect to reaffirmations, the standards for making the certification that an attorney must follow are undefined. With luck, the bankruptcy courts will establish standards in a civil context before some prosecutor defines them in a criminal one.

Last, the BRA also places all kinds of additional responsibilities on the debtor's lawyer, who may now find himself to be a debt relief agency (DRA), and places enormous burdens on the consumer bankruptcy lawyer, including disclaimers and disclosures both in public advertising and in private dealings with the client. These provisions are discussed in detail in Chapters 4, 9, 11, and 13.

In addition, Code § 707(b) creates a means test. An attorney may be tempted to cut corners in her responsibility as a DRA or to game the system with respect to the means test. While there is no shortage of civil penalties for the errant consumer bankruptcy attorney, nothing in these sections makes civil penalties the exclusive remedy. Violations of the DRA provisions or aggressive gaming of the system could constitute criminal violations as well.

WARNING!! ━━━━━━━━━
Bankruptcy professionals cannot bury their heads in the sand, or divorce themselves from their clients' conduct, and sail blissfully through bankruptcy. They must observe the new responsibilities under the BRA scrupulously, and not assume that any penalty will be a civil one.

While bankruptcy criminal liability seldom rises to the level of an indictment or conviction, even a criminal investigation—as the *Bagdan* case reveals—can be devastating. Bankruptcy professionals cannot bury their heads in the sand, or divorce themselves from their client's conduct, and sail blissfully through bankruptcy. They must observe the new responsibilities under the BRA scrupulously, and not assume that any penalty will be a civil one. Failure to pay close attention to the issues of bankruptcy crimes may result in too many additional shooting stars.

CHAPTER 17

No Good Deed Goes Unpunished:
Pro Bono Practice under the BRA

by Corinne Cooper and Thomas J. Yerbich

It would be easy to assume that the provisions of the BRA apply only to debtors' attorneys who receive payment. After all, what incentive could there be to subject *pro bono* attorneys to increased liability?

If one assumes that the law is intended only to apply to "bad" debtors' attorneys—that is, those who are assisting their clients to abuse the system—then it would make sense to exclude attorneys who receive no fee. But the unexpressed but thinly veiled intent of the attorney liability provisions is to keep consumer debtors from obtaining legal advice and learning their rights, which will decrease the number of consumer bankruptcies resulting in a discharge. All the consumer provisions (and the political rhetoric behind them) point to this goal:

- The means test will decrease the number of Chapter 7 filings;
- New barriers to entry, such as requiring credit counseling and demanding extensive documentation, will decrease the overall number of filings and result in many more dismissals without a discharge; and
- Imposing advertising restrictions and increasing liability on consumer debtors' attorneys will drive up the price of bankruptcy and decrease the number of available attorneys.

All these provisions will increase the number of debtors who enter bankruptcy without counsel. If that is the objective, discouraging even *pro bono* practice makes some sense. But if the true objective is—as the supporters of BRA have steadfastly maintained—to curb abuse by debtors, it makes no sense.

Debtors who qualify for *pro bono* representation are not abusers of the bankruptcy system. Eligibility for a *pro bono* program established under the auspices of the Legal Services Corporation is very limited. For example, income cannot exceed 125% of the poverty level.[1] In exceptional circumstances the recipient's income can be increased up to 150% of the eligibility level (187.5% of the poverty level).[2] The assets held by these debtors are pitifully small, even less than the exemptions Congress allowed under § 522(d)!

The vast majority of debtors receiving *pro bono* assistance are going to fall within the safe harbor of § 707(b)(7).[3] Since Congress has given debtors who have such minimal income and assets a pass from the means test, can't we assume that Congress didn't consider them abusers of the system? So what overriding public policy consideration is being promoted by making it more difficult for them to obtain legal assistance?

Many of the attorney liability provisions apply only to DRAs as defined in § 101(12A).[4] To qualify as a DRA, the attorney must provide "bankruptcy assistance to an assisted person in return for the payment of money or other valuable consideration. . . ."[5]

So, for example, the attorney advertising provisions do not apply to *pro bono* bankruptcy attorneys, and they wouldn't have to refer to themselves as "debt relief agencies" in their advertising. This won't matter to debtors' attorneys who provide *pro bono* representation, since they will already be DRAs. For creditors' attorneys, who make up a significant portion of the *pro bono* bankruptcy bar, this exclusion is significant.[6]

---

1.   45 C.F.R. § 1611.3(b). The current income caps are set forth in 45 C.F.R. pt. 1611, App. A.

2.   45 C.F.R. § 1611.4(a).

3.   The 2005 median income for a family of four in the lowest-income state (New Mexico) according to the U.S. Trustee Program is $47,256. The eligibility limit (125% of the poverty level for the contiguous 48 states and D.C.) for a family of 4 is $24,188.

4.   BRA Section 226(a)(3), amending Code § 101 by adding subsection (12A).

5.   *Id.* Bankruptcy petition preparers are not defined as DRAs by reference to the receipt of consideration in this section: "'debt relief agency' means any person who provides any bankruptcy assistance to an assisted person in return for the payment of money or other valuable consideration, or who is a bankruptcy petition preparer under section 110. . . ." *Id.* However, the definition of a petition preparer in § 110 requires compensation. *See* Code § 110(a)(1). Note that unless they waive it, private attorneys providing *pro bono* services are entitled to reimbursement of expenses incurred. This payment alone might make these attorneys DRAs, but it will not make them BPPs, since they usually will appear as the attorney for the debtor. So it's best for *pro bono* attorneys either to decline reimbursement or to work in programs that pay expenses for the debtors directly, rather than via reimbursement.

6.   Of course, as noted in Chapter 4, many creditors' lawyers will also wind up being DRAs.

But the certification and reaffirmation provisions do apply to *pro bono* practice, since they apply to all attorneys who sign documents, regardless of whether they receive a fee.[7]

Under § 707(b)(4), the attorney signing the petition certifies that "the attorney has performed a reasonable investigation" and "has no knowledge after an inquiry that the information in the schedules filed with such petition is incorrect." How much investigation or inquiry must the *pro bono* attorney conduct? More specifically, is the attorney entitled to rely upon the eligibility screening by the agency that referred the debtor?[8] Assuming that the agency is state-operated under LSC regulations, the agency uses a simple form and procedure to obtain eligibility information "in a manner that promotes the development of trust between the attorney and client."[9] Only if there is "a substantial reason to doubt the accuracy of the information" should the agency make reasonable inquiry to verify the information.[10] Attorneys performing *pro bono* work will quite understandably be reluctant to rely on the limited inquiry conducted by the referring agency to satisfy the requirements of § 707(b)(4).

Rules affecting attorney conduct regardless of payment are not new. Rule 11 and Rule 9011 are not limited to attorneys receiving payment. But when new, onerous liability provisions are added to the obligations imposed upon debtors' attorneys, the likelihood that lawyers will volunteer their services to assist debtors out of the goodness of their hearts plummets. For those who do provide *pro bono* assistance, the added requirements will mean more time for each client served. Since the number of available *pro bono* hours will be reduced by the loss of *pro bono* lawyers, and the time required to provide services to each debtor increased, the net result will be a decrease in the number of consumer debtors who receive legal assistance.

Even those who are not faint-hearted are likely to be instructed by their malpractice insurers that this area of practice is outside the scope of their coverage.[11] How many attorneys will put their homes on the line to ensure

---

7. The attorney providing services on a *pro bono* basis does not run the risk of being classified as a bankruptcy petition preparer because the definition of a bankruptcy petition preparer also requires the attorney to receive compensation. See note 5.

8. Screening for eligibility is conducted by the referring agency. 45 C.F.R. § 1614.4(d). Also, where reimbursed for expenses, which may be considered "compensation," the attorney is acting as an attorney for the debtor.

9. 45 C.F.R. § 1611.7(a).

10. 45 C.F.R. § 1611.7(b).

11. The malpractice issue is very real. Even before the BRA became effective, there were reports of coverage being cancelled for consumer bankruptcy practice. E-mail on file with the author reporting cancellation of a policy by Great American Insurance in Texas, from the Bankruptcy Roundtable Listserv dated April 18, 2005; e-mail on file with the author from Robert Minto, president and CEO of ALPS, a professional malpractice insurance company.

that debt-ridden consumers have assistance to file bankruptcy? Only consumer debtor bankruptcy lawyers (who are likely to be insured for this practice) will continue in the practice, and fewer of them will take on *pro bono* cases intentionally.[12] And creditors' attorneys are almost certain to give up these cases.[13]

The American Bar Association pointed to this problem in its opposition to the attorney liability provisions in the bill:

> These provisions will greatly reduce *pro bono* representation for the poorest Americans. Although the "debt relief agency" provisions in Sections 227-229 only apply to attorneys who receive payment for their services, the new certification requirements of Sections 102 and 203(a)[14] apply to *all* debtor bankruptcy attorneys, whether or not they charge a fee. As a result, these provisions will strongly discourage attorneys and law firms from providing essential *pro bono* bankruptcy services to the very debtors who need them most.[15]

What's particularly sad about this is that the American Bar Association, under the leadership of the Standing Committee on Pro Bono and Public Service and the Section of Business Law Pro Bono Committee, has been nurturing a *pro bono* bankruptcy practice program to provide legal service to consumers unable to afford attorneys.[16]

The potential dire consequences on the availability of *pro bono* services are real. As noted above, the malpractice insurance situation is, at best, troubling. We recognize that legal malpractice suits arising out of *pro bono* activity are extremely rare, but they do occur. With the increased requirements imposed on attorneys representing consumer debtors, the risk of such malpractice claims rises. It follows, as night does day, that when the insured risk increases, one of two things happens: insurers quit insuring the risk or increase the premium.

---

12.   Of course, many attorneys take on *pro bono* cases when they represent consumer debtors, because the check bounces or the work vastly exceeds that anticipated by the attorney. Perhaps one benefit of the BRA will be a reduction in those cases.

13.   If the attorneys themselves aren't concerned, their firms probably will be. *See* Chapter 4, which explains that firms are DRAs when attorneys become DRAs.

14.   Referring to §§ 707(b)(4)(C), (D) and 524(k)(5).

15.   Letter from Robert D. Evans, Director, American Bar Association Governmental Affairs Office, to members of the Senate (Mar. 1, 2005), *available at* http://www.abanet.org/poladv/letters/109th/bankrupt/bankrupt030105.pdf.

16.   *See, e.g.,* Business Law Section, Business Bankruptcy Committee, Subcommittee on Pro Bono Legal Services and the Section of Litigation, Bankruptcy and Insolvency Litigation Committee, Subcommittee on Pro Bono (2d ed. 1999), How to Begin a Pro Bono Program in Your Bankruptcy Court, *available at* http://www.abanet.org/legalservices/probono/publications/bankruptcy_starterkit.html.

WARNING!!

With the increased requirements imposed on attorneys representing consumer debtors, the risk of such malpractice claims rises. It follows, as night does day, that when the insured risk increases, one of two things happens: insurers quit insuring the risk or increase the premium.

Many legal services and public interest *pro bono* programs carry Employed Lawyers Professional Liability Insurance that also covers volunteer outside *pro bono* counsel. What happens if the carrier raises the rates for coverage of consumer debtor work?

The funding for legal services programs is primarily from the federal government through the Legal Services Corporation (supplemented by state grants and private contributions). Government funding of legal services has been steadily decreasing. If more available funds are required to provide malpractice coverage, legal services organizations will be faced with some very tough choices.

Will the practitioner (or firm) who might otherwise be willing to provide *pro bono* representation to consumer debtors also be willing to pay for a rider that provides malpractice coverage for it? The outcome is, to a significant extent, in the hands of the malpractice carriers. Will the sky fall or just sag a bit? We do not pretend to have the answers, just justifiable concern.

CHAPTER 18

Woe Unto You, Lawyers

by Catherine E. Vance

Throughout most of this book, the attorney liability provisions of the BRA have been put under a microscope. The authors have explored in detail the meaning of the words Congress has enacted, the interpretive difficulties, ethical conflicts, constitutional infirmities, and more.

Now it's time to take a step back and look at the policy implications of the attorney liability provisions as a whole. The big picture is not a pretty one. As one bankruptcy judge put it, "Without a shred of evidence, BAPCPA convicts debtors' attorneys as conspirators in an 'abusive' bankruptcy system."[1] For most of these lawyers, the only "crime" committed has been dedicating their careers to the welfare of their clients and providing competent and affordable representation to ordinary people who are in financial distress and need help.

Of course, there are exceptions. There are bankruptcy lawyers who are incompetent, who aid their clients in committing fraud, or whose work is just not up to the standard expected of attorneys.[2] But the BRA treats the exception as the rule. All consumer debtors' attorneys are treated as suspect and in need of regulation. Worse, the new regulations don't really address the problems that the incompetent or unethical lawyers create within the system.

But the real insult—the slap in the face to all consumer debtors' attorneys—is in the BRA's treatment of these lawyers in comparison to two groups with a demonstrated record of preying on the financially vulnerable: credit counseling agencies and bankruptcy petition preparers.

---

1. Hon. Keith M. Lundin, *Ten Principles of BAPCPA: Not What Was Advertised*, 14 AM. BANKR. INST. L.J. 1, 69 (Sept. 2005).

2. *See, e.g.*, Hon. Steven W. Rhodes, *An Empirical Study of Consumer Bankruptcy Papers*, 73 AM. BANKR. L.J. 653 (1999).

While Congress was considering the BRA, much was learned about the credit counseling industry, and the news was not good. According to a *Business Week* report in 2001 (the midpoint between introduction and enactment of the BRA):

> The billion-dollar credit-counseling industry is deeply troubled. Some clients end up in worse financial shape after using agencies. The fees they pay, usually labeled "voluntary contributions," are often steep. Some agencies are fraudulent; others are run by executives with questionable backgrounds. The agencies, which mostly operate as nonprofits, often pay their executives lavish salaries and make cushy deals for goods or services with related companies. They also steer consumers to affiliated for-profit companies that make debt-consolidation or home-equity loans. "This whole industry is fertile ground for scams," says Eric S. Friedman, a Montgomery County (Md.) consumer-protection official who with colleague Myriam A. Torrico has been tracking credit-counseling fraud.[3]

In 2003, the Federal Trade Commission announced it had filed suit against AmeriDebt, which has become the Enron of the credit counseling scandal.

> "We will not allow consumers to be duped into 'contributing' hundreds of dollars to these so-called 'non-profits,'" said Howard Beales, director of the FTC's Bureau of Consumer Protection. "There was nothing voluntary and nothing charitable about these payments. Consumers' money didn't go to creditors, it just ended up lining the pockets of the defendants."[4]

Also in 2003, the first comprehensive report on the credit-counseling industry was released.[5] Among the findings of the report, prepared by the Consumer Federation of America and the National Consumer Law Center, is abuse by these agencies of their "nonprofit" status:

> Nearly every agency in the industry has non-profit, tax-exempt status. Nevertheless, many of these agencies function as virtual for-profit businesses, aggressively advertising and selling DMPs [Debt Management Plans] and

---

3. Christopher H. Schmitt, Heather Timmons & John Cady, *A Debt Trap for the Unwary*, BUSINESS WEEK ONLINE (Oct. 29, 2001), *available at* http://www.businessweek.com/magazine/content/01_44/b3755094.htm.

4. Press Release, Federal Trade Commission, FTC Files Lawsuit against AmeriDebt; Agency Alleges that "Credit Counseling" Firm Misrepresents Costs and Nature of Its Services (Nov. 19, 2003), *available at* http://www.ftc.gov/opa/2003/11/ameridebt.htm.

5. Dean Loonin & Travis Plunkett, *Credit Counseling in Crisis: The Impact on Consumers of Funding Cuts, Higher Fees and Aggressive New Market Entrants* (2003) (report by the National Consumer Law Center & Consumer Federation of America).

a range of related services. Some agencies appear to be in clear violation of Internal Revenue Service (I.R.S.) rules governing eligibility for tax-exempt status.[6]

The congressional response to this abundant evidence of a systemic problem in the credit-counseling industry is inexplicable. Not only are these agencies expressly excluded from the debt relief agency provisions as nonprofits, the BRA requires that all consumer debtors be channeled through credit counselors as a condition of bankruptcy eligibility.[7]

The insult to attorneys is worse when attention is turned to bankruptcy petition preparers. Unlike credit counseling, this field has always carried the taint of illegitimacy. Indeed, when Congress enacted § 110 of the Code in 1994, it was motivated by concern

> that debtors would be at the mercy of fly-by-night "typing mills" that would lull the unsuspecting public into thinking that they had the expertise to offer valuable legal (or at least quasi-legal) bankruptcy assistance. Congress' fear was that bankruptcy petition preparers might "take unfair advantage of persons who are ignorant of their rights both inside and outside of the bankruptcy system." In short, one specific target of the statute was the inherently dangerous unauthorized practice of law by bankruptcy petition preparers.[8]

Courts have consistently set out a very narrow range of permissible activities for bankruptcy petition preparers: they are scriveners who may type the debtor's information on the official forms and not much else.[9]

---

6.   *Id.* at 2. On the eve of the BRA's effective date, the pervasive misuse of credit counselors' nonprofit status became even more clear:

> Steven T. Miller, the IRS commissioner of the tax-exempt and government entities division, said in an interview yesterday that his agency is auditing 40 credit-counseling firms to see whether they should keep their tax-exempt status. "We think by the end of this calendar year, we would have taken adverse action" in about half of the audits, Miller said. The agency plans to audit an additional 20 nonprofit agencies after the current audits are completed.
>
> So far, Miller said, no credit-counseling agency has received a clean bill of health from the IRS, which began its audits more than two years ago after hundreds of consumers complained about deceptive business practices, including high fees, high-pressure tactics and inadequate educational services.

Caroline E. Mayer, *Credit Counselors' Tax Status in Jeopardy*, Wash. Post, Oct.13, 2005, at D1. What's more, the law bars the IRS from providing the United States Trustee with any specifics from the audits, so it's possible the Trustee has approved a credit-counseling agency that's on the verge of having its tax-exempt status revoked.

7.   Code § 109(h).

8.   *In re* Guttierez, 248 B.R. 287, 295-96 (Bankr. W.D. Tex. 2000) (citation omitted).

9.   *See id.* at 297-98.

The BRA threatens to undermine this body of case law and the protections that have long been afforded unsophisticated debtors. It creates confusion about the services bankruptcy petition preparers may actually provide by attaching to them the label of "debt relief agency" and requiring the petition preparer to state in its advertisements: "We are a debt relief agency. We help people file for bankruptcy relief under the Bankruptcy Code." The public, sophisticated or not, will have a hard time reading this statement as encompassing nothing more than typing services. And if the past is any guide, petition preparers will certainly take advantage of their new, statutorily conferred designation:

> Notwithstanding the express prohibitions . . . some persons no doubt believe that § 110 *authorizes* or *legitimizes* quasi-legal assistance under the rubric of "bankruptcy petition preparer." Indeed, in many cities, there are persons who now advertise their services as "bankruptcy petition preparers" in newspapers and other media, suggesting by reference to § 110 itself that Congress *created* and *legitimized* their profession, thereby permitting them to hold themselves out to the public as federally recognized professionals and to offer their services for sale, so long as they comply with the statute.[10]

Through the BRA, petition preparers are granted a legitimacy they've never enjoyed before. In addition to the advertising statement, the BRA requires all debt relief agencies—including bankruptcy petition preparers—to provide consumer debtors information that constitutes legal advice, such as information about the relief available under the various chapters of the Code and advantages and disadvantages of filing under each, and how assets are supposed to be valued.

Yet in a bizarre twist, one of the required DRA disclosures needn't be provided by petition preparers at all. The content of the "How To" Notice, discussed in Chapter 11, unquestionably constitutes the practice of law because it is supposed to provide information such as how to value assets, determine the proper address for creditors, and compute income for purposes of the means test. A statutory exception is provided; the DRA doesn't have to provide the "How To" Notice if doing so is not authorized under non-bankruptcy law, meaning, of course, state statutes prohibiting the unauthorized practice of law.

---

10.   *Id.* at 297 (emphasis added).

The exception may be legally necessary, but it begs the larger policy issue: the BRA simultaneously elevates bankruptcy petition preparers from scriveners to "debt relief agencies" who "help people file for bankruptcy relief" at the same time that it provides less stringent regulation for a petition preparer than an attorney.[11]

It would be nice to pretend that this treatment was unintentional, the result of poor drafting or a poor understanding of bankruptcy practice. But you cannot escape the conclusion that this is intentional. While purporting to "strengthen professionalism standards,"[12] this law demeans lawyers and diminishes the practice of law to the level of petition preparers by:

- branding lawyers—and requiring them to describe themselves—as "debt relief agencies,"
- forcing lawyers to give bad legal advice and preventing them from offering some good advice, and
- placing unnecessary burdens, risk, and expense on the practice of bankruptcy law.

In the same stroke, Congress has offered an imprimatur to petition preparers engaged in the unauthorized practice of law, and anointed credit-counseling agencies as the gatekeepers—standing guard at both the entrance and the exit—to the bankruptcy courts and a discharge.

There's plenty of room to speculate about the motives behind the attorney liability provisions. One generally accepted theory among those who followed the BRA over the years is that Congress was less interested in punishing bad lawyers than in chasing the good ones away.

But there's also something bigger going on. As explained above, the BRA blurs the distinction between the services that trained, licensed attorneys provide to their clients and the largely unregulated fields of credit counseling and

---

11. The courts will, of course, have to reconcile the conflict the DRA provisions create with Code § 110, which governs bankruptcy petition preparers. When that time comes, I have little doubt that the petition preparers will see the value of hiring a lawyer.

12. H.R. Rep. No. 109-31, at 17 (2005), *reprinted in* 2005 U.S.C.C.A.N. 88, 103. There's more "strengthening" afoot in the 109th Congress. The House of Representatives has passed H.R. 420, the Lawsuit Abuse Reduction Act, which would reinstate mandatory sanctions for Rule 11 violations—even in certain state court litigation. Worse, H.R. 420 has a "three strikes" rule, requiring suspension of an attorney on a third Rule 11 violation. One supporter said H.R. 420 is "another prime opportunity to pass meaningful legislation to strengthen our court system." Laurie Kellman, *Measure Would Punish Attorneys for Filing Frivolous Lawsuits*, Associated Press, Oct. 28, 2005.

bankruptcy petition preparation.

Congress has injected a flawed free market theory into the practice of law. Without regard for the skill and training that separate lawyers from credit counselors and bankruptcy petition preparers, the BRA speaks generically about "bankruptcy assistance" and assumes it's appropriate to allow the panoply of "providers" of those services to compete on equal footing. Attorneys are treated not as a learned profession, but as offering a basic commodity, like the aspirin so many attorneys will need as they strive to comply with the BRA's many changes, all under greater pain of sanctions and liability. But the BRA is merely a successful battle in a larger war.

It's easy to take cheap shots at attorneys. Senator Hatch did when he described bankruptcy lawyers as just another special-interest group;[13] H.R. 64, introduced in 2005, describes the services estate-planning attorneys provide as "make work." And this says nothing of the now pejorative term "trial lawyers."

What's more important is official policy, which is plainly found in recent statements by the Department of Justice (DOJ) and the Federal Trade Commission (FTC). In state bar deliberations regarding how properly to define the practice of law, the DOJ and FTC have advocated a very limited definition:

> [T]he practice of law should be limited to those activities where specialized legal knowledge and training is demonstrably necessary to protect the interests of consumers. Otherwise, consumers benefit from preserving competition between lawyers and non-lawyers.[14]

The BRA is perfectly in keeping with the definition for which the DOJ and FTC advocated. One of the notices debt relief agencies must provide requires the following content:

- A brief description of:
  - Chapters 7, 11, 12, and 13 and the general purpose, benefits, and costs of proceeding under each
  - *the types of services available from credit-counseling agencies*
- Statements specifying that:
  - a person who knowingly and fraudulently conceals assets or makes a false oath or statement under penalty of perjury in connection

---

13.   146 Cong. Rec. S50 (daily ed. Jan. 26, 2000) (statement of Sen. Hatch).

14.   Letter from the Department of Justice and Federal Trade Commission to Jeffery Alderman, Executive Director, Kansas Bar Association (Feb. 4, 2005). The DOJ and the FTC have submitted substantially similar comments in letters to various state authorities and have advocated their limited definition of the practice of law as amicus curiae in various lawsuits. *See id.* at n.3.

with a bankruptcy case shall be subject to fine, imprisonment or both
- all information supplied by a debtor in connection with a bankruptcy case is subject to examination by the Attorney General.

A separate notice, the content of which is prescribed in the BRA, must begin with the following (or language that is "substantially similar"):

IMPORTANT INFORMATION ABOUT BANKRUPTCY ASSISTANCE SERVICES FROM AN ATTORNEY OR BANKRUPTCY PETITION PREPARER.
If you decide to seek bankruptcy relief, you can represent yourself, you can hire an attorney to represent you, or you can get help in some localities from a bankruptcy petition preparer who is not an attorney. THE LAW REQUIRES AN ATTORNEY OR BANKRUPTCY PETITION PREPARER TO GIVE YOU A WRITTEN CONTRACT SPECIFYING WHAT THE ATTORNEY OR BANKRUPTCY PETITION PREPARER WILL DO FOR YOU AND HOW MUCH IT WILL COST. Ask to see the contract before you hire anyone.

Each of these notices suggests to the client that the attorney might be providing nothing of value that he cannot receive from a credit counselor or bankruptcy petition preparer at a much lower cost. On the whole, these and other BRA provisions codify what the DOJ and FTC advocate: a more limited role for "legal advice" and an expanded role for non-attorneys—credit-counseling agencies and bankruptcy petition preparers[15]—in providing the services that the financially strapped debtor needs.

That people in financial trouble will be harmed when the door is opened for non-lawyers to provide legal services is a foregone conclusion. As discussed above, there's already a damaging body of evidence against credit counseling agencies and bankruptcy petition preparers.

In the final analysis, what's most troubling is that lawyers who practice in other fields are oblivious to the dangerous trend that is heading their way.

---

15.   Other non-lawyers who get into the debt relief game are people who peddle "advice" in a way that's the functional equivalent of weight loss programs. They'll promise debtors a way to get out of debt without increasing income or changing their lifestyle habits, just as the diet industry promises a svelte figure without the bother of exercising or giving up pizza. Although some self-help books and debt relief programs are legitimate, many will fall within the range from worthless information to outright scam. The irony is that the FTC, which can take action against the scammers, is helping foster an environment where so many more of them will enter the market.

INDEX

S